HAMLIN GARLAND

Hamlin Garland

A BIOGRAPHY

By Jean Holloway

BOOKS FOR LIBRARIES PRESS
FREEPORT, NEW YORK

INTERNATIONAL STANDARD BOOK NUMBER:
0-8369-5802-0

LIBRARY OF CONGRESS CATALOG CARD NUMBER:
70-157342

PRINTED IN THE UNITED STATES OF AMERICA

To Joan

FOREWORD

THE PLACE OF Hamlin Garland in American literature has been hotly debated ever since the publication of *Main-Travelled Roads* in 1893. The earliest critics were shocked by a realism which was in advance of its time. But soon the currents of American thought had eddied past Garland, leaving him stranded on the isolated reef of his "veritism." Naturalism had moved to the fore. Only once in his lifetime did Garland's inspiration synchronize with the taste of the public. *A Son of the Middle Border* was widely acclaimed, and the Pulitzer Prize for Biography followed. But immediately the socially-conscious writers of the twenties raised the cry:

> Just for a handful of silver he left us,
> Just for a riband to stick in his coat.

And academicians down to the present, usually basing their interpretations upon fragments of the Garland-Gilder correspondence, have tended to follow the same line.*

Unquestionably Garland's literary reputation must rest upon a sprinkling of short stories and a volume or two of autobiography. But criticism continues to raise the issue of his motivations, to present the enigma of a talented writer who squandered his talents. It has seemed to me that the biographical approach would elucidate not only Garland the man, but Garland the writer.

*A refreshing exception is B. R. McElderry, Jr., in his "Preface" to the most recent edition of *Main-Travelled Roads* (Harper & Brothers, 1956).

A great deal of nonsense is written on the subject of editorial dictation to writers, and on the corrupting effect of publishers upon their authors. My position is this: The *form* of an author's work is usually determined by the requirements of his audience, and inasmuch as editors and publishers interpret such requirements, they may be said to direct the author's performance. Shakespeare couched his thoughts in poetic drama because there existed an Elizabethan stage that demanded such productions. Present-day authors write novels, serious articles—and even biography—because there has developed an audience for those types of writing. But the *content* of a writer's work is dependent solely upon his own personal make-up. Only an editor who has attempted to inject into a manuscript what was not there in the beginning can appreciate the hopelessness of trying to dictate to any author what he should say. An author's choice of subject matter remains a psychologically forced choice, the result of an interplay of factors of character and experience. Thus to my mind the biographical study is necessary groundwork for criticism.

Someone has remarked that the life of an author is made up of "reading, writing, and arithmetic." In this study I have treated of such mundane matters as royalty statements and promotional campaigns, a part of the "arithmetic" of authorship. I do so without apology. For to any professional writer such matters are important. Moreover, I am not convinced that there is a fixed inverse ratio between art and financial success. Sales figures, while not the final criterion of literature, do indicate the extent of a writer's impact upon his own times.

It has been my intention to present in chronological sequence the genesis and composition of Garland's various works and the critical reactions of his contemporaries, including only sufficient references to modern controversies to give point to the narration. For the rest, this is the story of a man who was a writer of some merit and an individual of great interest, who lived a full life in an era of chaotic change but a few decades removed from our own.

It may be objected that biography is superfluous in the case of a man who indulged so extensively in autobiography. It is true that a round dozen of Garland's books record his personal history: the four "Middle Border" books, the four volumes of

"Roadside Meetings," two accounts of psychic investigations, *Boy Life on the Prairie,* and *The Trail of the Goldseekers.* But the very profusion of Garland's reminiscences discourages the casual reader of American literature, and few specialists in the field are completely familiar with all these five thousand printed pages of unindexed material. Summarization is certainly in order.

But to such a synthesis has been added the evidence of manuscript materials, the comments of Garland's contemporaries in public forums and in correspondence. Fortunately Garland's own letters and papers preserved in libraries constitute a running commentary upon his published accounts of his adventures in the literary world. Often these have been used merely as corroboration, or to settle the matter of a date, for Garland was inaccurate and contradictory on such details. They have been even more invaluable in developing a picture which must inevitably differ from Garland's self-portraiture.

Autobiography and biography are, finally, separate art forms. In an early version of *A Son of the Middle Border* Garland himself admitted as much:

As a conscientious historian, I must warn the reader against believing that this writing contains the whole truth about an author. It is not even the whole truth about a man. It is indeed the study of a family and of an epoch. The Middle Border as herein depicted is not the West as others saw it but as Lincoln Stewart saw it, and the pictures drawn are truthful only in the sense that they present conditions as he remembers them and contain characters as they appeared to his youthful eyes. Even when most precise the narrative is not exact and certainly no man writes of himself without restraint.

In the same spirit I offer this volume, not as "the whole truth about an author," not as the definitive biography of Hamlin Garland, but as a critical study of his development as it appears to one motivated by the particular prejudices and biases set forth in this foreword.

JEAN HOLLOWAY

The High Road
Austin, Texas

ACKNOWLEDGMENTS

IN MY STUDY of Garland I have been fortunate in having had the competent assistance of Mr. Lloyd Arvidson, the affable Curator of the American Literature Collection of the Doheny Library of the University of Southern California, who has co-operated with me in many instances far beyond the call of duty, allowing me the freedom to ransack, and to publish from, their extensive Garland collection.

It was my good fortune to have had, also, the encouragement and advice of Mrs. Isabel Garland Lord and Mrs. Constance Garland Doyle, both of Van Nuys, California.

To the reference librarians of the New York Public Library and the library of the University of Texas I also owe a debt of gratitude.

I am indebted to the Macmillan Company for permission to quote from *A Son of the Middle Border, A Daughter of the Middle Border, Roadside Meetings,* and *Afternoon Neighbors.*

The selections from the Garland-Gilder correspondence are by gracious permission of the Century Collection of the New York Public Library.

Quotations from Garland's *The Mystery of the Buried Crosses* (Copyright, 1939) are by permission of the publisher, E. P. Dutton & Company, Inc. Those from *With Walt Whitman in Camden,* Vol. II, by Horace Traubel, are by permission of Doubleday & Company, Inc. From Edward Wagenknecht's *Cavalcade of the*

American Novel I have quoted by permission of Henry Holt &
Company, Inc., and from Sidney Kramer's *A History of Stone &
Kimball and Stone & Company* by permission of the University
of Chicago Press.

I express my appreciation for reliance upon, and quotation
from, studies by various scholars in the field: my late friend Walter S. Campbell and his publisher the University of Oklahoma
Press; John T. Flanagan; and Donald Pizer, the last of whom has
been particularly helpful in the area of bibliography.

For the illustrations in this book I am grateful to Garland's
daughters, Mrs. Lord and Mrs. Doyle, who ransacked attics and
trunks to locate most of the family pictures shown here, and to the
Doheny Library, the University of Southern California, which
granted permission to use four photographs from the Garland
Collection: Garland as a small boy, Franklin and Hamlin Garland, the Garland homestead at Ordway, South Dakota, and the
Garland homestead at West Salem, Wisconsin.

J. H.

TABLE OF CONTENTS

LIST OF ILLUSTRATIONS

HAMLIN GARLAND

§1§

The Minister's Charge

IN THE AUTUMN of 1884 when Hamlin Garland came to Boston to make his literary fortune, the city lay bathed in the romantic afterglow of that blaze of creative activity which in mid-century had made it appear the "hub of the intellectual universe." But the giants of that earlier generation were passing from the scene. Emerson, Hawthorne, and Longfellow were dead. Holmes, Lowell, and Whittier, dwindling in production, were old men repeating themselves in cadences unsuited to the tempo of agrarian revolts and labor riots. The study of comparative literature had effected a Copernican revolution in critical standards, while the emergence of the local-color school of fiction had created a centripetal movement in literature, making the American hinterlands no longer peripheral, but centers of creative activity in their own right. Although its most talented son of the younger generation was rapidly becoming an expatriate, Boston would remain, for yet a little while, the center of literary life in America.

The Boston-published *Atlantic Monthly* still enjoyed the prestige of its long and distinguished history and an international reputation as "the best edited magazine in the English language." Its editorship, descending in apostolic succession from one man of letters to another, from James Russell Lowell through James T. Fields to William Dean Howells, was now held by Thomas Bailey Aldrich, one of Howells' protégés. And Howells, an adopted Bostonian, was rapidly emerging as the leading figure in American letters.

About the time that Hamlin Garland clambered down from the train at the Hoosac Station into "the center of a vaguely alluring literary universe," Howells was engaged in writing *The Minister's Charge,* a novel subtitled "The Apprenticeship of Lemuel Barker." Barker, Howells' prototype of the country boy with literary ambitions, comes to Boston as the result of casual praise of his poems by a vacationing Boston minister. Confronted by the actuality of his rural poet in search of a publisher, the Reverend can only retreat to honesty and tell the young man his efforts are worthless. Chagrined, Barker wanders onto the Common to fall into the hands of confidence men, be robbed of his meager funds, and spend a night in jail on a false charge. Ashamed after this episode to go home, he maintains himself for a season in the city through a series of demeaning jobs. Finally his tribulations force him to admit defeat and he returns to Willoughby Pastures from whence he came.

As the manuscript pages of this realistic view of Boston's lower classes piled up on Howells' desk, young Hamlin Garland, across the city, was living out episodes of a similar apprenticeship—although one with a more romantic ending. Howells makes an amusing scene of his country boy's conspicuous arrival in the city. Barker had no money to ride the horse cars, and, attempting to find his way back to the station, hit upon the expedient of keeping his directions by running beside the public conveyance labeled "Fitchburg, Lowell and Eastern Depots."[1] While Howells wrote, Garland was experiencing a similar dilemma. He had arrived by train from his homesteader's claim in South Dakota, "a stalwart, brown-bearded young man of middle height, wearing a broad-brimmed black hat and carrying an imitation leather valise which contained a few shirts and socks." After two nights and

---

[1] W. D. Howells, *The Minister's Charge* (1886), pp. 48–49.

a day in the smoking car, living on lunchcounter sandwiches, doughnuts, and coffee, he reports:

... I was so sick that I could hardly stagger under the weight of my valise. Ignoring the street car, partly because I could not afford the fare, and partly because I was afraid the driver would not permit me to take my valise inside, I started toward the Common. No aspiring youth ever entered this capital in less exultant mood. The weeping skies overhead and the mud under my feet were in perfect harmony with my feeling of weakness and despair. [2]

Garland's frontal assault upon the literary world was perhaps as ill-advised as any situation of Howells' imaginings. A few months earlier he had been in Ordway, South Dakota (near present Aberdeen), in the home of his parents, a shack adjoining the general store. A knock at the door announced a stranger, who turned out to be a minister from Maine, the Reverend James W. Bashford,[3] visiting some old Wisconsin neighbors of the Garlands. Young Hamlin poured out to him his disillusionment with the country, despite the claim he was proving up forty miles to the westward, and recounted his ambition to spend a year or two in an Illinois normal school fitting himself to teach literature and oratory.

With an insouciance equal to that of Howells' fictional character, Mr. Bashford urged: "Why don't you go to Boston and take special work along those lines? No other place offers the same advantages." On the strength of this stranger's casual suggestion Garland sold the equity in his homestead and, with something like one hundred fifty dollars and two introductory letters from Bashford, arrived friendless in Boston, impressed, despite the dripping skies and his ominous forebodings, that it was "a splendid capital, overpowering with the grandeur of its historic monuments and the wealth of its records of great men and greater events."

To a youth from the plains, its innumerable red, yellow, and green horse-cars tinkling along the streets and its thunderous horse-drawn trucks were confusing. At night arc lights sizzled menacingly at cer-

---

[2] *Roadside Meetings* (1930), pp. 4–5.
[3] The Reverend James W. Bashford was later President of Ohio Wesleyan University.

tain corners but ancient lamplighters still went their rounds lighting
with a long pole the gas jets in iron lanterns. . . . Beacon Street was a
synonym for grandeur, and the Public Library, a plain brown building on Boylston Street, a palace. . . . Music Hall and Tremont Temple
were shrines of music and oratory and the Boston Museum and the
Howard Atheneum were still centers of drama. . . . Here, too, was the
center of lofty oratory; Faneuil Hall suggested Daniel Webster, Wendell Phillips, and William Lloyd Garrison.[4]

Awed by the profusion of historic monuments, Garland resolved to make the most of whatever short tenure he could contrive in this city of unknown potentialities. [5]

It was not precisely Garland's first sight of Boston, although it
appeared to him in a new light as he surveyed it as a prospective
resident. With his brother Franklin he had spent two days of
sightseeing in the city during a summer's excursion through New
England in 1882. That year had been one of restless roaming for
young Hamlin. He had attained his majority and a diploma from
the Cedar Valley Seminary in Osage, Iowa, at about the time his
pioneering parents were on the move to the new frontier in
South Dakota. Intending to strike out on his own, the new-
fledged graduate spent the autumn of 1881 in desultory search
for work—at first for a teaching position—and at length for any
job to keep himself alive. His *Wanderjahre* included most of the
Middle Western states, with stopovers to earn funds at such di-
verse tasks as harvesting, book-selling, clerking, lecturing, and
finally carpentering. The last trade provided steady enough em-
ployment that he was able to save a few dollars with which to join
his brother Franklin on a tour of New England and the East
Coast. The boys slept in barns and helped out with farm chores
to eke out expenses.

The next winter of teaching in a country school in Grundy
County, Ohio, convinced young Hamlin that he needed more
training to fit himself for a professorship, and at the same time
enthusiastic reports of the land boom in the Dakotas persuaded

[4] *Roadside Meetings,* pp. 6–8.
[5] A detailed account of Garland's life during the period preceding his Boston sojourn and of his first months in the city is given in *A Son of the Middle
Border* (1928), Chapters 21–24.

him that the way to finance further education was to homestead a claim. That claim proved up and sold, he was now in position to pursue his vague educational ambitions, recognizing his program as "a kind of insanity . . . a blind following of a desire to see and know the capital" [6] which his father taught him to venerate as the center of the literary universe.

But the Bashford letters provided no entree to the world of education. The professor of English at Boston University and the teacher of "expression" to whom they were directed had no encouragement for an impecunious stranger; nor would Harvard College admit a nonresident student. Thus rebuffed Garland grimly settled down to educate himself, rigidly budgeting his resources "on a scientific plan for cheap living"—a chill north room on Boylston Place at six dollars a month and expenditures of five dollars a week for food being calculated to stretch his funds until spring. He scheduled his time with equal parsimony —mornings for excursions to the historic monuments of the city, afternoons for reading in the Public Library, and evenings for such free entertainment as the city offered.

Thus he came to know the voice and mannerisms of every notable preacher in the city. The book reviews of the Boston *Herald* and of the *Evening Transcript* kept him apprised of the activities of the literary figures, those "remote and radiant stars." For the moment he was content to observe from his obscurity their relative orbits in the world of letters. Unwilling to spend a nickel for carfare, Garland yet indulged in the extravagance of the theater. For thirty-five cents he could stand in the back of the balcony at the Boston Museum and hear Edwin Booth teach "the dignity, power, and the music of the English tongue." On one occasion he reconciled himself to the expenditure of an entire half-dollar to hear the debut of Edward MacDowell at Music Hall. With great eagerness he went to hear James Russell Lowell speak on "The British Dramatists," but the contrast between the young and ardent poet of his imagination and the mumbling greybeard of the lecture platform was a shock and a disappointment. Ingersoll, however, lived up to the young student's expectations, and

[6] *Roadside Meetings,* p. 7.

was ranked by him alongside Edwin Booth as one of the greatest living orators.[7]

All these experiences were part of the education of the prairie boy. But it was Bates Hall, the second-floor reading room of the old Public Library building, which provided the solid meat of his intellectual diet. The shelves of its alcoves stretched toward the vaulted ceiling; its handwritten card catalogue listed more than 300,000 volumes, a rich and sometimes indigestible feast for the book-starved boy from the Middle West. [8] Garland, for a lad of twenty-four with literary ambitions, had had shockingly little contact with the great writers and thinkers. [9] The McClintocks, his mother's people, had had only two books in their home, the Bible and a tract opposing Free Masonry. The Garlands, though by nature a bookish family, had been forced by their successive moves to leave behind whatever volumes they had once accumulated. Thus Hamlin's childhood acquaintance with literature was limited to *Aladdin* and *Beauty and the Beast.* When he was ten years old he had acquired for his own Franklin's *Autobiography,* a life of P. T. Barnum, and *The Female Spy,* and had managed to borrow copies of *Ivanhoe, Scottish Chiefs,* and *Sunshine and Tempest.*

He conned avidly, however, whatever ephemeral reading material there was available in the community, stray newspapers and almanacs. Such magazines as the *New York Saturday Night,* the *New York Ledger, Godey's Lady's Book,* and *Peterson's Magazine* frequently found their way to the Garland home. And in an issue of *Hearth and Home* Hamlin discovered Eggleston's *The Hoosier Schoolmaster,* with its Indiana scene so like the prairie life around him. His father kept up with the political news by means of the Toledo *Blade* and the New York *Tribune,* with the result that in young Hamlin's mind "Horace Greeley and 'Petroleum V. Nasby' were equally corporeal."

[7] *A Son of the Middle Border,* pp. 319–21, 330; *Roadside Meetings,* pp. 42–45; *Companions on the Trail* (1931), p. 115.

[8] Justin Winsor, *Memorial History of Boston,* IV, 291; H. G. Wadlin, *The Public Library of the City of Boston,* pp. 66–70.

[9] Garland's limited boyhood opportunities for reading are described in "Books of My Childhood," *Saturday Review, VIII* (November 15, 1930), 347, and *A Son of the Middle Border,* pp. 120–21, 187.

To counteract the effect of Beadle's *Dime Novels* the rural schools led their scholars through the full set of McGuffey's famous *Readers,* with their selections from the classic writers and orators. Joaquin Miller's poem "Kit Carson's Ride" so impressed young Hamlin that he committed it to memory for a declamation contest. And on his fifteenth birthday his mother presented him with a copy of *Paradise Lost,* which he read thoroughly but with more bewilderment than enthusiasm. "The extraordinary harangues of Satan," which greatly impressed him, became a part of his declamatory material, until one day when his audience, the team of mules before his plow, bolted in protest at the vigor of his delivery.

With such a limited background Garland had enrolled in the local seminary in pursuit of the will-o'-the-wisp of culture. Even so, his preparation was probably on a par with that of his fellow students, for the Cedar Valley Seminary was an institution of the border country offering what would be, by present standards, roughly equivalent to a high school education. For tuition of ninety-five dollars per year the "college" offered to its fewer than two hundred students a four-year course, which, according to its prospectus, included two years of Greek, three years of Latin, four terms of German, one year each of algebra, geometry, United States history, and general history, with one or more terms of physiology, physics, chemistry, botany, geology, astronomy, New Testament history, and Christian evidences. Yet even this outline of instruction must be read with some skepticism in view of the limitations of the faculty.

President Alva (or Alvah) Bush of the Seminary was a Baptist preacher "possessed of some training secured in Jamestown Academy," supplemented by a year's study at Burlington University. His teaching budget in 1878, when Garland was a student, was only $1,000, to cover the costs of a language teacher and a preceptress. All other instruction, presumably, was given by the president himself. In the following year, however, there was $846 available for seven assistant teachers. Some one of this faculty evidently expanded the curriculum to impart to Garland a reading knowledge of French. Acquisitions to the library, if there were any, must have been concealed under the budgetary appropriation of $225 for "general expenses."[10] Yet even with its obvious limitations, the school provided sufficient reading matter to broaden young Garland's horizons, sets of Dickens, Thackeray, and Scott—terra incognita to the farm lad. One day he discovered in his browsing *Mosses from an Old Manse,* and Hawthorne became his "first profound literary passion." "With these volumes," says Garland, "my boyish reading ended. Thereafter I read as a student, vaguely aware of the problems which beset the American novelist, the poet, and the playwright."

On a lonely Dakota outpost the ambitions aroused in the dormered brick building of the Cedar Valley Seminary persisted, proof that education of the Mark-Hopkins-on-the-log variety often bears the best fruit. Garland settled down behind the counter of his father's store to put himself through a course in the nature of literature, plodding through "an unexpurgated volume of Taine, a set of Chambers' *Encyclopedia of English Literature,* and a volume of Greene's *History of the English People."* With this background he came to Bates Hall at twenty-four with some knowledge of what he was seeking.

Every day at opening hour he presented himself at the sandstone-and-brick building, for years condemned by Bostonians as lacking in the two essentials of light and air. To Garland, shivering in his sleazy cotton overcoat and thin-soled shoes, it was not only a well of inspiration but a haven of physical comfort. With hurried breaks for meals he read avidly until closing time—Darwin, Spencer, Fiske, Helmholtz, and Haeckel unfolding before him the mysteries of science. There was no religious block to this new revelation, for years earlier Ingersoll's lectures, as reported in the press, had dispelled any credence in the supernatural.

For diversion from such weighty theories Garland dipped into early English literature, "weltering in that sea of song which marks the beginnings of every literature, conning the ballads of Ireland and Wales, the epics of Ireland, the early German, and the songs of the troubadours," a course of reading which set him to composing his own critique, a grandiose project to be entitled "The Development of English Ideals." "My mental diaphragm

[10] Clarence R. Aurner, *History of Education in Iowa,* III, 148–50; Leonard F. Parker, *Higher Education in Iowa* (Bureau of Education Circular of Information, No. 6, Washington, 1893), pp. 126–27.

creaked," Garland reminisced of this period, "with the pressure of inrushing ideas. My brain—young, sensitive to every touch—took hold of facts and theories like a phonographic cylinder, and while my body softened and my muscles wasted from disuse, I skittered from pole to pole of the intellectual universe like an impatient bat."[11]

Lanier he met through *The Science of English Verse,* and Whitman through the proscribed *Leaves of Grass.* The Elizabethan dramatists kindled to life as he reread each morning the text of the role which Edwin Booth had created the night before: Hamlet, Lear, Othello, Petruchio, Sir Giles Overreach, Macbeth, Iago, Richelieu.[12]

But when the doors of Bates Hall closed for the evening Garland was forced to leave empty-handed this world of philosophy and poetry. Library regulations forbade nonresidents of the city to check out volumes. Back in his chill, eight-by-ten chamber he would wrap himself in his overcoat and brood over the nebular hypothesis. In the interests of science and in an effort to escape boredom he set himself to chart a natural phenomenon new to his experience, the habits of the genus cockroach. As his funds steadily dwindled the young man at last rebelled against this unwarranted proscription of his study time, which deprived him of library resources on evenings, Sundays, and the five legal holidays of the year. Resolving to carry his case to higher authority he recalled the kindly face and generous reputation of one of the preachers whose services he had attended, Edward Everett Hale.[13]

Hale, whose portrait had been one of the set of "Authors" cards in Garland's Iowa home, was now a trustee of the library. When Garland presented himself at the pastor's study in the South End church where Hale kept office hours, the shaggy-bearded philanthropist himself opened the door and greeted his visitor with bluff kindliness. Garland outlined his difficulties, which he presented as those of twenty thousand other young students in the city. "Well, well," roared Hale. "I don't like that.

<hr>

.1 "Books of My Childhood," p. 347; *A Son of the Middle Border,* pp. 192, 219, 307, 323.

[12] "Some of My Youthful Enthusiasms," *English Journal,* XX (May, 1931), 363.

[13] *A Son of the Middle Border,* pp. 325–26.

I will look into it." Meanwhile he gave Garland a card to the librarian, which won for the student full privileges of the circulating department. As a consequence Garland increased his reading hours from ten a day to fourteen a day, and, under his Spartan regime, grew leaner and more ill-kempt as the winter wore on. The memory of this bedraggled student must have haunted Hale for some time thereafter, for twice he mailed to Garland lecture tickets to subscription affairs. [14]

The successful outcome of this encounter with Hale encouraged Garland to make himself known to another public speaker. At the Young Men's Union at the close of a series of lectures on "The Philosophy of Expression," given by Moses True Brown of the Boston School of Oratory, Garland moved to the rostrum and complimented the speaker on his use of Darwin's writings in support of his thesis. Brown, "a large man with a full beard, genial gray eyes, and a pleasant voice," invited his admirer to an inteı view the next day in his office on the fourth floor of No. 7 Beacon Street. The upshot of the meeting was that Garland became a pupil in Brown's school, discharging his obligations for tuition by doing research and French translations for use in Brown's proposed book on his lecture topic.

To his Public Library tutelage Garland could now add the stimulation of formal lectures given by Brown's faculty on such subjects as "George Sand," "Turgenev," "Lessing," "Victor Hugo," "Emotion vs. Ideas," "Poetry of Poverty," "Poets of the Invisible," "Poets of Indignation," and other broad topics. In his battered student's notebook his lecture notes are interspersed with attempts at fiction. The stories are crude and fragmentary, the fumblings of a youngster not yet in command of his medium, and totally unsure of his direction. One entitled "Haunted!" is clearly under the influence of Hawthorne, with its *outré* opening: "Confound the man—if he be a man!" Yet side by side with such extravagances are gropings toward realism, a sketch of "Boomtown" called "Uncle Billy Farrell," and attempts at popular magazine subjects. The lead line of one of these, "Love vs. Business," must have caused his teachers to discount completely

[14] E. E. Hale to Garland, November 8, 1884, and November 18, 1884, Hamlin Garland Papers. See Bibliography, Unpublished Primary Materials.

the possibility that Garland might one day earn a living with his pen. Wrote the young student, painfully establishing character and setting: "Joel Bingham sat in his sunny little law-office in the busy little city of Dubuque thinking very hard out loud." [15]

That spring of 1885 the connection with Reverend Bashford at last proved beneficial. Belatedly Garland rode out to Jamaica Plains and presented a letter of introduction to a friend of Bashford, the physician Dr. Cross, who, observing the pallor of his visitor and the evident signs of his poverty, offered to take him in as a lodger for a nominal fee during the summer months while the family were on vacation. Thus Garland was able to exchange "the sunless den on Boylston Place" for an attic room in a pleasant residential area and his fifteen-cent dinners for three square meals a day.

Despite this upturn in his fortunes Garland's cash resources continued to decline until at last he determined that he must quit the city and go to some rural community to take up again his trade of carpentering. When he announced this decision to Professor Brown, his mentor was incredulous and amused that a young man of such pronounced literary bent should consider shingling a house. Impressed finally that Garland was serious about the matter, Brown offered as alternative to include in the summer session of his school a course in American literature to be conducted by "Professor Hamlin Garland," with all receipts therefrom to be the earnings of the lecturer. On the strength of this prospect Garland wrote home to borrow twenty-five dollars from his father, with which he paid his arrears in board to Dr. Cross and had dyed the suit in which he had arrived in Boston, once a purple aniline now turning pink at the seams. With the addition of a new pair of shoes and a plaid Windsor tie he was ready to assume his professorship.

The summer school was attended by teachers from nearby towns and the Middle Western states and a sprinkling of local residents. Among the last was a certain Mrs. Paysen, whose maternal instinct led her to become the sponsor and fairy godmother of the young lecturer, launching him upon his oratorical

---

[15] Notebook headed "Begun Oct. 16, 1884–Literature," Garland Papers.

career. Upon all her friends, many of them influential in the intellectual world, she forced subscription cards to a series of lectures. [16]

THREE EVENINGS IN LITERATURE AND EXPRESSION

Studies by Hamlin Garland
(Graduate of the Boston School of Oratory)

First Evening   "Victor Hugo and his Prose Masterpieces"
Second Evening   "Edwin Booth as a Master of Expression"
Third Evening   "Some German and American Novels"

At Mrs. J. Wentworth Paysen's
136 Fairmont Avenue, Hyde Park

Three Evenings, $1.00   One Evening, 50 cents [17]

Thus suddenly metamorphosed into "Professor Garland of American Literature" young Hamlin could boast as previous oratorical experience, that is, exclusive of harangues delivered to a pair of mules, only school declamations and an unsuccessful platform appearance or two on the road in 1882. Yet recalling the examples of Ingersoll and Booth and the precepts of "The Principles of Expression," he faced "with a gambler's composure" the distinguished audience gathered in Mrs. Paysen's parlor. It included Charles Hurd, literary editor of the *Boston Evening Transcript*, the painter John Enneking, and professors from the normal school at Ottawa, Wesleyan University, Howard University, Princeton, De Pauw, and Chicago University. The newspaper reporters present treated his lectures respectfully. "He struck a deep key and did not sharp or flat at the close," [18] wrote one.

After Garland's lecture on Edwin Booth, a subject which had long engaged his emotions and his intellect, there were many per-

---

[16] *A Son of the Middle Border*, pp. 340–42; *Roadside Meetings*, pp. 13–21.

[17] Printed card in the Garland Papers. In the account of this episode in *A Son of the Middle Border* Mrs. Paysen appears as "Mrs. Payne." Garland states that his first lecture at her home, on "The Art of Edwin Booth," was followed by three other lectures on the topics listed in this announcement, a separate lecture being given on "The Modern German Novel" and one on "The American Novel."

[18] "An Evening with Victor Hugo," and other undated, unidentified clippings in the Garland Papers.

sonal congratulations. Overhearing Mr. Hurd's invitation to the
young orator to call at the *Transcript* office, Professor Brown
nudged his protégé, "Going back to shingling, are you?" he asked
quizzically.

There was no doubt but that Garland had graduated from his
carpenter's tools. However shaky his written style, as a speaker he
commanded his audiences. Not only did he realize ninety dollars
from this series of lectures but he found himself in demand for
further engagements. [19] Within a few months he conducted a
series of talks upon Shakespearean subjects for the Wentworth
Club and a course on Browning in Chelsea. He was bold enough
to conclude this latter series, according to a contemporary news
fully crowned the true criticism." [20]
report, with "a generous presentation of original work [which]

With his finances stabilized Garland continued to study and
to write. Between the composition of lectures and historical essays he again tried his hand at verse and fiction. Charles Hurd of
the *Transcript* was a kindly mentor, publishing without pay to
the author an occasional critical article or short piece of verse.
A crude short story, "Ten Years Dead," was accepted in March,
1885, by *Every Saturday Night,* a Boston weekly, for the sum of
five dollars. The tale deals with a man who returns "as one dead
for a space of ten years" to familiar scenes. This hero, making his
reappearance in the Chicago Public Library rather than in Bates
Hall, is in other biographical details a pure reincarnation of the
author. The Hawthornesque story was one of which Garland was
to be heartily ashamed in future years. [21]

More suggestive of his future subject matters were the series
of descriptive sketches which he began that winter. [22] Diffidently
he introduced his first essay:

I venture to present, therefore, the latest phases of corn-husking in the
West, though daunted at the outset by the doubting word of a friend

---

[19] *A Son of the Middle Border,* pp. 344–45.
[20] Undated, unidentified clipping in the Garland Papers.
[21] *A Son of the Middle Border,* p. 347; *Roadside Meetings,* p. 36; C. E.
Schorer, "Hamlin Garland's First Published Story," *American Literature,*
XXVI (March, 1953), 89–92.
[22] *American Magazine* (Brooklyn), January–October, 1888, VII, 299–303;
570–77; 683–90; VIII, 148–54; 296–302; 712–17.

who says, "Oh! There isn't any poetry in such wholesale methods of
corn gathering." I answer him by saying, "There is for me, and there
will be for many others who, like myself, grew up amid it and took
part in it."

.   .   .   .

Sometimes now, when I sit at my desk in the city, a man in the street
will shovel coal into a spout to somebody's cellar; and instantly I am
back beside that stove, listening to the ringing sound which the corn
makes as it leaves the scoop: first a little rumble and rattle—that is
the shovel being pushed along the box under the corn—next, that
ringing scrape, as the hard ears leave the steel. Then the faint crash
of the corn as it strikes in the crib. [23]

The acceptance of this first sketch called "The Huskin'" by
the *American Magazine* of Brooklyn encouraged Garland to go
on with his series of "Boy Life on the Prairie." This new-world
Shepherd's Calendar continues with a nostalgic description of
"The Thrashin'"; a tribute in mingled verse and prose to "The
Voice of Spring"; a paean on seeding, "Between Hay an' Grass";
a glorification of the harvest, "Meadow Memories"; and to round
out the year a sketch of autumn entitled "Melons and Early
Frost."

Garland's attitude toward his subject matter wavers between
a somewhat self-conscious nostalgia and an attempt at realistic
perspective. After one of his more extravagant flights he comments:

It is a delusion, the mere gilding of a hard task, a halo around a dull
and laborious life by the passage of time. Ah, well: there is no harm
done in looking back wistfully at this distance—it is safe enough. It is
a phase of life passed away. The "check-rowing-automatic-corn-plant-
er and coverer" has taken the place of the girls and boys with aprons
and hoes. [24]

But when he reaches his winter sequence he strikes the note
which was to become dominant in his best fiction:

It takes but a long cold rain to bring out the terrible contrast of the
brilliant landscape on fair days, and the gloom and narrowness of the

[23] "The Huskin'," *ibid.*, VII, 298.
[24] "Between Hay an' Grass," *ibid.*, VIII, 149.

home life at all times. There is no gilding of setting sun or glamor of poetry to light up the ferocious and endless toil of the farmers' wives. [25]

The pay for "Boy Life on the Prairie" was meager, publication slow. When, however, *Harper's Weekly* promptly paid Garland twenty-five dollars for a long poem called "Lost in a Norther," [26] he felt that his rigorous training was at last paying off. With this bonanza he hastened to send to his father a set of the *Memoirs of General Grant,* and to his mother the material for her first silk dress.

It was well that Garland was beginning to pay his own way, for the fortunes of his family had taken a down turn. A series of bad seasons combined with loosely extended credit had brought the failure of the Dakota store, and as the parents returned to the grim round of farm labor, Hamlin's brother Franklin came on to Boston, where he found work as a railway accountant. Hamlin's Sundays were no longer spent in brooding isolation but in showing Franklin the wonders of Boston and the beauties of the surrounding countryside. [27]

Gradually, too, he made friends within the peripheral circles of the arts. John Enneking, the landscape painter, introduced him to the studios where impressionism and socialism were urged with equal vigor. By this time Garland had become an ardent disciple of Henry George, whose *Progress and Poverty* he had read feelingly in Dakota, and could harangue with the best of them against individual ownership of land and the evils of capitalism. [28]

Garland's essential gregariousness came into play as these various contacts and his expanding lecture activities relieved the enforced isolation of his earlier Boston days. Like the reporter-hero of one of his novels he learned to explore the back streets of the city:

He soon knew every principal street. Next he studied the districts of the city. He found that the West End held most colored people, the North End most Italians, the South End most Irish, Harrison Avenue most Chinese. He studied the wharves till the longshoremen wondered

[25] "Melons and Early Frost," *ibid.*, VIII, 716.
[26] XXXI (December 3, 1887), 883.
[27] *A Son of the Middle Border,* pp. 348–52.
[28] *Roadside Meetings,* pp. 26–29; *A Son of the Middle Border,* pp. 313–14.

at him. He discovered a great deal about sailors, one thing being that they never talked in nautical metaphors. [29]

The Minister's Charge; or the Apprenticeship of Lemuel Barker, which had been appearing serially in the *Century,* was soon handed to Garland for review by his friends on the *Transcript.* With slight effort he could identify himself with the young hero of that novel, but the position which he should take on Howells as novelist was one to which he must give considerable attention in his new dignity as professor of American Literature.

He recalled the first of the Howells novels which he had encountered. In Iowa during his last term of school, while idling about the post office, he had opened a book lying on the counter, *The Undiscovered Country,* which the postal clerk roundly condemned, since the title had led him to expect a tale of travel or adventure. Garland read a portion of it as he waited and was "irritated and repelled by the modernity of William Dean Howells."

During his two years in Boston, Garland had become more and more aware of Howells as the rising luminary in that galaxy of literary figures whose orbits the young critic followed from afar, the subject of much literary gossip since the announcement of his association with *Harper's Monthly* to conduct the "Editor's Study." Howells' books were controversial material both in method and subject matter. His readers debated among themselves whether or not his women characters could be found in New England society, and the critics condemned them as woeful exaggerations. [30] Garland found fault with Howells on different grounds. In his lecture on "The Modern Novel" in connection with praise of Spielhagen he asked the rhetorical question *"Will you put Howells beside this man? Or Cable, or Crawford or James?"* and continued: "Howells in his *Undiscovered Country* started in bravely upon a study of modern spiritualism but soon became convinced of his inadequacy and after dabbling around the edges drew off. He was a tenderfoot who had forgotten his compass." [31]

[29] *Jason Edwards* (1892), p. 8.
[30] *A Son of the Middle Border,* p. 227; *Roadside Meetings,* p. 55.
[31] Extracts from this lecture, the manuscript of which is in the Garland

But as he studied further Garland came to reverse his position and to appreciate Howells as the foremost exemplar of that principle he was drumming into the ears of his new audiences:

American literature, in order to be great, must be national, and in order to be national, must deal with conditions peculiar to our own land and climate. Every genuinely American writer must deal with the life he knows best and for which he cares the most. Thus Joel Chandler Harris, George W. Cable, Joseph Kirkland, Sarah Orne Jewett, and Mary Wilkins, like Bret Harte, are but varying phases of the same movement, a movement which is to give us at last a really vital and original literature! [32]

By the time he came to review *The Minister's Charge* Garland had become Howells' enthusiastic advocate. His comments were given the lead position on the book page of the *Transcript*, set in larger type than the other reviews. [33] Garland's sympathetic reaction to the ordeals of Lemuel Barker had been spontaneous. As he explained in a later critical article on Howells, he saw Barker's life and experiences as "representative, in great measure, of those of thousands of young fortune seekers, students of music, painting, sculpture, journalism, who come and go in Boston and who make up a large and distinctive class. They do not all come with poems to sell, or with the avowed intention of succeeding Mr. Lowell, but they do have a vague, inarticulate desire for a more intellectual life, a broader and more public activity." [34]

He could also sympathize with the background figures in the novel, with "the silent, grotesque, and infinitely sorrowful figure of Lemuel's mother," seeing her plight as "a genuinely and characteristically American tragedy obscurely set forth . . . the inevitable and inexorable separation of parent and child, that comes with the entrance of the child upon wider and higher planes of thought and action." He elaborated his interpretation in this fashion:

Papers, have been reproduced by Lars Ahnebrink in "Appendix C" of *The Beginnings of Naturalism in American Fiction*, pp. 444–47.

[32] *A Son of the Middle Border*, p. 387.

[33] *Boston Transcript*, January 31, 1887.

[34] "Mr. Howells' Latest Novels," *New England Magazine*, II, n.s. (May, 1890), 243–50.

The cities are filled with children fighting for standing room, winning here and losing there, and the country is full of homes without sons and daughters to lighten up the gloomy passage of the toil-worn parents on their way to the grave. There they sit, as Lemuel's mother sat, waiting for the weekly letter—all too short in most cases—and dreaming of the success of their children. To many a man in the city the story of Lemuel Barker came with a directness that made the case his own. [35]

Edward Clement, the hitherto unapproachable editor-in-chief of the *Transcript,* sent for Garland as a result of his review, commending it as an "able article." Having sent a copy to Howells, he suggested giving Garland a letter of introduction to the author, but on second thought withdrew the offer for the moment, suggesting that in view of the controversy swirling around Howells it would be better for Garland "to keep his objectivity unsullied by a personal acquaintance."

It was not until a later date that Garland met William Dean Howells face to face. The impact of that encounter so impressed the younger man that he continued throughout his life to recount the story in the public print, with ever-increasing circumstantial details.

Presenting himself at "The Elms," the residential hotel occupied by Mr. Howells, Garland's nervous trepidation was increased by the hauteur of the clerk who informed him Mr. Howells was at luncheon. But his letter of introduction from the *Transcript* won him the privilege of awaiting an audience:

A light step reached my ears. I rose. The curtain parted and a short man with a handsome head stood before me. His face was impassive but his glance one of the most piercing I had ever encountered. In that single instant, before he smiled, he discovered my character, divined my state of mind, and probably inventoried my clothing. It was the glance of a student of men, of the author of "Silas Lapham."

His appraising scrutiny took but a second's time. Then his face softened, and he smiled winningly: "I am glad to see you," he said, and his tone convinced me of his sincerity. "Won't you be seated?"

He indicated a seat at one end of the sofa. I took it, finding him like his portraits, only kinder. He began by thanking me for my reviews,

[35] "Mr. Howells' Latest Novels," *New England Magazine,* II, n.s. (May, 1890), 245.

then proceeded to inquire concerning my own work and purposes. It took but a moment to start the story of my coming to Boston. In truth I was bursting with talk. I hurried on with rushing flow, developing my early antagonism to his realism and my recent conversion to it. I outlined my theory of criticism, and seeing that he listened intently, I described a work which I had in manuscript called "The Development of American Ideals." I was a torrent, a whirlwind, and a spring overflowing. . . . In the heat of my argument, I harangued like a political orator running at top speed. I didn't know how to stop—I don't think I did stop. I imagine he applied the brake, but if he did, he was so deft and so kindly in action that I did not understand exactly how he made use of it. . . .

How long he talked, or how long I talked, I cannot now recall (the clock stopped for me), but at last, in some deft way, he got me outside, and as we walked down the street toward the station he became still more friendly. He treated me not merely as a literary aspirant, but as a critic in whom he could confide. He spoke of his aroused interest in the Russian writers and asked my opinion with regard to certain questions in debate at the moment, and I answered with joyous vigour. I was, I fear, a mad orator, exalted and presumptuous, but in his gentle way he governed me and finally headed me for my train. [36]

To his previous encouragement of Garland's critical theories regarding the local-color school of fiction and of his ambitions to portray the West in literature, Howells added the final touch by pretending to consult the young critic on a proposed story of his own, agreeing then with Garland's comments. The younger man was exultant:

That any praise of mine, or any criticism of mine, could have any lasting effect upon a man whose fame was international, I could not believe, but to have him desire my impression of the fitness of a chosen theme, was like feeling on my shoulder the touch of a king's ennobling blade. My apprenticeship was over, I had been accepted by America's chief literary man as a fellow, a literary historian. [37]

---

[36] Garland referring to the interview in *A Son of the Middle Border* (1914) says "it must have been two years after" the *Transcript* review of January 31, 1887. In "Meetings with Howells," *Bookman*, XLV (March, 1917), 1–7, he states that this first meeting was "possibly in June of 1887," a date which appears to be approximately correct. In *Roadside Meetings* (1930), pp. 58–60, he gives the more detailed version here quoted, dating the incident, however, as of October, 1885, an obvious impossibility if it followed upon the *Transcript* review.

[37] *Roadside Meetings*, p. 61.

In such fashion began a relation which was to endure for more than thirty years, until Howells' death wrote an end to what Garland termed "the longest and most important friendship" of his life. [38] And as by-product of the meeting Garland acquired a formula for handling celebrities: a letter of introduction or an appreciative review as entering wedge, a certain brashness in forcing an appointment, an honest awe and admiration for the achievements of the great—there would be few doors in the worlds of art or politics which would remain closed to his approach.

[38] *My Friendly Contemporaries* (1932), p. 294.

❧ 2 ❧

Professor of Literature, "or Something Kin"

As a professional critic in the virgin field of contemporary American letters and as self-appointed press agent for the local-color school of fiction, Hamlin Garland now began to send out a barrage of inquiries to the great, the near-great, and the ephemeral, writers of the day. What did they consider their aim in writing? What was their critical theory? Their methods of work? The flattery of his interest produced a sheaf of replies. The names of many of the signatories are lost in the limbo of forgotten poets, but others of Garland's correspondents stand high in literary history. Both to the famous and to awe-struck aspirants Garland continued to write with cordiality and respect, establishing relations that often led to personal meetings, and in some cases to deep and lifelong friendships.

Whatever charge of snobbish opportunism may attach to the brash persistence of his epistolary methods, the catholicity of his choice of correspondents tends to soften the verdict. While he was capable of forcing himself to the attention of Edwin Booth, enclosing "a very scanty and incoherent synopsis of a lecture which

I have been delivering," and maneuvering himself into an introduction at a public gathering,[1] he was equally concerned to send
books and letters of encouragement to a woman on an Indian reservation who between preparing meals for twelve children had
written a sketch on "Life Among the Piutes." [2]

Apropos of a *Transcript* review of *A Moonlight Boy* in which
Garland claimed to have "some hand," he wrote to E. W. Howe,
proposing to include him in a more elaborate work of criticism:
"There are representative names, standing for 'local, scene and
character painting'; in which category you stand in solitary grandeur, in the midst of the great west (myself, your only rival, not
having published yet)." [3]

Howe replied, inaugurating a brisk correspondence. Sarah
Orne Jewett furnished a thoughtful analysis of the rationale of
her stories. Mark Twain was characteristically brusque: "I am
heels over head in work and cannot possibly spare the time for
giving the subject you speak of the proper thought so as to venture the least advice." But Mary Wilkins Freeman wrote extensively as to her theories of literature, and at length agreed to
Garland's arranging a meeting with William Dean Howells, insisting ("though not very conventional either") on the propriety
of Howells' coming to her hotel rather than her calling at his.
Edgar Fawcett, who in addition to writing novels and poetry
served as reader for Garland's publisher, the *American Magazine,* gave sales advice and criticism. John Burroughs corre-
sponded on his enthusiasm for Walt Whitman, a topic on which
Garland was also voluble. [4]

To his classes Garland lectured on Whitman as the living exponent of an indigenous literature, and to the poet wrote a report

[1] Garland to Edwin Booth, January 22, 1886, quoted in *A Son of the Middle Border* (1928), pp. 381–82.
[2] Sarah Wimemuscee Hopkins to Garland, February 16, 1887, Garland
Papers.
[3] Garland to E. W. Howe, July 2, 1886, Garland Papers.
[4] E. W. Howe to Garland, July 7, 1886; Sarah Orne Jewett to Garland,
October 24, 1888; Mark Twain to Garland, March 23, 1889; Mary Wilkins
Freeman to Garland, February 8, 1887 and January 21, 1891; Edgar Fawcett
to Garland, undated, and December 7, 1888; John Burroughs to Garland,
October 16, 1888; all in Garland Papers. Portions of the letters from Miss
Jewett and of the earlier letters from Mrs. Freeman are printed in *Roadside
Meetings* (1930), pp. 34–36. The Howe correspondence is summarized at pp.
95–96, and the letter from Burroughs is quoted, pp. 154–55.

of the reception of his talks. "I have demonstrated (what of course you know) that there is no veil, no impediment, between your mind and your audience, when your writings are *voiced*." Whitman kept this letter and later commented on this analysis: "That's a point to chew on. Read it again. I want to get it clear in my noddle for keeps!"

Garland continued, in the vein of neophyte to master, asking permission to quote Whitman in a chapter on "The Age of Democracy" in his book on "American Ideals":

I am a young man of very ordinary attainments, and do not presume to do more than give you a glimpse of the temper of that public which would not do you wrong, deliberately, but who by reason of the causes hinted at above, fail to get at the transcendent power of "Leaves of Grass." If I have given you the impression that I believe in you and strive to interpret you, you will not feel that I have overstepped the privilege of a pupil in the presence of a great teacher.

The enclosed slip is a meagre outline of a volume which I am writing and which I hope to get out this coming spring. As the motto page of this volume I have used a paragraph from your Collect which is entitled Foundation States—then Others. [5]

The invalid at Camden characterized this epistle "a dandy letter from Garland. . . . a first confession: not an obsequious obeisance made to the ground but just a manly equal shake of the hand. . . . I always seem to expect the men and women of the West to take me in—what shall I say?—oh! take me in one gulp.'"[6]

Despite his favorable reaction Whitman did not reply, being unsure where to address Garland. Some months later Garland, disturbed by this omission, seems to have appealed to Richard M. Bucke, one of Whitman's editors, for Bucke wrote Garland in March of 1887 to consider Whitman's silence as the equivalent of consent in the matter of permission to quote. [7]

But the manuscript of "The Development of American Ideals" was destined to languish unpublished, [8] for the influence of a new

[5] Garland's letter is dated November 24, 1886, and is quoted in *Roadside Meetings*, pp. 128–29.

[6] Horace Traubel, *With Walt Whitman in Camden*, II, 160–63. Whitman's comments were made upon rereading the letter on August 18, 1888, just prior to a visit from Garland.

[7] R. M. Bucke to Garland, March 12, 1887, Garland Papers.

[8] Donald Pizer, "Herbert Spencer and the Genesis of Hamlin Garland's

correspondent combined with personal experiences to set Garland upon a different tack. That May, for the *Transcript,* he reviewed *Zury, The Meanest Man in Spring County,* praising its homespun qualities. "To say that Joseph Kirkland has written the most realistic novel of American interior life is to state the simple fact. It is as native to Illinois as Tolstoi's 'Anna Karènina' or Tourgènieff's 'Fathers and Sons' are to Russia." [9] A copy of this review mailed to the author brought an invitation to visit him. Garland, who planned to pass through Chicago en route to his old home, promptly accepted, and found Kirkland, a sixty-year-old lawyer of literary bent, a most congenial companion.

The Kirkland ladies being away for the summer the two men could stay up to all hours discussing realism, Howells, and the land question. Kirkland, after reading some of his young guest's Western sketches, [10] urged him to write fiction. Garland demurred, claiming his inability to write dialogue. Kirkland brushed aside this excuse as mere laziness: "You must bend to your desk like a man. You must grind! . . . When your name is known all over the West, remember what I say. You can go far if you'll only work."

Garland left Chicago in a glow of encouragement. As the familiar landmarks of his boyhood flashed by the railroad cars his aroused sense of fictional possibilities warred with the happiness of homecoming:

Something deep and resonant vibrated within my brain as I looked out upon this monotonous commonplace landscape. I realized for the first time that the east had surfeited me with picturesqueness. It appeared that I had been living for six years amidst painted, neatly arranged pasteboard scenery. Now suddenly I dropped to the level of nature unadorned, down to the ugly unkempt lanes I knew so well, back to the pungent realities of the streamless plain.

Furthermore I acknowledged a certain responsibility for the condi-

Critical System" (*Tulane Studies in English,* VII [1957], pp. 153–68), has given an excellent analysis of this unpublished MS with particular relation to Spencerian ideas and to the development of Garland's critical system, "which served as the foundation for his defense, advocacy, and practice of local color."

[9] *Boston Evening Transcript,* May 16, 1887.

[10] Presumably in manuscript. "Boy Life on the Prairie" had not yet appeared in print.

tions of the settlers. I felt related to them, an intolerant part of them. Once fairly among the fields of northern Illinois everything became so homely, uttered itself so piercingly to me that nothing less than song could express my sense of joy, of power. This was my country—these my people. [11]

Back in the town of Osage, where at the height of the Garland fortunes Hamlin's father had once been in charge of the grain elevator, Hamlin wandered as a stranger. Unrecognized behind his growth of whiskers he observed his old neighbors with something of the detachment of his fictional hero "returned as one dead for the space of years." Few of his old intimates were on hand to watch the Fourth of July parade. Some were dead and some had married and moved away. Burton Babcock, the companion of his youth, was preaching on the frontier, and "Alice," the girl who had occupied his Seminary dreams, lived in another town. Garland listened as the old men complained of the crops. Even the young men seemed silent and sad. He was puzzled to note that "laughter was curiously infrequent" and wondered if in his days on the farm his companions "had all been as rude of dress, as misshapen of form and as wistful of voice as they now seemed. . . . At the moment nothing glozed the essential tragic futility of their existence."

Upon making himself known Garland found a hearty welcome from neighbors in Dry Run, the farming community where his elder sister Harriet was buried. But the habits and attitudes of his one-time associates revolted him:

All the gilding of farm life melted away. The hard and bitter realities came back upon me in a flood. Nature was as beautiful as ever. The soaring sky was filled with shining clouds, the tinkle of the bobolink's fairy bells rose from the meadow, a mystic sheen was on the odorous grass and waving grain, but no splendor of cloud, no grace of sunset could conceal the poverty of these people, on the contrary they brought out, with a more intolerable poignancy, the gracelessness of these homes, and the sordid quality of the mechanical daily routine of these lives.

I perceived beautiful youth becoming bowed and bent. I saw lovely

---

[11] *A Son of the Middle Border,* p. 355. The homecoming is described on pp. 354–74.

girlhood wasting away into thin and hopeless age. Some of the women
I had known had withered into querulous and complaining spinster-
hood, and I heard ambitious youth cursing the bondage of the farm.
"Of such pain and futility are the lives of the average man and woman
of both city and country composed," I acknowledged to myself with
savage candor, "Why lie about it?" [12]

In summary of his experience at Osage, Garland reports:

In those few days, I perceived life without its glamor. I no longer
looked upon these toiling women with the thoughtless eyes of youth.
I saw no humor in the bent forms and graying hair of the men. I began to understand that my own mother had trod a similar slavish
round, with never a full day of leisure, with scarcely an hour of escape
from the tugging hands of children, and the need of mending and
washing clothes. I recalled her as she passed from the churn to the
stove, from the stove to the bedchamber back to the kitchen, day after
day, year after year, rising at daylight or before and going to her bed
only after the evening dishes were washed and the stockings and
clothing mended for the night.
    The essential tragedy and hopelessness of most human life under
the conditions into which our society was swiftly hardening embit-
tered me, called for expression, but even then I did not know that I
had found my theme. I had no intention at the moment of putting it
into fiction. [13]

Garland fell further and further into disenchantment as he
studied the landscape across Iowa and into South Dakota, "the
familiar flimsy little wooden towns . . . like beads upon a string."
At Ordway there was a reunion with his parents and his younger
sister Jessica. But again Garland was shocked, this time by the
signs of age in his mother. "Hesitation was in her speech. Her
voice once so glowing and so jocund, was tremulous, and her
brown hair, once so abundant, was thin and gray." He realized
that in the three years of his absence "she had topped the high al-
titude of her life and was now descending swiftly toward de-
fenseless old age."
    The wheat was in the harvest and Hamlin took his old-time
place in the crew as "boss stacker," noting anew his physical sen-

[12] *Ibid.,* p. 365.
[13] *Ibid.,* p. 366.

sations, the callousing of his hands, the sweating of his scalp, and the all-pervasive grime of his labors. These details he set out at length for the benefit of his new-found friend Joseph Kirkland. Replied Kirkland:

Your observation of farm life so far toward the frontier, especially in harvest-time must be very valuable. The next thing is to be "bold, vigorous, and faithful" (as they used to say in bestowing the accolade of knighthood) to write it in truth and sentimental perception. I *do not* like your title "Boomtown. *A Social Study*": Our fiction *is* a social study, but we must conceal the study part. You might as well call it *an essay,* and so damn it at once. And if, as I fear, your study of the subject is perceptible in your *treatment* of it, you must write it all over again to eliminate self and make your characters seem to act and talk with perfect spontaneity. The "art to conceal art" is the one indispensable thing in realism. Of course you have to throw light on your theme, but you must fool the reader with the idea that the light shines from within it, outward. [14]

Kirkland's suggestion threw Garland into "a condition of tantalizing productivity. . . . Conceptions for stories began to rise from the subconscious deeps of my thought like bubbles, noiseless and swift—and still I did not realize that I had entered upon a new career," remembered Garland. [15]

Yet as he lay in the shade of the hay rick at nooning he was soon penciling lines of verse which he called "Color in the Wheat." [16] While yet on the farm he began to write out an anecdote told him by his mother—a simple tale of a farm woman who astonishes her husband and neighbors by insisting on making a trip back to her old home in York state. In Garland's version of "Mrs. Ripley's Trip," the old grandmother makes her journey, then returns to settle complacently into her old routine. "She took up her burden again, never more thinking to lay it down till her poor workweary, bony hands should be folded finally on her lean, pathetic

[14] Joseph Kirkland to Garland, July 30, 1887. In "Joseph Kirkland's Influence on Hamlin Garland," *American Literature,* XXIII (January, 1952), 458–63, Clyde E. Henson has quoted many of Kirkland's letters to Garland. The originals are in the Garland Papers. Where passages quoted or referred to are available in Mr. Henson's article that reference also will be given.
[15] *A Son of the Middle Border,* p. 371.
[16] "Color in the Wheat" appears in *Prairie Songs* (1893) at p. 26.

old bosom. Her next trip will be so far away she will never return
—far past the gates of space and time." [17]

The contrast between the lot of the Mrs. Ripleys of the world
and his own good fortune weighed heavily upon Garland as he
took the train back East:

It seemed a treachery to say good-bye to my aging parents, leaving
them and my untrained sister to this barren, empty, laborious life on
the plain, whilst I returned to the music, the drama, the inspiration,
the glory of Boston. Opposite poles of the world could not be farther
apart. Acute self-accusation took out of my return all the exultation
and much of the pleasure which I had expected to experience as I
dropped my harvester's fork and gloves and put on the garments of
civilization once more. [18]

Garland probably stopped over in Chicago to lecture under the
aegis of Joseph Kirkland, [19] but early in September was back at his
desk in the attic room of Jamaica Plains, working upon a multi-
tude of literary projects in a burst of disorganized activity which
led his mentor to complain: "While I am toiling over a chapter
you rattle off a volume. You write—I rewrite." Among Garland's
conceptions was an outline of a propagandist play in which he
hoped to play the lead. Of this proposal Kirkland commented:

Your play experiment is promising—your idea of acting in it is
alarming. All my folks (experienced playgoers, critics and amateur
actors) exclaimed at the idea. There is no road to the footlights except
through the back of the stage. The lecture platform does not help;
the elocutionary—declamatory experience positively hinders. . . .

The first manager you apply to will talk you out of it. A good professional playwright to prune and improve your play and some good
professional players to represent it.—I hope for a good income from it
for years to come. Nothing is so profitable as a successful play, as you
no doubt are well aware. [20]

[17] "Mrs. Ripley's Trip" was first published in *Harper's Weekly*, XXXII
(November 24, 1888), 894–95.
[18] *A Son of the Middle Border*, p. 373.
[19] On August 24, 1887, Kirkland wrote Garland discussing possible lecture
topics for Chicago, presumably for an engagement on Garland's return route.
Garland Papers.
[20] Joseph Kirkland to Garland, November 13, 1887, Garland Papers; Henson, *op. cit.*, p. 460.

With the opening of the school term Garland dropped back into his previous routine of lecturing and letter-writing. Only now his letters to authors and to editors were likely to include an original manuscript for criticism or for submission. With a beginner's confidence he addressed himself to the most exalted literary markets of the time. He seems, however, to have severed relations with the *Atlantic Monthly* before they had really begun. Aldrich rejected his "Art of Edwin Booth" on the grounds that he knew Booth intimately and was writing on the same subject himself. This so piqued Garland that he crossed the *Atlantic* from his list and transferred his addresses to the great literary triumvirate, *Scribners'*, *Harper's*, and the *Century Magazine*. [21]

Richard Watson Gilder, the editor of *Century*, was not unsympathetic to Garland's efforts, though crudities of composition and unflinching realism made his early stories unacceptable to a conservative magazine steeped in the traditions of a genteel literature. Garland accepted his rejections by the *Century* in good spirit, writing Gilder on one occasion: "I am very grateful for your criticisms of my story. They were very just." Again, submitting "two western stories," he wrote: "There may be some objection to the strong language—if so it can be easily softened down." Despite these attempts to conform to the *Century's* requirements it was not until some years later that Garland appeared in its staid pages. Nor was he successful at this time in breaching the gate at those other castles of conservatism, *Scribners'* and *Harper's Monthly*. [22]

But the "fighting arm of the House of Harper," the flamboyant family newspaper of *Harper's Weekly*—with its political news, its Thomas Nast cartoons, its full-page and double-page engravings, and its garish advertisements—had no such qualms about Garland's offerings. In its pages the work of the local-color writers, such as Sarah Orne Jewett and Mary Wilkins Freeman, was appearing side by side with the romances of H. Rider Haggard. And only a month after publishing Garland's poem, "Lost in a

---

[21] *Roadside Meetings*, pp. 39–41.

[22] Garland to J. W. Gilder, two undated letters from Jamaica Plains, and one of September 7, 1889, New York Public Library. Garland's notebook for this year shows several unsuccessful submissions to *Scribners'* and *Harper's Monthly*.

Norther," *Harper's Weekly* printed a prose version of the same episode, "Holding Down a Claim in a Blizzard." [23]

This sketch, based upon Garland's bitter experiences as a homesteader, opens with a sequence of wooden dialogue as several youths set out from "Boomtown" by buckboard to make one of the periodic visits to their claim prerequisite to establishing title. As the storm enfolds the party, Garland's poetic vision of nature emerges to save his piece from absolute mediocrity:

> The stability of the prairie seemed changed to the furious lashings of a foam-white waste of waters. Great waves of snow met, shifted, spread, raced like wolves, joined again, rose, buffeted each other till puffs of fine snow sprang into the air like spray, only to fall and melt in the sliding streams. All was unreal, ghastly.
>
> No sky but a formless, impenetrable mass of flying snow; no earth except when a sweeping gust laid bare a long streak of blackened sod that had the effect, the terrifying effect, of a hollow, fathomless trough between the hissing waves, and over all the night and tempest were spreading like the flight of twin eagles.
>
> Outside, the storm lashed and hissed like an ocean. There was a clattering roar, as of myriad wings, a rattle of distant musketry, the howling of innumerable wild beasts, and the wails of women in agony. There were vague sounds of rushing, of swirling, and the tinkling as of distant, falling, driving sand.

At the climax of his narrative Garland actually drifts into verse, brazenly repeating (with several improvements in diction) a dozen lines from his poem which had appeared in the same journal a few weeks earlier.

Despite this obvious identification of himself as a regular contributor to the *Weekly,* the by-line of this sketch was misprinted to read "Hamlen Garland." No mere compositor's error, however, could dampen the author's pride in his achievements, and within a short time he was writing to Kirkland calling attention to these two publications and outlining further plans so grandiose that Kirkland felt impelled to caution his charge on the dangers of too rapid production:

> Three novels at once under way! Your hands must be full. But you are as fluent as I am taciturn—*costive* I would say, only that throws a

[23] XXXII (January 28, 1888), 66–67.

bad odor about the matter produced. No; I did not see "Lost in a Norther" and "Holding Down Claims." I should think you could do those splendidly. As to your "occasional work" you are rather easily satisfied. You don't keep a thing revolving in your mind until some sharp, striking thought, dramatic, pathetic or humorous, starts into being, to compel the attention of the whole world. [24]

After reading "Boy Life on the Prairie," Kirkland pronounced it "capital." "If I had a store of such material I should use it in a great romance. But in magazine articles it will doubtless pay better."

During the succeeding months Kirkland continued to act as critic and agent for his protégé, mincing no words about the need for revision in Garland's manuscripts. "The style of Daddy Deering is *execrable*. How many times do you think you use the phrase 'the old man' in these 19 ms. pp. *I counted 64* times and doubtless missed some. . . . Editors and critics won't stand such slovenliness." With revision, however, Kirkland suggests that the story might appeal to the Chicago magazine *America,* "as I have rewritten it; shortening and thickening it so it isn't like chicken soup which has been chickened by driving an old hen through the pond where the water came from." To demonstrate the value of revisions Kirkland remitted a check for fifteen dollars for a poem of Garland's accepted by *America* after Kirkland's exten-

[24] Joseph Kirkland to Garland, February 13, 1888, Garland Papers; Henson, *op. cit.,* p. 460. Since Garland's half of this correspondence has not been preserved it is difficult to say with assurance what were the "three novels" upon which he was working. "Boomtown: A Social Study" had by this time become "The Rise of Boomtown," and may have evolved into "Under the Wheel," of which a portion of the action is laid in Garland's hypothetical railhead, Boomtown.

   The other two projects may have been the novelettes "Up the Coulé" and "The Branch Road," of which Garland dates the composition *(Roadside Meetings,* p. 119) as shortly after his first Western trip. The dates of composition of Garland's various works remain to some extent a debatable point. B. F. Gronewald ("Social Criticism of Hamlin Garland," unpublished Ph.D. thesis, New York University, 1943) attempts (Notes to pp. 111, 116, 117, 134, and pp. 134–37) to date many of the early stories and novels, relying largely on Garland's notations in an 1891 edition of *Main-Travelled Roads.* Garland's memory as to dates has proved inaccurate in so many instances that it has seemed wiser here to rely chiefly on the evidence of his contemporary notebooks and correspondence as taken in conjunction with original publication dates in the various periodicals.

sive revisions. [25] " 'Paid His Way,' " he wrote in a subsequent letter, "will appear on Saturday," adding the information that the editors, after examination of Garland's original version, pronounced it so faulty that they would never have considered it in its early form. Nonetheless, *America* soon printed another of Garland's verses. [26]

Certainly Garland had no reason to resent the paternalism which could produce such constructive results, and subsequent correspondence with Kirkland in the same year indicates that he was reciprocating these favors by approaching the Boston publishers Houghton & Mifflin in behalf of his friend's new novel *The McVeys*.

Meanwhile *Belford's* had printed Garland's study of the death of an overworked farm woman, "A Common Case," and *Harper's Weekly* had accepted another pair of his stories. "Mrs. Ripley's Trip" appeared in their November, 1888, issue followed the next year by "Under the Lion's Paw." [27] The paw of the lion, in Garland's tale, is the heavy hand of the landowner Butler, who rents to a newcomer in the community, with a vague verbal option to purchase, an unimproved piece of farmland. By the sweat of his brow the tenant adds fences and barns, doubles the value of the land. Faced with an increased rental he offers to purchase at the figure originally discussed, only to find that the asking price of the land has doubled also. The tenant's naïveté in Garland's illogical plot does much to emasculate this indictment of the capitalist system. Yet in the concrete details of his description of the struggle against nature Garland pens a moving plea for amelioration of the farmer's plight.

As such, his story chimed in with the rising dissatisfaction of

[25] Joseph Kirkland to Garland, March 20, April 27, April 28, 1888, Garland Papers. Portions of these letters are quoted by Henson, *op. cit.*, pp. 460–62. "Daddy Deering" first appeared in *Belford's Magazine*, VIII (April, 1892), 152–61.

[26] Joseph Kirkland to Garland, May 16, 1888, Garland Papers. The *America* poems were "Paid His Way," I (May 19, 1888), 6; and "The Average Man," II (July 25, 1888), 526.

[27] *Belford's Magazine*, I (July, 1888), 188–99; *Harper's Weekly*, XXXII (November 24, 1888), 894–95; *ibid.*, XXXIII (September 7, 1889), 726–27. The first and the last were immediately picked up by the *Standard*. See Garland Bibliography.

the later eighties, taking political form in the Farmers' Revolts, the Grange Movement, and the growth of the Populist Party. This was the period when Henry George was at the height of his influence, and Garland found himself increasingly allied with the dissident elements which rallied about George's *Standard*. [28]

In the autumn of 1887 when George lectured in Boston, both Hamlin and Franklin Garland were in the gallery of Faneuil Hall, looking down upon the crowded audience of working men, standing elbow-to-elbow, "a closely packed mosaic of derby hats and rough coats of all shades of black and tan." The next night at the Globe Theatre they heard George's famous address on "Moses and the Land Question." [29] Garland recalled, many years after the event, the singular powers of persuasion of the prophet of San Francisco, whose "graceful lucidity of utterance, combined with a personal presence distinctive and dignified, reduced even his enemies to respectful silence. His altruism, his sincere pity and his hatred of injustice sent me away in a mood of a disciple." Garland joined the local branch of the Anti-Poverty Society and soon was drafted as a speaker for one of their meetings. [30]

His friend Chamberlin, "The Listener" of the *Transcript*, wrote up the occasion, stressing the poetic qualities of Garland's address rather than its logic. Garland wrote to complain: "I am afraid, Friend Listener, that you have not got over your long dissipation on amusements, balls, theatres and the like! I was speaking on the abolition of poverty, not the abolition of prose." "We shall meet," he challenged, "at Philippi."[31] Chamberlin answered, signing himself "Yours utopianly": "I was impressed with the meeting and wanted to tell the story of it and couldn't really describe it except as it appeared to me. As to the meeting at Philippi, I shall be glad to have it take place as soon as practicable. I

---

[28] Garland frequently contributed to the *Standard*—poems, political reports, and editorials—and wrote for the *Arena* (see Chapter 3) and other magazines numerous articles on Georgian subjects.

[29] "Memories of Henry George," *Libertarian*, V (November, 1925), 280.

[30] *A Son of the Middle Border*, pp. 379–80. For a detailed study of Garland's relation to the Anti-Poverty League and the Single Tax Movement, see Donald Pizer, "Hamlin Garland and the *Standard*," *American Literature*, XXVI (November, 1954), 401–405.

[31] *Roadside Meetings*, p. 32.

am no good at an argument. I expect to be beaten." [32] Chamberlin's description of Garland at that period of his life is sympathetic, although tempered by amusement:

In appearance, in the '80's, Garland was a young man of certain
singularities, but of great beauty. He was of medium height, of supple
figure, with abundant brown hair, and wore a rather long, brown
beard, that gave him a sort of apostolic appearance. His grave, medi-
tative manner heightened his apostolic effect. He would have made
an excellent model for John, the Beloved Disciple. A very young man
then he had the weight of studious centuries on his excellent square
shoulders. Also he had joined the Anti-Poverty Society, and espoused
the doctrines of Henry George; and he deeply felt the sorrows of the
disinherited laboring man. I doubt if Garland has been as serious in
his life as he was in 1887 or if he ever will be again. [33]

In his early enthusiasm for the single tax Garland tried to en-
list his fellow authors under the Georgian banner. Howells was
interested, but skeptical of the effect of "land confiscation":

Besides, the land idea arrays against progress the vast farmer class
who might favor national control of telegraphs, railways and mines,
postal savings-bank-and-life-insurance, a national labor-bureau for
bringing work and workmen together without cost to the workman,
and other schemes by which it is hoped to lessen the sum of wrong in
the world, and insure to every man the food and shelter which the gift
of life implies the right to. Understand I don't argue against you; I
don't yet know what is best; but I am reading and thinking about
questions that carry me beyond myself and my miserable literary
idolatries of the past. [34]

Again Howells wrote Garland with openmindedness toward
George: "He is *one* of the great hopes, but not the only one, it
seems to me; and I'm not sure that his truth is the first in order." [35]
But when Garland's social theories crept into his literary judgments and biased the reviews of *Annie Kilburn* Howells was

[32] J. E. Chamberlin to Garland, November 29, 1887, Garland Papers.
[33] J. E. Chamberlin, "Hamlin Garland—The Hardy of the West," in *Hamlin Garland, A Son of the Middle Border,* pamphlet of the Macmillan Company [n. d.].
[34] W. D. Howells to Garland, January 15, 1888, Garland Papers; in *Life in
Letters of William Dean Howells,* ed. Mildred Howells (1928), I, 407–408.
[35] W. D. Howells to Garland, October 21, 1888, Garland Papers.

moved to mild protest. Garland, writing in the *Transcript,* had argued that Howells' book advocated "charity" rather than "justice," insisting that Howells through one of his characters should have given his solution of "the social riddle . . . that we may judge what line of reform he thinks must be pushed next." [36] Henry George's *Standard* had put the matter more bluntly:

Alas for "Annie Kilburn!" It promised to be so magnificent a story, so *true* a fiction. . . . Was Mr. Howells afraid of his own story? Howells does not see, Tolstoi only sees dimly, that the problem fronting humanity is not how to do good to the poor, but how to do justice to them and give them a chance to do good to themselves. [37]

Howells wrote Garland in humorous indignation at these misinterpretations:

And you and the Standard coolly ask me why I do not insist upon justice instead of alms.

Really, I hope you will read the story in justice if not alms to the friendless author. Read Mr. Peck's sermon. It could hardly have been expected that he should preach the single tax, but short of that, what more could you have? [38]

Another of Garland's reviews that autumn of 1888 reflects his personal acquaintance with Walt Whitman. In October, [39] Garland by prior arrangement called upon Whitman. As Horace Traubel, Whitman's companion and amanuensis, records the interview, Garland came for two minutes, and to the irritation of the nurse stayed for half an hour. Whitman was asked "What is he professor of?" The Good Gray Poet laughed and replied,

[36] *Boston Evening Transcript,* December 27, 1888, p. 6.

[37] The *Standard* review occurs in the issue of November 3, 1888, p. 8, and is unsigned. In content, although not in style, it closely resembles the *Transcript* review.

[38] W. D. Howells to Garland, November 6, 1888, Garland Papers, and in *Life in Letters,* I, 419.

[39] Garland in *A Son of the Middle Border* (Chapter 30) refers to this meeting as "after a trip to Dakota in the summer of 1889." In *Roadside Meetings* (p. 131) he dates it as of October, 1888, which corresponds with the dating of the letters by Traubel. E. C. Hill in "A Biographical Study of Hamlin Garland, 1860–1895," (unpublished Ph.D. thesis, Ohio State University, 1941), p. 88, makes out a case for the proposition that Garland's second return visit to the West occurred in 1888 rather than in 1889.

"That would be hard to tell—literature or something kin to it. I don't know. I think Kennedy [William Sloan Kennedy of the *Transcript*] knows him." But after the visit Whitman commented:

I am more than favorably impressed with Garland. He has a good voice—is almost Emersonee—has belly, some would say, guts. The English say of a man, 'he has guts, guts'—and that means something very good, not very bad. Garland has guts—the good kind: has voice, power, manliness—has chest-tones in his talk which attract me: I am very sensitive to things like those in a man. Garland seems to be enthusiastic about Leaves of Grass. [40]

Garland, unaware of Whitman's reactions, was in turn deeply impressed by the poet. Recalling the interview he wrote:

The house was a dingy, white frame building from which an odor of cabbage came, the paper was off the walls and the swing screen door was old and marred with much usage. A narrow stairway of faded green and gray led up from the door.

I entered the room and heard a cheery voice cry with a peculiar inviting implication—"Come in."

The old man, majestic as a stranded sea-God, was sitting in an arm chair, his broad Quaker hat on his head, waiting to receive me. He was spotlessly clean. His white hair, his light gray suit, his fine linen all gave the effect of exquisite neatness and wholesome living. His clear tenor voice, his quiet smile, his friendly handclasp charmed me and calmed me.

He spoke of one of my stories to which Traubel had called his attention and reproved me gently for not "letting in the light." [41]

Back in Boston after this memorable meeting Garland wrote up his impressions of "Whitman at Seventy," which the poet read and corrected in manuscript. " 'Again I would say to the young writer,' " Garland quotes Whitman, " 'do not use evil for its own sake.' "

[40] Traubel, *op. cit.* (September 26, 1888), II, 383–84.
[41] The first two paragraphs are taken from Garland's 1889 [?] notebook, Garland Papers [the dating is by another hand]. The last two paragraphs are from *A Son of the Middle Border*, pp. 408–409. See also *Roadside Meetings*, Chapter 11. An undelivered address of Garland's is included in *Camden's Compliments to Walt Whitman* (Horace Traubel, ed.).

Here the old man was seized with a figure which lifted his face and hand in a grandly suggestive gesture. "As in some vast foundry whose roof is lost in blackness—way up aloft, a scuttle lets the sun-light in and the blue sky in." [42]

Before reviewing *November Boughs* for the *Transcript* Garland insisted on having an autographed copy and suggested that Whitman send also a copy to Howells to secure his reaction. This interest continued to impress Whitman favorably. [43]

"We should hasten to do him honor while he is with us," wrote Garland in the *Transcript*. "Whitman is no longer a mystery; he is the serene, gentle, grand old man, living in Camden, who sends me what he thinks is his final volume." [44] Whether or not his writings are poetry, Garland urged, is beside the point. Call them merely "passionate descriptive speech" if you like. And as to the charge of pornography, there are "not ten lines in 400 pages that readers of Shakespeare would find objectionable." "I present my tribute," soared Garland in his panegyric, mingling sincere enthusiasm with his inevitable self-advertisement, "drop my bit of laurel into the still warm, firm hand of the victorious singer." The "laurel" was a lengthy tribute in Whitmanesque verse.

The Camden poet was generally pleased with the review. "It has spirit, movement . . . It is written by an admirer; that can be seen." Despite an occasional misgiving as to the "permanency" of Garland's friendship and enthusiasm, Whitman continued of the opinion that "Garland is much better mettle than his polished exterior would indicate." With Traubel he was accustomed to discuss Garland's earnestness, commending him for his courage in support of the single tax—and of Whitman. Traubel agreed: "A man can't be an upholder of W. W. and be altogether a man of peace." And Whitman elaborated on his hopes for Garland:

[42] The manuscript "Whitman at Seventy," with emendations which Garland indicates are in Whitman's hand, is in the Garland Papers. It was published in the New York *Herald* of June 30, 1889, p. 7.

[43] Traubel, *With Walt Whitman in Camden* (October 18 and October 2, 1888), II, 509, 530.

[44] *Boston Evening Transcript,* November 15, 1888, p. 6. Portions of this review are quoted in *Some of My Youthful Enthusiasms,* p. 362, and in *Roadside Meetings,* p. 139. Whitman wrote a brief note of thanks for the review on November 18, 1888. Garland Papers.

He seems started all right: is dead set for real things: is disposed to turn himself to the production of real results. Will he keep on or get discouraged by and by? So many of the fellows do go all right for awhile then suddenly stop—are arrested—develop no further—or go back, retreat: Those who have no faith, only cleverness. . . . Garland looks like a man who is bound to last—to go on from very good to very much better: but you never can tell; there are so many dangers—so many ways for the innocent to be betrayed; in the clutter, clatter, crack of metropolitan ambitions, jealousies, bribes, so many ways for a man unless he is a giant, unless he is possessed of brutal strength and independence—so many ways for him to go to the devil. I look for Garland to save himself from this fate. [45]

[45] Traubel, *With Walt Whitman in Camden* (January 1, 1889), III, 437–38. For an excellent and detailed study of Whitman and Garland see B. R. McElderry, Jr., "Hamlin Garland's Views of Whitman," *Personalist*, XXXVI (1955), 369–78.

❧ 3 ❧

The Dean

WITH THE NEW YEAR of 1889 Garland acquired a fresh field of activity, another cause into which to pour his prodigious energies. Already a convert to Ibsen, [1] he discovered, that January, the realistic drama of the actor playwright James A. Herne. Herne, with his wife Katherine, was presenting in an obscure South End theatre a problem play, *Drifting Apart,* which excited Garland by its similarity of theme and dialogue to forms of local-color fiction. He immediately penned a note of appreciation to the Hernes asking permission to call.

Herne replied at length analyzing his play and its chances of survival. "My task, and a difficult one at first, is to secure the attendance of the fine auditor—the others will follow. . . . the public likes to be led in all matters demanding thought. . . . the opinions and criticisms of a man like you carry great weight. . . .

[1] *Roadside Meetings* (1930), p. 65. For a discussion of Ibsen's influence on Garland, see Lars Ahnebrink, *The Beginnings of Naturalism in American Fiction,* pp. 363–78.

That is the only way in which a play like mine makes a mone-
tary success—purely by word of mouth." [2]

So engrossed were the Hernes in performances and rehearsals,
however, that it was not until some four months later after a road
tour, that they were able to invite Garland to their home. The
Hernes with their three small daughters made a delightful family
group, who immediately promoted Garland from "Professor" to
"the Dean." Their first evening together remained in Garland's
memory as "in effect a session of Congress, a Methodist revival,
and an Irish comedy. Our clamor lasted far into the night, and
when I went away at last, it was with the feeling that I had met
people of my own kind." [3]

This feeling was evidently reciprocated, for the very next morning Herne penned a six-page postscript to the evening's discussions. He was interested in the possibility that Howells might be
persuaded to dramatize *Silas Lapham,* and was seriously considering the problem of finding a place for Franklin Garland in his
troupe. The young aspirant he considered too inexperienced for
a major part in his next production, "Hearts of Oak," but he
might be worked into "the small but excellent character bit of
the Old Fisherman." Better yet, Herne offered to employ Franklin at twenty dollars a week, giving him "ostensible charge of the
stage," while he learned under expert supervision "the artistic,
mechanical and commercial parts of the dramatic profession from
the back door to the front." [4]

Evidently mindful of Joseph Kirkland's advice that this was
the only sure route to dramatic stardom, Hamlin persuaded his
brother to accept the offer, and soon Franklin was one of the
Herne company. Hamlin, for good measure, threw in his services
as public relations man and advance agent, traveling with the
troupe to Troy, to Brooklyn, and to New York, experiencing "the
desolate effect which the sound of slow-dropping seats in a half-
filled auditorium has on a manager," and "the deep discouragement of watching streams of people pass the open door." [5]

[2] James A. Herne to Garland, January 6, 1889, Garland Papers. Portions
of this letter are quoted in *Roadside Meetings,* pp. 68–69.
    [3] *Roadside Meetings,* pp. 69–70.
    [4] James A. Herne to Garland [postmarked April 29, 1889], Garland Papers.
    [5] *Roadside Meetings,* p. 73.

Garland's happiest times were those when the Hernes were back from tour in their suburban Ashmont cottage. Then he could preside as Dean over the turbulent discussions while Jim Herne told dialect stories, and Katherine, oblivious to time and space, argued on "Flammarion's supersensuous world of force, Mr. George's theory of land-holding, or Spencer's law of progress."[6] Meanwhile the group rewrote "Drifting Apart," attempted other dramatizations, and sketched out a new play dealing with the troublesome divorce question, *Margaret Fleming*.

Despite Garland's buttonholing of managers and producers no one would risk the public reaction to a realistic treatment of such a delicate subject. At last Howells, who had been drawn into consultation, suggested that the experimenters follow the example of Sudermann in Berlin, hire a hall and become their own producers. *Margaret Fleming*, after an earlier tryout in Lynn, Massachusetts, opened in Boston in Chickering Hall on May 4, 1891. Although Garland dropped all other activities in his efforts to promote the play, he was able to secure for his friends a critical success only. After a short run Herne was obliged to leave the cast and accept a position as stage manager in New York in order to support his family. For another four weeks Benjamin Orange Flower, the radical publisher, underwrote the continuance of this early Little Theatre project, but then the doors were forced to close.[7] It was not until the following year that the Hernes

---

[6] "Mr. and Mrs. Herne," *Arena*, IV (October, 1891), 552. Others of Garland's writings on the Hernes were: "Truth in the Drama," *Literary World*, XX (September 14, 1889), 307–308; "Mr. Herne's New Play," *Boston Evening Transcript*, July 8, 1890; "The Question of an Independent Theatre," *Boston Evening Transcript*, April 29, 1891, p. 6; "The Morality of Margaret Fleming," *Boston Evening Transcript*, May 7, 1891, p. 6; "The New Drama," *Boston Evening Transcript*, May 9, 1891, p. 12; "Herne's Sincerity as a Playwright," *Arena*, XXVI (1901), 282–84; "On the Road with James A. Herne," *Century*, LXXXVIII (August, 1914), 574–81; *A Son of the Middle Border* (1928), pp. 391–94.

[7] A circular with eleven signatures, headed by Edwin Mead and B. O. Flower, and with Garland as secretary, announcing "A Prospectus of the First Independent Theatre Association," and another circular announcing *Margaret Fleming* as "An American Play without a Soliloquy," are in the Garland Papers. They are reproduced by Ahnebrink, *op. cit.*, "Appendix D," pp. 451–55. The review of the Lynn tryout written by Garland for the *Boston Evening Transcript* (July 8, 1890, p. 6) is reproduced by Donald Pizer in *American Literature*, XXVII (May, 1955), 246–47.

managed a financial success with their colloquial drama *Shore Acres.*

Under the stimulus of this personal contact with the theatre Garland's writing turned largely to dramatic criticism and to dramatic efforts of his own. Soon Flower's new magazine, the *Arena,* printed his essay on "Ibsen as a Dramatist." In view of later identification of Garland with the beginnings of naturalism in America it is interesting to note his early distinctions in regard to dramatic art. "Realism," he wrote, "in its broadest meaning is simply the idea of progress in art. It does not despise the past, but on the other hand, it does not accept any age as model. . . . It has only one law, to be true, not to the objective reality, but to the objective reality *as the author sees it."* The realistic methods which he approved in Ibsen included naturalness of dialogue, loss of soliloquies, simplicity of plots, and sound motivation of characters. Regretting that Ibsen lacks Howells' "saving grace of humour," Garland complained: "There is a strain of morbid psychology here and there in one or two of these dramas which I do not care for." [8] Ghosts indeed!

The play of which he had previously written to Kirkland found its way into the following issue of the *Arena.* [9] *Under the Wheel,* which later became the novel *Jason Edwards,* was printed from the *Arena* plates under the imprint of the Barta Publishing Company in the same year. Howells kindly declined to introduce or endorse it, [10] and Herne was experienced enough not to attempt to produce it.

The early scenes of the novel (or play) are laid in the tenement districts of Boston where Jason Edwards, "an average man," struggles against the poverty of a mechanic's lot. His daughter Alice, a pure flower in the filth of the slums, aspires to rescuing her family by becoming a concert singer. Walter Reeves, the young editor whose background and viewpoints are Garland's own, urges her toward matrimony, but with all the tenacity of the "new woman" she insists on a life and a career of her own.

Their courtship proceeds against the backdrop of "Pleasant Avenue" where the Edwardses live:

[8] *Arena,* II (June, 1890), 72–82.
[9] *Ibid.,* II (July, 1890), 182–228.
[10] W. D. Howells to Garland, August 27, 1890, Garland Papers.

Through this street, moving toward its better quarters, Alice Edwards and Reeves were making their way slowly, oppressed by the heat and impeded by the riotous play of the children and the grimy babes rolling on the pavement before the doors.

"This dodging the babes on the pavement makes me think of walking in the country after a rainstorm, when the toads are thick. In the thousands of the city, these little mites of humanity have no more significance than toads. They lie here, squat in the way uncared for, and unlovely. What a childhood to look back upon." [11]

.   .   .   .

[Reeves] seemed to see more of the hideous future of these people, these young people born for a prison or a brothel in so many cases. How long can this disease go on intensifying, he thought. He stopped a moment, and looked at it all with a sudden sweep of the eye, a hot, unwholesome alley, swarming with vicious and desperate life—a horribly ugly, graceless, badly-lighted alley, poison-tainted, vice-infected. He thought of the miles of such streets in Boston, a street almost typical. Boston was predominantly of this general character, as he well knew. The real Boston does not get itself photographed and sent about the country. [12]

Reeves, with this indignation seething in him, attended a Single-Tax meeting. But he could not place much importance upon the "fine-spun theories of a dreamer like Mr. Henry George." The important thing, he editorialized, was "the fact that two thousand people met in Tremont Temple to cheer the sentiments that social conditions are unjust." [13]

Illustrating the injustice of social conditions, Jason Edwards' landlord raised the rent, and Jason, squeezed between cuts in wages and increased costs of living, decided to migrate West in search of free land. Alice, despite Reeves's importunings, decided her duty lay with her family.

Part Two of the novel is laid in "Boomtown"—this time located in western Minnesota—where Edwards was being ground beneath the wheel of mortgages and drouth. His illusion of free land had been a mirage generated by the speculators, and to make a fresh start he had been obliged to incur ruinous debts. When

[11] *Jason Edwards: An Average Man* (1892), pp. 26–27.
[12] *Ibid.,* pp. 89–91.
[13] *Ibid.,* pp. 83–84.

Reeves arrived for a final effort to persuade Alice to marry him, the Edwards family had nothing to show for four years of back-breaking labors but the prospect of being foreclosed. The final catastrophe occurred when prayed-for rain turned into devastating hail. At the height of the storm Jason Edwards was stricken with paralysis. Alice looked at his prostrate figure and exclaimed "with a terrible bitterness, 'See what God has done!' "

Reeves noted the broader implications of the situation. Although he could rescue Alice and her family, take them back to Boston and provide for the old age and illness of Jason, there were others not so fortunate. Reeves reflected that he had "been in the presence of a typical American tragedy—the collapse of a working man. The common fate of the majority of American farmers and mechanics—dying before their time. Going to pieces at forty, fifty or sixty years of age, from under-pay and over-work. 'Yes, Edwards is a type,' he concluded." [14]

Into the plays and stories of these years Garland poured his emotional frustration over the plight of his own family. On their Dakota farm, troubles multiplied. To the difficulties of ten-cent corn and ten-per-cent interest, which they shared with their neighbors, were added private misfortunes. When Garland and his friend Dr. Cross were visiting in Ordway in the summer of 1888 Garland's mother suffered a stroke from which she made only a partial recovery. The following year young Jessica, who had been sent to Cedar Valley Seminary at Garland's insistence, sickened and died. [15] Back in Boston Garland brooded in helpless sorrow and indignation. The mother who had borne him and nursed him, poured out her pennies to buy him *Paradise Lost,* argued for his chance at an education, and abetted his first literary efforts was now a feeble invalid who needed his presence. But to return to her and to the desolate life of the frontier was to cut off a career which promised at length to be the means of easing her lot. Torn by alternatives completely irreconcilable Garland turned doggedly to his desk, his writing at once an immediate release for his emotions and a potential solution of his difficulties.

His next *Arena* story dealt with a family incident which he had

[14] *Ibid.*, pp. 179, 208.
[15] *A Son of the Middle Border,* Chapter XXX.

heard told and retold, his father's return from the campaigns of the Civil War. The detail of the soldier's reunion with his family, as Garland dramatized it, is identical with the biographical account which he reconstructed many years later. From the intensity of his imaginings of this man and woman of the 1860's Garland created a scene which rises above the individual into the universal. "The private" takes on some of the characteristics of an unknown soldier, prototype of "the common soldier of the American volunteer army," as Garland closes on a somber note, bringing the story back into his present: "He is a gray-haired man of sixty now, and on the brown hair of his wife the white is also showing. They are fighting a hopeless battle, and must fight until God gives them furlough." [16]

Three more of Garland's stories found their way into *Harper's Weekly* at this time. [17] "Old Sid's Christmas" is a grim characterization of the village shrew whose lack of charity condemns an old man to death. "Among the Corn Rows" deals with the precipitous one-day courtship of a young homesteader. "Drifting Crane" records Garland's first published comment on the Indian question. A settler, outpost of a new civilization, discusses with an Indian chieftain, defiant remnant of a passing culture, their conflicting interests. "Each man was a type," sums up Garland, "each was wrong and each was right." Yet even the settler feels uneasy with his place on the wave of the future. "This is all wrong," he mutters. "There's land enough for all, or ought to be. I don't understand."

Totaling his publications to the close of the year 1890 Garland was forced to be satisfied with this handful of stories and articles. His fictional manuscripts, as yet unsalable and resting in his desk, would have tripled the number which had found their way into print. For the six years of his Boston sojourn Garland had been attempting fiction—at first in a desultory fashion turning out an occasional sketch in the midst of his reviewing and lecturing—but recently in a prodigious burst of production, writing and rewriting in narrative and dramatic form all the wealth of his Western impressions. Because of his methods of work, his habit of re-

---

[16] "The Return of a Private," *Arena*, II (July, 1890), 97–113.
[17] XXXIII (December 28, 1889), 1038–40; XXXIV (June 28, 1890), 506–507; XXXIV (May 31, 1890), 421–22.

vising, elaborating, cutting, combining, and recombining of materials, it is difficult to date with assurance the composition of any
particular manuscript. Yet by 1890 there existed in one form or
another all of the stories and novels associated with his early
period, including some materials which were not published until
many years later.

The *Century* was Garland's immediate target. He wrote from
Jamaica Plains assuring Gilder, "I am Western born and the dialect and descriptive matter can be relied upon," [18] and apologizing
for bombarding the editor "at wholesale" with his manuscripts.
When Gilder returned a story with suggestions for revision Garland acceded: "I have also stricken out most if not all of the profanity. It does not seem to me to be profanity at all but it does to
others and you are reasonable in asking its removal." In agreeing to alterations in another manuscript he reassured Gilder: "I
am as wax in the hands of the potter—and mean clay." [19]

Having attracted the attention of Parnassus Garland in the
autumn of 1889 indulged in a veritable spate of letter writing.
Gilder expressed an interest in "Old Pap's Flaxen," the story of
the adoption of a border waif by two homesteading bachelors, although obviously Garland's treatment of a frontier accouchement would have to be toned down for *Century* readers. Garland
was conciliatory about the matter:

In considering that "addenda" please remember that I will revise
it carefully—filling it out in detail—but the plan will remain the same.
I don't want you to misunderstand me, *I like it,* but it is a question
whether it detracts from the value of the whole as a work of art. I
don't know why the preceding part is not just as strong and artistic
with this added, but if it does not appeal to you strongly don't use it.
I wanted among other things to insist on the majesty and mystery
of maternity as Whitman does. I do a little toward *de-vulgarizing* it.
Is it not worthy of my art? [20]

A week later he wrote Gilder: " 'Ol' Pap' I like. In the main it
satisfies me. I can read it again and again and enjoy it as if it were

---

[18] Garland to R. W. Gilder, undated, New York Public Library.
[19] Three letters from Garland to R. W. Gilder, New York Public Library.
All are undated but tone and content indicate that they were written in the
early autumn of 1889.
[20] Garland to R. W. Gilder, October 2, 1889, New York Public Library.

written by someone else." But he had had a new inspiration: "I have planned a drama on 'Flaxen.' Mrs. Herne read it and was delighted with it—never tires of speaking of the men—'great, simple types.' "

This same letter answered Gilder's criticisms of another manuscript:

All you say is very true—"Prairie Heroine" in some phases is a little too obviously preaching. My tendency is to present things concretely and let others find the preaching. I knew when I did that final section that it was a falling off from the artistic standpoint, but I wanted to "let the light in" as Walt Whitman asked me to do. I wanted to give hope somehow.

But as far as the two first sections they are artistic—they exalt me with pity, and resolution to help these toiling men and women. I aimed to show (not that free-trade was right, not that the single-tax was a panacea and right—) but to show that the whole condition of the average American farmer was *wrong*. Had I stopped there your criticism would only have referred to minor points. As it is, you are right. [21]

There is no doubt that Gilder was somewhat disturbed by the radicalism of his new find, for he at length rejected "A Prairie Heroine," one of the most bitter of Garland's descriptions of the degradation of farm labor. He continued, however, to criticize the young writer, although proceeding with caution in the matter of actual acceptances. In January of 1890 Garland sent him a play, again recommended by the Hernes "from the actor's standpoint," and this time also by Mrs. Howells, which he hoped to publish either in fictional or dramatic form. Garland wrote confidently of his plans for a May production. Undoubtedly this manuscript was "Under the Wheel," or to give it its final book title, *Jason Edwards*. Of this manuscript Garland wrote to Gilder:

I'm praying like a dervish that "Jason Edwards" may win your sympathies to the point at least of giving me a chance to make his story suitable for your use. You couldn't do me more good than by the publication of my drama which is at least an *American* drama.

[21] Garland to R. W. Gilder, October 8, 1889, New York Public Library.

"Another plan of mine," wrote Garland, "is to ask Remington to go in with me and make a little book of the prairie west to be called 'On the Prairie' or something like it—He to furnish drawings and I to furnish poems of that life." At this time Garland was completely unknown to his prospective collaborator, for he added rather wistfully, "I'd like to meet him sometime and *sound* him." [22]

In April of 1890 Gilder was withholding a final decision on a story of Garland's entitled "A Girl of Modern Tyre":

I must tell you what embarrasses me in stories of this sort. As you know, the newspaper press nowadays is vulgarizing. It not only expresses the vulgarity of the American masses but increases it—that is, to a large extent. Every decent man and woman, including many newspaper men, deprecates this condition of things. Now if we print too many stories which are full of the language which should not be used, we seem to many persons to be continuing the work of vulgarization. On the other hand we value correct pictures of life—of even pretty common life—and the consequence is we are giving an undue proportion, possibly, of dialect fiction. People who are trying to bring up their children with refinement, and to keep their own and their children's language pure and clean, very naturally are jealous of the influence of a magazine—especially of the *Century Magazine*—in this respect.

Here is really a predicament, and feeling that predicament, we at least think a dialect story—especially this kind, where "youp" is used for yes, for example, and where all sorts of vulgarisms occur—should very strongly recommend itself before being sent into almost every cultivated household in the United States! Had you thought of the matter in this connection? I am very far from wishing to go to an extreme in the other direction—lords and ladies—but I think we should not go to an extreme in this direction. [23]

Garland's reply was conciliatory, agreeing "to soften down the lingual sins of Albert," but arguing the principle involved:

[22] Garland to R. W. Gilder, two undated letters which are obviously a continuation of a correspondence inaugurated on January 10, 1890, New York Public Library.
[23] R. W. Gilder to Garland, April 5, 1890, Garland Papers; also in *Roadside Meetings,* p. 182.

There is this saving clause about dialect (though parents may never think of it). It is *usually* spoken by one whom the child reading feels is illiterate and not to be copied. I believe in general that *dialect* does not corrupt a child so much as "high faluten language." The child says to itself. "This man talks funny—The writer knows he talks funny—I mustn't talk as he does."

However, I feel the pressure which is brought to bear upon you on these lines, and I am perfectly willing to make compromises to make your predicament less vexatious. I feel that you would not ask me to sacrifice unnecessarily, and I think you must know me well enough to know that everything I do has *lift* in it, that I want to bring beauty and comfort and intelligence into the common American home. All I write or do has that underlying purpose. [24]

Garland had sent Gilder his photograph, for which Gilder thanked him: "Many thanks for your photograph. I see you sign it 'for single tax.' But are you not in favor of international copyright, the Sermon on the Mount, and summer vacations?" To which Garland jocularly replied: "Yes, I believe in the single-tax, and 'the Single-Tax' with me means international copyright, the Sermon on the Mount, and Summer Vacations for everybody." [25]

Meanwhile Gilder's deliberate methods and conservative hesitations were no match for Garland's ambitious productivity. On November 1, 1890, he was writing to Gilder enthusiastic over his new play "A Member of the Third House," which he had been giving as a public reading and which "has stirred 'em up a little." If Gilder does not want it, Garland announces rather grandly that he may publish it himself. "The *Arena* prints next month a story I would have sent to you only you have two or three of my stories now." This veiled declaration of independence is softened by the promise to send Gilder the story upon which he is then engaged, "Up the Coulé," laid "in the La Crosse region of Wisconsin." [26]

[24] Garland to R. W. Gilder, undated from 12 Moreland Street, Roxbury, New York Public Library.
[25] R. W. Gilder to Garland, November 7, 1890, Garland Papers; Garland to R. W. Gilder, undated, New York Public Library.
[26] Garland to R. W. Gilder, November 1, 1890, New York Public Library.

More than a year after this hint of impatience the *Century* brought Garland's name into print above the story "A Spring Romance," and in the spring of 1892 brought out as a three-part serial "Ol' Pap's Flaxen," which had originally been submitted in 1889. "A Girl of Modern Tyre," [27] which Garland had first sent the *Century* in 1890, was in process of revision and "in press" until 1897, a lag which caused Garland to protest:

I hope the embargo on my writing is not perpetual. What is the matter? The *Century* prints a couple of my stories, then waits six years and prints another. Must I wait six years for the next? What have I done to be such a "Joner"? [28]

By this time Garland was a well-known author, and his first love affair with the *Century* had definitely cooled. Yet he continued through the years to keep on good terms with Gilder, although never completely happy with the delays in publication, nor for that matter with the rates of payment, which went with being a *Century* author. Meanwhile in the early years of the nineties he was turning elsewhere for publication rapid enough to keep pace with his racing pen.

The *Arena* story which he had mentioned to Gilder in November, 1890, was "The Return of a Private." In the *Arena*'s editor, Benjamin Orange Flower, Garland had found a publisher geared to his own swift tempo and temperamentally akin in his reforming zeal. When Garland first offered to Flower his drama "Under the Wheel," the publisher was immediately interested. His new magazine was prospering, he advised Garland, and was providing a spur to its older competitors. Now the *North American Review* was spending an unprecedented amount, "several thousand per month" on advertising. "This is the result of our starting the *Arena,* as before its advent they advertised but little except in the Autumn months." [29] Moreover, Flower was certain he saw more

---

[27] "A Girl of Modern Tyre" was published in the *Century,* XXXI (July, 1897), 401–23. "A Spring Romance" appeared in the *Century,* XX (June, 1891), 296–302, and the serial appeared from March to May, 1892, XXI, 743–51, 912–33, and XXII, 39–47.

[28] Garland to Gilder from 474 Elm Street, Chicago, undated, Century Collection, New York Public Library.

[29] B. O. Flower to Garland, May 3, 1890, Garland Papers.

liberal tendencies appearing in both the *North American* and the *Forum.*

In accepting "Under the Wheel" Flower outlined the dream which underlay his support of such radical drama as *Margaret Fleming* and his publication of Garland's preachments. He wanted to form a society to give poor people Sunday morning concerts of beautiful music and a short address on political or economic subjects, and on Sunday evenings such drama as would elevate or awaken them. For Flower believed with Victor Hugo that "nothing can educate the masses like the drama," and felt it his mission to "make the people acquainted with the world's miserables." [30]

All of this tied in with Garland's vague reforming impulses—and with his need for a publisher sympathetic to his brand of realism. He was amazed at Flower's reaction to one of the manuscripts which Gilder had rejected. The editor of the *Arena* wrote about "A Prairie Heroine" enthusiastically, "although one feels something like Oliver Twist after finishing it, as if there should be another chapter." Flower's advice to Garland was in sharp contrast to Gilder's:

If satisfactory to you I will send you a check for seventy-five dollars for this story. I notice you seem to suppress your thoughts in two or three instances, and have erased some lines from your story. In writing for the *Arena,* either stories or essays, I wish you always to feel yourself thoroughly free to express any opinions you desire or to send home any lessons which you feel should be impressed upon the people. I for one do not believe in mincing matters when we are dealing with great wrongs and evils of the day. . . . I do not wish you to feel in writing for the *Arena* at any time the slightest restraint. [31]

[30] B. O. Flower to Garland, May 5, 1890, Garland Papers.
[31] B. O. Flower to Garland, April 30, 1890, Garland Papers. In his quotation from this letter in *Roadside Meetings* (p. 176) Garland represents it as his first contact with Flower, an obvious error on his part, for at least the Ibsen article (which would appear in the June *Arena*) should by this time have been set in type. Garland also says that "A Prairie Heroine" had not previously been submitted to either *Harper's Monthly* or the *Century,* despite the previous correspondence with Gilder thereon. As he speaks of receiving $100 for this story, it seems likely that in memory he confused "The Return of a Private," for which Flower paid him that sum (See Flower to Garland, September 16, 1890, Garland Papers) and which actually was his first *Arena* story, with the later "A Prairie Heroine." The confusion probably

With such carte blanche Garland proceeded to flood the *Arena* pages with his writings. In January, 1891, there appeared his report of the Single Tax Convention in New York, a polemic more remarkable for its enthusiasm than for its constructive argument. In March came his exposé of frontier evangelism, "The Test of Elder Pill"; in July the much rewritten "A Prairie Heroine"; in September a quiet sketch of "An Evening at the Corner Grocery"; in October a tribute to "Mr. and Mrs. Herne"; and in December a humorous frontier anecdote, "Uncle Ripley's Speculation." [32]

Meanwhile Garland did not neglect other publishers. New stories appeared in the *Youth's Companion* and *Belford's Magazine* [33] and he continued to submit manuscripts to *Harper's Monthly*. Henry M. Alden, the editor of the latter, wrote him in February of 1891:

I liked your story "A Case of Embezzlement" very much, but you have not given to it the care it deserves & which is necessary not only to its intrinsic excellence but also to its effective impression upon readers. It is partly because of this negligence on your part that the story is much too long. It is much easier to make a story of 14000 words than to put the same structure within the limits of 9000—& yet the limitation gives better art & secures for the story twice the number of readers.

I return the MS. If you should revise it, I will gladly reconsider it. [34]

Thus the *Century* and *Harper's Monthly* remained interested, but somewhat aloof from Garland's writings. *Harper's Weekly*, however, was receptive and no market to scorn from either the financial or the artistic standpoint, for in that same year it pub-

---

originated in a statement by Flower in the *Arena* of July, 1902 (XXVIII, 103): "I well remember the first manuscript sent me by Mr. Garland. It was 'A Prairie Heroine.' "

[32] III (January, 1891), 157–84; (March, 1891), 480–501; IV (July, 1891), 223–46; (October, 1891), 543–60; V (December, 1891), 125–35.

[33] "Going for the Doctor," *Youth's Companion,* LXIV (March 12, 1891), 151; "A Queer Case," *Youth's Companion,* LXV (March 3, 10, 17, 1892), 105–106, 121–22, 133–34; "Daddy Deering," *Belford's Magazine,* VIII (April, 1892), 152–61.

[34] H. M. Alden to Garland, February 3, 1891, Garland Papers. A portion of this letter is printed in *Roadside Meetings,* p. 124. The story referred to is probably "A Good Fellow's Wife."

lished among others Sir James Barrie, Henry James, Conan Doyle, Jerome K. Jerome, and H. G. Wells. The *Arena* waited with open arms, and Flower was considering publishing Garland's stories in book form. William Dean Howells had moved to an editorial position with *Cosmopolitan Magazine* and would soon be soliciting Garland's manuscripts. To the young author it appeared that the tide was at the flood. He resigned his staff position at the Brown School of Oratory to devote himself to writing and to free-lance lecturing.

An additional backlog of security was a contract with William M. Alberti to join his summer school faculty in New Jersey as lecturer in American literature. [35] The prospectus issued by this institution indicates the breadth of topics upon which Garland was now prepared to expound.

The Seaside Assembly

Avon-by-the-Sea   New Jersey

Schools of Expression and Literature

Eighth Session, July 5—Aug. 28, 1891

Wm. M. Alberti, Dean of School of Expression

LECTURE—STUDIES IN AMERICAN LITERATURE AND EXPRESSIVE ART

by Professor Hamlin Garland

1. Colonial Age.
2. Revolutionary Age.
3. First Age of the Republic.
4. The Landscape School. Studies of Bryant, Cole and Cooper. Art Beginnings.
5. The Transcendentalists. Emerson, Thoreau.
6. The Balladists. Readings from Whittier, Longfellow and Holmes.
7. Hawthorne and Poe. The Romance.
8. The Civil War. Its Effect on Thought. Literature of the War.
9. The Literature of Democracy. The *Genre* and Landscape Poetry of Whitman.
10. The Epic of the Age. The Novel. The American Novel.

[35] William M. Alberti to Garland, January 22, 1891, Garland Papers.

11. Americanism in the Novel. William Dean Howells and Henry James.
12. Local Novelists. Their Significance as Precursors. Provincialism no Bar to a National Literature. The Spirit of the Age.
13. The Pioneers. Bret Harte and Joaquin Miller. *The New Eldorado.*
14. Some Representative Names. Joseph Kirkland and E. W. Howe: *The Prairie West.* Geo. W. Cable, Joel Harris, Miss Murfree, Miss Baylor: *The South.* Miss Wilkins, Miss Jewett, Rose Terry Cooke: *New England.* Unparalleled Vitality and Importance of the Movement.
15. Aristocracy of Democracy. The City in Fiction and the Drama. Sharpening Social Contrasts. Edgar Fawcett.
16. Poets from the Soil. Farm-life. *Dialect:* James Whitcomb Riley and Others.
17. Sidney Lanier and His Art. The Question of Future Verse-Form. The Modern Landscape School. Cosmic Feeling for Nature.
18. Summary of Principles and Results. Final Study of Race, Elements, Momentum, Surroundings. Social Problems.
19. Logical Prophecy. The Future of Poetry and Fiction.

Terms:	Single lecture	.50
	5 lectures	$2.00
	10 lectures	$4.00

H. Garland, Dean of School of Literature, Aug. 11–Aug. 25. [36]

In his new connection Garland had attained the title of Dean in the public eye as well as in the intimacy of the Herne family circle. By the standards of the time he deserved the promotion, for since the days of his first trembling debut in Mrs. Paysen's parlor he had acquired the polish of the experienced platform speaker. Moreover, almost all of the living American authors whom he discussed could now be numbered if not among his close friends at least among his correspondents: Howells, Joaquin Miller, Kirkland, Howe, Miss Wilkins, Miss Jewett, Edgar Fawcett, Riley, and Walt Whitman.

At Avon-by-the-Sea it was characteristic of the strange affinity which Garland possessed for the famous and those about to be famous that the reporter covering his lecture on Howells was a

[36] Circular, Garland Papers. Reproduced by Ahnebrink, *op. cit.*, "Appendix B–3," pp. 442–43.

youth named Stephen Crane, "slim, boyish, with sallow complexion, and light hair. His speech was singularly laconic." Impressed by the accuracy of Crane's report Garland sought him out, and the two were soon on friendly terms, finding themselves both devotees of the art of pitching a curved ball. The first chapter of their relations was a short one, however, for Crane's cynical reporting of a labor parade earned him a quick dismissal from his conservative paper. [37] Meanwhile Garland as a labor reporter for a more liberal paper, the *Arena*, set out on travels which were to keep him from Crane's orbit for a year or more.

[37] *Roadside Meetings,* pp. 189–90. See also "Stephen Crane as I Knew Him," *Yale Review,* III, n.s. (April, 1914), 494–501. Donald Pizer, in "Crane Reports Garland on Howells," *Modern Language Notes,* LXX (January, 1955), 37, has reproduced portions of this news story which appeared in the New York *Tribune,* August 18, 1891, p. 5.

❧ 4 ❧

Main-Travelled Roads and Byways

THAT SAME SUMMER of 1891 under the sponsorship of the *Arena* Garland published his first volume of stories. *Main-Travelled Roads: Six Mississippi Valley Stories* included three items from *Harper's Weekly,* "Under the Lion's Paw," "Mrs. Ripley's Trip," and "Among the Corn-rows," and from the *Arena,* "The Return of a Private." None of these was controversial in subject matter, and perhaps as a gesture of conservatism Garland omitted the much-disputed "A Prairie Heroine." To round out his volume, however, he included two hitherto unpublished novelettes, which in their realistic portrayal of farm conditions were calculated to stir up criticism. Both bear the marks of Garland's emotional turmoil and represent two versions of the theme of the prodigal's return.

"Up the Coolé" describes the efforts of a successful actor to recompense his family, and in particular his younger brother, for his years of neglect while pursuing his career. His efforts are of no avail, for his brother explains: "Life ain't worth very much to me. I'm too old to take a new start. I'm a dead failure. I've come to the conclusion that life's a failure for ninety-nine per cent of us. You can't help me now. It's too late."

Here Garland's rural scenes appear in the familiar terms. "The miry cowyard . . . the disconsolate hens standing under the wagons and sheds, a pig wallowing around its sty, and for atmosphere, the desolate falling rain." "A small barn, and poor at that. There was a bad smell, as of dead rats about it, and the rain fell through the shingles here and there." As the actor observes "the routine life in the little low kitchen, the barren sitting room, and this still more horrible barn," he broods: "Why should his brother sit there in wet and grimy clothes, mending a broken trace, while he enjoyed all the light and civilization of the age?" [1]

In his other novelette, "A Branch Road," Garland contrives a happier ending to his prodigal's return, though only by flouting the marriage bond. [2] As the result of a lover's tiff his hero leaves his sweetheart Agnes and Rock River. Having made his fortune in some mysterious fashion he returns after seven years to find Agnes married, and most unhappily. Her life is a round of toil and quarrels, of querulous in-laws and a bestial husband. His affection undimmed, the young man offers to take her away with him, arguing, "God don't expect a toad to stay in a stump and starve if he can get out. He don't ask the snakes to suffer as you do." Agnes succumbs to his persuasion:

She had lost the threads of right and wrong out of her hands. She was lost in a maze, but she was not moved by passion. Flesh had ceased to stir her; but there was vast power in the new and thrilling words her deliverer spoke. He seemed to open a door for her, and through it turrets shone and great ships crossed on dim blue seas. [3]

An unpublished Garland poem "Homeward Bound," bearing the endorsement, "The above lines were the original suggestion for the initial story 'A Branch Road' in Main-Travelled Roads," reads in part:

[1] *Main-Travelled Roads* (1899), pp. 5–44.
[2] *Ibid.*, pp. 45–87.
[3] *Ibid.*, p. 62.

> Seven long years since we parted in anger,
> Seven long years since that stormy goodbye—
> O, could I relive them—
> Could I destroy them!
> Ah, God, the irrevocable years, how they fly!
> I chide as I ride
> The engine's slow stride,
> That bears me to Agnes, my sweetheart, my bride!

.   .   .   .

> What if they lied who called you the faithless?
> Life would begin again, Agnes, my bride. [4]

In his autobiography Garland conjoins the publication of his first volume with a bit of veiled personal reminiscence:

And yet, by a singular fatality, at this moment came another sorrow, the death of Alice, my boyhood adoration. I had known for years that she was not for me, but I loved to think of her as out there walking the lanes among the roses and the wheat as of old. My regard for her was no longer that of the lover desiring and hoping, and though I acknowledged defeat I had been too broadly engaged in my ambitious literary plans to permit her deflection to permanently cloud my life. She had been a radiant and charming figure in my prairie world, and when I read the letter telling of her passing, my mind was irradiated with the picture she had made when last she said goodbye to me. Her gentle friendship had been very helpful through all my years of struggle and now in the day of my security, her place was empty. [5]

Whatever connection may be made between this shadowy "Alice" of the prairie world and the "Agnes" of Garland's Lochinvar phantasies, the personal connection between the other stories and the author's own experience is underscored on the dedication page of *Main-Travelled Roads:*

To

My Father and Mother

Whose half-century pilgrimage on the main-travelled road of life has brought them only toil and deprivation, this book of stories is dedicated by a son to whom every day brings a deepening sense of his parents' silent heroism.

[4] Notebook labelled "1899," Garland Papers. This is a penny notebook with unnumbered pages.
[5] *A Son of the Middle Border* (1928), pp. 419–20.

It is possible that in titling his volume Garland half-consciously echoed a phrase of Whitman's from the introduction to *November Boughs.* "So here I sit gossiping in the early candle-light of old age—I and my book—casting backward glances over our travelled road." Though Garland, unlike Whitman, was writing in the full vigor of young manhood, his prefatory fable has a similar nostalgic note:

> The Main-Travelled Road in the West (as everywhere) is hot and dusty in summer, and desolate and drear with mud in fall and spring, and in the winter the winds sweep the snow across it; but it does sometimes cross a rich meadow where the songs of the larks and bobolinks and blackbirds are tangled. Follow it far enough, it may lead past a bend in the river where the water laughs eternally over its shallows.
>
> Mainly it is long and wearyful, and has a dull little town at one end and a home of toil at the other. Like the main-travelled road of life it is traversed by many classes of people, but the poor and the weary predominate.

Garland's Boston friends were quick to review his work. Hurd of the *Transcript* claimed for him "a first-place among American short-story writers," commenting on his excellent characterization "and the bits of description which come into his stories like accidental lights in a painting . . . oftentimes as perfect as a picture by Millet, and as full of color." Garland, he urged, "had the audacity of a man who knew he had something to say and believed he could say it. He had no respect for the conventionalities in life or in literature."

In J. E. Chamberlin's review are echoes of the protests which Garland's unretouched photograph of rural life had evoked. Chamberlin conciliatorily agreed that Garland's picture of the Middle West was perhaps a shade too dark, but defended the writer's intentions. "He has no other earthly motive than the exact portrayal of truth in his stories. He has the poetic temperament strongly developed, and is the friend of men of letters and of artists. Nothing could induce him to seek success by factitious work or meretricious means." Chamberlin, himself a polished essayist, carefully avoided any discussion of the literary style of his friend's stories. [6]

[6] C. E. Hurd, J. E. Chamberlin, "Hamlin Garland," *Writer,* V (October, 1891), 207–10.

William Dean Howells, however, did not shirk from a full evaluation of Garland's book, both as documentary history and as literature. In a lengthy essay treatment in "The Editor's Study," [7] after discussing the relative merits of novel and short story, he turned to examine these stories "full of the bitter and burning dust, the foul and trampled slush, of the common avenues of life, the life of the men who hopelessly and cheerlessly make the wealth that enriches the alien and the idler, and impoverishes the producer."

If any one is still at a loss to account for that uprising of the farmers in the West which is the translation of the Peasants' War into modern and republican terms, let him read *Main-Travelled Roads,* and he will begin to understand, unless, indeed, Mr. Garland is painting the exceptional rather than the average. The stories are full of those gaunt, grim, sordid, pathetic, ferocious figures whom our satirists find so easy to caricature as Hayseeds, and whose blind groping for fairer conditions is so grotesque. . . . The type caught in Mr. Garland's book is not pretty; it is ugly and often ridiculous; but it is heart-breaking in its rude despair.

In his discussion of individual stories Howells calls "Under the Lion's Paw" a "lesson in political economy, as well as a tragedy of the darkest cast." "The Return of a Private" is "a satire of the keenest edge, as well as a tender and mournful idyl of the unknown soldier." "Up the Coolé" he sees as "the allegory of the whole world's civilization."

But the allegorical effects are not the primary intent of Garland's work: it is a work of art, first of all, and we think of fine art; though the material will strike many gentilities as coarse and common. . . . He has a certain harshness and bluntness, an indifference to the more delicate charms of style, and he has still to learn that though the thistle is full of an unrecognized poetry, the rose has a poetry, too, that even overpraise cannot spoil. But he has a fine courage to leave a fact with the reader, ungarnished and unvarnished, which is almost the rarest trait in an Anglo-Saxon writer, so infantile and feeble is the custom of our art; and this attains tragical sublimity in the opening

[7] W. D. Howells, "Editor's Study," *Harper's Monthly,* LXXXIII (August, 1891), 629–642. This entire article is used as an introduction to later editions of *Main-Travelled Roads.*

sketch, "A Branch Road," where the lover who has quarrelled with his betrothed comes back to find her mismated and miserable, such a farm wife as Mr. Garland has alone dared to draw, and tempts the broken-hearted drudge away from her loveless home. It is all morally wrong, but the author leaves you to say that yourself. He knows that his business was with those two people, their passions and their probabilities.

Such recognition from his elders and fellow craftsmen warmed Garland's heart and mitigated his disappointment over the sales of his book, which remained small despite the loyal efforts of his friends and publishers. While many in the West condemned him roundly as a traitor to his land, there were others who approved his frankness. Some of his fan mail came from Single-Taxers as far away as Australia. Garland must have known the true thrill of authorship now that he was receiving letters of the type which he himself had so often used in establishing literary relations. "I have never before in my life made a nuisance of myself by writing to a person whom I did not know," began Elia W. Peattie in complimenting his stories. [8]

Garland was soon to meet Mrs. Peattie, co-publisher with her husband of the Omaha *World-Herald,* for at Flower's suggestion he again traveled West to gather material for a new novel. When Flower first broached the subject of a serial to deal with the growth of farmer unrest and the People's Party, Garland was already one jump ahead of him. From the grab bag of fragmentary manuscripts in his desk he resurrected a story, thirty thousand words dealing with Bradley Talcott, his rise from hired man to lawyer to legislator. With Flower's blessing—and financing— Garland rode westward to bring his material in line with current political conditions. Full of reforming zeal he offered his services as speaker to frequent meetings along his route. And in Omaha it chanced that his father, as a delegate from Brown County, South Dakota, was among his audience. Next to him sat Garland's new-met friends the Peatties. His son's appearance as a speaker and his prestige as the salaried representative of the *Arena* moved the veteran pioneer to a reluctant pride. Elia Peattie overheard him confide to the old soldier beside him: "I never knew just what

[8] Elia W. Peattie to Garland, September 30, 1891, Garland Papers.

that boy of mine was fitted for, but I guess he has struck his gait at last." And Hamlin was able to introduce his father to the candidate of the hour, General Weaver, the chief advocate of a third party. [9]

A Spoil of Office, the novel which resulted from this excursion into politics, appeared serially in the *Arena* during the first half of 1892. Bradley Talcott moves at first through experiences familiar to Garland's as, under the inspiration of the silvery-tongued Grange orator Miss Ida Wilbur, he leaves his plow in its furrow and enters the village seminary. Under the tutelage of the Democratic judge he becomes a local orator in Rock River and a law student, and then moves on as a member of the state legislature to Des Moines. Up to this point the scenes and characters are handled with assurance.

In a short story for the *Century,* as yet unpublished, Garland had condemned a hero similar to Talcott to a small-town existence, arguing that love and a man's career were incompatible. [10] When Gilder, who wanted a more satisfying ending, questioned this conclusion, Garland defended it on the grounds of verisimilitude. The character, as he had projected him, was an ordinary chap, a "common case of Western ambition. A river lost in sands." "I don't know why he can't go to Congress—except that when love came it weakened him," argued Garland, citing his own observations of life:

> Out of twenty fine fellows who started with me, fellows of equal or greater powers of grappling or holding, seventeen are settled as Albert Lohr is settled in those dead or alive western villages, as pettifogging lawyers, principals of schools or shop keepers.
> I saw fifty bright fellows (at the very least fifty) during my six years of seminary life drop out and down as Albert did, growing at length indifferent and in a way content with husks to fill their bellies. [11]

Such might have been Bradley Talcott's fate had not verisimilitude run up against the exigencies of the farm movement. In *A Spoil of Office* Garland's hero moves on to Washington as Con-

---

[9] *A Son of the Middle Border,* pp. 423–24.
[10] XXI, n.s. (July, 1897), 721.
[11] Garland to Gilder, undated [obviously in reply to Gilder's letter of February 20, 1890, Garland Papers], New York Public Library.

gressman, eventually bolts the Democratic Party and joins the People's Party. At this point it becomes apparent why Garland's heroes should forego Congressional careers. Their author was too unfamiliar with legislative halls to carry his narrative forward with any conviction, once he had abandoned the familiar terrain of the Middle West. Verisimilitude, if not in the exact sense Garland had intended, indeed put a ceiling on the ambitions of his heroes. For in Washington Talcott and Ida Wilbur become merely animated political tracts. The love story between the two young idealists proceeds jerkily, wedged in between their respective platform appearances, while even these interludes are couched in terms of reform lectures. It seems a logical, if somewhat unrealistic, conclusion, that after four weeks of marriage they agree to separate indefinitely, Talcott to continue his work in Washington, Ida to return to her vocation as mentor to the farmers and their wives.

This bride who proclaimed, "I am cursed. I can't enjoy this life any more, because I can't forget those poor souls on the lonely farm grinding out their lives in gloomy toil; I must go back and help them," [12] was Ibsen's strong-minded woman with a vengeance. She was quite likely molded from Mary A. Lease, a young woman active in the Kansas Grange at that time and spoken of by enthusiasts as a possible senatorial candidate. [13] Garland's "Ida" must have seemed to him the logical antithesis to his farm-weary drudges, ever complaining of the fate into which marriage has led them. To Flower, an ardent advocate of woman's rights, she must have been a character doubly appealing as a farm crusader and as a career woman.

Garland describes his publisher in those days as "a small, round-faced, smiling youth with black eyes and curling hair . . . a new sort of reformer, genial, laughing, tolerant." [14] But the files of the *Arena* give no hint of geniality or tolerance in the personality of its editor. Even more than Ibsen, Flower seems to lack Howells' "saving grace of humor." His pages emanate a solemn fanaticism. There are turgid pleas for the single tax, for dress reform, for nationalization of the railroads, for—and this in a

[12] *A Spoil of Office* (1892), p. 384.
[13] See Mary A. Lease to Garland, November 29, 1893, Garland Papers.
[14] *Roadside Meetings* (1930), p. 176.

long-drawn-out symposium on "The Shame of the Nation"—legislative action to raise the age of consent. Among the "isms" to which Flower fervently subscribed was the investigation of the occult, a field to which he promptly introduced Garland.

Despite the not-forgotten deception of the spiritualists by the notorious Fox Sisters, there remained both in England and in America a hard core of enthusiasts dedicated to the investigation of psychic phenomena. In Boston one of the leaders of the movement was Minot J. Savage, who in the pages of the *Arena* and of more staid publications, continued to report his experiences with séance phenomena. At Flower's suggestion he organized the American Psychical Society, with Ernest Allen as secretary. To offset the known predilections of these three enthusiasts Flower recommended that three other men, notorious skeptics, be enrolled as officers to give the scientific viewpoint necessary to objective investigation. Amos E. Dolbear, physics professor of Tufts College, and Rabbi Solomon Schindler accepted the invitation as did Garland, who as a voluble disciple of Herbert Spencer seemed to qualify as a member of the opposition. [15]

Garland honestly considered himself an unbiased and skeptical observer, since his days of study in Bates Hall had confirmed his enthusiasm for scientific method, made him a follower of Darwin and Ingersoll in the most advanced nineteenth-century fashion. Yet in his family background were hidden other influences. His mother's family the McClintocks were Celts, possessed of a pronounced streak of mysticism. His grandfather McClintock, an Adventist, had been so preoccupied with the imminence of world's end as to be totally indifferent to the outcome of the Civil War. His maternal aunts and uncles had all been musicians, somber and brooding individualists, from whom Garland no doubt derived his own poetic intensity and idealism. And his own mother as a child had often acted the role of medium. Thus Garland entered into his psychic investigations with a mixed heritage, the Celtic streak of mysticism of the McClintocks at war with the practical skepticism of the Garlands, the whole overlaid by a hastily acquired veneer of intellectualism.

As Garland moved about the country speaking for the Farmers'

[15] *Forty Years of Psychic Research* (1936), pp. 1–5.

Alliance, scribbling on trains the serial installments of *A Spoil of Office,* he found time to attend numerous darkroom sessions where tables mysteriously moved and ghostly voices emanated from speaking-tubes. Much of all this he dismissed as the cheapest of charlatanry, yet there remained a nucleus of phenomena which he considered inexplicable and on which he reported duly to his colleagues. [16]

Meanwhile he wrote on assignment for the *Arena* a report on "The Alliance Wedge in Congress," and as by-product an amorphous sketch dealing with the reactions of a blind girl and of an Indian to the Capitol rotunda. Also a piece of literary criticism, "The West in Literature." Although Howells appealed to him from the *Cosmopolitan* to give them something "as good as The Return of the Private or Up the Coulé," or "a word study of the *personnel* of the farmers' Alliance as you met them lately in the West," [17] the best that Garland could do under pressure of his other obligations was to send along two descriptive sketches, one obviously of much earlier composition, and one laid on the New Jersey seacoast. Although Howells duly printed these contributions, they were never considered by Garland or his subsequent editors worth republishing. [18]

At this particular juncture Garland was too much a part of the personnel of the Alliance movement to report upon it with much objectivity. Having put himself in the hands of the State Central Committee of Iowa of the People's Party he campaigned assiduously, speaking almost every day for a period of six weeks. In February of 1892 he was attending the St. Louis convention which laid the groundwork for the formation of the Populist Party when a letter from his mother alarmed him as to her condition. "There was something in this letter which made all that I was doing in the convention of no account," Garland recalled. And he took train immediately to go to his mother, cooped up in a frontier shanty through the bleak Dakota winter. Garland resolved to bend every effort to rescue her from that deplorable

[16] *Psychical Review,* I (August, 1892), 43–44; (November, 1892), 136–37; (February, 1893), 226–29; with others II (November, 1893), 152–57.

[17] W. D. Howells to Garland, December 10 and December 20, 1891, Garland Papers.

[18] "At the Brewery," *Cosmopolitan,* XIII (May, 1892), 34–42; "Salt Water Day," *ibid.* (August, 1892), 387–94.

situation. His political activities, however worthwhile they might seem as striking at the root of the evil, would do little to ameliorate his own family's plight, and Garland turned again to the more immediate problem of furthering his own career. [19]

The dramatic reading "A Member of the Third House" Garland now revised into narrative form. Flower wished to publish it but hesitated over the possibilities of libel and insisted on an opinion from the attorney general. [20] In this story Garland followed closely the events of a recent lobbying scandal in the Massachusetts Legislature, into which he interjected another version of his young reformer-politician. Close enough to current events to be libelous it may have been, but Garland's treatment of situations with which he was unfamiliar again betrayed him into what now reads like the choicest melodrama, utterly removed from reality.

Nonetheless, F. J. Schulte & Company of Chicago brought out the tale in book form, almost at the same time as the publication of *A Spoil of Office* and *Jason Edwards*. Since D. Appleton & Company was simultaneously publishing the previously serialized novelette "Ol' Pap's Flaxen" under the title of *A Little Norsk,* Garland made good his earlier boast to Kirkland of "having three novels under way," by bringing into print within a single year not three but four novels.

A Spoil of Office was dedicated to William Dean Howells, "the foremost historian of our common lives and the most vital figure in our literature." In accepting this dedication Howells warned cryptically, "Be fine, be fine, but not too fine, and the game is yours." After publication he duly praised the novel, but as evidence that his critical approval was not to be won by flattery he soon thereafter returned a story to Garland with this curt comment: "I have read this story, and I do not like it. The reaction was to me unromantic, and the thing wilfully operated." He added the information that he was "in no editorial position" at the moment, for with the end of his short-lived *Cosmopolitan*

---

[19] *A Son of the Middle Border,* pp. 427–28. See also Herbert Edwards, "Herne, Garland, and Henry George," *American Literature,* XXIII (January, 1952), 359–67.

[20] B. O. Flower to Garland, September 3, 1890, Garland Papers.

connection Howells had taken up his residence in New York City. [21]

In this move Garland was soon to follow him. Franklin Garland was in New York playing one of the leading roles in the Herne play *Shore Acres,* which was to have a run of five years. To be with his brother, and close to such friends as Howells and the Hernes, Garland left Boston, which in the perspective of his recent travels was beginning to lose something of the glamor which had once surrounded it. In truth, Boston was no longer the literary capital which had beckoned him out of the West.

In New York the Garland brothers secured a furnished flat on 105th Street, tiny and crowded, but with a sun-drenched sitting room where Hamlin wrote of mornings while his brother slept. When the actor awoke they would broil a chop, and then board the elevated for the excitements of the city. Hamlin spent much time backstage with the Hernes, and was a frequent visitor at their home, on Covent Avenue. The conviviality of the Ashmont days blossomed anew, with theater shoptalk interspersed by economic debates. Garland now made the acquaintance of the Henry Georges, and with the Hernes, also ardent Single-Taxers, often called upon the prophet and his family. [22]

As Garland's acquaintance broadened he was summoned to dinner by no less a figure than Rudyard Kipling, then staying in New York in a rather obscure hotel. The invitation perplexed Garland, for he knew Kipling only through his writings and as an acquaintance of Howells. Somewhat abashed at the idea of meeting such a world-famed celebrity he accepted with the proviso that, lacking dinner clothes, he must appear in a frock coat. In substance Kipling replied, "Come in buckskin, if you like."

As he approached the hotel that rainy night to keep his appointment Garland observed a "moon-faced elderly man on the sidewalk peering up at the entrance as if to reassure himself of his destination." Recognizing James Whitcomb Riley, Garland concluded that he had met a fellow guest. As it turned out Riley was as much in the dark as he as to the nature of the dinner which they

[21] W. D. Howells to Garland, June 25, September 14, November 6, 1892, Garland Papers.

[22] *A Son of the Middle Border,* pp. 429–30.

were to attend, and equally perturbed as to the niceties of dress. Respect for British decorum had induced him to don a dinner jacket, but the Western prejudice against formal dress as un-democratic had made him compromise by concealing his costume beneath a worn reefer.

As they entered the elevator he checked Garland. "Wait a sec-ond. Wait till I ad-just a hame-strap." He reached under his over-coat and pulled out a pin. Down dropped one of the tails of his evening coat. With a muttered explanation of having loaned out his other coat he pulled out the second pin, and with the overcoat draped neatly over his arm was ready for their entrance.

At table with Mr. and Mrs. Kipling and their sister-in-law, Riley and Kipling "exchanged quip for crank" as it became obvi-ous to the Americans that they had been invited as walking ex-hibits of the vernacular school of Western writing. Any possible resentment they might have felt at this situation dissolved in the flattery of Kipling's wholehearted discharge of his duties as host. Over the cigars he expanded into a succession of anecdotes which had not yet found their way into print, a monologue gorgeous with the colors of India. "He dealt with cobras, typhoons, tropic heat, windless oceans, tiger-haunted jungles, and elephants . . . 'muttering among themselves like wise old men.' " When they re-joined the ladies Garland insisted that Riley read for the group. The poet unhesitatingly obliged with "Nothin' to Say," and "That Young 'Un." Kipling applauded vehemently: "By the Lord, *that's* American literature." [23] So in a West Side hotel in New York that night "there was neither East nor West, border nor breed nor birth," nor even differences over the punctilio of dress, as Hamlin Garland MC'd the meeting between those ends of the earth—India and Indiana.

Garland's enthusiasm for his new acquaintance, true to form, soon spilled over into his literary lectures, and a little later Kip-ling was writing from Brattleboro, Vermont, in acknowledgment of his tributes:

Many thanks for your kind letter. It seems a bit early to be lectur-ing about me; but if it amused the audience I suppose it is all right.

[23] *Roadside Meetings*, pp. 168–74.

I'd like to see what in the world you find to say. . . . I'm glad to know you approve of some of the things I do, but don't run away with the notion that they are unconventional. They are based on a very old convention—so old that most folks don't know about it—but they are as conventional as any other work really—as all work has to be.

No man can jump out of his skin. I'm busy with verses and things at present and intend going south for the Spring thaw. Give my best salaams to Riley when you meet him wandering about and remember if you're within hail of here anytime do come along. [24]

One day there came through the mails to the 105th Street apartment a book written—according to the title page—by one "Johnstone Smith," inscribed "The reader of this book must inevitably be shocked, but let him keep on till the end, for in it the writer has put something which is important." His curiosity aroused by this message from an unknown, Garland read with increasing interest *Maggie, a Girl of the Streets,* recognizing it unquestionably as the work of his young Avon friend Stephen Crane. The next morning he sent the manuscript to Howells for his opinion on it. Locating the author through the Albertis he invited him to the apartment. Crane at this time was living on East 23rd Street with a group of Bohemian artists and writers whom he described as sleeping on the floor, eating buns and sardines, painting on towels, and writing on wrapping paper. "Savages," he said, "all dreaming blood-red dreams of fame."

To the methodical Garland, a nonsmoking teetotaler, the idea of this harum-scarum existence was appalling, and he set out to supply the deficiencies in Crane's diet by frequently asking him to share a home-cooked meal. One day Crane arrived with a roll of manuscript. His sheaf of poems were "written in blue ink upon single sheets of legal cap paper, each poem without blot or correction, almost without punctuation, all beautifully legible, exact and orderly in arrangement." As Garland read he marveled at the originality. "They suggested some of the French translations of Japanese verses, at other times they carried the sting and compression of Emily Dickenson's verses and the savage philosophy of Oliver Shriner, and yet they were not imitative."

[24] Rudyard Kipling to Garland, January 24, 1895, pasted in Garland's copy of *The Day's Work,* Garland Collection.

Crane's account of his methods of composition was as amazing as the quality of his work, for he claimed that he had the poems in his head "in little rows" all ready to be written out. To prove his statement he then and 'there sat down and effortlessly transcribed another, equal in merits to those he had brought with him. It "flowed from his pen like oil," said Garland, "without hesitation or revision." Again in Herne's dressing room Crane repeated the performance, announcing it as the last: "That place in my brain is empty."

Another manuscript which Crane brought to the 105th Street apartment filled Garland with awed incredulity. As he read the vivid battle scenes of the opening chapters he was completely unable to relate them to the "sallow, yellow-fingered small and ugly" boy wolfing down Franklin's steak. Crane admitted that the other half of his manuscript was in pawn for fifteen dollars of typing costs. Garland promptly advanced that amount to redeem the missing pages and encouraged Crane to send it to the Irving Bacheller Syndicate. [25] He also wrote to Flower sending along some of Crane's other work, convinced that he had stumbled upon an inexplicable case of genius. Although Flower did not print Crane's stories until the following year, Garland managed to introduce into the November *Arena* a review of *Maggie,* which had been, in Crane's version, "privately half published and . . . entirely unsold," referring to the fact that the cheap printers whom he had obtained had refused to place their imprint on such a shocking tale. [26] Condemning "an ambitious French novel" included in the same review as marked by "morbid sexuality," Garland praised this "modest American story," which "deals with poverty and vice and crime . . . not out of curiosity, not out of salaciousness, but because of a distinct art impulse." "With such a *technique* already at command, with life mainly *before him,*

[25] Thomas Beer in *Stephen Crane,* pp. 246–47, suggests that Garland at this time could have seen only a rough-draft version of *The Red Badge of Courage.* Crane's work was indeed published in abbreviated form by the Bacheller Syndicate prior to book publication by D. Appleton & Company in 1896 (see p. 138 below).

[26] Beer, *op. cit.,* pp. 190–91, and "Stephen Crane: A Soldier of Fortune," *Saturday Evening Post,* CLXXIII (July 28, 1900), 6–7. Crane's "Ominous Baby" appeared in *Arena,* IX (October, 1894), 662–67; his "The Men in the Storm" in *Arena,* X (October, 1894), 662–67.

Stephen Crane is to be henceforth reckoned with," concluded his fellow writer. [27]

At this juncture Garland left New York on one of his Western trips and the paths of these two authors, so dissimilar in temperament, again drifted apart. Shortly thereafter Crane wrote reporting that Bacheller Syndicate was publishing his "war novel," *The Red Badge of Courage,* in abbreviated form, and apologizing for sometimes wearing "the appearance of having forgotten my best friends, those to whom I am indebted for everything." Another time he explained his absence: "I have not been up to see you because of various strange conditions—notably, my toes are coming through one shoe and I have not been going out into society as much as I might." [28]

Garland could not shake from his memory the lines which Crane had written out in Herne's dressing room, nor his conviction that they should be published. His efforts in this regard were baffled, however, by Crane's characteristic insouciance. To an inquiry in the spring of 1894 Crane reported that he was eating again "with charming regularity, at least two times per day," "content," and "writing another novel which is a bird," but had completely lost interest in his verse. He confessed: "That poem 'The Reformer' which I showed you in behind Daly's was lost somehow, so I don't think we can send it to the *Arena.* I can't remember a line of it." [29]

Such cavalier disregard for a completed work must have been inconceivable to Garland, who until the day of his death hoarded every scrap of paper with writing upon it, particularly the various versions of his own laboriously copied manuscripts. But for all of Crane's casualness he was not remiss in acknowledging his obligations. When the poems which had stood "in little rows" in his head appeared in 1895 as *Black Riders and Other Lines* their dedication was to Hamlin Garland.

Some time after the publication of Crane's poems there ap-

[27] "An Ambitious French Novel and a Modest American Story," *Arena,* VIII (November, 1893, supplement), xi–xii.

[28] Stephen Crane to Garland, n.d., Garland Papers. The first letter is dated in "Stephen Crane: A Soldier of Fortune" as of April, 1893. Portions of both letters are quoted in *Roadside Meetings,* p. 201.

[29] Stephen Crane to Garland, May 9, 1894, Garland Papers. Portions of this letter are quoted in *Roadside Meetings,* pp. 200–201.

peared another note: "I have just returned from my wanderings in Mexico. Have you seen 'The Black Riders'? I dedicated them to you, but I am not sure I should have done it without your permission. Do you care? I am getting along better—a little better than when I last saw you. I work for the Bachellers." [30]

Before Crane left the country forever the two men met briefly once or twice. But Garland was inclined to play a rather magisterial role, urging Crane to cut loose from his Bohemian associates and go to the country for a rest cure. They parted, with impatience on the one side and resentment on the other, never to meet again. Garland in later life was inclined to give Crane somewhat less than his due, remembering him not so much as a contemporary of great talent, but rather as a "strange, wilfull, irresponsible boy." [31]

An odd coda to their one-time intimacy was written in 1930 when Garland negotiated the sale of his brother's inscribed copy of *Maggie* for $500 and was debating whether to sell his inscribed manuscript copy plus an autograph of "The Old Swimming Hole" for $2,000, or whether "to hold out for more." [32] That the "irresponsible boy" would repay Garland's early generosity in coin of the realm was an event which neither of them could have anticipated in 1892.

In the autumn of that year Garland traveled to the West Coast. In Los Angeles, where his Uncle Addison had arranged a series of lecture engagements, he was interviewed at length by the *Herald* on November 27, 1892. He discussed his aims in his three recently published social novels, declaring that he had no intention of writing another political novel and suggesting that he might turn to Chicago or to university life for his next material. [33]

In Santa Barbara he was approached by a young woman who recognized in him one of the officers of the American Psychical Society, an earnest medium who wished to demonstrate for him her powers. In Los Angeles at an impromptu sitting at the home

---

[30] Stephen Crane to Garland [July 17, 1895], Garland Papers, and quoted in *Roadside Meetings*, p. 201.

[31] *Roadside Meetings*, p. 206. See also "Stephen Crane as I Knew Him," *Yale Review*, III, n.s. (April, 1914), 494–506.

[32] Garland to Harold S. Latham, June 1 [1930]; Garland to George Ulizio [1930?], Garland Papers.

[33] Los Angeles *Herald*, November 29, 1892.

of the local librarian this medium, whom Garland identifies as a "Mrs. Smiley," produced numerous psychic occurrences. Voices spoke through her trumpet, and although she was securely bound to her chair, objects were carried about the room, piano strings strummed, messages written on paper. Garland was convinced of the genuineness of the phenomena, if not prepared to grant the possibility that spirits were the motivating forces. He wrote to Flower honestly reporting his bewilderment:

> There can be no question of prearranged machinery. The sitting was held in a private library which Mrs. Smiley had never entered. The circle was of the highest character. I confess that it has made a radical change in my attitude toward the phenomena on which spiritualists base their faith. If this happened, anything can happen. [34]

The following year, with Garland's encouragement, the psychic came East to demonstrate her powers before the Society's committee. Under more rigid test conditions she produced on various occasions similar phenomena, and at last returned to California leaving her investigators convinced of her sincerity, but divided in opinion as to the interpretation to be given her results. With the shifting of his residence from Boston Garland dropped out of active work with the Psychical Society, but continued to maintain a lively interest in psychic research. [35]

[34] *Forty Years of Psychic Research,* p. 44.
[35] *Ibid.,* Chapters 4–6.

❧ 5 ❧

Prairie Folks

DESPITE OCCASIONAL LITERARY CONTACTS Garland at this time put down no abiding roots in New York City. Franklin and the Hernes were uneasy residents there, dependent upon "the run of the play," and Hamlin recognized that the eastern metropolis was no place to which he might bring his mother and father. The city would be as alien to them as to him, and he considered it "a veritable hell because of the appalling inequity which lay between the palaces of the landlords and the tenements of the proletariat." He felt no urge to use the urban setting as background for his writing. In *Jason Edwards* he had exhausted his comment upon slum life, and was apparently willing to abdicate that subject matter to the Cranes and the O. Henrys. As the winter passed, his thoughts turned more and more to the possibility of establishing his parents at some midway point between the frontier which they knew and which constituted the source of his materials and the markets of the East where that material must be sold to provide for them all. Just at this time the attention of the nation became focused upon the lusty city of Chicago, stridently ballyhooing its progress by preparations for a great World's Fair. The barker's call, breezy and familiar in its flat Middle-Western accent, reached Garland in his crowded New York flat, and like the yokel to the shell game he responded.

While the activities preparatory to the Columbian Exposition attracted Garland to Chicago as a coming literary center, beneath the city's raucous call sounded a softer, more compelling note. Beyond the scintillation of the White City gleamed a more constant lodestar, the remembered lights of home. A day's travel to the north and west of Chicago lay the Wisconsin coulee of his childhood. With the compulsive instinct of the homing salmon Garland struggled back toward the place of his origin. [1]

There where the wooded ridges of the glacial uplands dipped toward the Father of Waters nestled the valley homesteads where centered all the memories of his first eight years, and where now focused all his hopes of establishing a permanent home. There in Green's Coulee, just beyond the river road skirting the La Crosse, he had lived with his parents, his sister Hattie, and his small brother Frank. Together the children had roamed the swamps and woodlands, picked wild strawberries, and coasted on the hills.

In those years of the Civil War it was yet an untamed land. The wildcat on the cliff and the rattlesnake in the marsh were common hazards, and often a bear was seen snuffling through the berry patches. Bands of Indians drifted down from the northland, unwarlike, but truculently insistent upon their right to a wayfarer's meal. The Garland quarter section lay unevenly upon the slopes, its rocks and stumps and stagnant areas a constant challenge to the strength of the husbandman. Although Hamlin was too small for this work of clearing and sowing, his soldier-father early inducted him into the discipline of labor. There was firewood to be brought for the kitchen, nubbins to be broken for the calves, corn to be shelled for the chickens, and cows to be driven to pasture.

On winter days there were indoor tasks with which he should help his mother, the carding and spinning of wool, the molding

---

[1] Garland relates the early pioneering experiences of the Garlands and the McClintocks in *A Son of the Middle Border* (1928), Chapters 1–3; *Trail Makers of the Middle Border* (1927), Chapters 6 and 9.

of candles. The spread of the quilting frame made a glorious tent beneath which he and Frank camped on their way to "Colorado," and under the arch of the high-legged stove was a warm lair where he could curl, spelling out the continued stories in the country paper or the poems in the *Farmer's Annual*. In the evenings his mother sat with a basket of mending as his father told the wide-eyed children stories, tales of his own boyhood in Maine, of his three years as teamster and clerk in Boston.

Then Edwin Forrest and Brutus Booth walked the boards, as the narrator intoned in his deep voice, "Now is the winter of our discontent made glorious summer by this son of York." Then Daniel Webster thundered, and Rufus Choate; and Wendell Phillips pantomined the lashing of a slave. It seemed but the logical flow of history when the stories moved to grimmer scenes. The names of Sherman, Grant, and Lincoln rang out like trumpet calls as the children thrilled to the maneuvers of "Logan at Peach Tree Creek" and "Kilpatrick on the Granny White Turnpike."

Perhaps of all his father's stories Hamlin loved best those of his logging days before his marriage, when he was known as "Yankee Dick, the Pilot," the expert woodsman and riverman, boasting "God forgot to make the man I could not follow," as he ran the rapids of the "Old Moosinee" or of "Jinny Bull Falls." In the postoffice town of Onalaska at the mouth of the Black River where Hamlin went to school there was still this flavor of the lumbering camps. Saws clamored from the islands and huge floats of pine logs drifted toward the Mississippi. Rivermen and millhands met at the saloons, where a crude violence held sway.

But the town was remarkable to young Hamlin as the home of his grandparents on the Garland side [2] and of his Aunt Susan. Grandfather Garland was a transplanted bit of New England, pious without hypocrisy. His neat-spired church was the center

[2] The Garland family tree goes back to Peter Garland, "Mariner," who emigrated to this country from Wales in the 1620's. Richard Garland's great-grandfather signed the Resolution of Congress on March 14, 1776, promising to "oppose the hostile proceedings of the British fleets." In post-Revolutionary days the Garlands remained centered in the New England states as substantial farmers and merchants, until the removal of Hamlin's father to Wisconsin. (James Gray Garland, *Garland Genealogy* [Biddleford, Maine, 1897])

of his existence, serving as club, as forum, and as commercial exchange. By trade a carpenter, he was a precise workman, exact, orderly, and "sot in his ways." His wife was an invalid, pinned to her chair, her hands always busy at needlework. She it was who preserved the intellectual heritage of the clan, teaching the small children the poems of Whittier and Longfellow and passing on to them the ethical precepts of an unemotional Christianity.

Just across the divide lived Hamlin's other grandparents, in the valley of the Neshonoc, an alien world of mysticism and minstrelsy, a continent removed from the habitat of the sober Garlands. Grandmother McClintock, a Marylander, had reared seven stalwart sons and six gifted daughters. Three of her boys had found soldiers' graves in the Wilderness, but the uncles who remained to Hamlin were boisterous giants, prototypes of the Davy Crocketts and Paul Bunyans of the fabled frontier. The names of his young unmarried aunts fell on the ear like a Biblical chant: Rachel, Samantha, Deborah. And Grandfather Hugh McClintock had taken on the appearance of one of the Old Testament prophets, whose writings he constantly perused. A huge white-shocked old man, like a snow-covered mountain, dreaming his dreams of the Apocalypse, this Scotch-Irish Ezekiel lived in a world of religious imagery and prophetic utterances, momentarily expecting the Second Coming and the end of creation. About him eddied the tumultous activities of his family, who laughed affectionately at his absent-mindedness and by the vigor of their labors compensated for his unworldliness.

Yet it had been Hugh McClintock in earlier days who had first welcomed the immigrating Garlands to this new land, and his appearance to them in their time of trouble had taken on something of the miraculous aspect of a ministering angel sent from the heavens. For the Garland family, Dick Garland, then a young man, with his sister Susan, and his parents, had traveled westward by way of the Great Lakes, debarked at Milwaukee with Susan ill of an undiagnosed ailment. An accommodating teamster offered to take them to their destination in Spring Valley, but en route Susan broke out with the characteristic pustules of the dread smallpox. Inns were closed to them, and as the alarm spread fellow travelers fled at the sight of their wagon. At the town of Brownsville, which was their last hope of refuge, irate citizens barred the road, refusing them even passage through the community. At this juncture there appeared a giant with a plough on his shoulder and the look of a visionary in his eyes, who took charge of the situation, shepherding the exhausted and bewildered Garlands into a deserted cabin, where he nursed through the pestilence first Susan, then her father, and finally Dick Garland himself. At the end of the period of quarantine the Garlands settled beside the McClintocks. "And thus," ran the family saga, "the Garlands and McClintocks joined forces." For before many years young Dick had courted and won the hand of Isabelle McClintock.

The sons of Hugh McClintock, Hamlin's uncles, were the writer's boyhood heroes. William at fifty stood straight as an Indian, a two-hundred-forty-pound six-footer, powerful as a black bear, the champion weightlifter of the community. Frank, the smallest, at one hundred eighty pounds, was an agile acrobat, turning somersaults and cartwheels in the dooryard from sheer *joie de vivre*. David, a mighty hunter and woodsman, inevitably won the local turkey-shoot. The McClintock brothers owned the community threshing machine, and thus were masters of the revels at that frontier sociable, the "threshin' bee." Indeed their splendid vigor made all undertakings, barn-raisings, harvestings, and rail-splittings, seem heroic rivalries of strength and endurance, and prodigious labors a mere game. These champions of frontier skills were made to order for a boy's idolatry.

The McClintock home held a different atmosphere from that of its neighbors. A broad-roofed structure, half logs, half planking, it was flanked by two great chimneys. Its large living room, with its rare open fireplace, low ceiling, and plastered walls, combined the charm of a Scottish hall with the homeliness of a New England kitchen. When the girls were at home their courtiers' horses tied at the front rail would have mounted a troop of cavalry, and the house rang with song and laughter. All of the tribe were musical. The girls sang with true voices and played the dulcimer. The men were all adept on the fiddle, David a true genius of the bow. Although Grandsire McClintock had renounced the violin as "the Devil's instrument," he yet kept time on the arm of his ladder-backed chair as the ballads and hymns pealed forth.

The songs of dying maidens, "Nellie Wildwood," "Lily Dale,"

"Minnie Minturn," "Lorena," were typical of the lachrymose sentimentality of all folklore, but equally in keeping with the somber strains of Celtic melancholy which often turned the animal spirits of the McClintocks into cloudy brooding. To the repertoire of familiar hymns from "The Golden Circlet" and "The Family Choir" were added chants of Hugh McClintock's own choosing:

> The Chariot, the Chariot! Its wheels roll in fire,
> As the Lord cometh down in the pomp of His ire.
> Lo! Self-moving it rolls on its pathway of cloud.

Then the mercurial temperament of the Celt would shift to sunshine and the tunes would be of the plantation and the logging camp, "Camp Town Racetrack," or "Down the O-hio." But the music which was to remain with Hamlin as the theme song of his migratory people was a ballad of the Alleghenies:

> Cheer up, brothers, as we go
> O'er the mountains, westward ho . . .
> Then o'er the hills in legions, boys
> Fair freedom's star
> Points to the sunset regions, boys,
> Ha, ha, ha-ha!

For the lure of the sunset regions, of fairer lands to the westward, was to dissipate the McClintock-Garland clan before the sixties had passed. One branch of the family had reached Wisconsin by way of Maryland, Pennsylvania, and Ohio. The other had come from Maine by way of Massachusetts and the Great Lakes, to this point where their streams ran together. Soon the waves of migration would catch them up again and scatter them along the various overland routes to the Pacific. Once the magic circle of boyhood was broken naught would remain in the old Wisconsin coulees but the memory of song and laughter.

In his nostalgic gropings toward this remembered haven Hamlin Garland traveled westward again in February of 1893 to consult his parents and lay before them his plan to reunite the family. His crippled mother, trapped in a bleak box of a house by the Dakota blizzard, was the first to weaken to her son's importuning. But in the face of three bad years his sternly independent father could think of no other remedy than further pioneering, this time to the irrigated lands of Montana. At last Garland won him to the reluctant compromise of promising to visit the old home scenes.

Back in Wisconsin himself to scout the possibilities Hamlin found the landmarks of his childhood shrunk in dimensions. Green's Coulee, Onalaska, La Crosse, and West Salem, the four corners of the earth in his boyish geography, now lay within the circle of a few hours' travel. But the valley of his birth retained its quiet beauty:

> The bluffs were draped with purple and silver. Steel-blue shadows filled the hollows of the sunlit snow. The farmhouses all put forth a comfortable, settled, homey look. The farmers themselves, shaggy, fur-clad and well-fed, came into town driving fat horses whose bells uttered a song of plenty. On the plain we had feared the wind with a mortal terror, here the hills as well as the sheltering elms (which defended almost every roof) stood against the blast like friendly warders. [3]

But of the McClintocks only Uncle William remained. Of the Garlands only his father's sister Susan Bailey. This aunt welcomed the idea of a reunited household, offered to contribute to its purchase in exchange for a place to spend her declining years. And Hamlin turned toward Chicago and the business of authorship confident that before the year was out his dream of a "Garland Homestead" would become a reality.

Chicago at this time was a brawling, bustling Middle Western metropolis. Out of the prairies had sprung the gigantic plants of Armour and Swift, McCormick and Deering, the emporiums of Marshall Field and Edson Keith, of Montgomery Ward and Sears. Garland's friend Joseph Kirkland had just seen through the press Volume I of a profusely illustrated labor of love celebrating his native town. In these closing months of his life he was at work upon a second volume, to be brought out posthumously in 1894 by his daughter. *The Story of Chicago* covered the city's history from the time of the *voyageurs* to the present, and in his last notes Kirkland could speak of the phenomenal growth of population from 1,000,000 in 1890 to 1,650,000 at the time of

---

[3] *A Son of the Middle Border*, Chapter 33.

writing. The World's Fair, its planning, inception, and accomplishment, provided a mighty theme for this second volume. "Never was there such a feast," wrote Kirkland, "as that which Chicago set before the world in the summer of 1893. The banquet was spread from May to November, for all who would come to sup." [4]

In that unexampled summer of fair weather Hamlin Garland, like many another, was lured to the shores of Lake Michigan by the classic splendor of the White City, and remained to add a digit to Chicago's swelling population figures. The fair new buildings at Jackson Park marked an architectural swing which would sweep the country from Romanesque to Classic, jarring even the Boylston Street Public Library at Boston from its utilitarian structure into a Greek temple. Chicago's new Palace of Fine Arts was almost pure Ionic in design, and in the richness of its visiting exhibits that summer rivaled the Louvre. Machinery Hall, beyond its impressive colonnades, held the familiar booths and stalls of any state fair. The boardwalk was an all-American carnival whipped and whirled into a fantasy of feverish excitement, while above the singing gondoliers on the lagoon before the Court of Honor brooded a colossal statue of the Republic.

Chicago was conscious as never before of its progress in matters cultural and artistic. To its forty-year-old Northwestern University had been added the Rockefeller-endowed University of Chicago, the Gothic buildings of blue Bedford stone still under construction but housing 1,850 students in this second year of its operation. When the visiting exhibits of the Palace of Fine Arts would be dismantled there would yet remain permanent art treasures in the city's museums and in its private collections. Potter Palmer and Charles T. Yerckes were among the merchant princes who had branched out from old masters into the field of impressionists. At the Columbian Exposition Frederick J. Turner had read his paper on "The Importance of the Frontier in American History," but neither Kirkland, the city's historian, nor Garland, the champion of the frontier in literature, seem to have been aware of his discussion.

There were Chicagoans, however, who saw the city in less rosy

light than did the dying Kirkland. Henry Blake Fuller published
in that year of 1893 *The Cliff-Dwellers,* satirizing the shady in-
trigues of Chicago's financiers, its crackerbox real estate develop-
ments, its *nouveau riche* society, and its bewildered young
people. Fuller was to become one of Garland's closest intimates,
appreciating as few others could the literary problems of the
younger writer. To indoctrinate Garland into his new surroundings he wrote:

> "Chicago" means more than Chicago merely; it means Chicago and
> the outlying "provinces"—Iowa, Wisconsin, and the rest. Now if *I* have
> corralled the *town,* the next step in the process devolves on *you:* to
> hitch the town and the country together. Plant yourself on both legs
> and rock it to 'em;—one foot in Chicago, the other in La Crosse or
> Cedar Rapids or Rock River. Bring your small-town people to the big
> city; do the battledore-and-shuttlecock act . . . Bring your clean, hon-
> est, ambitious countryfolk to town, and make $40-flat Westsiders of
> them, and let them see (and perhaps judge) the metropolis from that
> point of view. Ain't that your real "lay"? . . . It may be a mighty fine
> thing to have one's feet in the Belgian blocks of the "business district";
> & better, I'm sure, to have it planted on the good honest soil of Wis-
> consin; but your legs, I feel, can develop a "spread" equal to the cov-
> ering of both fields. Be the Colossus, so to speak, of the G. N. W., the
> great northwest. [5]

There were others among the writing fraternity to welcome
the newcomer. Eugene Field gave Garland a hilarious send-off in
his "Sharps and Flats" column of the Chicago *Daily News* of
July 13, 1893:

> The chances are that to the end of our earthly career we shall keep
> on regretting that we were not present at that session of the Congress
> of Authors when Mr. Hamlin Garland and Mrs. Mary Hartwell Ca-
> therwood had their famous intellectual wrestling-match. Garland is
> one of the apostles of realism. Mrs. Catherwood has chosen the better
> part: she loves the fanciful in fiction; she believes, with us, in fairy
> godmothers and valorous knights and beautiful princesses who have
> fallen victim to wicked old witches.
> 	Mr. Garland's heroes sweat and do not wear socks; his heroines eat
> cold huckleberry pie and are so unfeminine as not to call a cow "he."

[5] H. B. Fuller to Garland, May 10 [?], Garland Papers.

Mrs. Catherwood's heroes—and they are the heroes we like—are aggressive, courtly, dashing, picturesque fellows, and her heroines are timid, stanch, beautiful women, and they, too are our kind of people.

Mr. Garland's *in hoc signo* is a dungfork or a butter-paddle; Mrs. Catherwood's is a lance or an embroidery-needle. Give us the lance and its companion every time.

Having said this much, it is proper that we should add that we have for Mr. Garland personally the warmest affection, and we admire his work, too, very, very much; it is wonderful photography. Garland is young and impressionable; in an evil hour he fell under the baleful influences of William D. Howells, and—there you are.

If we could contrive to keep Garland away from Howells long enough we'd make a big man of him, for there is a heap of good stuff in him. Several times we have had him here in Chicago for eight or ten days at a stretch, and when he has associated with us that length of time he really becomes quite civilized and gets imbued with orthodoxy; and then he, too, begins to see fairies and flubduds, and believes in the maidens who have long golden hair and cannot pail the cow; and his heroes are content to perspire instead of sweat, and they exchange their cowhide peg boots for silk hose and mediaeval shoon.

But no sooner does Garland reach this point in the way of reform than he gallivants off again down East, and falls into Howells's clutches, and gets pumped full of heresies, and the last condition of that man is worse than the first.

The fascination of realism is all the more dangerous because it is so subtle. It is a bacillus undoubtedly, and when you once get it into your system it is liable to break out at any time in a new spot. But Garland is not yet so far gone with the malady but that we can save him if he will only keep away from Howells. In all solemnity we declare it to be our opinion that Howells is the only bad habit Garland has.

So we are glad to hear there is a prospect of Mr. Garland's making his home here in Chicago, where the ramping prairie winds and the swooping lake breezes contribute to the development of the humane fancy. Verily there will be more joy in Chicago over the one Garland that repenteth than over the ninety-and-nine Catherwoods that need no repentance. [6]

Garland wrote back at length, and not without a humor to match Field's own:

[6] Eugene Field, *Sharps and Flats,* I, 47–51. For a report on the Chicago Literary Congress, see the *Critic,* XXIII (July 22, 1893), 3.

It certainly is a curious thing to see the lords and ladies who partake of ambrosia and sip nectar making a last desperate stand in the West— the home of Milwaukee beer and Chicago pork. . . . [But] the baleful influence of Mr. Howells seeks them out even there and makes life miserable for them. . . . Realism or veritism or sincerity or Americanism (at bottom these words mean practically the same thing) is on the increase. . . . Because (and this is the most terrible fact of all) realism or Americanism *pays* . . . and even Mr. Howells, contrives to live on $10,000 or $15,000 a year. [7]

At this point Mrs. Catherwood entered the fray with her bodkin. She contended merely for equal privileges for both realists and romanticists, conciliatorily appealing to Mr. Garland's sympathy in the matter. Field endorsed this letter:

We approve everything this lady says—everything except that passage in the beginning of her letter in which she speaks of what she is so indiscrete as to term Mr. Garland's "big, sympathetic, manly heart." This is an admission which we shall not make. In dealing with Garland and his piratical crew we propose to concede nothing, for we know full well that if those ravening heretics can get close enough to us they are going to disembowel us and all our kind. They are worse than iconoclasts; they are but one remove this side of anarchists. In his lucid moments Garland himself has confessed that one of his purposes is to subvert the Grand Old Republican Party—in fact, that shameful confession was the first thing that opened our eyes to the wickedness of the whole realistic brood. Then, too, he would burn up all fairy tales and ghost stories—just think of that! Do you suppose that any person bent upon such a purpose could, by any possible freak of nature, be possessed of a "big, sympathetic, manly heart?" [8]

At this point the subject might have been exhausted as material for Field's column, except for the fact that William Dean Howells visited Chicago. At this opportunity Field revived the mock battle, noting that Garland had "opened out headquarters in Dearborn Street, a locality long sacred to the uses of insurance agents, epic poets, mortgage brokers, and idealistic novelists," thus " 'carrying the war into Africa.' " Field pretended to inter-

---

[7] Charles H. Dennis, *Eugene Field's Creative Years*, pp. 130–31, quoting the "Sharps and Flats" column.
[8] *Ibid.*, pp. 132–33.

pret Howells' arrival as the drawing up of reinforcements, and thereupon sounded the alarm for the romanticists:

Mr. Howells loves Garland; he confesses that he is responsible for Garland, as Garland exists today. When he took Garland up, Garland was a mere boy hustling around the streets of Boston with his trousers fringed with burdocks and his hair thick with hayseed. Howells said, "Let there be light," and there was light—we'll leave it to Garland if there wasn't. Yes, Howells molded and shaped the plastic Wisconsin survival as a potter pottereth his clay, or, to use a contemporary realistic phrase, as the buxom country wench spanketh the golden butter into short-weight pound gobs.

Having created Garland, it is Mr. Howells's duty to protect him. Mr. Howells admits all this. Nobody can—metaphorically speaking—dispossess Garland of an ear or an eye or a tooth without receiving from Mr. Howells an intimation at least of his disapproval. [9]

Upon Howells' return East Field purported to see the final rout of the forces of evil. "Garland was for the utter annihilation of the audacious brood that stood in the path of realism, but Howells insisted that the poor creatures be conciliated, and proselyted rather than exterminated." Thus divided on strategy the realistic invasion failed. Howells had gone back to New York, reported Field, and Garland was "immured in a Wisconsin farmhouse, reading through Lew Wallace's latest quarto exploit in 32-mo romanticism." [10]

Field, of course, came off the victor in this exchange, operating as he was on the home territory of his own column, with a body of loyal readers who for ten years had accepted, in the spirit in which they were produced, a succession of drolleries, hoaxes, and exaggerations. When Garland's innings came the situation was somewhat different. He had accepted an assignment for the new magazine of S. S. McClure to write a series of interviews of famous American men of letters. He chose for his first subject Eugene Field, perhaps with the idea of getting back a little of his own. But he was working in an unfamiliar genre, the informal interview, for a new editor whom he doubtless wanted to impress,

[9] *Ibid.,* pp. 133–34.
[10] *Ibid.,* p. 134. For Garland's comments on this exchange, see *Roadside Meetings* (1930), pp. 252–54.

and for an unidentified group of readers, the potential subscrib-
ers to a new magazine of which this was the pristine issue. Garland must have visualized his audience in terms of the earnest
students who sat before him at Avon-by-the-Sea, for his interview is heavy-handed and pedantic in tone. The device of making
the two conversationalists address each other respectively as
"brother Field" and "brother Garland," instead of giving the
dialogue the folksy character probably intended, lends to the
report a note of camp-meeting sanctimony.

Garland describes in detail the cluttered library of the Field
home and his shirt-sleeved host, "a tall, thin-haired man with a
New England face of the Scotch type, rugged, smoothly shaven,
and generally very solemn—suspiciously solemn in expression."
Unable to convey on paper Field's puckish humor or to trans-
late adequately what must have been Field's ribaldries at the
business of being interviewed, Garland leads his subject plod-
dingly through the necessary biographical preliminaries to a discussion of literary art as a "war against sham." "Field became
serious at once," Garland reports, "and leaned towards the other
man in an attitude of great earnestness. The deepest note in the
man's voice came out 'I hate a sham or a fraud.' " The portrait
of Field loses all recognizable dimensions as Garland mounts his
soapbox. " 'Yet some of the finest things, I repeat, are your reminiscent verses of boy-life,' pursued Garland, who called himself a veritist and enjoyed getting his friend as nearly on his
ground as possible." By the end of the article Garland has reduced Field to a ventriloquist's dummy, placing in the mouth of
his erstwhile adversary this uncharacteristic speech: "I believe in
the West. I tell you, brother Garland, the West is the coming
country. We ought to have a big magazine to develop the West.
It's absurd to suppose we're going on always being tributary to
the East!" [11]

This interview provoked one commentator, "X. Y. Zed" in
the *Critic*, to damn generally all of Garland's work on the
grounds that "he has never put his pen to paper but to exploit
himself." Zed must have been one of Mrs. Catherwood's cohorts,
for the description of Field sitting in his shirt sleeves, conversing

[11] "A Dialogue between Eugene Field and Hamlin Garland," *McClure's*,
I (August, 1893), 195–204.

in "an illiterate dialect" so shocked his, or her, sensibilities, that the article concludes: "I suppose that Mr. Garland thinks that this 'conversation' is a good joke and that he has succeeded in his aim of offending Eastern readers, all of which may be true. . . . If this be the realistic way of treating one's friends, let us pray to be interviewed by romanticists." [12]

The *McClure* article, however, must have been a success from Garland's and his editor's standpoints, for it led to other similar assignments. To one of Field's biographers it remained a desecration, "a most remarkable jumble of misinformation and fiction, with which Field plied Garland to the top of his bent":

What Garland thought were bottom facts were really sky-scraping fiction. As if this were not enough, Garland made Field talk in an approach to an illiterate dialect, such as he never employed and cordially detested. Garland represented Field as discussing social and economic problems—why not the "musical glasses," deponent sayeth not. The really great and characteristic point in the dialogue was when something Field said caused "Garland to lay down his pad and lift his big fist in the air like a maul. His enthusiasm rose like a flood." The whole interview was a serious piece of business to the serious-minded realist. To Field, at the time, and for months after, it was a huge and memorable joke. [13]

Though his pen-portrait may have been to Field a "huge and memorable joke," it was not one which would interfere with the course of a friendship. As the article appeared Field wrote gaily to his interviewer reporting his remark to Mrs. Catherwood "that you were indubitably the anti-Christ." [14] He probably thought it poetic justice that he who had pricked Garland's seriousness with the darts of his humor should be bludgeoned by that same seriousness into appearing in the public prints as a moralistic ass. In 1895, a few months before he died, Field delivered a light riposte, writing a sketch of two lugubrious men of genius who meet on a Russian railway car. The air is heavy with

[12] [X. Y. Zed], "Realism with a Vengeance," *Critic,* n.s., XX (September 2, 1893), 158.
[13] Slason Thompson, *Eugene Field. A Study in Heredity and Contradictions,* II, 259–60. For Garland's comments on this interview, see *Roadside Meetings,* pp. 240–46.
[14] Eugene Field to Garland, August 1, 1893, Garland Papers.

Weltschmerz as the two solemnly discuss human misery and artistic realism. As the train pulls into the station, introductions are belatedly suggested:

"By all means," said the older genius with a profound sigh. "I am Leo Tolstoy."
"And I," said the younger genius with a half-suppressed groan, "I am Hamlin Garland." [15]

When, in June, 1893, Garland met in Chicago a poet of even greater seriousness than his own, Edwin Markham recorded his impressions on a scrap of paper: "In Hamlin Garland we meet an earnest man. . . . It would be impossible for him to write anything else than those dreary, hopeless stories of life upon Western ranches." The two authors discussed the possibility of a "western magazine" to "take up the literary uses of the problems discussed in the 'Arena.' " Garland advised Markham to put his boyhood experiences into a story with emphasis on the heroism of his mother. With a letter of introduction to Howells, Markham went on his way, jotting on a manuscript this message: "For Garland. We will have a great literature when we have set aside the atheistic formula of 'art for art's sake' and the inhuman doctrine 'every man for himself.' Let us have art for truth's sake." [16]

Meanwhile, in the *Arena*, Garland could argue more convincingly his theories of literature than had been possible through the lips of a dummy Eugene Field. Discussing "The Future of Fiction" he conjectured:

It is safe to say that the fiction of the future will grow more democratic in outlook and more individualistic in method. Impressionism in its true sense means the statement of one's own individual perception of life and nature, guided by devotion to truth. Second to this great principle is the law that each impression must be worked out faithfully on separate canvasses, each work of art complete in itself. Literalism, the style that can be quoted in bits, is like a picture that can be cut into pieces. It lacks unity. The higher art would seem to be the art that perceives and states the relations of things, giving atmosphere and relative values as they appeal to the sight. The realist or

---

[15] Dennis, *op. cit.*, pp. 135–36.
[16] J. S. Goldstein, "Two Literary Radicals: Garland and Markham in Chicago, 1893," *American Literature*, XVII (May, 1945), 152–60.

veritist is really an optimist, a dreamer. He sees life in terms of what it might be, as well as in terms of what it is; but he writes of what is, and suggests what is to be, by contrast. He aims to be perfectly truthful in his delineation of his relation to life, but there is a tone, a color, which comes unconsciously into his utterances like the sobbing stir of the muted violins beneath the frank, clear song of the clarionet; and this tone is one of sorrow that the future halts so lamely in its approach. [17]

As an established writer Garland now found other publications bidding for his services besides the new *McClure's.* The *Ladies' Home Journal* printed several of his sketches, [18] and about this time he joined Crane as a contributor to Irving Bacheller's newspaper syndicate. [19] The short-lived *Literary Northwest* published a poem and a story and in 1893 Garland made his initial appearance in magazines as far apart on the literary scale as the *Northwestern Miller* and the *Forum,* appearing in the latter in a critical article on "The Literary Emancipation of the West." [20] "While Boston and New York are debating which has the most literary men," gibed Garland, so recently a literary aspirant in both places, "the West and South are rising to say 'Pool your issues, good friends. You'll soon need each other's aid to maintain your hitherto unquestioned domination over American literature.' "

In this year even the *Atlantic Monthly,* third of the great literary magazines to succumb, published some of Garland's work.

[17] *Arena,* VII (April, 1893), 518–19.
[18] "Forgetting," X (December, 1892), 17; "Before the Overture," X (May, 1893), 13; "A Pioneer Christmas," XI (December, 1893), 11.
[19] Irving Bacheller in "A Little Story of a Friendship," *(Mark Twain Quarterly,* IV [Summer, 1940], 14) says that he bought a story "Mosinee Tom" from Garland in the "late 1880's," and thereafter "a number of sketches of country life in the west." In the Garland Papers is a transfer of copyright from the Bacheller Syndicate to Garland, dated March 4, 1897, which lists nine literary properties covered with their original copyright dates. The earliest, "A Lynching in Mosinee," was first copyrighted on November 12, 1894. In an unpublished Ph.D. thesis Mr. Donald Pizer lists as published in the New York *Press* on November 4 and November 11, 1894, respectively, "Old Mosinee Tom" and "A Lynching in Mosinee."
[20] "In Winter Night," *Literary Northwest,* II (December, 1892), 96, and "A Short-term Exile," *ibid.,* III (July, 1893), 308–315; "A Graceless Husband," *Northwestern Miller* (Christmas Number, 1893); "The Literary Emancipation of the West," *Forum,* XVI (October, 1893), 156–57.

The *Atlantic* had been only tolerant of his performance in *Main-Travelled Roads,* labeling it "one overwhelming impression of grinding, unremunerated toil," and regretting that Garland's characters were not individualized but were "a vast company, with worn stolid faces, toiling in the fields all day without remission." "Even the Angelus is denied them," the reviewer C. T. Copeland had complained in the parallel to Millet that Garland's work seemed always to evoke. "One reads and is convinced, and then cries out that it is impossible; that this writer, so terribly in earnest, must be mistaken; that in his enthusiasm for Mr. Howells he has married Russian despair and French realism." "Meanwhile," pontificated the *Atlantic,* "writing is writing, and Mr. Garland must accept and take to heart the warning that monotony is the danger of the earnest man." [21]

There was certainly nothing of monotony, nor of realism, nor despair, in the Garland prose-poems which the *Atlantic* now printed. They were literally the canvases against which Garland himself had recently fulminated, pictures that could "be cut into bits," disconnected descriptions from Garland's recent trip through the Western states. Their titles indicate the diffusion of subject matter: "Arizona," "Santa Barbara," "Oakland Ferry," "San Francisco Bay," "Sunset at San José," "An Oregon Landscape," "Washington State," and in conclusion "A Dakota Landscape," wherein Garland in the mellow mood of a tourist could even apostrophize his old enemy the prairie wind as "the voice of the sky, the felt presence of space," as "the menstruum of all life, the devourer of all flesh and blood, the purveyor of earth and sky." [22]

Garland's poems also appeared in various periodicals steadily throughout the year. [23] Not only were the magazines receptive to his offerings but his publishers had cause to be pleased with the reception of his most recent novel. The *Review of Reviews* had

---

[21] [C. T. Copeland], "The Short Story," *Atlantic Monthly,* LXIX (February, 1892), 266.

[22] "Western Landscapes," *Atlantic Monthly,* LXXII (December, 1893), 805–809.

[23] See: *Arena,* IX (December, 1893), 130; *Harper's Weekly,* XXXVII (August 12, 1893), 763; *ibid.* (August 19, 1893), 786; *New England Magazine,* n.s., IX (September, 1893), 64; (October, 1893), 240; *Review of Reviews,* V (May, 1892), 503.

praised *A Member of the Third House,* which "carries one on with intense interest to its dramatic denouement," and called it "particularly timely as being a story of American politics and a revelation of the corruption that prevails in the legislative life of some of the states." [24] With such encouragement F. J. Schulte & Company were willing to risk the public reaction to another book by Garland. Since his novel-length material was for the moment exhausted it needs must be another collection of short stories. Howells laughed off the idea of supplying a preface for the book:

A fellow who stands as strong upon his legs as you, wanting a hand from a dotard like me! I think the public would say, "Who is this pothering fool, who introduces a book of Garland's to us?"
Get out! [25]

Without Howells' public endorsement, but certainly with his encouragement, Garland ran through his files, polishing and re-titling stories which had appeared casually here and there in previous years, to make up the volume of *Prairie Folks* which appeared in the autumn of 1893. [26]

[24] V (May, 1892), 503.
[25] W. D. Howells to Garland, August 23, 1893, Garland Papers.
[26] For the publication history of the stories included in *Prairie Folks,* see Bibliography.

⚜ 6 ⚜

Prairie Songs and Prairie Publishers

Prairie Folks, which appeared in the autumn of 1893, was accorded a critical reception depressingly similar to that produced by Garland's other books. But the reviewers did take a somewhat more respectful tone, as befitted their dealing with an established author, albeit misguided. The story "Sim Burns' Wife," a new-titled version of "A Prairie Heroine" which had so shocked Gilder, came in for considerable comment. Even the caustic *Nation* admitted, however, that it was "undoubtedly true to life" and "almost tragic . . . a tale of toil that is never done." "But," complained the reviewer, "the tale is devoid of incident. If Mr. Garland would improve his stories and take less concern for their setting; if he would let us see more into the hearts of his prairie folk and less into their dwellings . . . the value of his work would be thereby increased. The well-known monotony of prairie scenery and plant life is likely to infect the delineator." [1]

With the exception of "Sim Burns' Wife" this collection was

[1] *Nation,* LVI (June 1, 1893), 408.

more cheerful in tone than Garland's earlier offerings, and he hoped for better sales. Before the book was through the press, however, F. J. Schulte became involved in business difficulties and was forced to suspend his publishing activities. In the spring of 1893 Garland mentioned these complications in a letter to Melville E. Stone, founder of the Chicago Daily News and, at that time, general manager of the Illinois Associated Press. Stone had a solution to suggest. His son Herbert, although only a junior at Harvard, had made a precocious start in the publishing business. With his classmate Ingalls Kimball he had founded the firm of Stone & Kimball which had two books then ready to appear. *The Terra Cotta Guide: Chicago and the World's Fair* was a revised edition of a guidebook which the boys had compiled and which had been sold in enormous quantities as a result of the aggressive advertising tactics of young Kimball. Another work already being oversubscribed from its prospectus was *First Editions of American Authors,* a checklist compiled by young Stone from the volumes in the Harvard library, and introduced to the public by a preface from the family's friend Eugene Field. The boys had tasted blood, and were eager to acquire new authors for their list. Herbert Stone, to whom Garland's letter had been forwarded by his father, wrote back:

The things about Mr. Garland's letter that attracted my attention first and preeminently was his remarks about his two books. I wish I had enough of a "pull" to get a chance at publishing them myself. I would see that they were as prettily gotten out as any books in the country. But I suppose Mr. Garland would hardly wish to have a new firm take hold of the thing—much less a boy. But I believe I could make the thing succeed as well as any of his books and as for the illustrating—I could get the artists perhaps better than he. I wish I could do it—I should like nothing better.

Although Garland was at first reluctant to cast in his lot with the young novices and had already begun negotiations with T. H. Carpenter for illustrations, he was shortly persuaded to give Stone & Kimball publication rights on *Main-Travelled Roads* and to agree to their publication of a book of verse to be entitled *Prairie Songs.* Flower released his rights to *Main-Travelled Roads,* which had gone into its tenth thousand under the *Arena* imprint, and Stone set out to make the new edition a model of the typographer's art. The type was reset by the Craig Press in Chicago, but Stone the perfectionist was unsatisfied by the results and discarded the entire first printing. The volume was again reset in the plant of John Wilson & Sons in Cambridge, from Elzevir type on English wove paper. Carpenter was retained as illustrator and contributed a frontispiece, six headpieces, and a tailpiece. The volume was bound in green buckram with gold stamped lettering. Upon the front and back covers appeared three tasseled cornstalks, and upon the spine a single stalk. It was indeed an attractive piece of bookmaking and a landmark in the history of American printing. Garland was extravagantly pleased with the result. Later in 1893 *Prairie Songs* was issued in a companion format.

In the same year the new firm published Eugene Field's *The Holy Cross and Other Tales,* and a manuscript which Garland had brought to their attention, Joaquin Miller's utopian romance *The Building of the City Beautiful.* [2] Garland had met the poet of the High Sierras on his trip to the West Coast of the previous year, having made a sentimental pilgrimage to "the Hights" to discover the writer who had provided his early declamation contests with the ringing lines of "Kit Carson's Ride." Touched by Garland's sincere admiration, the unworldly recluse seems to have come to rely greatly upon his new friend as literary advisor and agent. Early the next year he was writing to Garland asking him to edit at his discretion his manuscript for the *Arena,* and for future book publication, and making plans to visit Chicago himself. Garland was delighted to enact his favorite role of liaison officer by bringing together this artist of the West and the exciting new publishing firm of his newly adopted home town. [3]

But for all his enthusiasm for Stone & Kimball, Garland was still wary of financial hazards and impatient over publication delays. Before agreement was reached on two other volumes which

[2] Sidney Kramer, *A History of Stone & Kimball and Stone & Company,* pp. 16–19, 72n.

[3] *A Son of the Middle Border* (1928), p. 449; Joaquin Miller to Garland, February 17, 1893, Garland Papers. The letter is quoted in *Roadside Meetings* (1930), p. 223.

the publishing firm proposed to bring out for him, there was extensive correspondence. That the proposed volumes would be issued in identical format with the earlier two was a powerful inducement to Garland to give Stone & Kimball exclusive rights on all his work, although it was yet too soon to determine how effective the fledgling sales organization would be in marketing his writings. One encouraging sign was the fact that limited large-paper editions of one hundred copies each of *Main-Travelled Roads* and *Prairie Songs* had been sold out. [4] On January 16, 1894, Garland wrote young Stone at length about further publications:

Now with regard to "Prairie Folks." All would be simple if I had not become involved with Mr. Carpenter. The matter would stand thus. I would put in plates and share equally with you which is, of course, a thing I would not do on a new book. [5]

Since F. J. Schulte, the original publisher of *Prairie Folks,* was temporarily connected with Stone & Kimball, Garland was free to negotiate for a new edition of that volume. After considerable discussion of financial arrangements on *Prairie Folks* Garland passed to new matter:

Now we come to the essays. You say you can assure me of a profit on the first edition—well now *can* you. As we figured on the other books they were to pay me $187.00 on each book the first edition exclusive of the special edition. That would be 75%. Can you assure me of that?

Unless something definite is arrived at about cost, I am helpless. If the books cost $650. instead of $500. my profit is wiped out. This won't do for one who has made his start. This arrangement makes me to a certain extent (necessarily) [sic] a partner and I must know how things are going. If I let you have these books you have four of my best books and it is very important that the whole matter be carefully canvassed.

Your books are costing too much. No one but an expert can tell the

[4] Kramer, *op. cit.,* p. 58.
[5] This and the following quotations from the Garland-Stone correspondence appear in John T. Flanagan's "Hamlin Garland Writes to His Chicago Publisher," *American Literature,* XXIII (January, 1952), 448–53. All letters of Garland to Herbert Stone here quoted are in the University of Illinois Library. Additional letters of much the same tenor are in the Yale University Library.

value of a book like Miller's. "Crumbling Idols" should not cost above
$360. It is a small book. There are not above 40,000 words and I think
about 36,000. Say 180 pp at 80c and good paper and press work should
not bring it above 36c per copy. 40c at out-side.

I dont mind saying that I have been approached by several old firms
here for a book and that they are willing to pay unusual royalties and
make unusual concessions—but I am interested in your work and I
have not offered the book of essays and shall not do so until it becomes
certain that we cannot agree on terms. It is a very important venture
and I can't afford to run any risks on "Crumbling Idols."

1st   Can you assure me a profit of 75% or $187.50 on first edition.
2nd   Can you sell a limited edition.
3rd   Do you intend to make it uniform with the other books.
4th   Do you intend to make head-quarters in Chicago during the
      year.

These questions are important and I hope they will not seem out of
place. I think you can not blame me for taking great care about this
book. I confess to being very much distracted about the matter just
when I am swamped with demands for stories and essays.

Garland's demands must have been satisfactorily met by return mail, for two days later he wrote to Stone & Kimball, "Now
I think you may go ahead on both books," urging that they establish in Chicago "a snug little office and salesroom" and make
Carpenter their "genteel salesman and representative." His publishers must have expressed some qualms as to the reaction to be
expected on his critical essays, for he reassured them:

The effect of "Prairie Song" [sic] is going to be very great in
way of correcting any narrow view of my work. Making "Crumbling
Idols" date 1st of April, and the effect of the verse will have been very
wide. . . . Then again I am ready to send out purely literary books
thereafter. I shall not repeat either my economic writing or this literary and art reform. Having had my say I shall proceed on other things.

I have nearly ready a book to be called "Western Landscapes".
(like those in Atlantic) on which you can lavish all your book-making
skill. Also a book of purely dramatic and artistic stories called
"Glimpses of Women." Also a number of novelettes. One especially
called "Tregurtha." If things move forward so that you become
practically my publisher you need not fear repetition or monotonous
work. You dont know my plans and resources.

Keyed to a high pitch by the prospect of collaborating with the young and aggressive publishing firm, Garland was evidently throwing out proposals at random. Of the works projected in this letter none materialized in the near future, although "Glimpses of Women" finally evolved into *Wayside Courtships,* and "Tregurtha" in 1898 became a *Ladies' Home Journal* serial. Nonetheless Garland continued to reassure his publishers on his intention to produce fiction henceforth. "This will close my controversial work for the present. My next book can be two very strong and artistic novelettes or a vol. of Short Stories of my very best." [6] That *Main-Travelled Roads* and *Prairie Folks* had exhausted not only the very best of his published work in the short story, but practically all of it, troubled Garland not at all. Perhaps like Crane he had in his head "in little rows" a series of prairie stories ready to be written out. Perhaps in his desk drawer were other fragmentary manuscripts needing only a publisher's solicitude to revitalize. Meanwhile, he was at work rewriting material for the scheduled volume of essays and was blocking out scenes for a novel which would embody Fuller's advice and bring his country people to the city.

Garland had the ability to concentrate on his writing in any place and under any conditions. The move to Chicago scarcely interrupted his working routines. In his rooms at 474 Elm Street within a stone's throw of Lake Michigan he quickly established a bachelor's apartment and workshop. A hundred miles away at West Salem was the real home of which he had dreamed. According to plan his mother had come on from Dakota that summer of 1893 and he had established her and his Aunt Susan in a frame cottage on the edge of the village. Garland's father was contemptuous of this "four-acre onion patch," and returned periodically to his Dakota land to seed and harvest a crop. But for the other Garlands the new home symbolized security. It was a beatific haven amid remembered scenes, a refuge in a temperate climate from the rigors of the prairie. Thanksgiving, that great New England holiday, was the occasion of a celebration inaugurating the "Garland Homestead," with Franklin coming on from New York to join in the festivities. The younger Garland boy was de-

[6] Garland to Herbert Stone, undated letter.

lighted with the West Salem property, but after eighteen months of playing each evening the scene in *Shore Acres* in which a turkey was cooked and eaten on stage, he had difficulty in evidencing much enthusiasm for the traditional Thanksgiving bird. Again at Christmas time Hamlin Garland ran down to visit his mother and made West Salem a stopover whenever possible on the lecture tours which were taking him back and forth across the country. [7]

On February 23, 1894, he wrote to Herbert Stone asking for "a set of proofsheets of the entire book at *Memphis* AT ONCE. I am to lecture there on Friday the 2nd. . . . I had hoped to get the plates of 'Pra[i]rie Folks,' started but I couldnt spare the money." [8] The proofsheets to which Garland referred were those of *Crumbling Idols,* the book of critical essays to be published that spring.

Garland's elaboration of his artistic creed in the twelve essays of *Crumbling Idols* was a potpourri of earlier literary articles and lectures. In oratorical vein he announced himself a champion of the indigenous in literature, of realism as against romanticism, of the healthy West as against the decadent and derivative East, and of some form of evolutionary determinism. Many of his ideas had been more suavely expressed in 1891 by Howells in *Criticism and Fiction.* But Garland went beyond his mentor's restriction of the subject matter of literature to "the smiling aspects of life" to include within the artist's province all matters of human relations, though with strong reservations on the latitude of the "sex-mad" French novelists. Garland also made a substantial advance toward twentieth-century subjectivism beyond Howells' more conservative utterances, by advocating the approach of the impressionist painter, maintaining that art "is an individual thing,—the question of one man facing certain facts and telling his individual relations to them." [9] To distinguish this position from that of the simple objective reporting of "realism"—and also from the pornographic extremes of the French school—Garland coined the term "veritism."

On the initial page of his volume he evoked those authors who

[7] *A Son of the Middle Border,* pp. 462–67.
[8] Quoted by Flanagan, *op. cit.,* p. 455.
[9] *Crumbling Idols* (1952), p. 35.

had contributed such philosophical background as his theories possessed: Taine and Eugene Véron. Véron's *Esthetics* had made an early impression on the young veritist, and his well-marked personal copy bears the inscription in a bold hand: "This work influenced me more than any other work on art. It entered into all I thought and spoke and read for many years after it fell into my hands about 1886." [10]

Launching his criticism with a series of suggestions for the contemporary artist Garland expanded his previous article on "The West in Literature" to make up three essays dealing with "Provincialism," "New Fields," and "The Question of Success." With emphasis on the Pacific Coast as an area of unexploited possibilities, Garland advised:

> But the question forced on the young writer, even when he is well disposed toward dealing with indigenous material, is Will it pay? Is there a market for me? Let me answer by pointing out that almost every novelist who has risen out of the mass of story-writers in America represents some special local life or some special social phase. [11]

Broadening his previous article on "The Future of Fiction" to include the visual arts Garland composed his next three essays, "Literary Prophecy," "Local Color in Art," and "The Local Novel." His experiences with the Hernes furnished the material for a further essay on "The Drift of the Drama" in which he predicted: "Our stage is soon to be filled with the most amusing and interesting, because truthful, and most human characters ever grouped on any one national stage." [12] His first *Arena* article became a parenthetical essay on "The Influence of Ibsen." "Impressionism" grew out of his contacts with the new painters whom he saw as "veritists in the best sense of the word." [13] "Literary Centres" again revived the East-West controversy and the potentialities of regional magazines, with the *Southern*, the *Californian*, the *Midland Monthly* and the *Overland Monthly* cited as successful examples. In "Literary Markets" Garland's intensity throws the sectional dispute into dialogue form between East

---

[10] Garland's copy of Véron's *Esthetics* is in the University of Southern California Library.
[11] *Crumbling Idols*, p. 33.
[12] *Ibid.*, p. 95.   [13] *Ibid.*, p. 123.

and West. Haranguing his cohorts to pick up the gage thrown down by the convention-armoured East, Garland soars into a peroration:

Accept the battle challenge cheerfully, as those before you have done. What you win, you must fight for as of old. And remember, life and death both fight with you. Idols crumble and fall, but the skies lift their unmoved arch of blue, and the earth sends forth its rhythmic pulse of green, and in the blood of youth there comes the fever of rebellious art. [14]

The bravura of *Crumbling Idols* provoked numerous critical diatribes. " 'Contemporaneousness,' one finds, is the white robe of Mr. Garland's artistic faith, and mediocrity its palm branch," sneered the *Nation*. "Mr. Garland has written both prose and verse wherewith to illuminate his creed, and by them it should be judged no less than by its naked enunciation. The practice of most men is notoriously better than the worst of their dogmas, and Mr. Garland will not be found an exception to the rule." [15]

A writer in the *Atlantic* commented upon Stone's symbolic format, but insisted that to harmonize with its contents "the book should have been printed on birchbark and bound in butternut homespun, and should have had for cover design a dynamite bomb, say, with sputtering fire-tipped fuse, for the essays which it contained were so many explosions of literary Jingoism and anarchy. . . . Mr. Garland's message to the writer is this: Write of what you know. . . . His discovery of so trite a truth hardly justified a cataclysm in celebration."

The book reveals a man, who, if deficient in critical power and culture, has certain admirable qualities. True, these are moral rather than literary, but they may mean much to the future of his art . . . a splendid faith in America as a field for genuine literary art as opposed to literary exploitation, a deeply rooted interest in the common people and love for them, an enthusiastic devotion to what we must yet call his work rather than his art, and an almost Napoleonic self-confidence. . . . Pondering these qualities, one begins to under-

[14] *Ibid.*, pp. 191–92.
[15] *Nation*, LIX (July 19, 1894), 53.

stand how the same author could produce so foolish a book as Crumbling Idols and so admirable a one as Main-Travelled Roads. [16]

The past half century has curiously reversed the contemporary appraisal of Garland's fiction as surpassing his criticism. A modern authority, analyzing the manifesto of veritism, concludes: "A sensitive observer and chronicler rather than a great artist, he failed to realize in his own stories the possibilities of his theory. But in *Crumbling Idols* he made himself the public apologist for such young writers as Henry Blake Fuller, Harold Frederic and Stephen Crane." Garland "found in Crane the artist he could describe but could not himself become." "Garland's instant recognition of Stephen Crane was a tribute to his literary theory, for the boy practiced instinctively and with ease the impressionistic veritism of *Crumbling Idols*." [17]

At the time of publication, however, *Crumbling Idols* had few defenders. Howells loyally tried to take the sting from the vitriolic criticisms, writing Garland that the book was "very bold" and "largely true." "The kites that draw the electricity," he assured his protégé, "are the kites that go up. The kites that stay down are safe." [18]

The electricity of controversy was too diffused, however, to animate the sales register of Stone & Kimball, for Garland's new volume made a poor showing on the balance sheet. His earlier work continued to sell and was, in the words of the publishers' historian, indeed "the rock on which the firm was securely founded." More might have been expected of *Crumbling Idols*, for Garland quotes Walter Page as assuring him that that portion which had appeared in *Forum* had provoked "over a thousand editorials." Perhaps it was, as has been suggested, that "the savor of his summing up . . . evaporated in the periodicals where the essays were first published." [19] Perhaps it was that literary

[16] [C. M. Thompson], "New Figures in Literature and Art," *Atlantic,* LXXVI (December, 1895), 840–41.
[17] R. E. Spiller *et al.,* eds., *A History of American Literature,* II, 1017, 1020.
[18] W. D. Howells to Garland, October 28, 1894, Garland Papers.
[19] Kramer, *op. cit.,* p. 17, 72n, and quoting *A Daughter of the Middle Border,* p. 25.

criticism in America was too new a field to attract much popular attention. At all events, the volume of essays was neither a critical nor a financial success.

Garland acknowledged his disappointment to Melville Stone on September 18: "The boys write me a very discouraging letter. I don't know whether its the general stagnation in the trade or their lack of experience or my failure to reach the people." Disillusioned by the financial rewards of book authorship, he suggested: "If I had a manager with bright energetic methods I could do well in the lecture field. I wish Eugene [Field] would join teams with me." At about the same time he wrote to Kimball suggesting that the firm circularize the Middle Western colleges in his behalf: "If I had a manager to actively take hold of my lecturing I could make it profitable for us both." [20] But Stone & Kimball were too busy with publishing to encourage Garland in this idea.

Despite the discouraging reception of his artistic creed and despite reiterations that he would write no more polemics Garland stuck to his guns. The ink was scarcely dry on *Crumbling Idols* before he appeared again in print advocating in the *Forum* the identical formulae: "My own conception is that realism (or veritism) is the truthful statement of an individual impression corrected by reference to the fact."—"The difference between the veritist and the romanticist is expressed, first, by choice of subject. The veritist chooses for his subject not the impossible, not even the possible, but always the probable."—"The central figures do not necessarily marry or die at the end of the book—they walk over the hill."—"In advocating veritism I am not to be understood as apologizing for the so-called French realists. In fact they are not realists from my point of view. They seem to me to be sex-mad."—"Valdés advises the artist to treat of the thing he loves and it will no longer be prosaic or dull." [21]

As the anonymous scrivener of Chicago's Central Art Association Garland again delivered himself of his opinions in two pamphlets printed by that body. In *Impressions on Impressionism* an unnamed novelist [Garland], a conservative painter

[20] Quoted by Flanagan, *op. cit.*, pp. 456–57.
[21] "Productive Conditions of American Literature," *Forum*, XVII (August, 1894), 690–94.

[Charles Francis Browne], and a sculptor [Lorado Taft] conduct a didactic dialogue based on an exhibition of pictures, with the novelist summing up the discussion: "The public will rise to meet the impressionist half-way; we never will return to the dead black shadow, nor to the affected grouping of the old. Meanwhile the videttes of art will push on to other unconquered territory." The three characters continue the lecture after a lapse of months, this time with reference to another exhibition. *Five Hoosier Painters* finds Garland through his novelist protagonist again rendering a verdict for the experimental regionalists: "These men were isolated from their fellow-artists. They were surrounded by apparently the most unpromising material. Yet they set themselves to their thankless task right manfully—and this exhibition demonstrates the power of the artist's eye to find flood of color, graceful forms and interesting compositions everywhere." [22]

The impressionistic methods left their mark upon Garland's own work, both in prose and poetry. He, himself, had the ability to find, ofttimes in most unpromising materials, the "flood of color, graceful forms and interesting compositions" which he commends so highly in the impressionistic painters. But having the artist's eye for beauty, Garland unfortunately lacked the poet's ear. In spite of his intellectual acceptance of Lanier's theories of the relations between music and poetry, his own experiments in *Prairie Songs* are seldom entirely successful. Having abandoned the traditional verse forms of English prosody he is unable to achieve the powerful rhythmic effects and subtle tonal nuances of his models, Whitman and Lanier. His stanzas etch delicately perceptive word pictures of his prairie world, of the winter brook, the harvest field, the herald crane. But they are words without music—verse, not poetry.

Hamlin Garland, if no favorite with the critics, was a prophet of considerable honor by this time in his adopted Chicago. Soon after his arrival in the city and before he could be absorbed into the journalistic circle of Eugene Field and Opie Reed (if such

[22] *Impressions on Impressionism* (Central Art Association, Chicago, Autumn, 1894), p. 24; *Five Hoosier Painters* (Central Art Association, Chicago, Winter, 1894), p. 1. See also "Art Conditions in Chicago," *Chicago Art Institute United Annual Exhibition* (January 24, 1895), pp. 5–8.

might have been his logical destiny), he met Lorado Taft through
a lecture he gave on "Impressionism in Art." Through Taft he
came to know the "artistic gang" and to share their convivialities.
It was an informal camaraderie which Garland had never experienced in staid Boston or in crowded New York.

In Bessie Potter's studio the artists foregathered on Friday
afternoons, calling their association "the Little Room" after the
title of a current novel concerning "an intermittently vanishing
chamber in an old New England homestead." Later this group
moved their headquarters to the Fine Arts Building. Yet any day
of the week a few congenial spirits might be found in the Athenaeum Building at Lorado Taft's studio, nicknamed for obvious
reasons "the Morgue." [23]

Stone & Kimball had inaugurated the effete Eastern custom of
serving tea at their Chicago offices and soon the "artistic gang"
adopted the practice. Henry Fuller was later gently to satirize
the group and its adoption of a realistic writer, whom he names
Abner Joyce. This author of such tomes as *This Weary World*
and *The Rod of the Oppressor* could have been none other than
Hamlin Garland. Fuller writes of this newcomer to Chicago in
this fashion:

Abner, by this time, had enlarged his circle. Through the reformers
he had become acquainted with a few journalists, and journalists had
led on to versifiers and novelists, and these to a small clique of artists
and musicians. Abner was now beginning to find his best account in a
sort of decorous Bohemia and to feel that such, after all, was the atmosphere he had been really destined to breathe. The morals of his
new associates were as correct as even he could have insisted upon,
and their manners were kindly and not too ornate. They indulged in
a number of little practices caught, he supposed, from "society," but
after all their modes were pleasantly trustful and informal and presently quite ceased to irk and to intimidate him. Many members of his
new circle were massed in one large building whose owner had attempted to name it the Warren Block; but the artists and the rest
simply called it the Warren—sometimes the Burrow or the Rabbit-
Hutch—and referred to themselves collectively as Bunnies.
Abner found it hard to countenance such facetiousness in a world so
full of pain; yet after all these dear people did much to cushion his

[23] *A Daughter of the Middle Border*, pp. 6–8.

discomfort, and before long hardly a Saturday afternoon came round without his dropping into one studio or another for a chat and a cup of tea. To tell the truth, Abner could hardly "chat" as yet, but he was beginning to learn, and he was becoming reconciled as well to all the paraphernalia involved in the brewing of the draught. He was boarding rather roughly with a landlady who, like himself, was from "down state" and who had never cultivated fastidiousness in table-linen or in table-ware, and he sniffed at the fanciful cups and spoons and pink candle-shades that helped to insure the attendance of the "desirable people," as the Burrow phrased it, and at the manifold methods of tea-making that were designed to turn the desirable people into profitable patrons. That is, he sniffed at the samovar and the lemons and so on; but when the rum came along he looked away sternly and in silence. [24]

Garland himself in reminiscing of this period recalls that as a nonsmoker and a teetotaler he was "a dull and profitless companion" as a clubman. Likewise he suggests the belligerency which must have characterized his opinions. Upon being introduced one day to Lorado Taft's guests, including his sister Zulime and her friend Janet Scudder, who were en route to Paris to study art, Garland ignored the attractions of the two young ladies, one of whom was to become his wife, in his zeal to deliver to the two girls a blistering rebuke for deserting their native land in favor of foreign ateliers. [25] In Fuller's fictionalized version of this encounter events are somewhat telescoped and the hero's first meeting with the sister of his artist friend Stephen Giles occurs after she has completed her course of foreign study and is entertaining a dowager in her brother's Chicago studio:

It was for Mrs. Palmer Pence that the samovar steamed to-day in the dimly lighted studio of Stephen Giles, for her that the candles fluttered within their pink shades, for her that the white peppermints lay in orderly rows upon the silver tray, for her that young Medora Giles, lately back to her brother from Paris, wore her freshest gown and drew tea with her prettiest smile. Mrs. Pence was building a new house and there was more than an even chance that Stephen Giles might decorate it. [26]

[24] Henry B. Fuller, *Under the Skylights*, pp. 13–14.
[25] *A Daughter of the Middle Border*, pp. 5, 21–23.
[26] Fuller, *op. cit.*, p. 16.

But to the consternation of his host the somber Abner Joyce
snubs Mrs. Pence and her project of a training school for the un-
derprivileged:

Face to face with her opulence and splendour he set the figure of
his own mother—that sweet, patient, plaintive little presence, now
docilely habituated, at the closing in of a long pinched life, to unre-
mitting daily toil still unrewarded by ease and comfort or by any hope
or promise or prospect of it. There was his father too—that good grey
elder who had done so much faithful work, yet had so little to show
for it, who had fished all day and had caught next to nothing, who
had given four years out of his young life to the fight for freedom only
to see the reward so shamefully fall elsewhere. . . . [27]

Yes, in simple loyalty to his parents, Abner Joyce must snub
Mrs. Pence. He must also snub her niece, and must view Medora
with such distrust that she can read his opinion: "Why, I'm a
renegade, a European. I'm effete, contaminate, taboo." He must
certainly refuse to call on the Pences, churlishly pleading a lack
of time.

Abner made a good deal of time for the Burrow, but it was long
before he brought himself to make any for Eudoxia Pence. He came
to see a great deal of the Bunnies; in a month or two he quite had the
run of the place. They were friendly fellows who heaved big lumps of
clay upon huge nail-studded scantlings, and nice little girls who designed book-plates, and more mature ones who painted miniatures,
and many earnest, earnest persons of both sexes who were hurrying,
hurrying ahead on their wet canvasses so that the next exhibition
might not be incomplete by reason of lacking a "Smith," a "Jones," a
"Robinson." Abner gave each and every one of these pleasant people
his company and imparted to them his views on the great principles
that underlie all the arts in common. [28]

Such was Fuller's picture of "the Little Room" and its self-
elected spokesman. With due allowance for the impressionism
of satire the blue shadows of the sketch provide a corrective for
the floodlight glare upon the main figure in Garland's treatment
of the subject. In any case the fact remains that Garland's Chicago
years were deeply intertwined with the art movements of the

[27] *Ibid.*, p. 21.   [28] *Ibid.*, pp. 33–34.

city, its individual artists, and most closely of all with the complex personality of the author of *Under the Skylights.*

Henry Blake Fuller, although only three years Garland's senior, gave the impression of having been born old and a bit world-weary. Son of a banker he found himself more at home at studio teas than at directors' meetings, yet even in such a congenial atmosphere he remained a gnome-like, rather silent spectator instead of a participant. His first book *The Chevalier of Pensieri-Vani* had been praised by the discriminating for the reason "that the author did not try to prove anything." Strange companion for an ardent Single-Taxer and a crusader for veritism! Even Garland recognized the anomaly. In designating Fuller as his "most intimate friend and confidant" he added the ejaculation "antithetic pair!" Fuller delighted in the mastiff-terrier aspect of their relation and played the contrast to the utmost in "The Downfall of Abner Joyce." There the foil to the rugged, handsome, earnest Abner is the dilettante author Adrian Bond. "He was spare, he was meagre; he was sapless, like his books." Yet in a burst of confidence he discloses to Abner his philosophy of life:

"Well, then"—to Abner—"there *is* the great Human Problem, but it is not to be solved, nor was it designed that it should be. The world is only a big coral for us to cut our teeth upon, a proving-ground, a hot-bed from which we shall presently be transplanted according to our several deserts. No power can solve the puzzle save the power that cut it up into pieces to start with. Try as we may, the blanket will always be just a little too small for the bedstead. Meanwhile, the thing for us to do is to go right along figuring, figuring, figuring on our little slates, —but rather for the sake of keeping busy than from any hope of reaching the 'answer' set down in the Great Book above. . . ."

"Of course," Bond went ahead, less fantastically, "I know I ought to shut my eyes to all this and start in to accomplish something more vital, more indigenous—less of the marquise and more of the milk-maid, in fact—"

"Write about the things you know and like," said Abner curtly.

"If to know and to like were one with me, as they appear to be with you! A boyhood in the country—what a grand beginning! But the things I know are the things I don't like, and the things I like are not always the things I know—oftener the things I feel." Bond was speaking with a greater sincerity than he usually permitted himself. The right touch just then might have determined his future: he was quite as willing to become a Veritist as to remain a mere Dilettante.

Abner tossed his head with a suppressed snort; he felt but little inclined to give encouragement to this manikin, this tidier-up after studio teas, this futile spinner of sophistications. No, the curse of a city boyhood was upon the fellow. Why look for anything great or vital from one born and bred in the vitiated air of the town? [29]

Thus did Fuller chronicle the beginnings of a friendship. In real life the two men were a more antithetical pair than even the exaggerations of Abner Joyce and Adrian Bond could suggest, yet their friendship was warm and enduring. Fuller was not of the stuff to become a convert to veritism—or to any other creed. He continued, with one or two lapses into serious matter, a dilettante author, the writer of travel sketches. And Garland continued to sing his friend's praises, as fellow craftsman and as human being, albeit repeatedly confessing his bewilderment at the enigma that was "Henry B." Early in their association Garland jotted some notes on Fuller into his journal, describing him as "a ghost in flesh, a wraith in pantaloons." "His delicately perceptive personality is of the rarest and choicest kind—singularly born out of a commercial family in a commercial city." Unable to evaluate Fuller's pervasive irony Garland concluded hopelessly, "He values nothing in the world very highly." [30]

In a sketch in his *Roadside Meetings* [31] Garland describes Fuller at the time of the publication of *The Cliff Dwellers:*

In this fashion we began an acquaintance which was to ripen into friendship. He wore at this time a full brown beard and carried himself with fastidious grace, a small, alert gentleman who resented the mental and physical bad smells and the raucous noises of his native town. He studied me at our first meeting with bright eyes aslant as if only half liking my appearance, whilst I felt in him something puzzling and remote. He was reported to be more European than mid-Western, a man of independent means who had traveled widely in Italy and France. That he was the best informed man of my acquaint-

[29] Victor Shultz, "Henry Blake Fuller: Civilized Chicagoan," *Bookman*, LXX (September, 1929), 34–39; Fuller, *op. cit.*, pp. 17, 39–40.

[30] Journal, June 4, 1896, Garland Papers.

[31] *Roadside Meetings* (1930), pp. 265–75, presents an account of Garland's association with Fuller and of Fuller's work.

ances in Chicago was evident, although he made no direct display of his acquirements. He said little and his sentences were short, precisely controlled, and pertinent. He had little patience with fuzzy pretentiousness. Intellectually arrogant but never bitter, he worked away on the book to which he had alluded and when it came out a year later I found in it a mellower quality than I had hitherto perceived in him. [32]

This second of Fuller's Chicago novels was *With the Procession,* which Garland continued throughout the years to praise fulsomely. Of "The Downfall of Abner Joyce" there is little comment in all of Garland's voluminous reminiscences. Thirty years after its publication he wrote: "There he depicted our artist colony with quiet humor and authority. We are all there, reflected in his shrewd and laughing eyes. . . . He made game of me and my boyish plans for 'advancing Western Art.' " [33]

Though it is not remarkable that in autobiography Garland thus elides the caricature of "Abner Joyce," it is a matter for some comment that Fuller's satire apparently affected in no degree the even tenor of the relations between the two writers, as reflected by their correspondence. Perhaps subconsciously Garland recognized in his friend a veritism broader than his own, a fidelity of impressionism truthful enough to include self-caricature. Fortunately for Garland's equanimity the sketch in *Under the Skylights* appeared some eight years after the events it portrayed and after his protracted courtship of Zulime Taft had culminated in marriage. Moreover, in 1901, Garland's popularity was in the ascendant even as Fuller's small reputation had declined. In such circumstances "Abner Joyce" might well have been accepted graciously in private as well as in public, as merely another aberration of the unpredictable Fuller, who continued to be, in Garland's description, "a most desired guest at all our feasts." [34]

Amidst the newfound friends of "the Little Room" Garland in 1893 did not forget his old associates in Boston. For John Enneking, whose work he had praised in *Crumbling Idols,* he was active in his efforts to promote sales and exhibitions. Meanwhile

[32] *Ibid.,* p. 267.
[33] *Ibid.,* pp. 268–70. See also *Companions on the Trail* (1931), pp. 62–64.
[34] Garland to R. W. Gilder, undated [from 6427 Greenwood Avenue, Chicago], New York Public Library.

he wrote to Gilder in the interests of the Chicago Art Association
and of Lorado Taft, enclosing "some views of Taft's new group"
which he urged should be used in "an early number." "Can you
use them *soon?* If not send them back." [35]

Although Gilder continued stolidly unreceptive to this, and to
other of Garland's suggestions, Flower and other Eastern editors
remained loyal to their expatriate citizen. *Harper's Monthly*
printed a sentimental story entitled "God's Ravens," portraying
the hearts of gold which beat beneath the rude exteriors of the
prairie folk. [36] The *Arena* used a Single-Tax article, and an essay on "The Land Question and Its Relation to Art and Literature." [37] *McClure's* continued its series of "real conversations"
with "A Dialogue between James Whitcomb Riley and Hamlin
Garland," a piece in which the two conversationalists appeared
more en rapport than had those in the introductory experiment
with Eugene Field.[38] *McClure's* also offered Garland the assignment of an article on the Carnegie steel mills.

In "Homestead and Its Perilous Trades," which appeared as
their lead article for June, 1894, [39] Garland's indignation at the
fourteen-cent-an-hour twelve-hour day and labor "of the human
sort that hardens and coarsens" is overshadowed by his poetic
reaction to the physical background of the steel mills. Garland's
descriptions were magnificently supplemented by the illustrations of Orson Lowell. One of the four full-page engravings, that
facing the title page, is a representation of "The Converting
Mill: The Converter in Blast as Seen Near By," a boldly mod-
ernistic concept in which an erupting blast of light silhouettes
the huge ladle as it empties its molten steel, the peripheral figure
of the operator dwarfed by the mass of dark machinery in the
foreground. Garland's prose was equally vivid:

Out of each pot roared alternately a ferocious geyser of saffron and
sapphire flame, stressed with deeper yellow. From it a light streamed

[35] *Crumbling Idols,* p. 130; John Enneking to Garland, December 31,
1894, October 25, 1895, Garland Papers.
[36] LXXXIX (June, 1894), 142–48.
[37] "The Single Tax in Actual Application," *Arena,* X (June, 1894),
52–58; "The Land Question in Its Relation to Art and Literature," *Arena,*
IX (January, 1894), 165–75.
[38] II (February, 1894), 219–34.
[39] III (June, 1894), 1–20.

—a light that flung violet shadows everywhere and made the gray out-side rain a beautiful blue.

A fountain of sparks arose, gorgeous as ten thousand rockets, and fell with a beautiful curve, like the petals of some enormous flower. Overhead the beams were glowing orange in a base of purple. The men were yellow where the light struck them, violet in shadow. Wild shouts resounded amid the rumbling of an overhead train, and the squeal of a swift little engine, darting in and out laden with the com-pleted castings. The pot began to burn with a whiter flame. Its flut-tering, humming roar silenced all else. [40]

Reluctantly wrenching himself from this awe-inspiring vision of modern industry Garland returned to his theme of the exploi-tation of the workmen to conclude: "In the midst of God's bright morning, beside the beautiful river, the town and its in-dustries lay like a cancer on the breast of a human body." [41] His article was widely quoted at the time, [42] although it is question-able whether its impact lay so much in its moral indignation as in its graphic reporting.

In Garland's own section of the country, that is, in the terri-tory West of the Alleghenies, there were developing new outlets for his work. The newly founded *Midland Monthly* was receptive to his offerings, [43] while within Garland's own circle of associates a more important magazine was in its birth throes. On May 15, 1894, the first number of the *Chap-Book* was issued from Cam-bridge, as a sort of house organ of Stone & Kimball. The publish-er's imprint on this semi-monthly changed on August 15 from "Cambridge & Chicago" to "Chicago" alone, and the White City had its long-heralded periodical. The *Chap-Book,* however, was of a far different breed from the regional magazine which Gar-land had so strenuously advocated. Quickly expanded from its beginnings as "an attractive kind of circular" for advertising Stone & Kimball books into a lighthearted journal of personal flavor, it became the first important example of the outbreak of

[40] *Ibid.,* pp. 1–2.
[41] *Ibid.,* p. 20.
[42] *A Daughter of the Middle Border,* p. 10.
[43] "Boy Life in the West," *Midland Monthly,* I (February, 1894), 113–22; "Mount Shasta," *ibid.,* I (December, 1894), 481–83; "Night Landing," *ibid.,* III (February, 1895), 142–43; also ten poems (see Bibliography) from *Prairie Songs.*

"little magazines" which was to characterize the nineties. At the opposite pole from regionalism the *Chap-Book* was distinctly international-minded. In its short lifespan it published many distinguished British writers, Kenneth Grahame, Edmund Gosse, Israel Zangwill, Robert Louis Stevenson, H. G. Wells, and Max Beerbohm, as well as originals or translations from Paul Verlaine, Anatole France, Stéphane Mallarmé. Its pages were illustrated by prints from the best French artists, and even a Toulouse-Lautrec poster was once commissioned to advertise the magazine in France.

Yet the *Chap-Book* leaned heavily on American local-colorists, such as "Octave Thanet" and Maria Louise Pool, for its short stories and upon the younger group of American poets. [44] In such company Garland might feel somewhat at home. And he listened meekly to Herbert Stone's paternalistic advice, "You started right, Mr. Garland, but you've gone wrong. You're a bit of the preacher where you should be only the artist. The *Arena* was all very well once, but you need a different kind of publishing now. You must write for the *Chap-Book* and forget your cause." [45]

By way of compliance Garland contributed to the home-town magazine "The Land of the Straddle-Bug." [46] The "straddle-bug," Garland explained, was "three boards nailed together like a stack of army muskets to mark a claim." It was "the squatter's watchdog." Using the same setting of Boomtown, which had figured in so many of his earlier stories, Garland again described the harshness of the homesteader's lot. This time, however, his scene was background for a triangle of extramarital relations which he expounded with a ponderous solemnity quite at odds with the gay and chatty tone of the Stone & Kimball publication. Garland was congenitally incapable of joining in the "art-for-art's-sake" tendencies of the Gay Nineties or of becoming an enthusiastic contributor to the *Chap-Book*.

During this spring and summer of 1894 Garland spent most of his time in West Salem, reveling in the delights of land ownership, as he attempted to come to grips with a new theme:

[44] Sidney Kramer, *op. cit.*, Chapter 2.
[45] *Roadside Meetings* (1930), pp. 277–78.
[46] "The Land of the Straddle-Bug" was serialized through 1894–95 in *The Chap-Book,* and was republished in 1901 as *Moccasin Ranch.*

With a cook and a housemaid, a man to work the garden and a horse to plow out my corn and potatoes, I began to wear the composed dignity of an earl. I pruned trees, shifted flower beds and established berry patches with the large-handed authority of a southern planter. It was comical, it was delightful! [47]

Meanwhile he worked desultorily on his "Chicago novel," a task which he admitted later was "rather difficult." "After nine years of life in Boston, the city by the lake seemed depressingly drab and bleak, and my only hope lay in representing it not as I saw it, but as it appeared to my Wisconsin heroine who came to it from Madison and who perceived in it the mystery and beauty which I had lost. To Rose, fresh from the farm, it was a great capital, and the lake a majestic area." [48]

But if Garland was forced to hard labor to create enthusiasm for a city setting, an encounter with a new facet of nature, a new vista of open country, always served to start the flow of his inspiration. Acting on a suggestion he had thrown out in *Crumbling Idols* he turned to the Wisconsin "pineries" for the setting of two of his 1894 stories. "Only a Lumberjack" [49] is a sketch of a well-bred stranger mysteriously working as a roughneck woodsman, his talented performance on the violin the only suggestion of the estate which has been lost to him through drink. A holiday visit to the logging camps had obviously awakened in Garland the memories of his father's yarns of "Yankee Dick, the Pilot" and of his Uncle David's fiddling. "Woman in the Camp: A Christmas Sketch," [50] which was Garland's final appearance in the faltering *Arena,* also used the background of the "pineries."

In August of 1894 there came an opportunity for Garland to explore new territory, and gratefully shelving his slow-moving manuscript of "Rose" he set out for Colorado to be the guest of Louis Ehrich, a New York acquaintance and fellow reformer who had gone West for his health. In Colorado Springs he made the acquaintance of the Chief of the National Bureau of Forestry and accompanied him on a ten-day pack trip. In hunter's cabin and miner's shack Garland knew again the satisfaction of being

[47] *A Daughter of the Middle Border,* pp. 16–17.
[48] *Ibid.,* p. 26.
[49] *Harper's Weekly,* XXXVIII (December 8, 1894), 1158–59.
[50] *Arena,* XI (June, 1894), 90–97.

a man among men. The "High Country" thrilled him as potential fictional material. He recalls this first impact of the mountains upon his writer's imagination:

Thereafter neither the coulee country nor the prairie served exclusively as material for my books. From the plains, which were becoming each year more crowded, more prosaic, I fled in imagination as in fact to the looming silver-and-purple summits of the Continental Divide, while in my mind an ambition to embody, as no one at that time had done, the spirit and purpose of the Rocky Mountain trailer was vaguely forming. ... To my home in Wisconsin I carried back a fragment of rock, whose gray mass, beautifully touched with gold and amber and orange-colored lichens formed a part of the narrow causeway which divides the White River from the Bear. It was a talisman of the land whose rushing waters, majestic forests and exquisite Alpine meadows I desired to hold in memory, and with this stone on my desk I wrote. [51]

[51] *A Daughter of the Middle Border,* pp. 19–21.

❧ 7 ❧

Rose of Dutcher's Coolly

GARLAND'S DESK at the Homestead was littered with the disorderly sheets of the uncompleted "Chicago novel." Although the lichen-covered rock which weighted them was indicative of subconscious activity, the author's first order of business upon his return was the completion of this manuscript which he had been carrying back and forth with him across the country for the past two years. *Rose of Dutcher's Coolly,* a significant landmark in Garland's literary development, no doubt benefited by the length of time of its gestation. But it is true that the latter portions of *Rose* do not come up to the promise of its beginnings—perhaps a failing inherent in the novel's shift of scene, perhaps an indication of the shift of interest Garland experienced before the last chapters were composed.

It has been suggested that this novel was Garland's imaginary projection of the life his sister Jessica might have known had she survived to fulfill her early promise. There are undoubtedly familial, or autobiographical, touches as Garland outlines the career of a child of the coolly from birth through young womanhood. The first half of the book describes Rose's development in her rural setting, a motherless child, untrammeled by conventions, living the free and healthy existence of a child of the prairies. In the tenderly depicted scenes of farm and village life, of country schooldays and simple recreations, Garland is in the nostalgic vein of *Boy Life on the Prairie*.

Rose is the female counterpart of his earlier heroes, of the young men afire with ambition who went to Boston, or to Des Moines, to make their fortune. Like them, and like their creator, the girl is inspired by vague ideals of bettering herself. In Rose's case her idealism finds a symbol in the person of a trapeze artist, in whom she contemplates not only physical perfection but lofty intellectual and moral qualities. All this despite the fact that her one glimpse of this paragon is across the expanse of a circus tent. In endowing this schoolgirl crush with such weighty and persistent influence Garland was obviously attempting to recapture some adolescent experience of his own, for in later writings he has recourse to the same symbolism. [1]

Rose, true to formula, is encouraged to continue her education by a chance visitor to the district school, a childless physician of Madison, who provides for her a home with his family during her first two years at the university. That the doctor's interest evolves beyond the paternal escapes Rose's apprehension, for her patron, admitting the danger of propinquity, arranges for her to board elsewhere during the remainder of her college years. By this time Rose has matured into a striking beauty, her five-foot-nine physique, her "splendid line of bust" and "graceful limbs" evoking from her maiden companions the exclamation, "Oh, you gorgeous creature!" and from the young men on the campus the conventional attentions and at least one offer of marriage.

Rose, however, is too much the "new woman" to elect to walk the treadmill of matrimony. Yet, after her graduation, she finds herself unable to fit into her old place on the coolly farm, and faces the inevitable conflict between loyalty to her aging father who has sacrificed for her education and her own blind drive toward a fuller life. At last she sets out for Chicago determined

[1] See "Electric Lady," *Cosmopolitan*, XXIX (May, 1900), 73–83. Garland's 1888 notebook contains a sketch, "The Professor at the Circus," which is significant in this connection.

to become a "poetess." In the city her beauty and personality rapidly triumph over the limitations of her background to win her powerful supporters, a lady doctor, who proclaims Rose a genius on the strength of a few imitative poems, a society woman, who schemes to marry Rose to her attractive son, and a cynical newspaper editor, Mason, who, while ridiculing Rose's literary attempts, is strongly attached to her.

Mason, an older bachelor, exceedingly skeptical of the possibilities of romantic love, debates with himself long and earnestly the propriety of wooing such a girl, talented and perhaps on the verge of a successful career. But in the end he writes her a businesslike proposal of marriage, outlining his own deficiencies and uncertainties and offering her a matrimonial partnership based on mutual esteem "as comrade and lover, not as subject or servant, or unwilling wife." This offer Rose accepts in the closing chapters, and under the stimulus of love—or of "limited partnership"—produces her first significant poetry.

Thus, Garland's novel ends, not as he had advocated with the characters walking on "over the hill," but in a marriage, albeit a realistic rather than a romantic one. The narrative in its surface events developed no conflict, no idea, new to Garland's writing. But in selecting a woman for his central character Garland had deliberately ventured into deeper waters. From the outset he had concerned himself with depicting Rose's development in terms of sex-awakening as well as of intellectual growth. In a period of American literature when frank discussion, or for that matter any discussion at all, of relations between the sexes was completely taboo, *Rose* was a startling innovation.

The stress upon Rose's early knowledge of farm husbandry argued the acceptance of the physical facts of sex as the healthy heritage of the country child. Resolutely Garland developed the theme, indicating the first stirrings of passion toward her playmate Carl on the occasion of a school picnic, and suggesting the involvement of the two youngsters in adolescent experiments with sex when Rose was almost fifteen. This episode is terminated by Rose's confession to her father, who handles the incident wisely, leaving the girl repentant but untroubled by guilt. As she outgrows Carl the vision of the circus artist preserves her from intimacies with any of the other suitors who come to her. The memory of the stain of Carl's "thoughtless hands" returns to her on one occasion when she is taken to the theater by a young lawyer, the play dealing with a woman's premarital indiscretions. The facile acceptance of the double standard evidenced by Rose's escort is a compelling factor in her rejection of him as a suitor. And Rose turns from the boys of her acquaintance to dedicated pursuit of her ambitions, expressing the conviction that "a woman can set her foot above her dead self as well as a man."

There was nothing she did not think of during these character-forming days. The beauty and peace of love, the physical joy of it; the problem of marriage, the terror of birth—all the things girls are supposed not to think of, and which such girls as Rose must irresistibly think of, came to her, tormenting her, shaking her to the inmost center of her nature, and through it all she seemed quite the hearty young school girl she was, for this thought was wholesome and natural, not morbid in any degree.

She was a child in the presence of the Doctor, but a woman with her suitors. The Doctor helped her very much, but in the most trying moments of her life (and no man can realize these moments) some hidden force rose up to dominate the merely animal forces within. Some organic magnificent inheritance of moral purity. She was saved by forces within, not by laws without. [2]

Although the euphemisms of gentility tinkle quaintly upon ears accustomed to the gynecological blatancies of mid-twentieth-century fiction, such purple passages thoroughly shocked Garland's readers, as did his novel's conclusion with the heroine entering into what could only be construed as a "trial marriage." Even Garland's most intimate friends were uneasy at his outspokenness.

John Burroughs, a slow and painstaking reader, wrote Garland his reaction to the early chapters before he had encountered the more controversial material. At that point he praised the book except for "one disagreeable streak" in the first chapter. The point which had offended the old naturalist was the "little girl's curiosity" as to the facts of procreation, and he suggested "perfect candor or silence on such matters." By the time he had completed the book Burroughs was all for the latter, considering

[2] *Rose of Dutcher's Coolly* (1895), pp. 126–27.

Garland's emphasis on sex "too pronounced." "I think," he wrote, "all prurient suggestion in a story is to be avoided, especially when the hand of the author is so conspicuous. . . . I do not think Zola a safe guide in such matters." [3]

Howells, who in more than a dozen novels had permitted his own heroines no more than a rare and chaste engagement kiss, faced difficulties in reviewing his young friend's latest work. Howells had recently engaged on a new assignment of which he had written Garland:

> It is true that New York journalizes;—I'm always saying that. But I accept the conditions and mean to work in them for the Good True & Co. You will like my new dept. in Harper's Weekly, and you will see that I shall serve God in it. [4]

In his new column of "Life and Letters" Howells soon was called upon to express himself upon *Rose of Dutcher's Coolly*. Relating the new novel to Garland's earlier work he called attention to the seriousness of the author's artistic intentions, his absorption in his theme at times so complete as to detract from the "free movement of his characters":

> There is a frankness in his portrayal of the rustic conditions which Rose springs from, very uncommon in our fiction, and there is an acknowledgment of facts and influences usually blinked. But along with this valuable truth there is a strain of sentimentality which discredits it; and the reader is left in an uncertainty as to the author's meaning in one essential which is at least discomfiting. If fiction is to deal with things hitherto not dealt with in the evolution of character, it must be explicit.

Although unable neatly to categorize the extent of Rose's youthful indiscretions, Howells concluded that "the purpose in the present case is to prove that a woman may live down her past as a man may," a premise Howells was unwilling to grant. For, he argued, neither a man nor a woman can truly live down the past, since the past is absorbed into their characters and its evil overcome only by confession and repentance. The flaw in Gar-

---

[3] John Burroughs to Garland, January 7, 1896, February 14, 1896, Garland Papers.
[4] W. D. Howells to Garland, April 28, 1895, Garland Papers.

land's story, in terms of Howells' morality, was that Rose did not disclose her past to her husband.

With characteristic gentleness Howells went on to take the sting from the criticism he had felt impelled to make on moral grounds. Rose, he averred "is always, except upon the most intended side, strongly and attractively realized, but she is less interesting and charming to me in her Chicago phase than in her student avatar in Madison. That whole part of the book relating to the university . . . is beautiful, and in despair of fresher terms, I must call it a contribution to literature." [5]

Garland could be thankful that there was a Howells among the reviewers, for others were far less generous. The *Critic* considered the Chicago novel reminiscent of Zola and of Mr. Howells, admitting "a measure of maturity and a consciousness of strength about this story which marks a certain stage of achievement." With that introductory concession it turned to berating Garland for stylistic deficiencies and for his choice of subject:

"Rose of Dutcher's Coolly" leaves a more disagreeable taste in the mouth than "Jude the Obscure." Mr. Garland's word "sex maniac" is barbarous enough; but the continual dwelling on (we had almost said gloating over) the thing is far worse. Here we do not care to particularize; we content ourselves with saying distinctly that what the author is so fond of calling a "clean-minded" young man or woman would be, if not simply puzzled, shocked and repelled by page after page of this book. [6]

Garland had used the "barbarous" phrase in a single casual context in describing an incident of Rose's first railroad journey: "The brakeman came through and eyed her with the glare of a sex-maniac." Since no actual sexual aberration enters into the book the grammatical purist of the *Critic* in referring to "the thing" upon which the novel dwelt or gloated must have been equating all sex itself with sex-mania. *Honi soit qui mal y pense.*

The confusion of Garland's readers indicates the difficulties

---

[5] W. D. Howells, "Life and Letters," *Harper's Weekly,* XL (March 7, 1896), 223. Garland in *Roadside Meetings* (p. 455) erroneously attributes this review to Henry James.

[6] [Anon.], "Rose of Dutcher's Coolly," *Critic,* XXVIII (o.s.) (February 8, 1896), 89.

of the problem he had attacked, that of dealing in fiction with a "thing" for which there was no accepted literary vocabulary. It is remarkable that within the confines of permissible language Garland was able to produce a convincing psychological study, to create a prototype of career woman as true for her generation as Kitty Foyle and Marjorie Morningstar would be for later eras.

There were those among his readers who discerned his achievement, mostly readers abroad. James M. Barrie wrote in appreciation of a gift volume:

I thank you most heartily for your book, which only reached me this week. It is certainly the best novel I have read for a long time, and I expect when Mason publishes his novel he will find himself forestalled. Rose herself is the triumph of the book, very subtle and fresh. That is a beautiful scene where they find the old father in grief. I am coming to America in a few days and you give me a keen desire to see Chicago, which had seemed too far afield for me. If possible, we shall go now. In any case I hope to meet you. [7]

The loyal Fuller, at this time also in England, was acting as advance press agent for Garland's book. In June of 1895 he wrote that he had given H. L. Nelson "a toot or two about your latest— 70000 words (as I reported it) of town and country." Later when a British edition of *Rose* actually appeared, by virtue of Stone & Kimball's arrangement with Neville Beeman, Fuller gleefully spotted for his friend each favorable review, [8] including the highly commendatory comments in the *Academy:*

The theme is the development of a country girl of more than ordinary intelligence from childhood to womanhood; the treatment is truthful and at the same time restrained.

The growth of ideals in her mind as she ceases to be a child is told with remarkable knowledge, and full of truth and insight is the account of the sudden crystalization of these ideals round the figure of an athlete whom she sees in a travelling circus.

Is she to be drawn under by marriage? As her history thus far may be taken as a scheme of education for women, so may the plan on

[7] J. M. Barrie to Garland, September 22, 1896, Garland Papers, and quoted in *Roadside Meetings,* p. 326.
[8] H. B. Fuller to Garland, June 7, 1895, April 17 [1897], May 15 [1897], Garland Papers.

which Mason and she seek to arrange their married life be taken as a workable compromise for an intellectual and ambitious woman. Here is a book to be read, and we commend it to the attention of the English reader. [9]

But to a French reviewer, otherwise an ardent admirer of Garland's work, his picture of the "new woman," and his facile acceptance of the single standard, posed an incomprehensible problem. Rose's idealization of a circus acrobat appeared to this Frenchwoman as arrant nonsense, which Garland could hardly have meant to be taken seriously. Rose totally lacks religion. What, then, is this "force within" which Garland conjures up to save his heroine from moral degradation? Completely at a loss to understand this prairie heroine, Mme. Blanc complains: *"M. Garland ayant prêté à son héroïne des sentimens et des sensations que ne sont guére de son sexe. . . . elle est, réflexion faite, un garçon déguisé. . . . En croyant proposer un modèle, Hamlin Garland a créé un monstre."* [10]

The amount of concentrated effort Garland had expended on the completion of *Rose of Dutcher's Coolly* may be gauged by the paucity of his periodical publications during the succeeding months. In April of 1895 the *Ladies' Home Journal* printed a sketch which the associations of West Salem had obviously called up, "My Grandmother of Pioneer Days," and in July there appeared in the *Forum* a follow-up report on the activities of the Art Association. Also that summer *Harper's Monthly* brought out a story of earlier composition "Evangel in Cyene," and in the *Bookman* for November there appeared a slight sketch "Opposites," evidently a by-product of Garland's preoccupation with the reciprocal attraction of men for women. [11] (One other magazine story, three sketches for the *Philadelphia Press,* and two poems, completed his publication for 1895, the total a small trickle compared to his former inundation of the editors.)

The single article to which he seems to have devoted much

[9] [Anon.], "Rose of Dutcher's Cooley," *Academy,* LI (May 15, 1897), 520.
[10] "Mme. Blanc" [Th. Bentzon], "Un Radical de la Prairie," *Revue des Deux Mondes,* CLVII (1900), 170–77.
[11] *Ladies' Home Journal,* XII (April, 1895), 10; *Forum,* XIX (July, 1895), 606–609; *Harper's Monthly,* XCI (August, 1895), 379–90; *Bookman,* II (November, 1895), 196–97.   .

thought at this time was another contribution to *McClure's* series of "real conversations." The subject of this interview was the sculptor Edward Kemeys. As usual, more can be divined from the article as to the state of Garland's thinking than can be reliably imputed to the interviewee. Garland was impressed with Kemeys, as he had been in the case of Riley, by the essential mysteriousness of the artistic process. Previously he had reported Riley as saying of his poetic creation: "I don't know how I do it. It ain't me." According to Garland the voice of the Hoosier poet at this time "took on a deeper note, and his face shone with a strange sort of mysticism. . . . He put his fingers to his lips in a descriptive gesture, as if he held a trumpet. 'I'm only the "willer" through which the whistle comes.' " [12] When Garland came to analyze the art of the Welsh sculptor he specifically endowed his subject with fey gifts and powers of divination. Before he can knock at Kemeys' door the sculptor appears. " 'I felt ye,' he said, with a curious intentness and gravity. 'I knew ye were near. Come in.' " The two men engage in conversation upon such subjects as fatalism, predestination, and Indian psychology, in accord with Garland's conception that "Edward Kemeys is a mystic":

His mysticism is not of books; it arises, rather, from a knowledge of woods and wild spaces, from a love of mountains, from the breadth of the plains. Like the American Indian, he has come to feel nature as something very close and very sentient. This phase of his character (half-jocular in its expression) is perceived first of all. [13]

The third volume of the *Chap-Book* carried a poem by Garland, "Wagner," [14] and the fourth volume featured on its opening pages his long poem "The Cry of the Artist." The first and last stanzas read:

> I am afloat now!
> O strange and treacherous power,
> Where will you carry me?
> I swim like a swimmer at sea.

[12] "A Dialogue between James Whitcomb Riley and Hamlin Garland," *McClure's,* II (February, 1894), 219–34.
[13] "Edward Kemeys," *McClure's,* V (July, 1895), 120–31.
[14] The *Chap-Book,* III (October 1, 1895), 379–80.

My arm is strong now,
My face is to the sky,
I see my ideals soar like eagles above me—
But how long can I swim?

.   .   .   .

I know that I must fail.
The green deeps are waiting me!
    They reach their cold hands for me!
When the sun fails and the clouds grow grey,
    Then I must sink
But help me to live out the day,
In the night I will not care.
I will sink with folded hands,
    Content in caves of silence
    When the dark night comes—
But not now—not now! [15]

The introspective mood which these productions reflect was a new note for the customarily objective and aggressive Garland. Brooding over the mechanics of inspiration had hitherto been no part of his operating procedure. So long as there had been fellow-authors and editors to correspond with, so long as there had been blank paper on which to dash off his thoughts, he had been content to write, to write anything, letters, stories, articles, outlines of projected novels, novels themselves. Now, drained by the creative effort of *Rose* he sat at his desk, brooding through the writer's dark night of the soul. Spiritualism, mysticism, Indian lore, filled his thoughts and before his eyes the lichen-covered rock paperweight took on a talismanic significance. The attraction of the "High Country" seemed somehow the pull of destiny.

Late in June, 1895, with *Rose* put to bed Garland was free to indulge his wanderlust. On this trip through the Rockies he had companions of his own choosing, Herman MacNeill, a Chicago sculptor, and Charles Francis Browne, who had appeared as "the Conservative Painter" in the Chicago Art Association dialogues. Of the three artists Garland was the only one who had been west of the Mississippi River, and he found himself guide and exposi-

[15] *Ibid.,* IV (November 15, 1895), 7–8.

tor of the mountain country which he had cursorily explored the year before. From Colorado Springs the party staged into the roaring mining town of Cripple Creek. Leaving his companions to their sketching Garland rode on into the high plateaus of the Pikes Peak region to watch his first cattle round-up. Later he and Browne traversed the Royal Gorge on foot. Garland's notebooks bulged with descriptive notes and sketches of the characters who would appear in his later fiction, wrangler and prospector, trader and boardinghouse keeper. Crossing the Continental Divide near Silverton they turned south to join MacNeill in "The Happy Hunting Ground of the Utes," where, as Browne sketched, Garland picked up from the trader the elementary words of the Ute language. Through the Navajo country into the land of the pueblo tribes wandered the three travelers, and for the nine-day duration of the snake dance ceremonies shared the rude shelter of a Hopi woman.[16]

The immediate impressions of Garland's vacation in the West went into two articles for *Harper's Weekly,* one on the Ute country, and one on the Walpi snake dance, and into a sketch for the *Ladies' Home Journal* on "The Most Mysterious People in America," the sum of Garland's magazine appearances for 1896. [17] Some of his Indian articles were also syndicated at this time for the newspapers by Albert Bigelow Paine, [18] and he continued to write, principally Indian and mountain stories, for the Bacheller Syndicate. [19]

---

[16] Garland's 1896 notebook, Garland Papers, contains a six-line outline of "The Honor of a Miner" which would become *The Spirit of Sweetwater,* "The Vulture," a poem, an untitled paragraph recognizable as an outline for "The Man at the Foot of the Mountain," and many other suggestions for future works. *Roadside Meetings,* pp. 284–98.

[17] "Into the Happy Hunting Grounds of the Utes," *Harper's Weekly,* XL (April 11, 1896), 350–51; "Among the Moki Indians," *ibid.* (August 15, 1896), 801–807; *Ladies' Home Journal* (October, 1896), pp. 5–6.

[18] I am indebted for this information to an unpublished master's thesis, "A Bibliography of Hamlin Garland," by Lloyd Arvidson, of the University of Southern California.

[19] Copyright certificates to the Bacheller Syndicate which were transferred to Hamlin Garland on March 4, 1897, covered: "A Lynching in Mosinee," November 12, 1894; "The Wapseypinnicon Tiger," February 25, 1895; "A Grim Experience," August 12, 1895; "Grace," October 14, 1895; "A Girl from Washington," January 16, 1896; "Captain Hance," October 27, 1896; "A Division in the Coulé," November 7, 1896; "Whole Troop Was Water

The long summer in the Rockies had had a tonic effect upon Garland. Again he wrote with eagerness, piling superlative phrase upon flamboyant clause in an effort to convey the grandeur of the scenes he had traversed, the charm of the primitive civilizations he had encountered. But from the inspiration of the heights the autumn slid quickly into the depressing trough of economic difficulties. The Stone & Kimball books were selling poorly and there was slight market for descriptive articles on Indian lore. For all his declarations of independence from the East, Garland found it necessary to travel to New York to make the round of editors, hat in hand.

He had maintained his contacts with Gilder of the *Century* and Alden of *Harper's Monthly*. There were old friendships to renew in the city, with Burroughs, Howells, the Hernes, but the literary men seemed, Garland noted, to foregather in militant cliques: "They know one another, but have few good words for one another. The struggle for place is sharper than in Chicago, where something of the get-together spirit of the boom town still lingers." [20]

The most aggressive publisher in the field at the moment was the Irish immigrant S. S. McClure, whose early newspaper syndicate had serialized the novels of such writers as Kipling, Howells, Hardy, Stevenson, and Frank Stockton. *McClure's Magazine* with John S. Phillips as managing editor had brought this fiction to a wider audience, and was expanding into the factual and historical fields, the prelude to its muckraking campaigns of the next decade. When Garland called upon S. S. McClure during this New York visit the magazine was running a "Life of Lincoln," the first work of Ida M. Tarbell under the *McClure* masthead. It was the editor's suggestion that Garland follow up this biography with a "Life of Ulysses S. Grant," a project Garland had once casually mentioned as a possibility. Grant had been one of Garland's childhood heroes. Now McClure's offer of a fifty-dollar-a-week drawing account and traveling expenses combined with Garland's admiration for the Civil War general to

Drunk," November 7, 1896; and "Stern Fight with Cold and Hunger," November 16, 1896. Garland Papers.
[20] *Roadside Meetings*, p. 302.

overcome his instinctive reluctance toward such an extensive commitment outside the fictional field. "I don't suppose I shall really lose anything by the years of work upon Grant," Garland confided to his journal shortly after the interview with McClure. "The truth is I am beginning to take a delight in the glory of days gone by. If so—then a year from now will enhance the value of these recollections. Each year will add to the depth of the emotion." [21]

Whatever of nostalgic emotion Garland was nurturing was to be recollected in anything but tranquillity in the years while *Grant* was on the stocks, for the necessary research kept him in constant motion about the country. In March of 1896 he was in New Orleans, in San Antonio, Corpus Christi, and planning a swing into old Mexico to visit the scenes of Grant's campaigns under Generals Taylor and Scott. In Ohio, and at West Point, in St. Louis, in Galena, in Detroit, he talked with Grant's relatives and neighbors. He visited the battlefields of Vicksburg, the Wilderness, and Chattanooga, and searched out the veterans of the thin grey lines, covering an estimated total of 30,000 miles in his reconstruction of Grant's career. Hundreds upon hundreds of letters in Garland's files, from the great and from the obscure, testify to the persistence with which he tracked down every scrap of information that eye-witnesses could give to authenticate his manuscript. [22] But for all his preoccupation with military and political history he did not forget his duties as "Dean of American Literature." As opportunity presented itself he called upon the literary figures of the towns he visited, upon Ellen Glasgow in Richmond, Ruth McEnery Stuart in New Orleans, Joel Chandler Harris in Atlanta.

These occasional professional contacts to a degree relieved the monotony of Garland's round. For the most part his work was that of the newspaper legman, fruitless interview after interview in the hope of unearthing some single scrap of pertinent information—and at the day's end the cheerlessness of some provincial hotel room. By autumn when his itinerary brought him back to

[21] Journal, February 14, 1896, Garland Papers.
[22] Letters of John H. Phillips to Garland, 1896–98, Garland Papers. See also *Roadside Meetings*, Chapters 23 and 27.

New York, Garland was starved for shop talk and for association with his own kind. The place for it was awaiting him. Brander Matthews, short-story writer and dramatic critic, just entering upon his long and distinguished career at Columbia University, had been in 1889 one of the founders of "The Players." Now he proposed Garland to membership in that exclusive club of practitioners of the various arts. At 16 Gramercy Park in the rooms hallowed by the presence of Edwin Booth the weary journalist found the intellectual stimulus from which he had been too long absent.

On October 3 James Barrie landed in New York to consult with Charles Frohman over the staging of *The Little Minister*. Ingalls Kimball tendered him to a luncheon at the Players, where he and Garland met face to face for the first time. Ernest Thompson Seton was another of the guests, as was the Commissioner of Police, Theodore Roosevelt. With both Garland had in common a knowledge of America's "Wild West."

Garland and Barrie found each other congenial, and though the shy and silent Scotchman remembered with awe the dynamic vigor of the future president ("I once had the distinction of supping with Colonel Roosevelt. . . . We began at eleven and I left at two. He was still supping."), it was Garland's association he most valued. One of Barrie's biographers sums up the residue of his American visit in terms of friendships made: "All those literary New Englanders—the Nortons, William James, and many others, especially, perhaps, Hamlin Garland, who would remain a friend and correspondent until the end." [23]

When Barrie had gone on to New England and to the South to visit George Cable, Garland continued to see Theodore Roosevelt upon various occasions, usually in the company of big-game hunters and western writers. There was an exchange of autographed books between the two authors. Roosevelt offered *The Wilderness Hunter* in return for *Prairie Folks* or *Prairie Songs,* and promised to read at once Fuller's *The Cliff Dwellers.* In the same note he continued: "Next week I shall be away, but the week after I shall be back here, and if you can come around to the office, I will do everything I can to put you in contact with the

[23] *Roadside Meetings,* pp. 326–28; Denis Lackail, *The Story of J. M. B.* (London, 1941), p. 254.

police machinery. Perhaps the best way would be for you to make a tour with me some night around the precincts." [24]

So it was that with Roosevelt as companion Garland saw a section of the night life of the tenement districts that was unknown to him. When Roosevelt held court, hearing cases of police delinquency, Garland was by his side. One officer charged with sleeping at his post was an abashed country boy. Garland whispered to the Commissioner, "Lemuel Barker from Willoughby Pastures!" Roosevelt smiled, recognizing the allusion as a plea for leniency, and with only a reprimand dismissed the charges. [25]

Garland's enthusiasm for the West brought him other acquaintances, Owen Wister, not yet renowned as the author of *The Virginian,* and William Allen White. With White he had only accidentally crossed paths. They had met on a train when Garland was traveling as lecturer for the Farmers' Alliance, but, as was Garland's practice, the casual contact was not allowed to fade. And the Kansas journalist was writing him intimately in December of 1896, asking that Howells' attention be called to his work, including a summary of a "long story" which he had in progress, and asserting that "Your ideals have been mine and your work my model for many years." [26]

At this time Garland made another acquaintance which was to ripen into one of his deepest friendships. In Chicago in June of 1896 one of the music critics urged that Edward MacDowell then playing a concert in that city had expressed a desire to meet the author of *Crumbling Idols.* Flattered, Garland called upon the composer, and found him akin in many respects, of the same Scotch-English ancestry, of about the same age, and as determined to create an American music as Garland was to evolve a native literature. In New York that autumn the friendship progressed as Garland compared his remembrance of Indian fireside chants with the Omaha songs of Alice Fletcher which MacDowell was studying. With the apartment lights turned low to simulate the atmosphere of the Navajo lodges, Garland essayed with tambourine and humming to convey the primitive throbbing of Indian

[24] Theodore Roosevelt to Garland, September 25, 1896, Garland Papers. Portions of this letter are quoted in *Roadside Meetings,* p. 329.

[25] *Roadside Meetings,* pp. 330–31.

[26] W. A. White to Garland, December 9, 1896, Garland Papers.

music. It was in this year that MacDowell, recently appointed Professor of Music at Columbia University, produced his *Indian Suite.* [27]

Admission to the inner circle of the arts, however pleasant, brought Garland little sense of furthering his career. During his year of wandering the position of his books had deteriorated. On top of unfavorable reviews and slow sales he now had to contend with a dissolution of the partnership of Stone & Kimball. In April of that year differences of opinion arose between the two principals as to the conduct of their business, and Ingalls Kimball purchased the seventy titles of Stone & Kimball, exclusive of the *Chap-Book,* for the sum of $10,000, moving his headquarters to New York, where he continued to publish under the name of Stone & Kimball. Garland realized at this point that he was in no position to protest this change of management. However competent Herbert Stone and his partner had been in the matter of book design, their business arrangements with their authors had been decidedly on the sketchy side.

On October 15, 1896, Garland wrote to Kimball, in exasperation using the firm's own stationery for his epistle, demanding some definite royalty agreement on his books, particularly on *A Spoil of Office* and the English edition of *Rose of Dutcher's Coolly.* He pointed out that there was no contract covering these books, and for that matter none on *Prairie Songs* or *Crumbling Idols.* "Now," he insisted, "please let us get down to accurate business." [28] Garland must have overlooked the fact that his contract signed the previous year on November 1, 1895, on *Rose of Dutcher's Coolly,* contained a paragraph extending for a period of five years the original one-year agreements covering *Main-Travelled Roads,* and *Prairie Songs,* and containing standard clauses as to foreign rights. As a business man the author was as careless as his publishers. None of the enthusiasts of the halcyon period of the founding of the new publishing firm seem to have worried too much about the technicalities of financial arrangements.

[27] *Roadside Meetings,* pp. 318–22.
[28] Sidney Kramer, *op. cit., passim;* Garland to Ingalls Kimball, October 15, 1896, Merle Johnson Collection, New York Public Library.

Within weeks of Garland's demands, however, Kimball signed a two-year contract for publication rights on *Prairie Folks* and *Crumbling Idols,* agreeing to pay the author one-half of the net profits after publication expenses, a gesture of little significance in view of both the firm's and the books' obvious lack of prospects. [29] At this moment the one bright spot on the Stone & Kimball horizon was the *succès de scandale* achieved by one of the three books published in 1896 under the old imprint of "Chicago," Harold Frederic's *The Damnation of Theron Ware.* That title immediately sold 20,000 copies and went on to larger editions. *Rose of Dutcher's Coolly,* equally shocking to the critics, had had no such good fortune.

Another contract which Garland signed within the same week was on more current matters. Just before the appearance of the first installment in *McClure's* of "The Early Life of Ulysses S. Grant," the agreement under which Garland had worked all year was legalized. For the material used in the magazine John S. Phillips as Treasurer of S. S. McClure Company agreed to pay Garland fifty dollars per thousand words, not to exceed five thousand dollars, with advances of fifty dollars per week for time actually used in research or composition, with traveling expenses and board and lodging, except while the author was in Chicago. For the book version there was the customary royalty of 10 per cent on the first edition, on later editions, a graduated royalty running from 10 per cent on the first three thousand to 15 per cent on sales above ten thousand. [30]

The timing of this formal agreement provokes speculation. If the imbroglio of Stone & Kimball had produced in Garland's mind a resolve to be more businesslike in his arrangements, it would have been natural for him while in New York to push for a written contract with *McClure's* on his own initiative. But there were reasons why S. S. McClure Company might well have been eager to bind their author in certain respects before the actual publication of his material. The contract as signed gave the pub-

[29] Contracts between Garland and Stone & Kimball, August 11, 1893, November 1, 1895, November, 1896, Garland Papers.
[30] Letter of John S. Phillips, Treasurer, to Garland, outlining terms of agreement, November 14, 1896, Garland Papers.

lishers rights of "editorial suggestion and supervision," and rather broad powers relating to space considerations. In the event of disagreement between the parties Howells was selected to arbitrate the differences. In the months ahead Garland was to have occasion to meditate the differences between the gentlemanly, if haphazard, methods of Stone & Kimball, and the high-handed practices of the journalistic tycoons.

❧ 8 ❧

Wayside Courtships

GARLAND GREW increasingly dissatisfied with *McClure's* as the monthly installments of his biography appeared throughout the first half of 1897—"Grant at West Point," "Grant in the Mexican War," "Quiet Years at Northern Posts," "Grant in Missouri," "Grant at the Outbreak of War." [1] The drastic cutting which his manuscript received in editorial offices was for him the butchery of a year's hard work, and he suspected McClure's motives to be those of economy rather than of literary judgment, as the total compensation was to be based upon the amount of accepted wordage. The disagreements with his publishers were bitter, but they did not reach the stage of calling for outside arbitration as provided by the contract. It is doubtful whether Howells would have agreed to act in any such official capacity had the necessity arisen. But as a friend he was most sympathetic to Garland in his ordeal.

[1] *McClure's,* VIII (January–May), 195, 366, 402, 514, 601.

After the publication of the first two articles he wrote Garland, praising his work as "fresh and strong":

If the papers have been cut, that accounts for a certain roughness and abruptness that troubles me. You have got some newspaper diction on your pen point, and you must shake it out. . . . It is a shame for McClure to touch your work. You ought to make a mighty row whenever he does it. [2]

From Sicily Henry B. Fuller wrote offering Garland his condolences. By way of consolation he pointed out that his own latest book with the Century Company [3] had sold only six hundred copies in America and two hundred in England:

Ain't I jes payin' for my devotion to art?
So are you. Well, that's what you get for dealing with a concern that is purely mercantile.
                    McClure
                    You'n
                    A lovely American type, sure.
Well, if the magazine articles don't go quite right, be stiff about the book. That's what will last. Is the damphool completely without a realization of the notable thing you have done in collecting and shaping all that material? Does he think Grant needs firecrackers and tin horns? I ask.
Yes, go to Appleton and rest yourself. You've had enough of crank firms and upstart firms. At your time of life you're entitled to a little repose.
This need not be saved for my Life & Letters, 10 vols. [4]

Garland, writing of the firm of S. S. McClure & Company from the vantage point of 1930, elides the controversy, mentioning only that he intended to treat Grant "at every stage of his career, as if he were the chief character in a novel," without any devices to foreshadow his eventual prominence. McClure, Garland mentions casually, "was not convinced. He wanted each installment to be successful in itself, not as a step in a dramatic progress." [5] But this difference of opinion which Garland presents so cava-

[2] William D. Howells to Garland, January 8, 1897, Garland Papers; also in Life in Letters (Mildred Howells, ed., New York, 1928), II, 73–74.
[3] The Puppet-Booth: Twelve Plays, New York, 1896.
[4] H. B. Fuller to Garland, March 2, 1897, Garland Papers.
[5] Roadside Meetings (1930), pp. 308–309.

lierly in his reminiscences was matter for tragedy for the author in 1897.

Difficulties pursued Garland in other fields. Kimball's financing for the reorganized publishing firm was obviously shaky. As the letter from Fuller suggests, Garland in the early months of 1897 was already leaning toward D. Appleton & Company as his chief publishers. It was well that he could do so, for the overextended firm of Stone & Kimball went to the wall that summer, after having issued thirty-six new titles since the move to New York. Gradually their copyrights had been depleted by assignments to creditors, and on October 21 the remainder of the assets of the firm were sold at public auction. Garland attended this "rather melancholy affair" and noted "the walls of the pretty office dismantled—the furniture in disorder. The dust moving over all. The sheriff a consequential little Dutchman was bustling about seeing that the goods were in order."

Kimball received the guests, referring to himself as "the corpse" of the occasion and to the authors present as "the chief mourners." Edmund C. Stedman, who was co-editor of the firm's ten-volume set of Poe, remarked, "If we could but contrive to have Kimball's insouciance put up at auction we would all be paid in full." Garland noted of his publisher's behavior: "He smoked his pipe and shook hands with the sorrowful authors quite unmoved by the affair—apparently," but added, "It may have been a brave show merely." [6]

Herbert S. Stone & Company, of Chicago, which soon after the split had re-entered the book publication field, bought up practically all of the printed sheets and plates, and many of the copyrights. [7] Among these assets were the unsold copies of three of Garland's books. In the trade journal that month Stone & Company's double-page advertisement appears, the recto page devoted to display type featuring the ten-volume Poe and *The Damnation of Theron Ware*. On the verso page were listed thirty other titles which had been acquired at the auction. Near

[6] "Literary Notes," unpublished MS in Garland Papers, p. 17, quoted in Sidney Kramer, *A History of Stone & Kimball and Stone & Company*, pp. 88–89. A somewhat similar description appears in *Roadside Meetings*, pp. 313–14.

[7] Sidney Kramer, *op. cit.*, p. 89.

the head of the list were *Prairie Folks, Main-Travelled Roads,* and *Crumbling Idols.* In the same issue Isaac Mendoza, a bookseller, advertised forty-nine other Stone & Kimball titles as remainders at half price, an ignominy which the Garland books escaped.

But the title of Stone & Company to its purchases of copyright was brusquely challenged the following week when New York attorneys for certain judgment creditors purchased a half-page advertisement in the same journal to protest in heavy type "A WARNING" addressed to Stone & Company against selling books "manufactured for you from certain sheets purchased by you without right of publication." Although Stone & Company countered the next week with another full page listing the identical volumes as in its previous advertisement, none of this litigation was calculated to improve the situation so far as the long-suffering authors were concerned. [8]

Fortunately for Garland, D. Appleton & Company, which in 1892 had published his *Century* serial, *A Little Norsk,* now stood ready to take over such other titles as he could deliver to them. Garland's connection with the Appletons had remained friendly throughout the *Chap-Book* years, and their firm was indebted to him for what in time would become one of their most valuable literary properties, Stephen Crane's *Red Badge of Courage.* In 1894 Crane had appeared at the Appleton offices, poverty-stricken and emaciated, bearing an introductory letter from Hamlin Garland and some Philadelphia newspaper clippings 'of his graphic war story. Appleton's published it the following autumn, and while Garland was depositing his own manuscripts with Stone & Kimball, issued three other Crane titles, *The Little Regiment,* a new edition of *Maggie,* and *The Third Violet.* [9]

In February of 1897 Garland signed a contract with D. Appleton & Company providing for a straight 15 per cent royalty on *A Spoil of Office* (which had evidently been released to him by Stone & Kimball before the debacle) [10] and on a new volume of

---

[8] *Publishers' Weekly,* LII (October 30, 1897), 701–702, 733; (November 6, 1897), 777; (November 13, 1897), 807.

[9] Samuel C. Chew, *Fruit among the Leaves,* pp. 48–49.

[10] It must be presumed that the Arena Publishing Company had released to Stone & Kimball the copyrights on all three of Garland's books, although only *Main-Travelled Roads* was reissued by the latter.

short stories to be entitled *Wayside Courtships*. For this collection Garland assembled eleven stories of uneven length and considerable disparity of theme. Some had appeared in print before in early numbers of the *Arena, Belford's,* and other journals. One appeared simultaneously with book release in the current number of the *Century*. Others apparently were published first in the collected form. [11]

It was evidently considered that the fact that all these dissimilar contributions dealt with relations between men and women constituted a sufficient rationale for the volume. To suggest, however, as did the title, that it was a collection of romances was somewhat stretching the point. It is true that of the three long tales which occupy the first half of the book each ends with a wedding, or the promise of a wedding. But in one of these, "A Stop-Over in Tyre," Garland makes obvious his conclusion that marriage and a man's career are completely disjunctive pursuits. Other sketches touch on such complications to marriage as dipsomania, brutality in the husband, blindness, illusion, divorce, prostitution, and death from cancer. Nonetheless, in the closing "Upon Impulse" the book ends properly in a lovers' meeting, for once unalloyed by forebodings or regrets. To bind this rather somber collection of stories into a whole Garland attempted the device of short introductory and concluding mood pieces, the first an impression of a man's and woman's response to each other and to life as young lovers, and the last a glimpse of a couple after the vicissitudes of life have drained them. The man urges his wife to forget the intervening years:

He lay with closed eyes, tired, purposeless. The sweet sea wind touched his cheek, white with the indoor pallor of the desk worker. The sound of the sea exalted him. The beautiful clouds above him carried him back to boyhood. There were tears on his face as he looked up at her.

"I'm forgetting!" he said, with a smile of exultation.

But the woman looked away at the violet-shadowed sails, afar on the changeful purple of the sea, and her throat choked with pain. [12]

[11] For publication history of stories included in *Wayside Courtships* (1897), see Bibliography.

[12] *Wayside Courtships*, p. 281.

With such an ambiguous and despondent leave-taking of his readers Garland bundled together for the printer the hastily assembled manuscript of this, his third collection of short stories. It was not the "vol. of short stories of my very best" which he had promised Stone & Kimball in the happier days of 1894, but it was the best that he could produce at the moment to meet the offer from Appleton. Meanwhile, the Grant articles were grinding to a standstill, in a fashion which certainly neither Garland nor Mc-Clure had anticipated when the biographical project was undertaken.

The June issue of *McClure's* carried the installment dealing with "Grant's First Great Work in the War," with this editorial note:

> This series of papers will conclude in the July number with a paper on Grant in the Vicksburg campaign, where his military genius comes to its full maturity and recognition. The aim here has necessarily been only to indicate the general course of Grant's progress as a great commander, and give some close glimpses of his character and personality at the important points in it. A detailed history of movements and battles would not have been practicable, though it will be so in the book form which the papers are ultimately to take. [13]

To Howells and others in Garland's confidence this announcement could have meant but one thing, that author-publisher relations had strained to the breaking point. The next installment on "Grant in a Great Campaign," as promised, dealt with the Vicksburg campaign, though in summary fashion, and concluded with a note:

> The capture of Vicksburg brought to its full development and recognition Grant's genius as a military commander, and marks a clear division in his career. With the present paper, therefore, Mr. Garland concludes his series of interesting studies in Grant's life, his design having been only to exhibit, by close personal presentations, the course and character of Grant's progress to his high destiny. [14]

Thus, lamely, *McClure's* broke off what had originally been contemplated as a full-length biographical study. It is true that Garland published the following month a sketch of "Grant's

[13] *McClure's*, IX (June, 1897), 721.
[14] *Ibid.*, IX (July, 1897), 811.

First Meeting with Lincoln," and that after a lapse of almost a year there appeared in *McClure's* two more excerpts from the biography: "A Romance of Wall Street—The Grant and Ward Failures," and "Ulysses S. Grant—His Last Year." [15] But the continuity of the original project was broken, and it is to be suspected that these excerpts were delivered under pressure as settlements for advances which Garland had long ago drawn. At all events, the total length of the combined installments did not draw near the one-hundred-thousand-word maximum originally provided for the series. It was closer to one-half that figure.

Meanwhile, on June 29, D. Appleton & Company brought out simultaneously in a uniform edition, selling at $1.25 each, four titles by Hamlin Garland: *Jason Edwards, A Member of the Third House, A Spoil of Office,* and *Wayside Courtships.* [16] Thus Garland, whatever his tribulations as a biographer, had the satisfaction of knowing that all of his books were again in print.

With his commitments to Appleton met and with the Grant project in abeyance Garland turned westward. His first stop was the Homestead at West Salem, where Franklin, with his show closed for the summer, was waiting. The original frame cottage had expanded along with Hamlin's list of titles. With *Rose* had come a two-storied bay window, and to the amazement of the rural community, a trim-clipped lawn and a tennis court. With the bonanza of the Grant advances (Garland admitted that the fifty dollars a week was "more money than I had ever hoped to earn") there had been added such refinements as a piano and new dinner china. The place was not only a home for the two elderly ladies, but an anchorage for the two young men, a home port in which they could take shelter when the waters of their precarious professions were swept by storms. This time, however, the actor and the author did not linger long in the quiet backwash of West Salem. Hamlin was eager to show his brother the wonders of the Indian country. Within a week they were off to Standing Rock Reservation in North Dakota, Hamlin primed with letters of introduction to the various army posts. For the next month the brothers lived among Sioux, Crow, and Cheyennes, endeavoring

---

[15] *Ibid.,* X (April, 1898), 488–505; XI (May, 1898), 86–96.
[16] "Index of Books Published in 1897," *Publishers' Weekly,* LIII (June 29, 1898).

through interpreters to recapture the excitements of the frontier wars.

When they reached the western ranges of Montana, however, they found excitement which momentarily wiped out the heroic vision of Custer's last stand. The news of the Yukon gold strike had come by steamer to Seattle, and the West Coast was aflame with the madness which would soon sweep the entire country. Another gold rush was on. The Garlands were caught up in the enthusiasm of the moment, and Franklin was all for joining the exodus to the north. Burton Babcock, Hamlin's boyhood friend, had become a woodsman and prospector near Seattle. He added his plea to be "grub-staked" for the adventure. But in the end calmer counsel prevailed. Franklin returned to New York to rejoin the Herne troupe, and Hamlin settled down in Washington to complete his biography. But there was a promise, half in jest, that in the spring when the book was finished the two old friends, Burton Babcock and Hamlin Garland, would hit the trail together in search of wealth in the Klondike gold fields.

The Washington winter brought new associations for Garland. There were the scientists whom he met in the Cosmos Club. There was Edward Eggleston, whose *The Hoosier School-master* had first suggested the use of Mid-Western materials. The Grant researches led to the acquaintance of such men as John Hay, Senator Lodge, and General Longstreet. Theodore Roosevelt was now in Washington as Assistant Secretary of the Navy, and the friendship which had begun at the Barrie dinner the year before prospered on their common interest in the West. On one side Roosevelt expressed it: "I can't tell you how I enjoy having a man at my table who knows the difference between a *parfleshche* and an *apparejo.*" On the other, Garland noted in his journal: Roosevelt is "a man who is likely to be much in the public eye during his life. A man of great energy, of noble impulses, and of undoubted ability." [17]

But for all these casual contacts Garland spent a weary and depressing winter. His journal reflects an unaccustomed melancholy, as he brooded over public affairs, over his father's struggles, his mother's illness, and his own financial difficulties. In the

[17] *A Daughter of the Middle Border, passim* and pp. 56–57.

damp fogs which hung over the Potomac he dreamed of the sun-drenched lands of the "High Country." The pioneering spirit of the Garlands and the McClintocks had been reawakened by the sight of the Seattle prospectors outfitting for the northern trail, and as he turned over musty pages in the Library of Congress he yearned for the freedom of the wilderness. One gray day, alarmed at the introspection which close application to work had brought, he jotted this rhyme into his diary:

> I will fling the scholar's pen aside
> And grasp once more the bronchoe's [sic] rein,
> And I will ride, and ride and ride,
> Till the rain is snow and the snow is rain. [18]

Meanwhile he had need of funds to see him through the Grant book, since McClure's subsidy had been withdrawn. Three stories from the Indian country found their way into the *Youth's Companion*, [19] but other editors were apathetic to his Indian materials. Earlier he had sent to Gilder "a little story suitable it seems to me for your 'Lighter Vein' dept. It is a true story and gives what we seldom get the *Indians point of view.*" But nothing came of this overture. In fact, the *Century* still held unpublished Garland's story "A Good Fellow's Wife," originally submitted to them in 1893. [20] When Garland called on Gilder on April 1 of 1898 to mention the delay he obtained little satisfaction, and reported dejectedly in his journal that the editor's "manner was by no means enthusiastic. It was merely respectful. He has not been enthusiastic since the first year of my success with him." [21]

[18] Journal, *passim*, 1897–98, and February 23, 1898, Garland Papers. How greatly Garland used his journal for source materials may be seen from the fact that this rhyme in more polished form appears as the introductory verse of *The Trail of the Goldseekers* published the following year.

[19] "Joe, the Navajo Teamster," *Youth's Companion*, LXXI (November 18, 1897), 579–80; "The Story of Buff," *ibid.* (December 2, 1897), 606–607; "The Stony Knoll," *ibid.* (December 18, 1897), 635.

[20] On July 17, 1894, Garland wrote Gilder asking the return of "A Good Fellow's Wife," "for revision and strengthening of names." On January 10, 1898, he was still asking for publication on the pretext that he wished to include the story in a new volume of short stories. Gilder's penciled note on the letter is noncommittal, suggesting that Garland had better put over his book to fall. The offer of the story for the "Lighter Vein" is dated only June 19 and was sent from West Salem. All in Century Collection, New York Public Library.

[21] Journal, April 1, 1898, Garland Papers.

There were other editors, however, who were solicitous to ob-
tain Garland's work, although not the Indian stories which he
wished to send them. Edward Bok of the *Ladies' Home Journal*
readily accepted a four-part serial called "The Doctor," a pot-
boiling romance, dating in composition from 1895, and Garland
was persuaded to commit himself on another romance, although
this time one with a Western setting, "The Spirit of Sweetwater." [22] Garland debated with himself the advisability of these
new commitments. "It is harder to say no than I used to
think it would be [although] the public will tire of any name
iterated constantly." He recorded a resolution not to publish
more than the Grant biography and the Sweetwater romance
that year.

To finance the final Grant researches Garland was obliged to
rely in part on his lecture fees. Under the sponsorship of the
Arena a sheet advertising his "Seventh Season" tour was circular-
ized, describing the attraction offered in these terms:

For example, [sic] program first leads off with some poems of spring,
full of suggestions of wild prairie-chickens and soaring cranes. The
second selection tells about "Uncle Ethan's Speculation" in patent
medicines.
The third number is a bunch of lyrics in dialect, of which Mr. Garland is thoroughly master "Horses Chawin' Hay," and "Goin' Back
To-morrow."
The fourth number is "Among the Corn-rows," one of the famous
stories of "Main-Travelled Roads," and the program ends with a
group of horseback poems, in which the prairies with their wild
horses, and the splendid free life of the herder, are brought very close
to the hearer. [23]

The half-promise to accompany Babcock to the Yukon began,
despite the discouragement of friends, to take on the aspects of
a serious intention. Garland began to assemble information on
overland routes to the Klondike and to expound the merits of his
proposed journey. Fuller in Washington in January for a visit
and preoccupied with the imminence of war with Spain, was un-

[22] *Ladies' Home Journal*, XV (December, 1897–March, 1898).
[23] Journal, March 28, 1898, and Circular "Hamlin Garland, Seventh Season," Garland Papers.

sympathetic to Garland's project. Howells wrote Garland in March, apparently accepting the excursion as inevitable: "When do you begin throwing yourself away on the Klondike? (I hate your going too much to care whether I spell it rightly.)" [24] As Garland collected camping equipment, pack saddles, cooking utensils, and sleeping bags, he weighed the objections of his more sedentary associates, and something of their horror of the dangers of the wilderness must have impressed him with the potential danger of the undertaking. In a solemn and testamentary mood he undertook to leave behind him a literary legacy, the recollections of his boyhood and of the pioneering experiences of his immediate forefathers. The manuscript, hastily dictated in the Library of Congress, was in the third person, although the "Grant McLeod" of its episodes afforded only a thin disguise for the autobiographical nature of the narrative. "Within a week," Garland recalls, "the manuscript had grown into a bulky volume." [25]

Leaving this rough draft for the bewilderment of his executors should he not return from Alaska, Garland started from Washington in April to meet his friend Babcock in British Columbia. But a stopover at the Homestead added his mother's protests to those of his friends. The adventure was almost abandoned at this point. For a day Garland debated whether to go "or to settle down with my books. This is the young man and the old man in almost equal contest." He concluded gloomily: "The old man will win in a few years." [26] But like "The Cry of the Artist," the cry of his wanderlust was *"Not now, not now!"* And Babcock was waiting at the head of the trail. Garland lovingly packed his new equipment as through the village of West Salem passed five trainloads of soldiers, alerted for a possible attack from Spain. [27]

Given the knowledge of Garland's financial disappointments of the past few years it might be possible to conceive of his having joined the gold rush for the same stakes as the other Klondikers.

[24] W. D. Howells to Garland, March 14, 1898, Garland Papers.
[25] *Companions on the Trail* (1931), p. 490. An apparently even earlier version in a notebook marked "Cr. Stone & Kimball, Chicago, Illinois," is entitled "Lincoln Stuart. A Brother to an Actor."
[26] Journal, April 3, 1898, Garland Papers.
[27] Journal, April 18, 1898, Garland Papers.

Indeed, the *Nation* read the record in this fashion and sneered at the metamorphosis of the author of *Rose of Dutcher's Coolly* into the "rough-shod would-be miner of 1898." [28] But such an interpretation ignores the deepest facts of Garland's nature. Nothing in the daily jottings of the journal, which he began this year to keep with religious regularity, nor in the equally ingenuous printed accounts of his journey indicates any more than an observer's interest in the prospecting activities which he encountered.

His motives for making the arduous journey, so reckless and incomprehensible to his friends, were at once more simple and more complex than the mere craving for sudden wealth. Simply, he loved the life of out-of-doors with all its hardships. More complexly, he was at a plateau of development, the youthful concentration of his energy expended on goals which, now achieved, proved partially illusory. His future course appeared uncertain. In the self-evaluation which comes with the middle years Garland was turning more and more to thoughts of his origin, to nostalgia for the simpler conditions of his boyhood. Tentatively he had been writing in reminiscent vein, sketches of his grandmother, of frontier Christmases, and in a last confused burst of activity before setting out for the northern wastes, the long autobiographical account of "Grant McLeod." But however vivid his memories, the physical frontier of the Middle West was vanished, the prairie turned under by the plow. Garland's first sight of the unoccupied lands of Colorado and the Northwest had led him to exult that here was the land of his youth—only minus the buffalo. When he reached the savannas of British Columbia he exclaimed: "It was like going back to the prairies of Indiana, Illinois, and Iowa, as they were sixty years ago, except in this case the elk and the deer were absent." [29] In view of this persistent searching to recapture the experiences of his past it seems fair enough to take at face value Garland's contemporary assertion of his intentions in heading for the Yukon. "I believed that I was about to see and take part in a most picturesque and impressive

[28] "Three Books on the Klondike," *Nation*, LXIX (August 24, 1899), 155–56.
[29] *The Trail of the Goldseekers* (1926), p. 60.

movement across the wilderness. I believed it to be the last great march of the kind which would ever come in America, so rapidly were the wild places being settled up. . . . I was not a goldseeker, but a nature hunter." [30]

The route by which Garland hoped to reach the Klondike was chosen after due consultation with experts and government officials in Canada; the relative merits of proposed itineraries were discussed in his published articles.[31] The overland trails, including his own preference, "The Telegraph Trail," were known as "poor men's routes," since they avoided the costly steamer charges along the Pacific Coast as well as the duties levied upon those who approached the gold fields through United States territory along the southern fringes of Alaska. But the Telegraph Trail was long, and in great part across poorly mapped and treacherous country.

Outfitting at the town of Ashcroft, British Columbia, Garland, with his friend Burton Babcock, set out on the third of May on the long trek. Fifty-nine days later, the last crumb of their food consumed, they emerged some seven hundred sixty miles distant on the banks of the Stikeen River, and floated down to Wrangell in United States territory. Here they found that earlier arrivals who had attempted the final rugged route to the headwaters of the Yukon at Teslin Lake were turning back in discouraged droves. Garland, already six weeks behind his allotted time schedule, could not risk the chance of being frozen in for the winter and was forced to leave Babcock, a true prospector, to continue the journey in other company. Summing up his impressions Garland, in a more realistic mood than that of anticipation, surveyed the route which he had traversed:

The trail was a disappointment to me, not because it was long and crossed mountains, but because it ran through a barren, monotonous, silent, gloomy, and rainy country. It ceased to interest me. It had almost no wild life, which I love to hear and see. Its lakes and rivers were for the most part cold and sullen, and its forests sombre and de-

[30] *Ibid.*, p. 8.
[31] "Ho, for the Klondike," *McClure's*, X (March, 1898), 443–54, a digest of which was printed as part of a symposium on Alaska by *National Geographic*, IX (April, 1898), 113–16.

pressing. . . . As a route to reach the gold fields of Teslin Lake and the Yukon it is absurd and foolish. It will never be used again for that purpose. [32]

But he was reluctant to return home without having seen an actual gold field. With the Yukon out of the question Garland joined forces with a newspaper man to make a shorter trip to a newly reported strike near Skagway. By steamer the two went up the coast, then packed inland to Atlin Lake, where Garland spent a few days observing the frenzy of a true placer camp, and even went so far as to sluice a few pans of gravel—but on another man's claim. Then being out of funds for a *full* return steamer ticket, he crossed afoot to the coast over the famed Chilkoot Pass and went back by steamer to Wrangell to retrieve his faithful saddle horse Ladrone. Early on the trip he had resolved that nothing would induce him to leave his four-legged companion to the sure death of a northern winter.

But the problem of obtaining transportation back to the States for the animal caused him to miss steamer after steamer. At one point it seemed that Garland was to suffer a similar fate to that of his colleague Joaquin Miller, who spent the winter of 1898–99 frozen in on the Yukon on the steamer *Weare*. [33] At last, however, the *Forallen* made room for both passengers, and Ladrone rode to Seattle in aristocratic comfort in the ship's hold while mere mules and work horses crowded the outside decks. At Seattle, the Canadian-born Arabian horse, now a licensed American animal, was transferred to the railway cars. Across the two thousand miles between the Pacific Coast and West Salem Garland hopscotched, jumping off and on passenger trains to intercept the freight cars at intermediate points to feed and exercise his mount. Such concern for a mere animal aroused the curiosity of the loungers at one railroad junction. "Does it pay to bring a horse like that so far?" one inquired innocently. "Pay?" shouted Garland, remembering the times when he had owed his life to his surefooted pony," Does it pay to feed a dog for ten years? Does it pay to ride a bicycle? Does it pay to bring up a child? Pay—no; it does not pay. I'm amusing myself." [34]

[32] *Trail of the Goldseekers*, pp. 180–81.
[33] *Publishers' Weekly*, LIII (January 22, 1898), 103.
[34] *Trail of the Goldseekers*, pp. 255–56.

That exasperated outburst might have summed up Garland's entire Alaskan trip. A wealth of amusement, of experience, gained, but little in the way of financial returns. In his original prospectus he had advocated that, although actual expenses of the overland route might come to only some three hundred dollars, no one should undertake the trip without at least five hundred dollars in hand. The warning was well put, for by his own confession the trip (including Ladrone's passage, no doubt) cost him double what he had anticipated.[35] From the material he had accumulated in his notebooks, *McClure's* published a single article and two blocks of short poems, while the *Century* printed a single poem.[36] The book of travels published the following year had to compete with a tremendous spate of books on the Northwest, and was crowded into reviews only as one "Among the Late Books on Alaska."[37] Needless to say, the grubstake to Babcock, who reached the Klondike at last and spent the winter prospecting on Thistle Creek, brought no returns on Garland's investment.

But the intangible values of the excursion remained. In one of his most polished essays Garland thoughtfully analyzed the residue of his experiences:

The trail has taught me much. I know now the varied voices of the coyote—the wizard of the mesa. I know the solemn call of herons and the mocking cry of the loon. I remember a hundred lovely lakes, and recall the fragrant breath of pine and fir and cedar and poplar trees. The trail has strung upon it, as upon a thread of silk, opalescent dawns and saffron sunsets. It has given me blessed release from care and worry and the troubled thinking of our modern day. It has been a return to the primitive and the peaceful. Whenever the pressure of our complex city life thins my blood and benumbs my brain, I seek relief in the trail; and when I hear the coyote wailing to the yellow dawn, my cares fall from me—I am happy.[38]

---

[35] *A Daughter of the Middle Border*, p. 78.

[36] "Hitting the Trail," *McClure's*, XII (February, 1899), 298–304; "The Trail of the Golden North," *ibid.*, XII (April, 1899), 505–507; "The Trail of the Golden North," *ibid.*, XIII (May, 1899), 65–67; "The Ute Lover," *Century*, LVIII (June, 1899), 218–20.

[37] "Late Books on Alaska" (H. M. Stanley), *Dial*, XXVII (August, 1899), 72.

[38] "Hitting the Trail," p. 304. This passage was reworked into rhythmic form as "Vanishing Trails," in *Iowa, O, Iowa* (1935).

On September 22, 1898, Garland noted in his journal, "Home again after five months." Four days later as he was at work with his father fencing a pasture for Ladrone a neighbor delivered a package from the post office. It was an advance copy of *Ulysses S. Grant, His Life and Character* from Doubleday & McClure. Garland opened it eagerly, but his father, still the captain as of old, would permit no dawdling on the job. "Bring that spade," he commanded, and Hamlin was forced to leave his volume on the top of a fencepost until the day's work was done. [39]

Examined at leisure, the *Grant* pleased Hamlin greatly, wiping out the memories of the disappointing serial version. To the end of his life he would consider it "one of my best books." Brander Matthews in the *Bookbuyer* commended the volume for its anecdotal approach. The *Critic* reviewed it favorably, and even the austere *American Historical Review* gave it serious and sympathetic consideration. [40] It yet remains an authoritative sourcebook on the personal aspects of Grant's career. At the time of publication Garland and McClure were disappointed with sales, for the current hostilities had eclipsed Civil War materials in the public interest. But the biography remained a steady producer of moderate royalties down through the years. When much of Garland's fiction was being remaindered, Macmillan brought out a second edition of the *Grant*. [41]

After a protracted visit with his parents Garland returned to Chicago, to his desk at 474 Elm Street, and to the camaraderie of the studios. "The Little Room" had acquired another member in his absence. Garland's journal records his growing interest in the newcomer: *"November 3:* Miss Taft is just back from four years in Paris and is full of the latest theories of art. She was dressed in a red gown and looked very handsome." *"November 13:* Her four years of France have developed her as a woman as well as an artist. [She is] capable of meeting any social demand." *"Thanksgiving Day:* Better that I should save every dollar and

[39] Journal, September 22 and 26, 1898; *A Daughter of the Middle Border*, p. 72.

[40] *My Friendly Contemporaries* (1932), p. 305; *Bookbuyer*, XVII (December, 1898), 484; *Critic*, XXXIV (March, 1899), 257–58; Frederick W. Moore, *American Historical Review*, IV (March, 1899), 377–78.

[41] Miscellaneous financial statements in Garland Papers; *Ulysses S. Grant, His Life and Character* (New York, The Macmillan Co., 1920).

secure myself against want. If all goes well by next Thanksgiving I can have a home of my own." [42]

But the prospect of a home of his own was a matter only for daydreams. Garland's financial insecurity and his mother's increasing psychological dependence argued its improbability. Although Mrs. Garland continually urged her son to marry, she made it clear that Hamlin should choose not so much a wife as a "new daughter" for the Garland Homestead. Moreover, Hamlin, now aged thirty-eight, had developed into a wary old bachelor, repeatedly delivering himself of the opinion that marriage was the graveyard of ambition. Meeting Zulime Taft frequently in the studios and at the home of her sister Mrs. Charles Browne, he no doubt checked his emotions by recalling "the fifty bright fellows" of his seminary days, whom he had cited to Gilder as having dropped out and down, "growing at length indifferent and in a way content with husks to fill their bellies." Possibly he remembered the matrimonial deadlocks he had grimly portrayed in a long procession of fictional works. At all events, with his relations with the charming Miss Taft no more than those of cordial friendship Garland bundled up his manuscripts and left for New York. [43]

Israel Zangwill, whom Garland had helped to entertain in Chicago, was also in New York engaged in a dramatization of one of his novels. It was Garland's pleasure to introduce this new acquaintance to the American public, proclaiming in the *Conservative Review* that "the *Dreamers of the Ghetto* and the Ghetto's young dreamer, the author and his latest book, appeared together on our shores." [44] Kipling was back in America and Garland made occasion to renew the acquaintance begun years before at the dinner with Riley. Having reported to the Howells and the Hernes on his Alaskan experiences (he was also giving a professional lecture on "The Joys of the Trail") Garland turned again to the round of editorial offices. [45]

Publication of the *Grant* in book form seems to have healed the breach between Garland and *McClure's*, for the magazine

---

[42] Journal, Garland Papers.
[43] *A Daughter of the Middle Border*, Chapter VI.
[44] "I. Zangwill," *Conservative Review*, II (November, 1889), 404–12.
[45] *A Daughter of the Middle Border*, pp. 80–81.

not only published an article and several poems from the Alaskan journal but also began to print a few stories of Garland's red men. [46] As a reader for *McClure's* Garland discovered a manuscript which he recommended for serial publication called "The Gentleman from Indiana." The author was unknown and all agreed that "Booth Tarkington" was too unreal to be other than a pseudonym. Tarkington arrived in person shortly to dispel this illusion and to express his appreciation of Garland's encouragement. [47]

The situation with Richard Watson Gilder remained as Garland had earlier described it—"not enthusiastic." After a four-year lapse of time and after considerable prodding the *Century* had at last published "A Good Fellow's Wife." The correspondence between the author and his publisher in this connection is typical of the arm's-length attitude which pervaded Garland's early dealings with the *Century*. Wrote Garland:

I've forgotten just the length of "A Good Fellow's Wife" but it seemed to me to be worth a little more than the check—measured by your rates to me on the others—may be mistaken, however—I'm full of plans for new work and I'm glad to think you'll get started on printing my stories. When can I look for another appearance? [48]

"Yes," Gilder crabbedly noted his response, " but long stories are not so desirable as short." [49]

Garland's "plans for new work" were a part of his general whistling in the dark at this moment. By force of habit he had begun another novel as soon as he was back in Chicago, but he admitted that his pen "lacked direction." The New Year found him in a mood of bleak despair. The Players was practically deserted in the post-holiday doldrums as Garland sat brooding in the lounge. Suddenly the clouds rifted as George Brett, of Macmillan and Company, approached and drew up a chair. He proposed that his firm pick up three of the old Stone & Kimball titles

[46] See Note 36 *supra;* "General Custer's Last Fight as Seen by Two Moon," *McClure's,* XI (September, 1898), 443–48; "Rising Wolf, Ghost Dancer," XII (January, 1899), 241–48.

[47] *Roadside Meetings,* pp. 403–404.

[48] Garland to Gilder, undated, New York Public Library.

[49] Gilder, as was his custom, penciled notations on the original letter suggesting the substance of the answer to be sent.

with an advance of five hundred dollars against future sales, and advance three times that amount against two new books, one to be based on Garland's Klondike adventures and the other to be the long-projected reminiscent volume of boyhood experiences. Garland accepted eagerly, and chortled as he recorded the transaction in his journal: "I begin to think that I may soon be able to pay out a dollar for a dinner without a fearful pang. That West Salem farm begins to loom up as a possibility, and also a trip to London." [50]

Hastily renting a room Garland set to work on revising his books for Macmillan. *Rose of Dutcher's Coolly* was the only volume upon which he expended any great effort. His changes were not structural, but stylistic only. Going over it carefully, he tightened an occasional phrase, blue-pencilled an occasional word, being careful to substitute for the offensive "glare of a sex-maniac," *"an insolent glare,"* [51] and making a few other changes in the interests of euphemism. *Rose* would remain a "shocker," however, for a good many more years.

To *Main-Travelled Roads,* now with its third publisher, were added three stories, one lifted from *Prairie Folks* and the others from recent publications. [52] The volume met Macmillan's requirements for thirty-five pages of new matter and could be advertised as including "additional stories." *Prairie Folks* lost two stories, one dropped to its companion volume and one into oblivion. To fill the gap Garland searched out additional materials, stories from odd corners like the Bacheller papers and poems lifted from *Prairie Songs.* [53] The device of interspersing fiction with verse was one that Garland had used before in individual pieces. Now for a season he became addicted to the practice in all his volumes. When he came to write *The Trail of the Gold-*

[50] Journal, January 3, 1899, Garland Papers; *A Daughter of the Middle Border,* p. 79.

[51] *Rose of Dutcher's Coolly* (1899), p. 77.

[52] The additional stories were "Uncle Ethan Ripley" ("Uncle Ripley's Speculation" from *Prairie Folks*), "The Creamery Man" from the December, 1897, *Outlook,* and "A Day's Pleasure" ("Sam Markham's Wife" from the *Ladies' Home Journal* of July, 1898).

[53] Stories omitted were "Uncle Ethan's Speculation," and "A Saturday Night on the Farm." Added were "A Day of Grace," "Black Ephram," "The Wapseypinnicon Tiger," and "Aidgewise Feelin's." The first, third and fourth were from the Bacheller Syndicate.

seekers he included more than forty verses, most of them composed on the route, but a few reprints. [54] In his *Boy Life on the Prairie* he reprinted more than thirty items from *Prairie Songs*. [55] Thus he achieved what was in effect a new edition, although scattered through three volumes, of half the material of *Prairie Songs*. Garland was ingenious in keeping his work in print, his capital investment as an author out at interest.

Boy Life on the Prairie involved considerable new work. "This book," Garland explained in his preface, "is the outgrowth of a series of articles begun as far back as 1887. It was my intention, at the time, to delineate the work and plans of a boy on a prairie farm from season to season, beginning with seeding and ending with threshing, and I wrote some six or eight chapters in conformity with this plan. It occurred to me then that twenty-seven was too young to write reminiscences, and I put the book aside until such time as it might be seemly for me to say, 'I remember.' " [56]

The 1899 book was based indeed upon a reworking of Garland's first published sketches in the *American Magazine*—and of other materials, such as the fight of Steve Nagle originally described in "At the Brewery." While in the earlier *American* articles Garland had employed an impersonal essay treatment, now he threaded his episodes of frontier life into a loose history of the youngster Lincoln Stewart, his family and friends. The original scheme had covered the seasons of but one calendar year. In the longer semi-fictional organization the period covered is some twenty years of Lincoln's life, beginning with his arrival by prairie schooner to the Rock River country at the age of six and continuing through his departure in young manhood from the already vanishing frontier.

Although Lincoln Stewart was but a renaming of the "Grant McLeod," concerning whom Garland had dictated an autobiographical outline before leaving for the Klondike, the author disclaimed for *Boy Life on the Prairie* any autobiographical char-

[54] Oddly enough, one of the poems which was not original to this volume was the tribute to a horse entitled "Ladrone." It had previously appeared in *Prairie Songs,* and is mentioned in an undated letter to Gilder during negotiations over *Old Pap's Flaxen* [1890].

[55] For the publication history of individual poems, see Bibliography.

[56] *Boy Life on the Prairie* (1899), Preface.

acter, contending, "I have aimed to depict boy life, not boys." The result was a pleasantly vivid juvenile, too leisurely ever to be read by boys but attractive to those adults who had once known a rural boyhood.

With the readying of these volumes for Macmillan, Garland took stock of his situation. The connection with his new publishers had come most opportunely, for in this year William Henry Appleton, the last survivor of the sons of D. Appleton, the founder of the publishing firm, had died, and his company shortly became involved in financial difficulties which resulted in a "friendly bankruptcy." [57] Garland could well complain that he was a Jonah to any concern which undertook to publish his works. The reorganization of D. Appleton & Company, however, represented no such debacle as the downfall of Stone & Kimball, and Garland continued to receive a modest trickle of royalties from his five titles with that firm—the four of the uniform series of 1897 and the older *A Little Norsk*. As for the Doubleday & Mc-Clure books, while *Grant* had proved a disappointment, the slender romance *The Spirit of Sweetwater* had surprised both author and publisher by its sales. Garland's first royalty check covering only a part of the year 1898 was for over four hundred dollars, more than all of his Stone & Kimball books had netted him. [58] From the Stone & Kimball failure Garland had resurrected two of his volumes—not to mention the legerdemain that revived a part of *Prairie Songs*—and could look with satisfaction upon his list of fourteen volumes, eleven of them in recent editions and with substantial publishing houses. In the spring of 1899 Garland could well afford to dream of acquiring a new home or of a trip to London.

[57] S. C. Chew, *op. cit.*, pp. 51 ff.
[58] Journal, January 3, 1899; miscellaneous financial statements, Garland Papers.

❦ 9 ❦

Her Mountain Lover

ON FEBRUARY 11, 1899, Garland atttended in New York a meeting of the newly organized National Institute of Arts and Letters, an offshoot of the American Society of Science, devoted to the allied arts. Howells was the chief figure present. Charles Dudley Warner presided, and among others of Garland's friends within the group were Brander Matthews, Owen Wister, and the playwright Augustus Thomas. "Only a few men were out," Garland reported, "and those few were chilled by a cold room but nevertheless, this meeting is likely to have far-reaching consequences." [1]

Meanwhile in Chicago the members of the Art Institute were engaged in activities in which Garland took an even more acute interest. Their plan was to establish a summer art colony on Rock River, at Oregon, Illinois, some hundred miles west of Chicago. Garland was appointed one of the trustees of the new establishment, "The Eagle's Nest," and took up his duties with

---

[1] *A Daughter of the Middle Border* (1921), pp. 81–82.

enthusiasm, well aware that Zulime Taft was one of the moving spirits of the enterprise. But at this juncture Garland's romance suffered an abrupt check. Lorado Taft bluntly informed his friend that his sister Zulime "was definitely committed to another man."

Garland, according to his own account, without giving Miss Taft an opportunity to speak for herself, accepted this second-hand rejection with unloverlike equanimity, and set his face toward England. A visit to the London office of Macmillan provided the pretext for the journey; the recent royalty advances provided the wherewithal; but Garland's inner motivation for this excursion remains as obscure as that of his Klondike adventure. Apparently it was but a part of the general restlessness and lack of direction which pervaded his actions at the turn of the century. Despite a previous promise to his mother to remain close to West Salem, Garland, with the gift of a mechanical piano to assuage his guilt, set sail for England in April.

It was a rough crossing, and Garland proved himself no sailor. Nor, it may be suspected, did England quite meet the expectations of the gregarious Garland. To be sure, Zangwill was most hospitable, his study "the only warm place in London." There was a luncheon with Sir James Barrie, a weekend visit to Bernard Shaw, which produced a meeting with the neighboring Conan Doyle. There were calls upon Bret Harte and Thomas Hardy. And to climax the British interlude there was a dinner of the Authors' Society to which Zangwill procured Garland an invitation. Not too reluctantly, though protesting vigorously, the Middle Westerner had himself measured for a dress suit for the occasion. With a seat at the speakers' table between the editor of the London *Chronicle* and Henry M. Stanley, Garland, for one night at least, was in full glory. He recorded conscientiously every tidbit of his conversations with the great, material which would appear and reappear in his reminiscent volumes. Of such recollections are made up the official history of this London visit. [2]

[2] *Ibid.*, pp. 81–94; *Roadside Meetings* (1930), *passim*. It has been pointed out by B. R. McElderry, Jr. ("Hamlin Garland and Henry James," *American Literature,* XXIII [January, 1952], 433–46) that the incidents concerning Henry James which Garland includes in *Roadside Meetings* as having taken place in 1899 in reality pertained to his 1906 visit to England as recorded in his diary of that period. John R. Dove, ignoring this discrepancy, in "The

But they are recollections softened by the years, distilled through the screen of self-justification, reminiscences artfully interwoven to stress the meetings with celebrities and to suppress his private disappointments. A more accurate index to Garland's personal reactions to England in 1899 may be found in the "humorous extravaganza" which he composed from day-by-day events, *Her Mountain Lover*. The Colorado "hustler" whom Garland chose as spokesman in his volume finds little to commend in the mother country. The tight, little island suffers severely by contrast to the grandeur of the "High Country," its inhabitants exhibit only decadence and lack of initiative. Garland's continued fondness for his quite impossible yarn of a mountain miner in search of British capital leads one to suspect that the "hustler" was the mouthpiece for certain private impressions of the author which international amity and the pose of cosmopolitan author suppressed elsewhere.

A week in Paris gave Garland opportunity for a literary contact which redounded greatly to his reputation. Calling upon a friend of one of his Chicago acquaintances, Mme. Blanc, a distinguished critic, he made a profound impression, which resulted in a forty-page article in the *Revue des Deux Mondes* celebrating his works. The Frenchwoman was delighted with this "primitive man of the savage West," whose "powerful personality" made her tiny house bulge at the seams, who walked among the Gallic peasants "like Gulliver in Lilliput," who seemed "to say farewell to a Europe which doubtless affected him like an antique shop." Charmed by her visitor Mme. Blanc sat down to interpret to the Gallic mind the complexities of American life as reflected by this "radical" poet and novelist. She struggled with the Grange Meeting of *A Spoil of Office*, finally describing it as "a picnic of reforming farmers," explained the mortgage of "Under the Lion's Paw" as "the curse of all farmers in America," was baffled by that monster Rose Dutcher, but waxed lyrical over Garland's poetry, his sincerity, his reforming zeal. Garland in his turn made a short article out of his impressions of Paris when

---

Significance of Garland's First Visit to England" (University of Texas *Studies in English*, XXXII [1953], 96–109) notes the contrast between Garland's fictional and nonfictional accounts of this interlude but elicits psychological significance which seems exaggerated.

he had returned to America to pick up the threads of his normal existence. [3]

Back in West Salem, with royalty money still unspent, he began a remodeling program at the Homestead, designed to incorporate a bathroom in the floor plan. At his mother's urging and with the encouragement of his Chicago friends he now returned to the attack upon the affections of Miss Zulime Taft, who apparently was no further "committed" than at the time of his departure. At the "Eagle's Nest" the artists laid side bets as to the outcome of the affair as Garland moved in, lock, stock, and barrel of manuscripts, to the neighboring Heckman home to conduct his siege.

Garland remained sublimely unconscious of the interest he was arousing in the colony, being under the illusion that he was "proceeding with extraordinary caution, wearing the bland expression of a Cheyenne chieftain. I could not imagine anyone discovering in my action anything more than a frank liking, a natural friendship between the sister of my artist comrade and myself." Garland's letters to his brother, however, openly reveal the progress of his courtship. Soon he was writing to "Junior":

We are planning our campaign. Zuliema [sic] and I are very busy. She is a great girl. I have discovered that she plays the piano very well and reads music with care. She is a superb housekeeper and *likes* it. She paints landscapes with a modern touch and may be able to illustrate my work. [4]

As the prospects of Zulime's consenting continued favorable, Garland expanded his remodelling plans to include not only a new bathroom and dining room but an entire new story to the Homestead. And at last on his thirty-ninth birthday he brought himself to have "a long talk" with Zulime. [5] The content of that talk may be well imagined. Garland had put his ideas of matrimony on record in the form of Mason's proposal to Rose of Dutcher's Coolly. The substance of his own proposal four years

[3] Th. Bentzon, "Un Radical de la Prairie," *Revue des Deux Mondes,* CLVII (1900), 139–80; "Impressions of Paris in Times of Turmoil," *Outlook,* LXII (December 16, 1899), 968–73.

[4] Garland to Franklin Garland, undated, courtesy of Constance Garland Doyle.

[5] *A Daughter of the Middle Border,* Chapter VIII.

later was likely to have been couched in similar terms. In his classic address to the "new woman" Garland had written:

Dear Miss Dutcher:

I must begin by asking pardon for not writing before, but as a matter of fact I have not found this letter easy to compose. It represents a turning point in my life, and contains an important decision, and I have never been less sure of my judgment than now.

This letter may be considered an offer of marriage. It is well to say that now, and then all the things which come after, will be given their proper weight. Let me state the debit side of the account first, and if you feel that it is too heavy you can put the letter down and write me a very short answer, and the matter will be ended.

First, I say to you: whoso weds me weds sorrow. I do not promise to make you happy, though I hope my influence will not be always untoward. I cannot promise any of the things husbands are supposed to bring. I cannot promise a home. My own living is precarious, dependent upon my daily grind of newspaper work. For though I hope to achieve a success with my novel, great successes with novels do not mean much money. I do not feel either that I shall ever be free from money cares; luxury and I are to continue strangers.

I cannot promise to conform to your ways, nor to bend to your wishes, though I will try to do so. I cannot promise to assume cordial relations with your relatives, nor accept your friendships as binding upon me.

I cannot promise to be faithful to you until death, but I shall be faithful so long as I fill the relation of husband to you. I shall not lead a double life, or conceal from you any change in my regard toward you. If at any time I find a woman whom I feel I should live with, rather than with you, I shall tell you of her with perfect frankness. I *think* I shall find you all-sufficient, but I do not know. Men and women change, grow weary of things, of bonds, of duties. It may be that I shall become and continue the most devoted of husbands, but I cannot promise it. Long years of association develop intolerable traits in men and women very often.

On the other hand, let me say I exact nothing from you. I do not require you to cook for me, nor keep house for me. You are mistress of yourself; to come and go as you please, without question and without accounting to me. You are at liberty to cease your association with me at any time, and consider yourself perfectly free to leave me whenever any other man comes with power to make you happier than I.

I want you as comrade and lover, not as subject or servant, or un-

Garland as a Child

Isabelle McClintock Garland

Richard Garland

Garland's Parents

Grandmother McClintock

Hugh McClintock, Wife, and Daughter

Grandfather McClintock

Richard Garland at Eighty Years of Age

Ordway Dakota
the house in which "Main
Traveled Roads" was began. 1847

Early Homes of Garland

Garland Homestead, West Salem Wis. 1893

Franklin and Hamlin Garland

Jessie Garland (Hamlin's Sister), 1889

Isabelle Garland, 1865

Garland, 1881   *Garland, 1883*

At the End of Telegraph Trail, 1898

Henry B. Fuller

Zulime Taft Garland

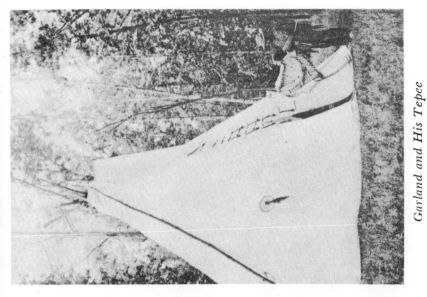

Garland and His Tepee

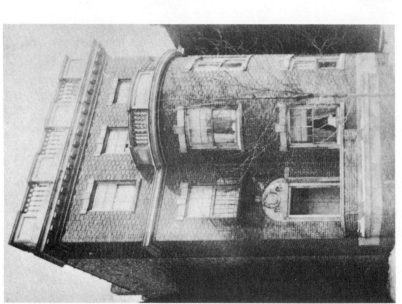

Garland's Chicago Home

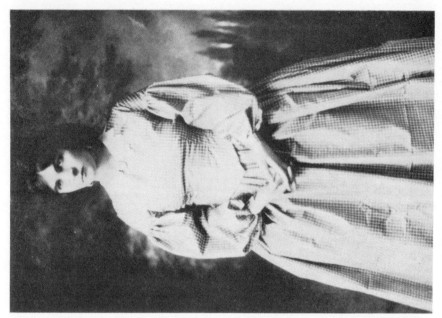

Isabel Garland in Stage Costume

Constance Garland at Eighteen

Line Drawings by Constance Garland for
Back-Trailers from the Middle Border

Garland as Lecturer

Garland at the Century of Progress

Garland and Grandchildren

willing wife. I do not claim any rights over you at all. You can bear me children or not, just as you please. You are a human soul like my-self, and I shall expect you to be as free and as sovereign as I, to fol-low any profession or to do any work which pleases you. It is but just to say that I have never been a man of loose habits. No woman has any claim upon me for deed or word. I have thought at various times that I could marry this woman or that woman, but I have never be-fore made a proposition of marriage to any woman.

I have written you in good, set terms what you may expect of me. I am not a demonstrative man by nature, and my training from child-hood has made me saving of words of endearment. My love for you must be taken largely for granted after it is once stated, for I regard the word "love" as a jewel not to be carelessly tossed from hand to hand.

Doubtless I shall make a dull companion—that I cannot judge for myself.

. . . .

I have written frankly because I believed it would prejudice you in my favor. Had I believed otherwise, doubtless I should have written in terms of flattery and deceit, for of such is man when seeking woman in marriage.

If you return the affirmative answer I shall be very happy to come up and spend the rest of my vacation at your father's home—provided it is agreeable to you. [6]

To this austere declaration Garland's heroine Rose tele-graphed a succinct reply: "Come up tomorrow if you can please." [7] The real-life heroine of Garland's romance was less precipitate, but after taking the matter under advisement for a week, she wrote him from the Eagle's Nest, "I am still undecided, but you may come." Within another week she had consented, and the wedding date was set for November twenty-third.

Garland reported immediately to "Junior":

Zuliema [sic] has yielded to my plans and on mother's account will come into our family home Thanksgiving week. . . . Of course all our plans are contingent on mother's health. . . . [Zulime] is yielding a great deal but does it most graciously. I make no demands. I merely stated the case and she concedes because she knows mother's life is

---

[6] *Rose of Dutcher's Coolly* (1895), pp. 378–81.
[7] *Ibid.*, p. 384.

insecure. Mother was radiant when I told her. It gives her something new to brood over.[8]

The decision once made, Garland became restive, impatient with feminine preparations. Packing his bag he went West, then on an impulse doubled back on his tracks early in November to intercept his bride-elect in St. Joseph, Missouri, as she was en route to her parents' home in Hanover, Kansas. The time of cautious courtship was over. Garland had become the importunate lover. Despite wedding announcements already with the printer he urged Zulime to advance the nuptial date by a week so that they might include in their wedding itinerary a trip to the mountains.

Fortunately the family into which he was marrying were no sticklers for convention. Don Carlos Taft, his future father-in-law, who had metamorphosed from a natural science professor into a country banker, was greatly relieved to find that his daughter's choice was a man of his own agnostic persuasion. The difference between one date and another was of no consequence to him. What Don Carlos had been dreading was the prospect of participating in a religious ceremony. He was delighted when Garland, always the dogmatist in his beliefs, or lack of them, insisted on a civil ceremony performed by the highest authority available, in this case the district judge. With Don Carlos siding with him to override any feminine hesitations over furbelows or announcements, Garland had his "judicial wedding" on November eighteenth, and the bridal pair were off for a whirlwind tour of Garland's beloved mountains. To the groom the trail was a familiar one: Colorado Springs, the Uncompahgre Range, across the Continental Divide at Silverton. But the splendors of the scenery were a new revelation to the bride, as also must have been the breakneck pace of travel maintained by the man she had married. The honeymoon was fitting prelude to a married life of which Zulime complained that for the first ten years her husband was always packing or unpacking a bag, just arriving from one place in time to leave for another.

Back in Chicago the Garlands had scant time for welcomes

[8] Garland to Franklin Garland, postmarked Chicago, October 24, 1899, courtesy of Constance Garland Doyle.

from their studio friends. They must be off to West Salem to spend Thanksgiving at the Homestead. Zulime, with the tact and social grace which had first attracted Hamlin, fitted admirably into this somewhat difficult household, completely captivating the old folks, and giving Hamlin's mother all the satisfaction she had hoped for in "the new daughter." The visit was not unduly prolonged, for by Christmas the Garlands were in Washington, and by New Year's Day in New York City, where they settled in an apartment in a Fifteenth Street Hotel, ready for a literary winter. [9]

Henry Fuller left an oblique comment on Garland's marriage in "The Downfall of Abner Joyce":

Yes, Abner had brought down, one after another, all the pillars of the temple. But he had dealt out his own fate along with the fate of the rest: crushed, yet complacent, he lay among the ruins. The glamour of success and of association with the successful was dazzling him. The pomp and luxury of plutocracy inwrapped him, and he had a sudden sweet shuddering vision of himself dining with others of the wealthy just because they were wealthy, and prominent, and successful. Yes, Abner had made his compromise with the world. He had conformed. He had reached an understanding with the children of Mammon. He—a great, original genius—had become just like other people. His downfall was complete. [10]

There are those critics of Garland who would consider that Fuller was gifted with foresight: that once Garland became a Benedict his "great, original genius" was lost; he became a writer of pot-boiling romances. To adopt this interpretation is to ignore at once the complexity of the change in Garland's work and the value, as well, of much of his later writing. True, after the first creative outburst of the nineties he turned aside from his "veritistic" pictures of farm life to an entirely different subject matter, and in many regards to an entirely different manner. But to link this shift with his entrance into matrimony is to rely too completely upon a correlation with publication dates, and with *book*-publication dates, at that. It is to ignore the evidence of the writer's notebooks, where outlines for specific stories appear an-

[9] *A Daughter of the Middle Border,* Chapters IX and X.
[10] Henry Fuller, *Under the Skylights* (New York, 1901), p. 139.

tedating by many years their actual composition. It is to ignore the evidence of Garland's correspondence, wherein stories are offered and reoffered to various publishers, sometimes for decades, before they find their way into print. It is to ignore a certain psychological continuity, and indeed an ethical continuity, which becomes apparent in his later development. And it is to ignore the fact that after severe illness and a world at war had altered his outlook he again returned to his original subject matter, albeit with a viewpoint which the alterations in economic trends and personal psychology of a quarter century had radically modified. Garland's marriage, no doubt, accelerated certain changes in his writing. It cannot be considered a unique cause of any such change.

Nonetheless, it is true that at the close of the century he began to deal with publishers in a new attitude of confidence. With the solid achievement of his five Macmillan books behind him, he could dicker for terms, play one house off against another, in a fashion which was impossible in the days of Stone & Kimball. The sale of *The Eagle's Heart,* the novel of a runaway boy turned Western bad man, which he had written in the intervals between running away himself, to the Klondike and to London, is a case in point.

The tone in which on November 15 he addressed Gilder (who was obviously considering publishing this novel) is an interesting change from his earlier obsequiousness. "I have decided," wrote Garland lordly, "to let Mr. Appleton bring out my little story. I do this because he does it at once and because he is to give me place of honor in his summer series of American novels. I'm getting *old* and I must make hay while the sun shines. . . . I hope that your people will see that my extreme age and poverty make it necessary for me to get things moving." [11]

With a tentative sale of serial rights on his novel to the *Saturday Evening Post* Garland was approached by S. S. McClure with an offer of $2,500 on all serial rights to the story, "you to sell such rights to the *Evening Post* for $2,000, we to recoup ourselves by having other serial rights than the *Post*, their rights expiring with the completion of the story in that paper. We will sell, if possible,

[11] Garland to R. W. Gilder, November 15 [1899], New York Public Library.

'The Rocky Mountain Hustler'." . . . And McClure added another offer which he felt might entice Garland back into the McClure fold:

> We will pay you $50. a thousand words for such of the Indian stories as we can use up to 20,000 words, and will get you as much as possible from other sources. If, on account of your previous arrangement, "The Eagle's Heart" must go to Appleton's, I would be willing to take another novel in its stead, but of course you would not expect me to render myself responsible for the serial rights of the next novel.
> We are to pay you a royalty of 20% on any of your books that we publish, including "The Heart of the Indian," "The Rocky Mountain Hustler," and "The Eagle's Heart," if about the same length. [12]

Garland and his wife had swung that autumn through Philadelphia to cinch the sale of *The Eagle's Heart* with George Lorimer of the *Post*. It began to appear serially the following June, and with that and its book publication by Appleton's Garland was content. To McClure he turned only a single Indian story, "The People of the Buffalo."[13] While in Philadelphia he saw Edward Bok in an effort to sell to the flourishing *Ladies' Home Journal* the manuscript of his British sojourn, variously entitled "Jim Matteson of Wagon Wheel Gap," "The Rocky Mountain Hustler," and "The Plainsman Abroad." But Bok was uninterested. [14]

The phenomenal rise of the *Ladies' Home Journal* was typical of the new journalism. In 1883 three pages of women's materials had been thrown into the Philadelphia-published *Tribune and Farmer* to fill out the dummy of that trade magazine. Encouraged by the response of readers, the three pages grew to eight, published separately as the *Ladies' Journal*. Readers added the word *Home* from illustrative material of the masthead, and boosted circulation in the first six months to 25,000 copies; doubled that by the end of the first year; and by geometric progression made the *Journal* one of the most remunerative markets in the United States, under the editorship of Scribner-trained

[12] S. S. McClure to Garland, January 30, 1900, Garland Papers.
[13] "The Eagle's Heart," *Saturday Evening Post*, CLXXII and CLXXIII (June 16–September 8, 1900); D. Appleton & Company, 1900; "The People of the Buffalo," *McClure's* XVI (December, 1900), 153–59.
[14] *Companions on the Trail* (1931), pp. 12–13.

Edward Bok. Howells' reminiscences of "My Literary Passions" had shared the opening pages of the December, 1893, issue with Garland's "A Pioneer Christmas," and by 1900 what had begun as a farm-journal supplement was a literary market challenging the old citadels of respectability for the work of established artists. [15]

Despite his friendly relations with Bok, Garland was unable to interest him in "Jim Matteson." With this refusal he turned again to Gilder and the *Century*, suggesting on April 12, 1900, that Gilder might like to consider his travel book in its unfinished state with the idea of using one or two chapters serially. For some time he was actively corresponding with Gilder on the matter, and by June 19 was suggesting that Gilder make him an offer on serial rights first, and settle the matter of book publication later. Garland at this point insisted that he had had a number of offers for book publication at twenty per cent royalty, with a $1,000 advance. As to the hesitations of the *Century* he reassured Gilder: "The points that trouble you would get rubbed off in the revises I intend to give it. I don't want to hurry you but I was afraid you were rejecting me and my time is short in which to settle several important matters."

Faced with an ultimatum from Garland that if Gilder did not want the story he send it to F. A. Duneka of Harper & Brothers, Gilder evidently tabled his objections, for by August 29 Garland confirmed their agreement: "You can go ahead on the announcement and God be on our side." In November the story began to appear serially as "Jim Matteson of Wagon Wheel Gap." But neither author nor publisher was satisfied with the title. At last after interminable correspondence on the subject Garland wrote wearily:

I haven't another suggestion. I've thought and thought till my brain is tired. Her Mountain Lover, a Transatlantic Comedy, or something like that ought to explain the situation. I will let you decide the matter then, for it is quite beyond me now. I know when a title suits me. I don't know a thing about pleasing the public with a title or anything else. [16]

[15] Edward W. Bok, "The Story of the Journal," *Ladies' Home Journal,* X (November, 1893), 13–14.

[16] Garland to R. W. Gilder, April 12 [1900], May 3 [1900], June 19, 1900,

The story became *Her Mountain Lover* as a Century book.

Meanwhile the Garlands had been called home from New York by the death of Susan Bailey. Along with normal sorrow at his aunt's death Garland felt also some measure of relief as a result of the easing of the financial pressures under which he had labored. His father as inheritor of a small legacy from Mrs. Bailey was now able to pay part of the expenses of maintaining the Homestead. And the married Garlands settled into somewhat the same pattern of commuting which Hamlin had established in his bachelor days. March and April of 1900 they spent in his old rooms in Chicago. With the coming of May and spring weather they reappeared at the Homestead. But despite visits from Lorado Taft and Edward MacDowell the country routine soon palled on Garland. He was at work upon stories laid in the Indian country and soon felt the need to get closer to his materials.

Most of the summer was spent at Fort Reno, Oklahoma, and the young Garlands had scarcely returned to West Salem in July when they set off again for Montana, Hamlin intent on research upon the life of Sitting Bull. Later Garland *père* joined the young couple for a ten-day camping trip through Yellowstone Park. Then Hamlin and his wife pushed on to Tacoma and Seattle to camp in the country around Lake MacDonald while Hamlin visited more Indian reservations.

It was a typical Garland summer, but a strenuous one for the young bride, and she was relieved when they returned at last to the now familiar Homestead. But Hamlin was off again immediately, this time to accompany his father to a reunion of the Grand Army of the Republic in Chicago. [17] After this he settled for a while to his desk in West Salem. Again he deluged Gilder with letters, with "Colorado stories," and a 27,000-word novelette, hoping for "another pleasant arrangement." [18] This latter may have been an abbreviated version of *The Captain of the Gray-Horse Troop*, which was beginning to shape itself beneath his pen. But Garland was having the usual difficulties with naming his production. Fuller, consulted about possible titles, advised:

June 21 [1900], August 29 [1900], New York Public Library; October [?], 1900, Century Collection, New York Public Library.
[17] *A Daughter of the Middle Border*, Chapters X–XIII.
[18] Garland to R. W. Gilder, September 23 [1900], New York Public Library.

" 'Lieu. Curtis of the Tetong Troop' is possible—'On Special Duty,' 'On Civilian Duty' preferred. Drop the others!" [19]

Fuller continued a faithful friend and astute critic, with no slightest break in relations following upon the publication of "The Downfall of Abner Joyce." Already an admirer of Zulime Taft he visited the young Garlands in West Salem, amusing his fellow author by his reactions to the country fair, which was all that offered by way of entertainment:

Fuller, who timed his visit to be with us during the exhibition, professed a keen interest in every department of it. His attitude was comically that of a serious-minded European tourist. He not only purchased a catalogue, he treated it precisely as if it were the hand-book of the Autumn Salon in Paris. Carrying it in his hand, he spent busy hours minutely studying "Spatter Work," and carefully inspected decorated bed-spreads. He tasted the prize bread, sampled the honey, and twirled the contesting apples. He was alert, and (apparently) as vitally concerned as any of the "judges," but I knowing his highly-critical mind, could only smile at his reports. [20]

Fuller was fortunate in maintaining his close relations with Hamlin Garland. His publication at his own expense in 1899 of "The New Flag," a diatribe against the Philippine campaign, had alienated him from a community of which he had never really been a part, had made him more than ever the recluse, the "passionate spectator" of human affairs. The affection of the forthright, humorless Garland must have been a help to Fuller in combatting his natural tendency for withdrawal from the world, while to Garland this oddly charming and urbane introvert remained an anchor and a stay. Garland freely admitted Fuller's literary judgment to be "second only to Howells'," and rarely submitted a manuscript without Fuller's critical appraisal having been passed. Yet as the years went on the contrast between the two men was accentuated rather than diminished.

In November the Garlands were again in New York, intending to pass the winter in the city. The stimulus of a literary center was one of Garland's basic needs. In addition to the old friends of other New York winters there were new acquaintances. At

[19] Henry B. Fuller to Garland, September 10, 1900, Garland Papers.
[20] *A Daughter of the Middle Border*, p. 208.

the Doubleday & Page offices Garland had met a young author named Frank Norris, whom both he and Zulime admired. Edwin Markham on the strength of the success of "The Man with the Hoe" had resigned the principalship of his school in Oakland and come East to make his living by his pen, a temerity which Garland, an old hand at the game, viewed askance.

Since Garland was actively engaged in writing upon Indian subjects he was much in the company of men who had a common interest, with Ernest Thompson Seton, and with Dr. Mitchell Prudden, head of the bacteriological department of Columbia University, whom he had first met in Walpi in 1895. And there were the colleagues of the National Institute of Arts and Letters, which held its first public meeting that autumn, with Howells presiding. [21]

No sooner were the winter activities in full swing than the Garlands were again recalled to West Salem by a death message. This time the victim was Mrs. Garland. The sorrowing son did not reach her in time for a last farewell, but on the day following her funeral he poured out his grief in a heartfelt memorial to "The Wife of a Pioneer":

> To me she was never young, for I am her son, and as I first remember her, she was a large, handsome, smiling woman—deft and powerful of movement, sweet and cheery of smile and voice. She played the violin then, and I recall how she used to lull me to sleep at night with simple tunes like "Money Musk" and "Dan Tucker." [22]

Giving credit to his mother for the drive in him toward education and culture Garland recalled her splendid singing voice, encompassing even in illness and old age "three octaves and one note." "I have always believed that a great singer was lost to the world in this pioneer's wife." [23]

As Hamlin sat in his West Salem study brooding over the history of the woman who had given him birth—"her toilsome, monotonous days rushed through my mind with a roar, like a file of gray birds in the night"—he pondered the whole enigma of

[21] *Companions on the Trail,* pp. 10–11, 18–19.
[22] "The Wife of a Pioneer," *Ladies' Home Journal,* XX (September, 1903), 8, 42.
[23] *A Daughter of the Middle Border,* pp. 212–19.

human endeavor. His musings recalled a promise he had made to Gilder the previous year, to write "a sort of epic of that splendid life now passing away. I can do it and shall do it if I never do another thing." [24] But with his immediate grief ameliorated by the catharsis of his written tribute, the epic theme appeared too demanding and was set aside for the healthy-minded, if more prosaic task, of revising *Her Mountain Lover*.

[24] Garland to R. W. Gilder, May 1, 1899, New York Public Library.

✣ 10 ✣

"Manly Poetry and a High Ideal"

THE COMPLETION of the tribute to his mother, Garland recalled, "eased my heart of its bitter self-accusation, and a little later I returned to my accustomed routine, realizing that in my wife now lay my present incentive and my future support. . . . To remain longer in the old home was painful, for to me everything suggested the one for whom it had been established. The piano I had bought for her, the chair in which she had loved to sit, her spectacles on the stand—all these mute witnesses of her absence benumbed me as I walked about her room." [1]

In this mood Garland returned to Chicago with Zulime, and at last settled down to the writing of his Indian novel. To Gilder in January of 1901 he wrote:

I am started upon a new novel which I call "On Special Duty." It deals with the affairs of an Indian Agency, with cowmen, Indians, artists, soldiers and cowboys as actors. I have laid out a big canvass and hope to do the right kind of thing.

[1] *A Daughter of the Middle Border* (1921), p. 220.

Would you like to read the first 10,000 words and make me an offer to begin publishing, say next October. Under favorable conditions book rights might go to the Century Co. This is not an offer of the story but the preliminary barter [?]. I shall sell in the best market. I shall "block the thing out" during the spring months and go into the wild country for the summer to freshen my studies. [2]

"On Special Duty," which became *The Captain of the Gray-Horse Troop*, reflects the life of the reservations as Garland had seen it during his intermittent visits to the Indian country since 1897, and in particular the experiences of the past summer when he and his wife were guests of Major George Stouch, the Indian agent on the Cheyenne reservation at Darlington, Oklahoma. John Homer Seger, the founder of the Indian school and town at Colony, Oklahoma, was likewise a valuable source of interpretation and information for the book.

In Garland's novel Captain Curtis, a soldier of the regular army, is detached on special assignment to replace a corrupt Indian agent. Curtis, a bit of a scholar, and completely sympathetic to the problems of the red men, attributes his assignment to the influence of "two literary chaps who camped with us on our trial march two years ago." [3] He arrives at his new post with his sister and fellow worker Jennie to find a tense situation, the cattlemen determined to drive the Indians from their grazing lands, and the agent working hand in glove with these evil interests. Also to complicate the situation there are present at the agency a group of scholars and artists, one of whom, Elsie Brisbane, is not only the niece of the corrupt agent but the daughter of a powerful politician and ex-senator.

Curtis falls in love with Elsie and must convert her from her conception of the Indian as a naked savage into an appreciation of the red man as an individual of dignity and culture. Thus Garland develops a vehicle for an exposition on Indian rights. In this novel, as in the earlier *The Eagle's Heart*, the cattlemen are definitely cast in the role of villains, Curtis expounding on the white settlers: "The best of them . . . are foolhardy pioneers who have exiled their wives and children for no good reason. The

[2] Garland to R. W. Gilder [January, 1901], Century Collection, New York Public Library.
[3] *The Captain of the Gray-Horse Troop* (1904), p. 7.

others are cattlemen who followed the cavalry in order to fatten their stock under the protection of our guidon." [4]

The wrath which in his earlier stories had been directed against the land speculator rather than the "foolhardy pioneer," against the desolation of frontier life and Fate itself, now turns against the moneyed interests represented by the encroaching cattlemen. This time the victim is not the pioneer woman but the native redskin.

As Garland maneuvers his story through a series of violent scenes culminating in the delivery of an Indian outlaw, killer of a sheepherder, into the hands of justice by Captain Curtis, and the final climax of a mob riot outside the prison, there are sympathetic descriptions of Indian councils and customs. The outlaw, killed at last by the angry mob, has attained in the end the dignity of a tragic hero, while Senator Brisbane, stricken by an attack in the middle of a rabble-rousing oration, is a pitiable figure of a crumbling tyrant. In a day when Charles Lummis, Oliver La Farge, Mary Austin, Stanley Vestal, were unknown, Garland's interpretation of the red man was a fresh note in American literature.

New also to Garland's writing was the complexity of his plotting. For the local divisions between cattleman, soldier, and Indian, between the responsible elements of the town and the desperadoes, are but reflections of the conflict on a national scale between predatory interests, reactionary sentiments, and the humanitarian efforts of the Department of the Interior. All of these elements also enter into the love themes which Garland introduces, the major romance between the Captain and the painter Elsie, the rivalry for the Captain's sister between a ranch scion and the young scientist studying the burial customs of the Tetongs. Indeed, as he had claimed to Gilder, Garland had laid out a big canvas, and the blending of the various elements is well achieved.

Garland's efforts to bring a "love-interest" into his fiction is no new phase, though perhaps now emphasized by the advice of Edward Bok and George Lorimer. As early as 1887 he jotted in his notebook after meeting some of his old school companions in

[4] *Ibid.*, pp. 70–71.

Ordway: "It would be a great thing to interpret the thoughts of these young girls, to get at what they actually know of the world and the color which thought imparts to it. If I could do this I could write one of the greatest books." [5] In effect he had attempted this in *Rose of Dutcher's Coolly* where the love story *is* the book, with no ideational conflict implied beyond that of marriage versus a career.

In fumbling for a title to his last collection of stories in 1897 Garland obviously wished to give them a romantic imprint. Among the titles he suggested were "Glimpses of Women," "A Preacher's Choice and Twelve Other Kinds of Women," "A Silent Wife and Twelve Other Kinds of Women," "Some Western Women," and simply "Wives." [6] The final selection of *Wayside Courtships* was consonant with this objective, although the contents of the book somewhat belied the title. Several of Garland's novelettes, "The Doctor," and *The Spirit of Sweetwater,* had been love stories, pure and simple. Now in *The Captain of the Gray-Horse Troop* it appeared that Garland had mastered the technique of combining a popular love story with what he liked to call "sociological background."

In the midst of the novel's composition he wrote confidently to Fuller:

I am in the position of a man with a good market for his produce and little time to produce. The demand for my short sketches and novelettes is strong, but my power for imagining them is diminishing. My romance [*The Captain*] absorbs all my energies. In casting up what I have done during the last year I find that I have written 225,-000 words, notwithstanding two trips to Oklahoma, one to the Pacific Coast, and another to the Atlantic. Evidently marriage has not interfered with my work to any noticeable degree. [7]

The second Oklahoma trip to which Garland refers was not a literary excursion. In May he discovered that his income had for

[5] Notebook, 1897, Garland Papers.
[6] Penciled list of titles in Garland Papers. This list includes fourteen alternate titles for a collection which as projected includes many of the stories eventually contained in *Wayside Courtships*, although often under variant names.
[7] Quoted in *Companions on the Trail* (1931), p. 71, under date of June 3, 1901.

once so far exceeded his expenses as to leave him with a surplus of five hundred dollars. Immediately he set out to buy a half section of land near Colony, Oklahoma, explaining wryly to his father: "Like Henry George we both understand the value of unearned increment." Franklin Garland was also this year succumbing to the lure of capitalism. When Hamlin out of his affluence offered to buy out Franklin's interest in the Homestead, the younger Garland accepted and departed with his capital to invest in Mexican rubber plantations, deserting the stage as a career. [8]

That summer the Hamlin Garlands again went to Colorado. With Zulime pregnant, her husband kept for once to the well-traveled trails. They visited as guests of the Ehrichs in Colorado Springs, as they had on their honeymoon. Zulime felt honored to receive a call and a breakfast invitation from an old and distinguished friend of her husband who happened to be in the city, Vice-President Roosevelt. With the Ehrichs the Garlands were guests of General Palmer on his seven-thousand-acre estate, a "camping" trip complete with valets, five-course luncheons, and a private Pullman car in the background. Garland, as an old trailer, enjoyed the contrast of such a luxury expedition, though with a certain uneasiness understandable in the prototype of Abner Joyce. "Strange to say," he reported, "I got nothing out of this summer, in a literary way, except the story which I called *The Steadfast Widow Delaney*. . . . All the beauty and drama, all the humor and contrast of the trip with the Palmers had no direct fictional value to me. It is hard to explain why, but so it was. I did not so much as write a poem based on that gorgeous experience." [9]

Yet in "The Steadfast Widow Delaney" (published the following year by the *Post*) Garland sketched with almost Dickensian flair a memorable pair of comic characters, the aggressive boardinghouse keeper of a mining town and the Milquetoast ne'er-do-well whom she grubstakes. The Palmers' hospitality had at least induced a mood of relaxation which brought to light an unsuspected quality of humor in the preternaturally solemn Garland.

Meanwhile the summer's lack of inspiration caused Garland

[8] *A Daughter of the Middle Border*, pp. 226, 238.
[9] *Ibid.*, p. 236.

no uneasiness. Two short sketches and *The Captain of the Gray-Horse Troop* had been sold to the *Post*; in addition he could count on a substantial income from his lecturing. Under the management of "The Inter-State Lecture Bureau of Cincinnati, Ohio," Garland in the season of 1901–1902 was prepared to give to any interested audience a choice of three subjects: "Prairie Song and Western Story," "The Joys of the Trail," or "Impressionism in Art." His notebooks reflect that he was frequently in demand as a platform performer. [10]

Zulime's son was stillborn. [11] After her recovery she and her husband returned to New York to settle into the Fifteenth Street apartment. A regular pattern of life was beginning to develop for the Garlands, winters in New York City, spring and fall visits to the Homestead, and summers in the High Country.

The first order of business upon their arrival East was to find a book publisher for *The Captain*. Frank Norris, who had read and criticized the manuscript, was enthusiastic about its possibilities, and reported that he had sold parts of his own *Pit* to a syndicate for $3,500.00. [12] Garland, recognizing that the literary market was at the moment highly competitive, carried out his resolution expressed to Gilder to sell his own work "in the best market." The newly organized firm of Harper & Brothers, to whose staff had been added the Pulitzer-trained journalist George Harvey and his lieutenants, F. A. Duneka, F. T. Leight, and A. D. Chandler, bought the book rights on *The Captain* on January 15, 1902, reserving for a period of one year all dramatization rights. [13] A play based upon Garland's work must have been considered a real possibility during the negotiations, but it was many years before dramatization occurred, and then only after the appearance of a new art form, moving pictures. Harper's set up a promotional campaign for *The Captain* which in its magnitude was new to Garland's experience. That the book remained a saleable item for more than thirty years justifies the firm's decision.

[10] Circular, Notebooks, Garland Papers.

[11] Conversation with Isabel Garland Lord, January 21, 1957.

[12] Frank Norris to Garland, two undated letters, Garland Papers.

[13] Contract of Harper & Brothers with Garland, January 15, 1902, Garland Papers.

Upon the book's appearance in March of 1902 it was widely reviewed, and generally favorably. Perhaps the comment which most delighted Garland was that of B. O. Flower who, in promising a July review in the *Arena*, wrote:

> In very many respects this is your best work. It combines the excellencies of your more recent long books with the strong altruistic and moral motive which was so marked a feature of your earlier novels. I felt in reading it that you were camping on the old trail again. [14]

Other reviewers were more impressed with Garland's new narrative powers than interested in his crusade. "The efflorescence of his genius," wrote one. "A capital story . . . a well-informed and warm-hearted book," agreed another. The *Athenaeum,* with a supercilious sneer at wild-western materials, concluded: "Elsie is on the whole a pleasant character and her love affairs . . . are skillfully interwoven with the development of the main idea." [15]

The publicity attendant upon the launching of this novel had the effect of interesting magazine editors in Garland's Indian subject matter. In 1902, in addition to appearances which might have been expected in *Harper's Weekly* and *McClure's,* Garland sold to *Frank Leslie's Magazine* "The River's Warning," and to the *North American Review* a lengthy article on "The Red Man's Present Needs." In 1903 he published in *Harper's Weekly* five more of the stories included in his category of "The Heart of the Indian." For the *Booklovers' Magazine* he discussed "The Red Man as Material."

From his platform in the *North American* Garland expounded his stand on the Indian question, advocating small settlements on water courses, with a competent "farmer" and "field matron" assigned to each district, the curtailment of missionary activities, and the abolition of Indian agents in favor of free economic competition. In the educational field he advanced the suggestion of John Seger that there be established an "Old Folk's Home" near

---

[14] B. O. Flower to Garland, March 31, 1902, Garland Papers. His review appeared in the *Arena,* XXVIII (July, 1902), 103–105.
[15] *Harper's Weekly,* XLVI (April 5, 1902), 432; *Dial,* XXXII (June 1, 1902), 387; *Athenaeum,* 1902 (2) (October 25, 1902), 547. For complete list of Garland's Indian stories, 1902–1903, see Bibliography.

each school to avoid the cruel separation of families under the present boarding-school arrangement. Education should be local and on a practical level, with encouragement of the native arts. And citizenship should be given to these native Americans with all its associated rights of freedom of movement and choice of occupation.

Garland argued the case for civil rights:

> I count it a virtue in that Northern chief who said: "I will not clean the spittoons of the white man's civilization." Hatred of tyranny is a distinctly American attribute, and one that deserves honorable consideration on the part of the department.... There should be some way to conserve and turn to account the lofty pride of the Sioux and the Cheyenne.

"Only when we give our best to these red brethren of ours," concluded Garland impassionedly, "do we justify ourselves as the dominant race of the Western continent." [16]

As an Indian expert Garland was also active on the political front. His friendship with Theodore Roosevelt, now President, gave him entree to the Department of Interior where he could urge such matters as the preservation of Indian tribal names, and the ear of the President himself on matters involving the Indian wards. The cordiality of "T. R." reached into social affairs, with the Garlands as guests at a White House musicale to hear a command performance of Paderewski. Throughout the years of the Roosevelt administration Hamlin was occasionally summoned to lunch with the President to give first-hand reports of conditions on the reservations. [17]

In October of 1902 Roosevelt so far took his fellow author into his confidence as to submit to him a draft of a paragraph of his message to the Congress dealing with Indian questions, asking for corrections or suggestions. "Let them be brief. But I wished either you or Mr. George Bird Grinnell to go over what I said." [18] With Stewart Edward White, and particularly with Albert Shaw, editor of the *Review of Reviews*, Garland was in constant correspondence during these years on matters affecting In-

---

[16] *North American Review*, CLXXIV (April, 1902), 476–88.
[17] *A Daughter of the Middle Border*, pp. 245–46, 264.
[18] Theodore Roosevelt to Garland, October 19, 1902, Garland Papers.

dian welfare and on appointments within the Department of the Interior. [19]

With Shaw he had another piece of business, a grandiose proposal, originated by Franklin Garland, for the formation of a syndicate to purchase 50,000 acres of Mexican land at one dollar per acre, "keeping the subscription among the 'literary chaps.' "[20] Although for a year or more Hamlin wrote constantly to Shaw and other "literary chaps" about this proposal, it seems never to have attained much substance. Garland's dreams of becoming a landed proprietor had to be satisfied by the acquisition of additional small tracts in Oklahoma near his original half-section. John Homer Seger, and after him his children Jesse and Neatha, acted as Garland's agents in these enterprises. [21]

With Stewart Edward White he had another common interest, the occult. For Garland was again interesting himself in psychic experimentation. The "Mrs. Smiley" whom he had brought East ten years before was now living in Cleveland, and Garland persuaded her to come to Chicago for a series of tests, with the scientist Robert Millikan and his wife among the group of participants. She was unable to reproduce the phenomena which had once so amazed Garland's Boston confreres. But there were other mediums, other experiments to be investigated, among them Professor Quackenbush's work in the field of hypnosis. [22] Among the friends of these years who shared this "hobby" of Garland's there were—besides White, whose interest would become at last all-consuming—Lew Wallace, the author of *Ben Hur*, Henry B. Fuller, and Edward MacDowell. On the other side of the unknown there were now not only Garland's aunt and mother but James Herne, who had died in the year of 1901.

Death was an ever-present figure in the streets of West Salem where so many oldsters waited out their last years. In the summer of 1902 Garland's uncle William McClintock, the giant mentor

[19] Stewart E. White to Garland, correspondence from 1902 forward, Garland Papers; Garland to Albert Shaw, correspondence from 1902 forward, particularly letters of February 19 and 26, April 29, June 24 [1902], New York Public Library.
[20] Garland to Albert Shaw, undated, New York Public Library.
[21] Correspondence between Garland and John H. Seger, 1902–1922, Garland Papers.
[22] *Forty Years of Psychic Research* (1936), pp. 123–24.

of his boyhood, was the victim of a stroke, and the same cloud
hovered over Garland's father, then passed on. In the sorrow of
watching the gradual failing of those dear to him Garland turned
again to verse, his poem appearing with full-page illustration in
the austere *Century* under the title "The Stricken Mountaineer":

> Once he was king of forest men.
> To him a snow-capped mountain range
> Was but a line, a place of mark,
> A view-point on the trail. Then
> He had no dread of dark,
> No fear of change.
> Now an uprolled rug upon the floor
> Appalls his feet. His withered arm
> Shakes at the menace of a door,
> And every wind-waft does him harm.
>
> God! 'Tis a piteous thing to see
> This ranger of the hills confined
> To the small compass of his room
> Like a chained eagle on a tree,
> Lax-winged and gray and blind.
> Only in dreams he sees the bloom
> On far hills where the red deer run,
> Only in memory guides the light canoe
> Or stalks the bear with dog and polished gun.
>
> In him behold the story of the West,
> The chronicle of rifleman behind the plow,
> Typing the life of those who knew
> No barrier but the sunset in their quest.
> On his bent head and grizzled hair
> Is set the crown of those who shew
> New cunning to the wolf, new courage to the bear. [23]

No oldster, but one of Garland's youngest colleagues, Frank
Norris was the next victim of the Grim Reaper. He was "the most
valiant, the happiest, the handsomest of all my fellow craftsmen,"
Garland wrote. "Nothing more shocking, more insensate than
the destruction of this glorious young fictionist had come to my
literary circle, for he was aglow with a husband's happiness, gay

[23] "The Stricken Mountaineer," *Century*, LXXIV (October, 1907), 928–30.

with the pride of paternity, and in the full spring-tide of his powers." [24] At the request of the *Critic* Garland wrote an essay on his
friend's work, concluding:

> Youth makes a savage realist, for youth has boundless hope and ex-
> ultation in itself. When a man begins to doubt his ability to reform,
> to change by challenge, he softens, he allows himself to pity. Norris in
> "The Pit" is more genial, that is to say, more mature, than in "Mc-
> Teague" and "The Octopus." He was thirty-two and successful. He
> was entering on a less inexorable period. He was not written out, as
> perhaps Stephen Crane was; on the contrary, his mind was glowing
> with imagery. His ideals were fine, his life without stain, and his small
> shelf of books will stand high in the library of American fiction. [25]

Throughout the year 1902 Garland wrote steadily on his new
novel. Sometimes he worked in the Indian tepee which he had
brought back with him from the reservation to set up at Eagle's
Nest where he and Zulime spent part of the summer. Complete
with blankets, parfleches, willow beds and other accessories, this
lodge was an exact replica of a Cheyenne dwelling and filled Garland with an inordinate pride. Seton came by one day to assist
in the dedication of its firehole, and the two old campers smoked
together a symbolic pipe of meditation. This primitive shelter
Garland found an appropriate study in which to write of Indian
lore and to compose the lectures he was scheduled to give that
autumn at the University of Chicago on "The Outdoor Literature of America."

Again the Garlands traveled to Colorado to investigate the
circumstances of the "Cripple Creek War," which formed the
background of the novel in progress. Garland "visited a ranch on
the plains of eastern Colorado, joined a round-up in the Sierra
Blanca country, explored the gambling houses and mines of Cripple Creek and Victor, and spent two weeks re-exploring the
White River Plateau," then for two weeks camped high on the
shoulder of Pike's Peak. [26] Despite all this activity and despite the
advice of a local newsman who had covered many phases of the
miners' controversy, Garland's portrayal of a labor war in *Hesper*
is not particularly effective.

[24] *A Daughter of the Middle Border*, p. 262.
[25] "The Work of Frank Norris," *Critic*, XLII (March, 1903), 216–18.
[26] *A Daughter of the Middle Border*, pp. 250–51, 258–59.

In the three-cornered squabble between free miners, union men, and mine owners, Garland's sympathies were clearly with the free miners, the prospecting individualists who were the counterparts of his beloved trailers. As consequence, the union viewpoint is never effectively stated, and despite Garland's recent entry into the ranks of landowners, he seems unable to treat intelligibly the psychology of the capitalists. The novel suffers also from Garland's efforts to superimpose upon the economic conflict a love story. Although he tried to integrate the two themes, his romance remains almost entirely extraneous to the conflict, a mere repetition of the equation which he has juggled before, of an eastern-oriented heroine set opposite a western-conditioned lover. As in all of Garland's writings, however, the descriptive backgrounds are excellent, and the spectacular mountain-top setting of his drama, its impressionistic scenes of storm and sunlight, do much to relieve the other mediocrities of *Hesper*. [27]

At summer's end the Garlands returned again to West Salem, this time to a home entirely their own, for Garland's father had set up a smaller establishment, leaving the Homestead to Hamlin and Zulime, who were again expecting a child. But not even a home completely his own could keep Garland from his autumnal restlessness. The need for the life of the city swept over him, and the final work on *Hesper* was done in New York, with the manuscript turned over to Harper's in March of 1903.

With *The Captain* selling steadily, and with *Hesper* in the printers' hands, Garland devoted himself to his family. To compensate his father for the loneliness of the past winter he now arranged a series of excursions for the old man's enjoyment. In April Richard Garland made the trip back East, which he had talked of since leaving Boston fifty years before—like the "Mrs. Ripley" of his son's first story. Sightseeing in Washington and Philadelphia under Hamlin's guidance stirred his patriotic emotions. The bustle of New York, and particularly his son's acceptance in the places of the mighty, moved him to wonder. At The Players he gazed with awe at the relics of Edwin Booth, the hero of his young manhood. But at the prospect of further "back-trailing" to Boston he quailed: "I've had enough. I'm ready to go

[27] *Hesper* (1903).

home. I'm all tired out 'seeing things,' and besides it's time to be getting back to my garden."

A little later Hamlin and his father continued their sentimental pilgrimage with a visit to old scenes in Iowa. Hamlin spoke to the alumni of the Seminary where he had spent his college days, but there was little joy in noting in old friends the toll of years and in counting the vacant places of those who had gone on. A much more pleasant excursion was the trip which Garland and his wife made the following month up the Mississippi on the houseboat of their friends the Eatons.

Back in West Salem Garland toyed with writing "the epic poem" which the life of Sitting Bull had suggested to him, and toward which he had once made a start in a *McClure's* article on "General Custer's Last Fight as Seen by Two Moon." But the work lagged, and at last he laid the manuscript aside, convinced that he was inadequate to the task. Meanwhile, something of his father's enthusiasm for Edwin Booth had reawakened his own memories, and he turned with growing interest to a series of lectures on the great actor to be delivered at the University of Chicago that summer. "The Art of Edwin Booth" was a revision of the manuscript so long ago rejected by Fields of the *Atlantic*.

At last Zulime's time arrived and she was delivered of a daughter who was christened Mary Isabel. Hamlin Garland at forty-three experienced belatedly the joys of parenthood, and like so many older parents, became completely fatuous in his adoration of this unique babe who had come to brighten the old Homestead. But soon he was forced to tear himself away from the fascination of watching his child's development to fulfill his lecture engagements in the East and to supervise the final proofs of *Hesper*.

Harper's enthusiasm for the novel encouraged Garland to pursue the course toward which both habit and inclination drove him. Even with the increase in his family he was determined to have his winter in the East, and as his book went through the press, he uprooted Zulime, the baby, and a West Salem maid, and established his ménage in a seven-room apartment overlooking Morningside Park.

With the check which he had received for "A Pioneer Mother" he bought his wife a set of silver initialled "I. G." in the playful

conceit that it was family heirloom handed down to her by Isabel
Garland. With the money from his article on "The Work of
Frank Norris" he bought a handsome clock for the hallway as a
memorial to his departed friend. [28] All these extravagances seemed
justified as *Hesper* rolled from the presses. The reviewers were
even more ecstatic than they had been over *The Captain of the
Gray-Horse Troop.*

"Hesper," wrote James MacArthur in *Harper's Weekly*, "ex-
emplifies the new uplift which has come to Mr. Garland's art. [It
is] a worthy successor to *The Captain of the Gray-Horse Troop*,
and will undoubtedly enjoy a still greater popularity." [29] This recommendation was something of a piece of house advertising, for
in the Harper reorganization the *Weekly* had become even more
closely linked with the publishing house, and the previous month
George Harvey's name had begun appearing on its masthead as
editor.

But others joined the chorus. The *Dial* was impressed by "the
consistent development of character in the case of the heroine,
if not in that of the hero," and continued:

We do not hesitate to say that "Hesper" represents the best work
that Mr. Garland has done; in it he has sloughed off most of his earlier
defects of thought and expression; his asperities have become softened,
and his rawness has undergone a transformation into something very
like urbanity. And all this evolution has been accomplished without
any diminution of the earnestness and the energy which first directed
attention to him as a writer. It is a far cry from "Main-Travelled
Roads" to the present volume, it seems almost too far to be accounted
for by a mere matter of fifteen years. [30]

The *Athenaeum*, in a rather puzzling summary of Garland's
development, claimed that he "has at last returned to the old trail
and we hope he will keep to it." *Rose of Dutcher's Coolly* and
Garland's "Chicago studies" were condemned as merely clever.
"He had deliberately discarded the romantic elements of his own
nature." While *Hesper* is "a novel in which all things happen
out of the average, and the result is a striking and interesting

[28] *A Daughter of the Middle Border,* pp. 260–70, 279–92.
[29] *Harper's Weekly,* XLVII (November 28, 1903), 1921.
[30] *Dial,* XXXVI (January 1, 1904), 19.

story . . . It is in the passage of this girl's [Hesper's] soul to the awakening, its return to the healthier condition of nature, that the psychological interest of Mr. Garland's book lies." [31]

The *Critic* put its finger on one cause of the enthusiasm which seemed so unanimous over Garland's new phase of development: "The Indian," it commented sagely, "is not likely to write to the newspapers and object to being championed, as did a Kansas farmer's wife in the days when Mr. Garland was the champion of the oppressed inhabitants of Wisconsin, Kansas, and Nebraska." "Incidentally," it added, *"The Captain of the Gray-Horse Troop* is an extremely readable tale of life on Indian reservations and at Western Army posts." [32] *Hesper,* in the estimation of early twentieth-century readers, was likewise a readable tale, and the problems of the Cripple Creek miners as remote from Eastern critics and from people inclined to write letters to the magazine editors, as had been the tragedies of the red man.

William Dean Howells added his word of praise on *Hesper* to the tributes of the public reviewers. He had sat up until twelve the previous night with the book, he wrote Garland: "It is a fine book, full of a manly poetry, and a high ideal." [33]

The only discordant note to the triumphal chorus which welcomed Garland into his new residence in the literary metropolis was the cryptic comment of Henry B. Fuller: "I do not think," ventured this old and trusted advisor, "you have a distinct call to write about women—no more a call than had Kipling." [34]

---

[31] *Athenaeum* (November 28, 1903), p. 614.
[32] *Critic,* XLI (September, 1902), 278.
[33] W. D. Howells to Garland, November 3, 1903, Garland Papers.
[34] H. B. Fuller to Garland, September 23, 1903, Garland Papers.

❧ 11 ❧

The Tyranny of the Dark

HESPER, despite its artistic defects, was commercially one of the most successful of Garland's books. He claimed for it and for *The Captain of the Gray-Horse Troop* a sale of over 50,000 copies, a figure consistent with the surviving records. [1] In the cheaper Grosset & Dunlap edition *Hesper* sold one year to the extent of providing a solid contribution of $1,462.50 to the Garland exchequer. Secondary rights were sold in the course of years to the *Louisville Post,* the New York American Press Association, the *Pittsburgh Times,* the *Baltimore Herald,* the *New York Press,* and other journals. When Garland's book became the subject of movie contracts *Hesper* led the list bought up by the Vitagraph Company for filming, at an advance of $500.00 apiece. [2]

[1] Garland makes this claim in *My Friendly Contemporaries* (1932), p. 2. His royalty statements from Harper & Brothers in the Garland Papers are not complete prior to 1909, but thereafter in both the Harper and Macmillan editions *Hesper* showed a steady sale.

[2] The Grosset & Dunlap statement (Garland Papers) is undated. Information on secondary rights is contained in a letter to Garland from Fred Duneka of Harper's, June 22, 1914. The Vitagraph contract is dated June 28, 1916.

The backlog of security represented by the *Hesper* and *Captain* royalties stood the Garlands in good stead in the decade that followed, for after the publication of these two novels Garland entered upon a period of diminished productivity. The impetus which had driven him to produce and market his Western materials died out, and for some time he turned from subject to subject, unable to capture the creative enthusiasm for another major effort. True, from 1903 to 1913, his bibliographical record shows a not unimpressive list of titles. But analysis reveals that many of these are reworkings of earlier materials, novelettes revamped and expanded into novels, snippets of articles culled from the file of his rejected manuscripts. Until *Cavanaugh* in 1910 there was fresh creative effort only in experimentation with psychic themes.

In *The Light of the Star,* published in 1904 as a *Ladies' Home Journal* serial, and as a novel by Harper's, Garland turned to the world of the theater for material for a love story. An actor's crusade for realism in the drama provided a thin thread of "sociological background" for a romance which both Garland and his publishers hoped would capitalize on the current popularity of the author. Echoes of Garland's experiences with the Hernes make the story of some biographical interest, but hasty writing and lack of intense conviction rob the work of any survival value. [3]

Garland's next project, however, was one for which he had unlimited enthusiasm, the attempt to portray in the realm of fiction the experiences which he had garnered through his many years of psychic experimentation. The mediums he had met, in darkened rooms in a dozen cities, the charlatans and the sincere believers, had always interested him both as novelist and as experimenter. These pitiable shadowy figures, strapped with adhesive to their chairs through the long hours of séance—in the interest of science, of a cult, or of earning a fugitive dollar—surrendering their personalities to outside forces, or to the vagaries of hysterical trance—had always awakened his sympathetic consideration. The more so as he remembered the confession of one of his maternal aunts that for two years the spirit forces "had made

[3] *Ladies' Home Journal,* XXI (January–May, 1904); book publication, 1904.

her life a hell." The isolation of the "Mrs. Smiley's" in the borderland of psychic research impressed Garland as a subject for
fiction equally valid with the loneliness of the "Mrs. Ripley's" of
the physical border. To interpret their predicament he began
the writing of a novel of which the heroine was a young medium.[4]

The Tyranny of the Dark dealt with the development of Viola
Lambert, whose parents having discovered her capacity as a
medium subordinate all normal activities of young girlhood to
the cultivation of her powers. In this they are abetted by a spiritualist pastor who proposes to marry Viola so that he can enjoy
communication with his dead wife. Viola is rescued from this
fate by the courtship of a young bacteriologist, who is interested
in the spiritualistic hypothesis to the extent of discrediting himself as a scientist, but refuses to allow his future wife to continue
in her bondage to unknown forces. While giving a convincing
portrayal of his heroine's doubts, divided loyalties, and indeci-
sions, Garland was able to summarize in lively conversational ex-
changes the arguments for and against the validity of psychic
phenomena. As author he maintains a judicial balance, avoiding
any more definite commitment than that of one of his characters:
"We assume that we've corralled and branded all facts, when, as
a matter of history, there are scattered bunches of cattle all
through the hills." [5]

The Tyranny of the Dark was coolly received by the public,
and Garland admitted in later years: "To turn aside from a sunlit landscape and explore dark chambers of a religious controversy was, I now confess, a mistake." [6] But upon publication the
book drew from his immediate friends and from psychic experimenters around the world a varied and interested response.

Among the correspondents it revived were Garland's old associates of the American Psychic Association. Minot J. Savage was
somewhat disappointed that his friend had not committed himself wholeheartedly as a spiritualist in his fictional study. [7] But
Professor Dolbear of Tufts College wrote goodhumoredly in
reminiscent vein:

[4] Discussed in *Forty Years of Psychic Research* (1936), pp. 136–38.
[5] *The Tyranny of the Dark* (1906), p. 257.
[6] *Companions on the Trail* (1931), p. 272.
[7] M. J. Savage to Garland, May 16, 1905, Garland Papers.

Bless me what a name for a book! Down I sat in my spare hours for
a day or two and read it thru—in the same room where we had those
tyrannous happenings twelve years ago! I got so absorbed in your
story that every little noise gave me a start. "Wilbur" was expected
and I would have welcomed him heartily.

That "delicate finger" high on the window. That horn touching my
forehead and the voice saying "I ain't dead," and the alarm clock
suddenly stopping, and the candy box being brought to the table!—
Every happening is a mystery until it is explained by a deeper mystery.

Another scientist accepted the story as the fiction which was
intended. Dr. T. M. Prudden, the Columbia bacteriologist, who
had served as model for Garland's hero, wrote jocularly:

Of course you story-telling folk wouldn't scruple to make a promising scientific man drop his career like a hot potato just as soon as an
alluring bit of femininity appears upon his horizon. Think what
that chap might have done for science if you had been willing to let
him alone with his ideas! But there would have been no story, so you
may be absolved.

William Stead, the spiritualist editor of the English *Review of
Reviews,* championed violently the opposite side of Garland's
human equation. Asking for a sequel "when your own ideas are
a little clearer on the subject," he blasted the novel from the viewpoint of his own fixed position:

As you have left it, the story is an ethical outrage. The destruction
of such a human telescope into the Great Beyond as Viola is painted,
merely to provide a very self-sufficient dogmatic prig of a young biolo-
gist with a wife, is an offense against ethics, against science and against
the sense of proportion.

Garland had the satisfaction, at least, of having stirred up controversy in psychical and scientific circles, and, in addition,
among his fellow novelists his aims were fully appreciated. Israel
Zangwill assured him that it was "the most engrossing book you
have written. . . . You hold the balance so impartially that you
achieve all the thrill of a detective novel." [8] Howells contented
himself with sympathizing with the difficulties of Garland's un-

[8] The letters from Dolbear, Prudden, Stead, and Zangwill are quoted in
Forty Years of Psychic Research, at pp. 140–43.

dertaking: "It is hard to beat the professional mediumship into the proper relation. I can say this frankly to you because I have wrought in the same field." [9] But Edwin Markham wrote with full enthusiasm: "We are now in the midst of your herd of ghosts and strongly drawn by your sorcery." [10]

The letter of William Dean Howells continued: "The other day I took down your Main Travelled Roads and read into it. ... It is a great, simple, individual work. I wish you had some such theme as the theme of that book to work out on the scale of a novel." There were reviewers of *The Tyranny of the Dark* who shared Howells' wish. *Public Opinion* expressed itself on the subject of the new novel that "compared to some of Mr. Garland's earlier writings ... it is a disappointing piece of work." "It is very delicate and exacting material that Mr. Garland has chosen for his latest novel," carped the *Critic*, "and very crudely has he handled it." The *Forum* was inclined to agree with William Stead that the author had dodged the basic issue, the validity of the spiritualist hypothesis.

The *Arena*, however, stood stanchly behind its one-time author, devoting space to an 8000-word review. Although the essay was somewhat facetiously titled "Garland in Ghostland," it seriously considered both the subject matter and the artistry of the novel, concluding: "Pleasing and interesting as is the romance considered merely as a novel, its supreme excellence lies in its detailed presentation of certain psychical phenomena." [11]

While Garland the writer was thus adventuring in ghostland his counterpart in the world of reality led a prosaic enough existence. The routine of domesticity more and more absorbed him, although he "managed to sandwich the writing of an occasional article between spells of minding the baby—and working on club committees." [12] The New York winters had been abandoned in favor of an apartment in Chicago where Zulime could be near her brother and her father, who had established himself

[9] W. D. Howells to Garland, August 20, 1906, Garland Papers.
[10] Edwin Markham to Garland, June 2, 1905, Garland Papers.
[11] *Public Opinion*, XXXIX (July 1, 1905), 26; *Critic*, XLVII (September, 1905), 284; *Forum*, XXXVII (July, 1905), 113; "Garland in Ghostland," *Arena*, XXXIV (August, 1905), 206–216.
[12] *A Daughter of the Middle Border* (1921), p. 293.

in that city. Eventually the Garlands purchased a house on Wood-lawn Avenue, a narrow-fronted three-story brick which enabled Hamlin to speak expansively to the uninitiated of his "town resi-dence," and in the same breath to refer casually to his "country home," the West Salem farmhouse which remained for some years the Garlands' summer abode.

In a burst of enthusiasm one autumn Garland designed and commissioned a fireplace for the Homestead, the only outside chimney in the entire village. "Building a Fireplace in Time for Christmas" was his report from the domestic front on this epi-sode to the readers of *Country Life in America*. [13] The triviality of the subject is indication of the paucity of imaginative materi-als at Garland's command at this time. Out of his brooding over the symbolism of his hearthstone, however, came a successful story of the problems of old age. "The Fireplace," published in the December, 1905, *Delineator,* is the single twentieth-century Garland item included in later editions of *Main-Travelled Roads,* appropriately enough, as it sounds something of an elegiac fare-well to his Middle Border characters. [14] Of the period when it was written Garland retrospectively admitted: "Marriage, paternity, householding, during these years unquestionably put the brakes on my work as a writer, but I had no desire to return to bachelor-hood. . . . Concerned with the problem of maintaining a com-fortable winter home for my family and happy in maintaining the old house in West Salem as a monument to the memory of my mother, I wrote, committed carpentry and lectured." [15]

But one September while the family still lingered in the coun-try Mary Isabel contracted diphtheria. Because of the isolation of the village she suffered lack of adequate medical attention, and for a time her life was despaired of. Although the child at last recovered, the shock of this incident so alienated her father from the Homestead that for several years the family shunned the Homestead, and Chicago became their year-round abode. [16]

[13] *Country Life in America,* VIII (October, 1905), 645–47.
[14] *Delineator,* LXVI (December, 1905), 1051–56; as "Martha's Fireplace" in future editions of *Main-Travelled Roads.*
[15] *A Daughter of the Middle Border,* p. 320.
[16] *Ibid.,* pp. 322–25.

Meanwhile Zulime Garland had entirely abandoned her career as painter and sculptress. The decision was made cheerfully and without repining as she had been convinced that her talents would never carry her beyond the field of the copyist. The bold feminism of Garland's blueprint for matrimony had been quietly discarded in the day-to-day responsibilities of marriage. Zulime, in the common pattern of women, found the demands of wifehood and parenthood, the duties of playing hostess for a gregarious writer, left no time for artistic activities. Although Lorado Taft might mutter about the wastage of his sister's talents, the obvious contentment which reigned in the Garland home offered its own rebuttal.

In Garland's case, while matrimony brought some curtailment of his activities, it did not materially check his restless wanderings. He was continually off on lecture tours, trips to New York to consult his publishers, journeys to Northern Mexico to inspect the mirage of Franklin's mining ventures. And always his energies were expendable on matters pertaining to the various organizations of which he was a member. In New York he continued to frequent the Players and to work on various committees. He was one of the moving spirits behind a testimonial dinner to Henry George, the occasion, the twenty-fifth anniversary of the publication of *Progress and Poverty*. Indefatigably he wrote letters to his friends selling tickets to the affair and soliciting testimonials. Even Bernard Shaw wrote lengthily in response to Garland's appeal, recalling having first heard George speak in London in the early eighties: "Henry George has one thing to answer for that has proved more serious than he thought when he was doing it—without knowing it," Shaw charged, continuing with a detailed analysis of George's influence on the Fabian movement. [17]

Armed with such evidences of the strength of the Georgian message Garland presided as master of ceremonies at the dinner given at the Hotel Astor on January 24, 1905, where William Jennings Bryan was one of the principal speakers. One can but wonder what the denouncer of unearned increment would have

[17] *Ibid., passim; Companions on the Trail*, pp. 233–38, 265–67; G. B. Shaw to Garland, December 29, 1904, carbon copy in New York Public Library.

made of the occasion, of the roster of opulent writers, editors, and politicians in attendance, the silver medals struck for each guest, the menu progressing solidly from "Canapé de Caviar" to "Fromage et Café Noir." [18]

Throughout the years the organization closest to Garland's heart was the American Academy of Arts and Letters, a select body representing the inner circle of the earlier established National Institute of Arts and Letters. The ritual by which one became a member of this august assemblage was inaugurated in 1904, partly under Garland's initiative. Seven men were selected from the parent body—William Dean Howells, Augustus St. Gaudens, Edmund C. Stedman, Samuel L. Clemens, John Hay, John La Farge, and Edward MacDowell—to serve as a nucleus and as representative electors. These seven immediately chose another eight to augment their ranks. The fifteen artists then balloted for another five, who joined the ranks of eligible voters to elect another ten. The final roster of thirty (later increased to fifty) constituted the "American Academy," which its founders trusted would have a dignity and an influence upon American arts comparable to that of the French Academy. [19]

Garland, like Brander Matthews, one of the prime instigators of the organization, was enthusiastic over the possibilities of the movement. Sometimes he was able to communicate his enthusiasm to his fellow craftsmen and secure their support and allegiance to the Institute and to the Academy. More often than not the individualism of the artist recoiled from the formalities of such an artificial body. Owen Wister at first fought shy of the matter, bluntly declaring his indifference: "I never did any public service or am likely to do any." [20] Edwin Markham was remote from the cause, but finally admitted to Garland that his arguments had swung him into line. [21] Henry B. considered the maneuverings of the literary elect with his usual irony:

[18] Program, 25th Anniversary Dinner for Henry George, January 24, 1905, Garland Papers.

[19] *Companions on the Trail*, pp. 251–53; Brander Matthews, *These Many Years* (New York, 1917), pp. 447–48.

[20] Owen Wister to Garland, April 4, 1903, December 2, 1907, Garland Papers.

[21] Edwin Markham to Garland, April 8, 1900, Garland Papers.

My "perfectly candid opinion of the Institute"! Well, Well! Really I have none. I don't quite understand what it's for. I never did. It doesn't function because there is nothing for it to function about. Will biggening its body give it more reality, when what it needs is a definite endowment of spirit? [22]

William Dean Howells, though a charter member of the Institute, and one of the first choices for the Academy, never really approved the evolution of the latter body. When Garland wrote congratulating him on the publication of *The Son of Royal Langbirth* he replied:

But I was an author before I was an Academician, and I would rather have written a book that brought such a shout from you than sit in one of the cerulean chairs which the good Underwood wishes some millionaire of letters to provide for us. [23]

In contrast to such lukewarm interest on the part of many of his friends among the authors, Garland remained throughout his lifetime a stanch and ardent supporter of the Institute, and of the Academy, to which he was himself elected in 1918. The work of its committees occupied him extensively in correspondence and in conferences, and he often spoke in its defense, "The American Academy of Arts and Letters—Is it Democratic?" "The American Academy and its Future," "The Mission of the American Academy." [24]

In Chicago Garland continued to work with various artistic and literary groups, and in March of 1905 had the honor of introducing Henry James, whom he had recently met in New York, to his friends of "the Little Room." James found the Latin Quarter atmosphere a welcome change from "the extraordinarily close corporation" of millionaires who were his official hosts on this lecture tour. [25]

With the University of Chicago Garland also maintained cordial associations, speaking often to one University group or another. At the fall convocation of the University that year he delivered an address entitled "Vanishing Trails," a poetic distilla-

---

[22] H. B. Fuller to Garland, December 9, 1907, Garland Papers.
[23] W. D. Howells to Garland, December 20, 1904, Garland Papers.
[24] Unpublished MSS, Garland Papers.
[25] *Companions on the Trail*, pp. 258–64.

tion of his personal experiences as a trailer mingled with a nostalgic sorrow for the passing of the frontier. On his return from the Klondike Garland had written in this vein: "The trail is poetry; a wagon road is prose; the railroad, arithmetic. My blood always leaps under a spur of dimly remembered joys as I turn from the dusty, rectilinear turnpike into the trail." [26]

Now, faced by the rows of youthful faces, Garland elaborated this theme, launching into an impassioned elegy on the vanishing trails of the middle border:

The trail is itself a sign—the sign of things vanishing. It is lost out of the lowlands of Ohio and Kentucky. The plows of Minnesota and Dakota have buried it deep. Its tracery is fading from the valleys of Montana and Colorado. Only in the high ranges, where the peaks jostle the stars, will you find it, its beauty, the sign of the unsubdued. It begins where the thoroughfare leaves off, and ends where the unscared ptarmigan broods beneath the wind-warped pines.

A whole world, an epic world, is vanishing, fading, while we dream. The land of the log cabin, the country of the cayuse, the province of the trapper, the kingdom of the cow-man, are passing never to return. All this hardy and most distinctive life will soon be but a dim memory, enduring only faintly in romance, its tone and quality but feebly reflected in our verse. I cannot but feel that something brave and buoyant, something altogether epic, is passing with the men of this, my father's generation, the last of the pioneers.

"Yes, the trail with all it subtends is fading from the earth; and the white trailers, like the red, are dying," lamented Garland, as he urged his young listeners while opportunity yet remained to experience the joys of the wilderness. "Out of such desert experiences the scholar of the right metal comes with fresh courage to face his work in the world."

> Do you fear the force of the wind,
>   The slash of the rain?
> Go face them and fight them,
>   Be savage again.
> Go hungry and cold like the wolf,
>   Go wade like the crane.
> The palms of your hands will thicken,

[26] "Hitting the Trail," *McClure's*, XII (February, 1899), 300.

The skin of your forehead will tan,
You'll grow ragged and swarthy and weary,
But you'll walk like a man! [27]

The verse of Garland's exordium was already beginning to find its way into anthologies of nature poetry, where it has remained a perennial favorite. In preparing this oration Garland must have become convinced that he had far from exhausted the materials of his Alaskan adventure, for shortly thereafter there appeared a new edition of *The Trail of the Goldseekers,* and Garland turned to the writing of a boys' serial based upon the same material which was subsequently published by the *Youth's Companion.* [28]

A short story of a frontier boy's night ride for a doctor had recently appeared in the English journal *Pall Mall.* [29] Henry James on his Chicago visit had extended Garland an invitation to visit him in Rye. On the basis of such trivialities Garland suddenly decided in the summer of 1906 to go abroad, a repetition of the sequence of associations of 1898 when he had returned from the Klondike only to set off immediately for England. This time he justified his excursion by consulting a doctor, "who, with fine understanding of my wishes, *ordered* me to spend the summer 'abroad.' " [30] In England Garland retraced the course of his previous journey by paying visits to Bernard Shaw and Israel Zangwill. Conan Doyle motored over to Zangwill's Shottermill cottage to take his colleagues for a ride in his new machine, and in London presided at an author's luncheon at which Garland was an honored guest. Similar experiences in 1899 had thrilled Garland to the core. This time no longer the impressionable young man of his earlier visit, he knew a sense of anti-climax. The Cecil Hotel now seemed "several degrees less splendid" than he had recalled it, and the authors' dinner devoid of well-known personages. But Garland could record in his diary: "With Kipling, as with Shaw

[27] "Vanishing Trails," *University Record* (Chicago: University of Chicago), X (1905), 53–61. Garland tells of the occasion in *Companions on the Trail,* pp. 278–91, quoting portions of his address. In revised form it also occurs in *Joys of the Trail* (1935).
[28] "The Long Trail: a story of the Klondike," *Youth's Companion,* LXXX and LXXXI (December 6–February 7, 1907).
[29] "Doctor's Visit," *Pall Mall Magazine,* XXXV (May, 1905), 585–90.
[30] *Companions on the Trail,* p. 292.

and Doyle, I resumed acquaintance almost as if six weeks instead of seven years had intervened—of such quality are the friendships established in youth." [31]

He and Kipling discussed, among other subjects, the English dialect. It is always a shock to an American going back to the home of his ancestral speech to find that to his ear the cadences of the English tongue, Cockney or Oxonian, have the sound of foreign speech. Garland jotted in his 1906 notebook:

> This extraordinary lingo is tiring. I worked hard to understand what they say, and only partly succeeded. My brain is filled with pictures of narrow-winding clean streets . . . with odds and ends of old buildings occupied as saloons mostly, and with pink and green hawthorne, purple wisteria, mighty elms in unkempt parks, splendid chestnut trees and very gnarled brick walls.

According to plan, Garland visited Henry James at Rye, noting:

> J. met me at the depot a portly figure. He was like a keen and kindly curate, brusk in movement, hesitant of speech. "If I were to live my life again I would [do so] in America—steep myself in it—know no other." [32]

One episode of this English visit was characteristic of Garland. In crossing he had discovered in the ship's library a copy of *Dialstone Lane* by W. W. Jacobs, and upon landing had made inquiries about this newly discovered author. The result was an invitation to visit Jacobs near Epping Forest. Turning then from the attentions of Zangwill, Shaw, and others of the mighty, Garland took train from London to spend a pleasant weekend with the Jacobses, reporting: "I had no sense of being in a strange country as I sat with these delightful people." [33]

Paris had "lost much of its charm and all of its mystery" after seven years, and Garland lingered only a weekend for conventional sightseeing. On the advice of Shaw he traveled south to Roman France, passed a day or two in Toulouse and Avignon, and with a friend of Lorado Taft's toured the Monet country,

[31] *Ibid.*, pp. 293–97.
[32] 1906 Notebook, Garland Papers.
[33] *Companions on the Trail*, pp. 293, 298–99.

pausing for a visit with an old acquaintance, Thomas Sargent Perry. Back in Paris he called upon Mme. Blanc, his *Revue des Deux Mondes* critic, finding her "old and poor and sad."

The first of August found Garland in Italy, doing Florence under the enthusiastic tutelage of Lorado Taft, and writing paragraphs headed "Lecture Notes," and "The Mountaineer Abroad." For Garland planned a repetition of his novelette *Her Mountain Lover* as the result of this Grand Tour, the sequel to bear some such title as "Jim Matteson's Old World Pasear." But the traveler's disillusionment with things Italian increased as the days went by. "Florence is hot and dusty as Omaha. The Arno, shrunk to a foul little stream, lies gasping in the sand. [Venice] has all the vices of a show place ... its malodorous streets ... its canals, noisome as sewers (bearing dead dogs, garbage, and sewage on their currents) ... the leather-lunged gondoliers, the raucous bellowing of street singers, the childish, theatric, passionate, unreasoning roaring of the people (with no reserve—no dignity—always fiercely affectionate or dramatically savage) wearied me and repelled me. I can't understand how Fuller and Howells could overlook the squalor, the ceaseless turmoil, of this city. Damn this bellowing mob!—Fifty men and women are this moment howling outside my window. They yowl and screech from the love of it. .... To-day I leave Venice. I have seen it and have nearly died in the midst of it." [34]

Garland's disgust with Southern Europe sprang from deeper sources than mere concern with insanitation and acoustics. The isolation of frontier life in which he had grown to manhood had impregnated him with a lasting xenophobia. Already in his writings had appeared many scathing references to the "foreigners" appearing in America, the Poles, the Germans, and the Danes. While toward these Nordic races Garland's antagonism went no further than suspicious unease, toward darker-skinned peoples (the dusky red man as a native American, of course, excepted) he exhibited an overt hostility. Although he had written feelingly of a Negro slave, an abstractly conceived figure, in "Black Ephram," his description of Booker T. Washington reveals a curious quirk of rationalization: "He thinks as a white man thinks. He is not really a negro, black as he is." [35] The color of skins influenced Garland more deeply than he was prepared to admit.

August 1–August 8, Switzerland: "By contrast with the people of Venice the Swiss are a blessed relief." August 8–August 15, Paris: "I do not care if I never see it again." August 16–August 20, London: "The people of England seem very clean and neighborly after six weeks of Italy and France. I feel almost at home." August 20–August 23, rural England, Scotland and Wales. August 24, a ship from Liverpool and the end of "Jim Matteson's Old World Pasear," a manuscript which Garland's unsympathetic attitude toward his experiences almost inevitably made unsaleable. [36]

Back in Chicago on September 3 Garland turned to his work table. Unable to capitalize as he had planned upon the summer's travels he was constrained to salvage what scraps he might from previous writings. An introductory section added to the 1898 novelette *The Spirit of Sweetwater* gave it reissuance by Doubleday & Page under the title of *Witch's Gold*. The *Youth's Companion* serial on the Klondike was published by Harper & Brothers in the hope that it would be as good a juvenile seller as *Boy Life on the Prairie*. And Garland turned to the notes of his previous Colorado summer for two short tales, one the story of a child's death on the prairie, and the other a sketch of the Indian turned farmer. [37]

Colorado Springs provided the setting for his next novel, a study of the development of an unpolished Western girl who marries a wealthy saloon-keeper and gambler. Garland recorded the genesis of this story which he originally called "Mark Haney's Mate":

The chief characters of this novel were suggested to me by a young girl, the manager of a hotel in a little Colorado town, and her lover, a big Irish gambler I once observed in Cripple Creek. I had no talk

[35] *Ibid.*, p. 344.
[36] The itinerary dates are from the 1906 Notebook, the quotations from *Companions on the Trail*, pp. 305–309.
[37] "In That Far Land," *Circle Magazine*, II (October–November, 1907), 204–205, 298–300; "Red Plowman," *Craftsman*, XIII (November, 1907), 180–182; *Companions on the Trail*, pp. 275, 316–18.

with the girl, but as I watched her in her defensive warfare against the cattlemen, drummers, and miners who frequented the hotel, I wondered what would happen if Mark Haney of Cripple Creek should chance to lunch at the Golden Eagle Hotel. [38]

But Bertha of the Golden Eagle Hotel is not so clearly realized as had been Rose of Dutcher's Coolly, and her story, published serially and in book form by Harper's as *Money Magic*, is definitely inferior to Garland's early study of maturing girlhood. Some of Garland's dialogue might be indicative of his own changed attitudes toward women and toward society. "If I were a poor girl who wanted to earn a living in the world," asks Bertha as she contemplates leaving her aged, crippled husband, "what would you advise me to do?" "Get married!" replies her artist friend. "A woman *can* do other things, but marry she *must* if she is to fulfill her place in the world—and be happy." A change, this, from the feminism of a William Mason!

And on the theme which dominated the book, the power of money, Bertha—or Abner Joyce?—philosophizes:

She felt herself up-borne by money. Without Haney's bank-book she would have been merely one of those minute insects who timidly sought to cross the street, and yet philosophers marvel at the race men make for gold! So long as silken parasols and automobiles mad with pride are keenly enjoyed, so long will Americans—and all others who have them not—struggle for them; for they are not only the signs of distinction and luxury, they are delights. A private car is not merely display; it is comfort. To have a suite of rooms at the Park Palace is not all show; it makes for homely ease, cleanliness, repose. And these people riding imperiously to and fro in Fifth Avenue buy not merely diamonds, but well-cooked food, warm and shining raiment, and freedom from the scramble on the pave. [39]

Money Magic was indifferently received by the public. It lacked the stirring action and the magnificent descriptions of Garland's other "western novels," and so far had public attitudes changed since 1895, its treatment of sex and the extra-marital triangle not only did not shock the public but seemed in 1905

[38] *Companions on the Trail*, p. 311.
[39] *Money Magic* (1907), pp. 277, 237.

somewhat coy and old-fashioned. Be that as it may, the editorial taboos of the *Saturday Evening Post* restricted Garland's serialization to a bowdlerized first six chapters which ended demurely at the point of Bertha's betrothal. [40]

Although his writing lagged, Garland continued with unabated enthusiasm to promote various literary activities. During 1907 he agitated unceasingly for the formation in Chicago of a club to parallel the Players of New York, a caravanserai to shelter practitioners of all the arts and provide a field of cross-fertilization among writers, painters, sculptors and musicians. Fuller scoffed at the idea, but on June 13 a luncheon nucleus which included Taft, Browne, Robert Millikan, Herbert Stone, and Wallace Heckman, began the mechanics of organization. In the autumn the club was formed with Garland its first president. Although the name selected was "The Cliff Dwellers," in remembrance of Fuller's Chicago novel, the author of that work continued to fight shy of the project, refusing so much as to lunch with Garland at the new club.

The honor of the presidency brought Garland "something of the responsibility of a hotel-keeper as well as the duties of a lecture agent," but he welcomed the distractions and reported himself "more content in my Chicago residence than I have been for several years." [41]

The Cliff Dwellers and the Players continued to provide Garland with contacts with most of the important figures of his time. His notebooks were crammed with references to publishers, politicians, actors, and authors. The names of Orlénieff, Nazimova, Emerson Hough, Horace Lorimer, Edward Bok, Mrs. Humphrey Ward, Gutzon Borglum, Rex Beach, Walter Hampton, Thomas W. Higginson, Zona Gale, Frank Lloyd Wright, William Lyon Phelps, and scores of others of equal prominence, dance through the jottings on his pages, a treasure trove of anecdotal materials which he was later to mine to advantage. Now they were merely encounters incident to an active life.

Since the Garlands lived in modest circumstances the chair-

[40] *Saturday Evening Post,* CLXXVIII (November 18, 1905), 1–3, 27–32.
[41] *Companions on the Trail,* pp. 323–25, 352, 370–72; *A Daughter of the Middle Border,* p. 330.

manships of all these cultural affairs taxed Zulime's ingenuity to the utmost. Gamely she accompanied her husband to all the evening parties, arriving by public conveyance, "her silver brocade gown pinned up under the pony coat with safety pins, her party slippers in a black velvet bag. And when she came home, she would get down on her hands and knees and scrub the kitchen floor, looking," in the eyes of her daughter, "thoroughly regal both times." [42]

Zulime was a beautiful woman. Her aristocratic carriage set off an excellent figure. The masses of her light brown hair poised gracefully upon a slender neck. Her husband, who liked to be seen with lovely ladies, complained often of the iniquities of social intercourse which placed his ornamental wife at the right of the lion of the hour and left him squiring the lion's frump of a spouse. Manlike, Garland ignored the limitations of his wife's wardrobe. Once returning from a dinner he turned enthusiastically to Zulime, "Now take Mrs. Potter Palmer. She dresses the way I like to see a woman dress."

"What did she have on, dear? I didn't notice."

"Oh, just a simple black gown," replied Garland, "with a bunch of *passementerie* at the neck."

Zulime smiled. Mrs. Palmer's imported models and her latest sunburst diamond brooch had been copy for the fashion writers for weeks.

One such dinner resulted in a new commission for Garland. The talk turned upon the occult, and the author of *The Tyranny of the Dark* came in for general quizzing, in the course of which Garland related the substance of his many séances with "Mrs. Smiley." After dinner the host, John O'Hara Cosgrave, editor of *Everybody's Magazine,* suggested that the interest of his guests presaged a commensurate interest from his reader-audience in the subject. In the form of just such an after-dinner conversation as had transpired, Garland wrote for *Everybody's* a non-fictional account of "The Shadow World." [43] Harper's loyally accepted the

[42] Isabel Garland Lord to the author, August 25, 1956, and January 21, 1957.
[43] *Companions on the Trail,* p. 383; *Forty Years of Psychic Research,* pp. 149–51.

manuscript for book publication, but demurred at the size of advance which Garland requested:

Your *Shadow World* is a book so peculiar—it must either be a great go or only a moderate success. Don't you think it is a little hard to ask the publisher to take more of a gamble on this than on any other of your books? [44]

For *Everybody's* Garland served as judge for a contest among the readers for the best report of real life psychic occurrences. Introducing the prize winners Garland commented that "very few of the experiments were conducted systematically with careful notations at the time of the happenings," but concluded from the vast response to the competition that "this fund of evidence makes it certain that the human body is a much more complex and marvelous machine than any of us had hitherto imagined it to be, and it has given all its readers a profounder realization of the essential mystery of life." [45]

At a dinner of the National Institute of Arts and Letters that spring of 1908 Garland undertook a sorrowful task, the presentation of a memorial to his friend Edward MacDowell, who had died as Garland was engrossed with *The Shadow World*. Mac-Dowell's end had not been unexpected, for he had never recovered from a breakdown in 1905, when Garland had taken a room in the same New York apartment building as his friend in order to be near him in his illness. But the loss of such an intimate, however well prepared for, bore heavily upon Garland. He had already set in motion the wheels of organization for a MacDowell Memorial Club, and now turned with all his customary zeal for such undertakings to the promotion of this project, arranging concerts in Chicago and New York, and presenting obituary resolutions at meetings of musical organizations. [46]

Meanwhile another daughter, Constance, was born to the Garlands on June 18, 1908. A few of Garland's Western stories were published that year, and he worked in desultory fashion revising his old *Chap-Book* novelette "The Land of the Straddle-Bug"

[44] Fred Duneka to Garland, April 28, 1908, Garland Papers.
[45] "The 'Shadow World' Prize Winners," *Everybody's Magazine*, XIX (November, 1908), 665–79.
[46] *Companions on the Trail*, pp. 376–81, and *passim*.

for book publication, and made an unsatisfactory attempt at playwriting. [47]

Of the slump in creative activity during these years Garland could write objectively a decade later:

My convictions concerning my literary mission were in process of disintegration. My children, my manifold duties as theatrical up-lifter, and club promoter, together with a swift letting down of my mental and physical powers, caused me to question the value of all my writing. I went so far as to say, "As a writer I have failed. Perhaps I can be of service as a citizen," with my Oklahoma farms bringing in a small annual income, the scrape of my pen became a weariness. . . . Altogether and inevitably my work as a fictionist sank into an unimportant place. I was on the down-grade, that was evident. Writing was a tiresome habit. I was in a rut and longed to get out—to be forced out. [48]

[47] "The Healer of Mogalyon," *Circle Magazine,* III (March, 1908), 140–45; "The Outlaw and the Girl," *Ladies' Home Journal,* XXV (May–July, 1908); "A Night Raid at Eagle River," *Century,* LXXVI (September, 1908), 725–34; "The Land of the Straddle-Bug" was published in 1909 by Harper & Brothers as *Moccasin Ranch.*

[48] *A Daughter of the Middle Border,* pp. 331–32.

❧ 12 ❧

The Sunset Edition

THE YEARS 1909 and 1910 afforded Garland opportunity of further consolidating his literary properties. The contract which he had made with Macmillan & Company in 1899 expired on January 23, 1909. According to its provisions Garland was allowed to purchase the plates of five of his volumes at one-half their cost, together with any unsold volumes or sheets. Promptly upon expiration of this contract Garland turned to Harper & Brothers these five titles: *Main-Travelled Roads, Prairie Folks, Rose of Dutcher's Coolly, Boy Life on the Prairie,* and *The Trail of the Goldseekers.* These volumes and five earlier works upon which publication rights had lapsed—*A Little Norsk, A Spoil of Office, Jason Edwards, Wayside Courtships,* and *The Eagle's Heart*— were transferred to Harper's on February 15, 1909. [1] In the seven years that Garland had been with Harper's that firm had published another seven of his titles as first editions.

[1] Contracts, Macmillan & Company and Garland, January 23, 1909, Harper & Brothers and Garland, February 15, 1909, Garland Papers.

Now in 1909 eight volumes were culled from this list to make up a collected Garland edition. From the older works were selected *Main-Travelled Roads, Prairie Folks, Rose of Dutcher's Coolly,* and *The Eagle's Heart;* from the more recent novels, *The Captain of the Gray-Horse Troop, Hesper, Money Magic,* and *The Tyranny of the Dark.* To encourage Harper's in setting up this edition Garland substituted for his royalty of 20 per cent on individual volumes a mere fifty cents per set on the eight-volume edition. As a collective title Garland suggested—in what can only have been a *lapsus linguae*—"The Corn Edition." [2] Probably a fondness for the cornstalk design on the spine and cover of the Stone & Kimball books provoked this egregious boner. Naturally Harper's overruled the suggestion, but their choice of "Sunset Edition" had its own unfortunate connotations, sounding as it did a valedictory note for a writer who had not yet passed his fiftieth birthday.

As though to disprove the suggestion that he was on the sunset trail Garland immediately turned to write with something of his old verve a novel based on the life of a forest ranger. Conservation of natural resources was a "sociological" theme for which he had great enthusiasm. His contacts with Theodore Roosevelt and Gifford Pinchot provided a wealth of authentic material on the Forest Service. And for background he had his intimate knowledge of the mountain West:

The actual composition of *Cavanaugh* began as I was riding the glorious trails around Cloud Peak in the Big Horn Mountains of northern Wyoming in the summer of 1908, one of the most beautiful of all my outings, for while the Big Horns are low and tame compared to the Wind River Range, yet the play of their lights and shadows, their clouds, and their mist was as romantic as anything I had ever encountered.

I recall riding alone down the eastern slope one afternoon, while prodigious rivers of clouds—white as wool and soundless as light—descended the canyon on my right and spread above the foothills, forming a level sea out of which the high dark peaks rose like rocky islands. This flood came so swiftly, flowed so marvelously and enveloped my world so silently that the granite ledges appeared to melt beneath my horse's feet.

[2] Memorandum in Garland's handwriting on latter contract.

"To get into my story some part of this glory, my hero must be something of a nature lover—as many rangers are," I argued, and this was true. Before a man will consent to ride the lonely road which leads to his cabin high in the forest, he must not only have a heart which thrills to the wonder of the lonely places, he must be self-sufficing and fearless. I rode with several such men and out of my experiences with them I composed the character of *Ross Cavanaugh*.

Thus Garland describes his original enthusiasm for the novel, one-half of which was written in a six-weeks period during the spring of 1909. Revision was not so exciting:

Practically all of the spring months of 1910 were given to revising and proof-reading *Cavanaugh, Forest Ranger,* which had genuinely interested me and which should have been as important in my scheme of delineating the West as *The Captain of the Gray-Horse Troop,* but it wasn't. It was too controversial, and besides I did not give it time enough. I should have taken another year to it—but I didn't. I permitted myself to be hurried by Duneka, who was (like most publishers) enslaved to a program. [3]

Indeed, *Cavanaugh,* for all its deeply sensitive rendering of the beauties of the wilderness, is obviously a pot-boiler. The exponent of veritism had once vehemently protested the devices of the romancers, insisting that men who had been killed stay dead instead of turning up conveniently to further the plot, and that characters neither die nor marry in the end of a novel but "walk over the hill." Now he perpetrated the same stale tricks himself, producing from the grave a supposedly dead father, then killing him off conveniently in the end, converting the supposed mother of his heroine into a stepmother in the denouement, and describing his reunited hero and heroine as "entering the New West together."

It is small wonder that Howells, though commenting kindly on the novel, allowed himself a note of reproof:

One day, I hope you will revert to the temper of your first work, and give us a picture of the wild life you know so well on the lines of *Main-Travelled Roads.* You have in you greater things than you have done, and you owe the world which has welcomed you the best you

[3] *A Daughter of the Middle Border* (1921), pp. 344–45, 347.

have in you. "Be true to the dream of thy youth"—the dream of an absolute and inspiring "veritism;" the world is yours. [4]

Harper & Brothers evidently shared in Howells' desire for a reversion to Garland's earlier style. In 1910 they reissued a group of stories culled from *Prairie Folks* and *Wayside Courtships,* under the title of *Other Main-Travelled Roads.* But Garland seemed unable to follow the lead of his critics and his publisher. His mind was turned not toward the border land of his early successes but toward the borderland of the unknown. [5]

Publication of *The Tyranny of the Dark* had brought Garland back into active participation in psychic research. One day in 1907 he met a woman who was reputed to be a medium of the highest powers. This "Mrs. Hartley" congratulated him on the authenticity of his novel, saying "You couldn't have kept closer to the story of my life as a girl if you had taken it down in shorthand." She refused to give Garland a sitting in Chicago, explaining that as a widow and the mother of a twelve-year-old son she was careful to avoid public sitting and newspaper notoriety. The following year, however, when Garland was in Indianapolis, Mary Jameson Judah, the aunt of Booth Tarkington and an old friend of Garland's, arranged a sitting with Mrs. Hartley, whom she frequently patronized. Before attending, Garland dropped by the University Club and wrote a note: "Edward, write a few bars from one of your unpublished manuscripts to establish your identity, and for M's sake."

The Edward of this epistle into the unknown was Edward Mac-Dowell, who had but recently died, and the "M" represented Marian, his grief-stricken widow. At the séance, Garland was impressed by the fact that the medium worked in full light, and produced messages upon folded slates within his own grasp. At her request he wrote several names upon a piece of paper, including that of Edward MacDowell, this time pencilling a request for a few bars of his *Tragic Sonata* as identification. Although Garland retained possession of this paper, the slates subsequently produced messages signed "E. A. McDowell" and some musical

[4] W. D. Howells to Garland, March 27, 1910, Garland Papers; *Life in Letters of William Dean Howells,* II, 282.

[5] Garland's account of his psychic experiments at this time occurs in *Forty Years of Psychic Research* (1936), pp. 194–256.

notations. In later séances more musical sketches appeared, signed "E. A.," a factor which puzzled Garland, as he had never known his friend to use his initials alone nor the contracted spelling of his surname.

At length Garland wrote Fuller an urgent message to come and use his musical training in interpreting the events which were occurring nightly in Mrs. Hartley's home. When Fuller had joined the group the ghostly "composer," speaking through Mrs. Hartley, dictated additional compositions, and conversed with Garland in phrases characteristic of MacDowell. All the observers were convinced that the results were beyond the possibilities of trickery or ventriloquism. But to attribute them to thought-transference raised additional problems, for the psychic was unversed in musical notation, and the dictated melody was beyond Fuller's powers of composition. Indeed he found it difficult to play.

Fuller and I walked away fairly stunned by the significance of this beautiful test. "If this melody, so like MacDowell, can be found among his manuscripts, it will be a marvelous case of mind reading. Either MacDowell knows it or the psychic is able to take it from the manuscript," I said. [6]

Later, Mrs. Hartley was persuaded to hold other séances. To rule out the possibility of physical pre-arrangements the sittings were held in the Judah home. The psychic took her seat at a small table in a bay window with the sun shining directly upon her, and in this position produced writing upon closed slates, four being written upon simultaneously, according to Garland's notes. There were messages for all the sitters including more material from "E. A."

Neither Fuller nor I was a man of science, but we were in our prime and were keen observers. In addition to my realistic habit, I had been educated by seventeen years in psychic research. Judah, a lawyer, while of theosophic trend of thought, was a business man, humorous and clearsighted, and Mrs. Judah, too, though predisposed to believe in these phenomena for the reason that psychic power had discovered itself in her family, was a realist. We all agreed that these tests were evidential. "A singular power resides in Mrs. Hartley." [7]

[6] *Ibid.*, p. 225.   [7] *Ibid.*, p. 236.

Thus did Garland sum up his uncanny experiences in a book on psychic phenomena published some eighteen years later. Upon their return to Chicago Garland and Fuller analyzed the score of their ghostly composer, finding in it many of the technical devices employed by MacDowell in his published works. Fuller, who was familiar with the MacDowell scores, was unwilling to rule out the possibility of thought-transference from his subconscious mind to that of the psychic. But he was forced to agree with Garland that, given this hypothesis, the process of communication by slate writing was inexplicable.

When Garland took the slates and the other records of the sittings to Marian MacDowell in New York the bubble of identification burst. For Mrs. MacDowell was emphatic that the musical score called "Ungarie" by the "spirit-composer" was not among MacDowell's manuscripts, nor did a message to recover a manuscript from the publisher Schubert have any validity. Schubert denied the existence of any such manuscript. The widow, however, started in surprise at a signature on one of the slates "Edward McDowell," identifying it by the spelling and by its peculiar flourishes as an old form her husband had used years before in Leipzig. The enigma was resolved into a simpler problem by Garland's discovery upon the walls of the studio a framed letter relating to the Leipzig period, bearing the exact signature reproduced on the slates, a letter which he must often have observed in the MacDowell home.

That these experiments, however inconclusive, produced a deep effect upon Garland is evidenced by the tone of his next novel. In *Victor Olnee's Discipline*—which is essentially the story of Mrs. Hartley and her son—Garland seems deliberately to have followed the advice of William Stead, who had asked him to write a sequel to *The Tyranny of the Dark,* when his "ideas were a little clearer on the subject," the implication of clarification, of course, being that of more definite commitment to the spiritualist position. It is obvious that the author of *Victor Olnee's Discipline,* while yet the skeptic as to the hypothesis of survival, is firmly convinced of the "supernatural" quality of psychic experiences. But the experiments, which in Garland's later factual account carry a certain amount of conviction, in fictional form seem the wildest of romancing. The novel was both a commercial and a critical failure. Like *The Shadow World* of a few years before, *Victor Olnee's Discipline* was roundly damned by the reviewers as "spiritualistic propaganda." [8] The failure was so complete that Garland in his 1921 autobiography completely omits the episode.

Discouraged, Garland continued to reiterate to Fuller and to Howells that he was through with fiction, was tired of writing love stories. Howells gently pointed out to him that novels need not necessarily be love stories. [9] There the matter rested as Garland continued to occupy his time with work for the Cliff Dwellers and for the Theatre Society of Chicago, an organization which had developed from Donald Robertson's "Players," and of which Garland became secretary. This club, formed to present plays of literary quality which lacked the box-office appeal to attract commercial producers, failed to find the backing necessary for an endowed theater, and the project was short-lived. [10]

Meanwhile Garland, through an article in *Current Literature*, had "discovered" Vachel Lindsay. [11] A subscription to *The Village Magazine*, which Lindsay was sending out from Springfield, Illinois, brought a whimsical reply: "I am honored indeed that you should inquire about my humble plans. It is a little flustrating to admit that I have none in especial ('Come, eat the bread of idleness, said Mister Moon to me.') What I produce, if I may say so, is not a definite plan, but *yeast*—if it is anything. The other man, once leavened, must produce the plan and do the work. In short, brother Garland, I am an inert gentleman who makes a loud noise."

The format of *The Village Magazine* excited Garland. "It was

---

[8] *Literary Digest*, XLIII (November 4, 1911), 808. For other reviews see *Independent*, LXXI (December 7, 1911), 1265; *Nation*, XCIII (November 9, 1911), 445; *New York Times*, October 15, 1911; for reviews of *The Shadow World*, see *Independent*, LXV (November 26, 1908), 1245; *Outlook*, XC (November 28, 1908), 90; *New York Times*, October 24, 1908.

[9] *A Daughter of the Middle Border*, p. 347; W. D. Howells to Garland, July 2, 1912, Garland Papers.

[10] See the *Dial*, XLIII (October 16, 1907), 237–39 and XLIV (May 16 1908), 293–95. The Robertson Players produced in February, 1909, a play of Garland's, "The Miller of Boskobell," dealing with the conflict between capital and labor (*Bulletin*, Chicago Art Institute, II [April, 1909], 56).

[11] This discovery is described in *Companions on the Trail* (1931), pp. 462–471.

a large, square paper-bound volume filled with handmade script which was almost illegible by reason of its minute characters but as beautiful in its way as a medieval manuscript." The effect, Garland told Fuller, was "at once medieval and modern and slightly mad." Nothing so novel had appeared in the Middle West since the days of the *Chap-Book*. Garland at once extended an invitation to Lindsay to bring his message of regionalism to the Cliff Dwellers. Lindsay agreed exuberantly: "I was an art student, you know, in the Art Institute from 1900 to 1903 and recognition from that quarter is just like being able to please one's cousins and aunts. At that time I read Mr. Fuller's books and was able, I thought, to identify a good many of the characters in 'Under the Skylights.' It is like taking up a half-read poem after many years to have contact with Mr. Fuller, Mr. Garland, and the rest."

Already Vachel Lindsay was a pronounced individualist, and his address at the Cliff Dwellers' had a mixed reception. As he vehemently urged the artist not to run away to some art colony but to stay in his home town and help elevate it, his arguments, Garland reported, "failed in grace rather than in logic." Convinced that he had met a genuine example of genius, Garland stopped in on his next visit to Springfield to urge upon Lindsay's parents an appreciation of their son's abilities. In later years Garland lost enthusiasm for Lindsay's "bizarre posturings and experimentation," his "platform show pieces." Indeed, as with others of Garland's "discoveries," it was the element of untutored genius which appealed to him in 1911 rather than an objective appreciation of Lindsay's work. In more self-conscious fashion eighteenth-century litterateurs, pursuing theories of primitivism, had sought out their minor Burnses and Ossians. The later-day regionalists seem often to have been influenced by an unconscious primitivism in some of their literary judgments. Garland's original enthusiasm for such writers as Crane and Lindsay, so soon rescinded as their work became recognized, may be a case in point.

Not even the appearance of a Lindsay upon the western horizon, however, could convince Garland that Chicago and its environs would ever attain its earlier promise of becoming a literary center. More and more he yearned toward the cosmopolitanism of New York. Yet, when a fire partially destroyed the Homestead in October, 1912, the ties of sentiment were too strong for him to accept this as an intervention of Fate nudging him toward a break with the Middle West. As he brooded over the charred wreckage of his home, visualizing the mellow charm it had possessed, with its accumulated souvenirs of a lifetime, Indian rugs, pictures by artist friends, autographed books, he was torn with grief:

I thought of it as it had been the night before, with the soft lights of the candles falling upon my children dancing with swinging lanterns. I recalled Enneking's radiant spring painting, and Steele's "Bloom of the Grape," which glowed above the mantle, and my heart almost failed me—"Is this the end of my life in Wisconsin?"

For twenty years this little village had been the place of my family altar, not because it was remarkable in any way, but because since 1850 it had been the habitat of my mother's people and because it was filled with my father's pioneer friends. "Is it worth while to rebuild?" I asked myself. For the time I lost direction. I had no plan.

The sight of my white-haired father wandering about the yard, dazed, bewildered, his eyes filled with a look of despair, at last decided me. Realizing that this was his true home; that no other roof could have the same appeal, and he could not be transplanted, I resolved to cover his head; to make it possible for him to live out his few remaining years under this roof with his granddaughters. [12]

The Homestead—with a new fireproof metal roof—was restored in time for the traditional Thanksgiving family reunion. But as Garland re-established himself in his old rooms he was weary and disillusioned. In the entire year of 1912 he had published only one small snippet, the running text for a pictorial essay in *Country Life* on "Middle West—the Heart of the Country." [13]

His file of unpublished manuscripts had been scraped close to the bottom. And what new material he produced was unacceptable to the established magazines. But to *Sunset,* the struggling Pacific Coast journal, he turned several items, an *outré* story of the supernatural, an article on Joaquin Miller, and a sketch of "Tall Ed Kelly," a character evolved from one of the

[12] *A Daughter of the Middle Border,* p. 361.
[13] *Country Life in America,* XXII (September 15, 1912), 19–24, 44.

Rangers who had furnished material for *Cavanaugh*. To the *Craftsman* went an article on "The New Chicago." This was the total of Garland's publications in 1913. [14]

His literary career seemed to be approaching a dead end. With depressing unanimity the critics had disparaged his recent fictional attempts. The result had been a paralysis of Garland's creative facilities. Physically ill and mentally weary, he was unable to summon the energy to block out new materials. His writing hours were spent in futile attempts to recompose the story of Sitting Bull, which he now entitled "The Silent Eaters," and in tinkering with the autobiographical manuscript which he had begun in the far-off days in the Library of Congress when he was completing the Grant volume. In this latter project he was following the advice of friends and critics. Howells and others kept wistfully calling for a repetition of the theme of *Main-Travelled Roads*. And ironically enough the same corps of reviewers who in the eighties had rejected his Middle Western stories now cheered the same materials reprinted in the twentieth century. *Moccasin Ranch,* which had gone almost unnoticed in its *Chap-Book* version, had been jubilantly hailed by the *New York Times* in 1900: "Mr. Garland has written longer and more important novels than this, but he has written nothing finer or more powerful in its presentation of human passions or more beautiful in style."[15] *Other Main-Travelled Roads* met with wide approval, although the critics felt compelled to compare it unfavorably with its 1891 predecessor. "Most of the stories, however, lack the force and convincing truthfulness of the earlier volume, though they are, as a whole, superior to the author's later work." [16] They are "a second gleaning from that early field. Three or four of them might well have deserved to be added to the half-dozen which made up the original volume." [17]

Garland, privately aware that the composition of many of the stories of his recent volume had been simultaneous with, or even

[14] "Nugget," *Sunset,* XXX (April, 1913), 335–42; "Poet of the Sierras," *ibid.,* XXX (June, 1913), 765–70; "Kelly Afoot," *ibid.,* XXXI (November, 1913), 919–26; "The New Chicago," *Craftsman,* XXIV (September, 1913), 555–65.

[15] *New York Times,* XIV (October 16, 1900), 611.

[16] *A.L.A. Booklist,* VII (November, 1910), 127.

[17] *Nation,* XCI (October 27, 1910), 39.

antecedent to, the stories of the 1891 volume, must have been puzzled by this persistent distinction. Indeed, "A Prairie Heroine" had been omitted from *Main-Travelled Roads* because of its controversial aspects. It had thus missed being damned, along with Garland's other output, in the 1890's. Now in 1910 it missed out on the acclaim accorded those "little classics of Middle Western literature," [18] and must take inferior ranking as part of the "second gleaning."

Probably feeling a good deal like the man with the boy and the donkey of Aesop's fable, Garland could get little constructive help from the advice of the reviewers, nor from those friends who continually urged him to repeat the work of *Main-Travelled Roads*. For those stories had been told, those roads travelled, those fields harvested. After the "second gleaning" there could remain to be garnered only stray straws of reminiscence. Yet Garland's writer's instinct agreed that somewhere within those fields of his memories was fertile soil, capable of maturing another harvest. Month after month he worked over his tattered manuscripts, revising and changing, destroying and reconstructing, writing and rewriting, until his desk was a jumble of untidy screeds.

It was a frustrating and unproductive labor from which he was only too willing to escape to more extroverted activities. The Progressive campaign for Roosevelt absorbed a great deal of his time and energies, and when the political excitement died down there was the fanfare of the meeting of the National Institute in Chicago. Garland, as president of the Cliff Dwellers, had charge of arrangements for the entertainment of the Eastern guests, obligations which he discharged fulsomely and with gusto. At the November, 1912, meeting he was in his element as representative host to old friends and visiting dignitaries at what was described as "the most successful session the Institute had ever had." [19]

In circulation at the time of the meeting was a generous word of commendation from Howells in the form of a *North American Review* article on "Mr. Garland's Books," a most timely reinforcement of the younger writer's faltering morale. Tracing the

[18] *Nation,* **XCIX** (February 26, 1914), 210, reviewing *The Forester's Daughter.*
[19] *Companions on the Trail,* pp. 505–525.

history of their long friendship and literary relations Howells praised the group of novels comprised by *Rose of Dutcher's Coolly, The Eagle's Heart, Hesper, The Captain of the Gray-Horse Troop, Money Magic,* and *Cavanaugh.* Eliminating from his discussion the psychic novels, and making his customary ambiguous reservations as to Garland's treatment of sexual motifs, Howells nonetheless defended in public what he had sometimes deplored in private, Garland's expansion of his subject matter. The fickle goddess of inspiration, said Howells, "seems to have known what she was about in guiding his talent from West to Farther West, from the farms to the wilds, and liberating it to the freer and bolder adventure which he must always have loved." Howells' choice of Garland's later work was *Money Magic,* "possibly the most masterly of the author's books. More than any other since the stories of *The Main-Travelled Roads,* it expresses constancy to his old young ideal of veritism." [20] It might be suggested that *Money Magic* appealed to Howells by reason of the similarity of its social themes to his own writings.

From this peak of conviviality and acclaim Garland descended into the Slough of Despond. His autobiographical manuscript was rejected again and again. Such friends as Fuller and Bacheller continued to encourage him in his efforts, however, and again he returned to his interminable recastings and revisions.

The entire material with which he worked was a bit shopworn, the oft-handled memories of his prairie youth. The nucleus was his first published series, the long-ago *American* sketches of the seasonal cycle of farm activities, then treated in the leisurely impersonal style of the contemplative essay. In 1898 he had revived these reminiscences, dictating hastily before leaving for the Klondike the story of "Grant McLeod." In 1899 he had reworked this manuscript into fictional form as the story of a frontier youngster Lincoln Stewart, and published it as *Boy Life on the Prairie* in his Macmillan debut. Something was gained by way of continuity in this second published version, but something lost of the freshness of the original by the artifice of the fictional form. Nonetheless, *Boy Life on the Prairie* had been a charming tale, and a successful venture. Garland now hoped to repeat that success on a

[20] *North American Review,* CXCVI (October, 1912), 423–28.

larger scale. But the form in which to cast his expanded version eluded him, and the advice of friends and editors was contradictory and confusing.

When the manuscript had grown to 100,000 words Garland submitted it to Harper's. Major Leigh recoiled from its autobiographical character, convinced that the public would take it as Garland's " 'swan song' as a novelist." Garland discussed this aspect with Howells, [21] revised the manuscript further, and six months later submitted it to the *Ladies' Home Journal*, which had published so many of his reminiscent sketches.

Edward Bok wrote him sympathetically in December of 1912:

> I have read the manuscript, and well as I know you I confess that I had no idea of the story that you have lived through. . . . But as a book I cannot see it. I think your belief in realism has led you to go too much into details. . . . I cannot get away from the intimate quality of it all, and on that ground I shouldn't like to see it published. [22]

Bok's further suggestion was that the story be recast in the third person as a small book on "A Prairie Boyhood," with another and smaller book developed on "A Prairie Mother." Not wishing his judgment to be final he passed the manuscript on to Horace Lorimer. Lorimer likewise rejected it.

Sterling Yard, Gilder's successor as editor of the *Century*, kindly refused the manuscript. [23] Edward Wheeler, editor of *Current Opinion*, at Garland's instance read another version and was quite encouraging:

> I have just finished the "Son of the Border West," and I have had a jolly good time reading it. To me it is very interesting, and I think it will be to a great many others. It has historical value as well as personal interest, for it presents vividly an important era that has disappeared forever, not only from American life, but from the world. It is not so romantic an epoch as Bret Harte and others have put into literature, but it is far more representative. I don't know of another book where one gets such a convincing view of that life.
>
> I was a little disturbed at first by your method. The constant change from the first person to the third and back again interfered with my pleasure. This annoyance wore away and disappeared after a time,

---

[21] Garland to W. D. Howells, June 29, 1912, Garland Papers.
[22] Edward Bok to Garland, December 12, 1912, Garland Papers.
[23] *Companions on the Trail*, p. 516.

but I think it is going to be a handicap to the book. I hardly think it can prove a serious handicap, and I would not feel like advising a change, for I can see the reasons that led you to adopt this method. Yet, I am not sure that the first person throughout would not be best. There is a slight trickiness in the present method which would be all right in a romance, but is not quite in harmony with a work the great value of which is its convincing verity.

I can see why you shrink from the straight autobiographical form, and perhaps your instinct is right. I am not quite in the same position as other readers would be, for I knew at once (partly from your letter, partly from my personal knowledge of you) that it was autobiography and not fiction, and the little subterfuge was therefore very transparent. To others it might not be so. [24]

On the strength of this advice Garland laboriously recast his entire manuscript in the third person in the hope of making it impersonal and of emphasizing its historical content. Again he submitted it to Harper's. Duneka suggested that his firm might publish it, but only on speculation, without any advance royalty: "In all our talks about 'The Middle Border,' and in some of your letters, you voiced your own belief (and ours) that the book would never sell in paying quantities, and that we might even be out of pocket on the venture." Since such a halfhearted acceptance was insufficient for Garland, Duneka a few days later courteously released any claim to Garland's work: "If you can sell 'The Middle Border' or your short stories at better rates and under better conditions, why good luck to you and God go with you." [25]

But no other publisher was interested in "The Sons of the Middle Border," and Garland's dejection deepened. In January of 1914 he started East again, stopping off to lecture in Pittsburgh, where he missed his scheduled train. "Pittsburg, January 17, Midnight," he headed the entry in his journal:

My lecture, delivered in the dining room of the club was a failure. ... I am writing this in my room at the University Club to which I returned for the night with a feeling that my whole trip is doomed to failure.

[24] *Ibid.*, pp. 519–20.
[25] F. A. Duneka to Garland, April 14 and April 18, 1913, Garland Papers.

I was strongly minded, while at the station, to give up my trip to New York. I thought of taking the train back to Chicago, but my trunk was already on its way to the East. With no expectation of selling any of my manuscripts I shall go on to-morrow morning and have another talk with Duneka.

In New York Duneka was still unenthusiastic about Garland's autobiography, but suggested *Collier's* as a possible market. Feeling, as he said, "like a squeezed orange" which had been cast aside, Garland delivered his manuscript to Mark Sullivan at Collier's, who promised it a quick reading. Garland was inclined to put small faith in this prospect. [26] A meeting of the Authors' League deepened his depression:

As I meet the men who are the chief purveyors in present-day book and magazine markets, I am more and more impressed with the ephemeral character of their output. They are for the most part opportunists; their talk is concerned almost wholly with the question of pay. Seldom do I hear a word concerning the nobility of the writers' craft. Thirty years ago, when I began to write, rewards were small and authorship less of a trade.

Another and still more disturbing change is in process. New York is becoming each year more European, more antagonistic to what certain of its writers call "New England Puritanism." Month by month these critics, contemptuous of "the American tradition," join in celebrating the novelists and dramatists who sound the sexual note most insistently. A claque for the pornographic has developed. It is becoming fashionable to sneer at marriage, chastity, home life, and the church, and to bring into the dining room the phrases and jokes of the roadhouse. Certain so-called philosophers openly advocate the morals of the barnyard in their essays on "freedom" and their attacks on "the puritanical ideal." Others, however, have achieved a success by the cheap and easy device of putting into print the stories and phrases of the saloon and the brothel. This is the most disturbing phase of the whole situation. Young writers, perceiving that the pornographic experts are the highest paid men and women in the field of authorship, are led to write their confessions and voice their defiances.

[26] Garland describes his efforts to market his manuscripts on this trip in *Companions on the Trail*, pp. 527–37.

In a few days Garland's outlook brightened. In quick succession Mark Sullivan commissioned a cutting of six installments from the Middle Border narrative, and accepted for *Collier's* a story of "Tall Ed Kelly." Yard of the *Century* purchased an article on James A. Herne. "I am returning to Chicago," chortled Garland, "four thousand dollars richer than when I left home a month ago."

❧ 13 ❧

A Son of the Middle Border

THE MARCH 28, 1914, issue of *Collier's* carried a cover illustration of a soldier in G. A. R. uniform leaning against a fence rail, and in display type announced "A Son of the Middle Border" by Hamlin Garland. The serial version which had at last evolved from the jumble of interlined manuscript and clipped and pasted typescript must have seemed a familiar story to purchasers of Garland's "Sunset Edition." For the narrator was "Lincoln Stewart" of *Boy Life on the Prairie,* and the events which he described followed the general outline of those of the juvenile volume. Moreover, many of the incidents related had appeared elsewhere in Garland's short stories, the first installment of "A Son of the Middle Border" being merely a slightly altered version of "The Return of a Private."

The series [1] carried the subtitle "A Personal Record," and opened with this ambiguous explanation:

[1] *Collier's* LIII (March 28, April 18, May 9, June 27, August 8, 1914).

In writing this story I have not only had the advantage of a some-what similar life in the West, I have also enjoyed the use of a volumi-nous mass of manuscripts called "An Abandoned Autobiography," from which at critical points I have freely quoted. In this way I have been able to retain something of that intimate quality of utterance which comes from the first-hand narration, while indulging myself in the historian's privilege of arrangement and comment.

Stewart's notes, and especially certain of his letters, have been of very great services in all that portion of the manuscript which deals with the vague world of childhood and the almost equally mystical region of early youth.

"It is now over a quarter of a century," he states in his foreword, "since I began to write of the West, and here (midway on the trail) I am moved to pause and look back on the long, hard road over which I have trudged, eager to make a final record of my joys before they escape me, and in order that I may preserve to my children some few of the intimate details of a life which is already passing if not com-pletely vanished.

"And yet, as a conscientious historian, I must warn the reader against believing that this writing contains the whole truth about an author. It is not even the whole truth about a man. It is indeed the study of a family and of an epoch. The Middle Border as herein depicted is not the West as others saw it, but as Lincoln Stewart saw it, and the pictures drawn are truthful only in the sense that they present conditions as he remembers them and contain characters as they appeared to his youthful eyes. Even when most precise the narrative is not exact and certainly no man writes of himself without restraint."

In the spirit of Lincoln Stewart's own philosophy I have made use of the materials at my disposal.

                                                            Hamlin Garland.

Garland's characterization of his hypothetical source as an author, and of that sparse variety, the Western author, his use of actual place names associated with the Garland family, the con-stant echoing of his earlier writings, all make the claim to be editing another's reminiscences a most transparent subterfuge. But, ostrich-like, he continued throughout the series to burrow deeper into the sands of anonymity.

The narrative opened in this fashion: "In beginning this story of Lincoln Stewart, I am almost wholly dependent upon the man's own words in order to account for his boyhood." It progressed in a series of jerky passages introduced by such phrases as, "Lincoln says of it," "Lincoln remarks of this." The result is monologue, not dialogue, recorded in a style approximating that of a newspaper interview. Only when Garland forgot his devices of concealment and threw long columns of descriptive matter into quotation marks does the narrative capture the charm of personal reminiscence. But in these passages the flavor of the prairie world, its sun-drenched landscapes, the wind in the wheat, the booming of the prairie cock and chirp of meadow lark, are projected with the emotional impact which had characterized Garland's earliest writing.

Doggedly he worked into his awkward mélange the set-pieces of his memory's recall. " 'Saturday night on the farm!' exclaims Lincoln. 'How it all comes back! I see a whisky-mad Wappsipinicon farmer walking barefoot up the middle of the street defying the world.' "—" 'As I hobbled to the barn,' explains Lincoln, 'The sinews of my legs seemed shortened.' " It was such detail which Duneka had complained was carrying realism to the extreme, which in the first person had shocked Bok as being overly intimate. In the third-person *Collier's* version which followed their suggestions, the realism is blurred, the intimacy veiled, but the result can scarcely be called a happy one.

In April appeared the second installment "Following the Sunset." In May, "Woods and Prairie Lands." In June, "The Passing of the Prairie." Into these sections Garland had worked most of the materials from his original series in the *American Magazine,* descriptions of plowing, threshing, haying, and of wildlife, and had brought his hero Lincoln Stewart up to the point of the family's removal to the town. These quiet reminiscent sketches contrasted oddly with the other materials currently appearing in *Collier's,* political articles and on-the-spot coverage of the uprisings in Mexico. "Woods and Prairie Lands" was followed by Jack London reporting on "The Red Game of War." "The Passing of the Prairie" was preceded by an article on "Our Adventures in Tampico," in which the correspondent described an oil boom which "out-Klondiked the Klondike." As once before in Garland's literary career tumultuous events south of the border had crowded from *McClure's* his historical study of Grant, now the Huerta revolution drew the public's attention from the so-

cial history of post-Civil War days which he was publishing in
Collier's.

After a lapse of six weeks Chapter V of his serial appeared,
"Lincoln Enters Hostile Territory," describing the first year
of Seminary life. Despite the announcement that the next installment "Golden Days at the Seminary" would appear in an
early issue, the series was abandoned at this point, unable to compete with the news of the assassination of an archduke. Garland
wrote his wife on May 18 from the Players:

> The blow has fallen! Sullivan has decided against the additional
> papers. This is not bad for I got $3,300, for the eight chapters, and
> have a chance to sell the four chapters for a thousand more. I am
> touching up the moving picture business also and must stay till I
> make a trial of that. I am taking part of the M. S. to the *Century* this
> afternoon. Also I am going to see the American and *Scribners*. [2]

But the round of editors was fruitless. No one at this juncture
was interested in the Middle Border story.

It is difficult to conceive, in any event, how Garland could have
carried his awkward disguise much farther. He had thrown into
the words of Lincoln Stewart his own recollections of "the vague
world of childhood and the almost equally mystical region of
early youth," but the events of his manhood would inevitably
have burst through this device of anonymity. Mark Sullivan was
aware of the corner into which his author had written himself
and was wise in abandoning the series. In later years, however,
he encouraged Garland to continue his reminiscences, but in
their original first-person form.

The *Collier's* publication, inconclusive though it was, had
been a partial justification of Garland's long labors, and a financial boost at a time most opportune. Few read this "personal
record," if the lack of comments in Garland's correspondence is
any indication. But his daughter Mary Isabel was delighted to
see in print the familiar bedtime stories of her childhood, and
the entire narrative was a personal triumph to aging Richard
Garland. Of his son's characterization of "Duncan Stewart" as a

² Garland to Zulime Garland, May 18 [?], courtesy of Constance Garland
Doyle.

strict family disciplinarian, he commented half-proudly: "Aren't you a little hard on me?"

The old soldier was unaware of the series' interruption, for, in Garland's sentimental phrase, he was "mustered out" during the second month of World War I. [3] His death broke the last tie with the Valley of the Neshonoc, and Garland, spending more and more of his time in the East, resolved to abandon Chicago and the Middle West, and establish his family again in New York. Harper's had just published the last of his novels, *The Forester's Daughter,* which brought the usual complaints from critics: "It is hard to believe that this story comes from the same hand that once gave us a book of real strength 'Rose of Dutcher's Cooley'." [4] *Collier's* continued to use his novelettes of the West, and Harper's had agreed to publish a book of Western short stories. But the fact which convinced Garland that an upturn in his fortunes was at hand was the interest of some of the infant moving picture companies in his Western materials.

One day in February, 1916, Wilfrid North, an actor and an old friend of Franklin Garland, was seated next to Hamlin at the Players. He revealed that he was employed by the Vitagraph Company, a concern making pictures in Brooklyn, and invited the author to visit their studios. There Garland met Stuart Blackton, the president of the company, and Colonel Brady, its scenario director. The latter knew Garland's books and suggested further meetings to explore the idea of filming *The Captain of the Gray-Horse Troop.* Garland saw a roseate vision of the future, a mirage confirmed by the reports of his fellow authors:

Scarcely a day passed without some new report of cinema prosperity. On Monday Black appeared, staggering under the weight of a fifteen thousand dollar check. On Tuesday White entered into partnership with a million dollar producing firm, and on Wednesday Black announced the sale of all his books. Can you wonder that I, notwithstanding my Scotch ancestry, my early training, and my grey

[3] *A Daughter of the Middle Border* (1921), pp. 379, 397.

[4] *Bookman,* XXXIX (April, 1914), 206. For other reviews of *The Forester's Daughter,* see *A. L. A. Booklist,* X (April, 1914), 325; *New York Times,* XIX (February 15, 1914), 72; *Outlook,* CVI (February 28, 1914), 504; *Publishers' Weekly,* LXXXV (April 18, 1914), 1342.

hairs, imputing wisdom, should have permitted myself on Friday to hope that a thin trickle of this cataract of gold might fall into my hands? [5]

Garland's humorous account of his adventures in movieland stresses his naïveté and somewhat distorts the actual sequence of events. The fact was that his Scotch caution kept him negotiating for many months with the Vitagraph people while he explored alternative possibilities with William E. Griffith. [6] The contemporary diary entries which he selected for publication reflect his increasing disillusionment with the methods of movie production, as *Hesper* was rushed into scenario form and onto film.

On April 1, 1916, the scenario was "hopelessly bad. I can't let them bring out a play of mine with such scenes in it. I will not sanction this scenario." April 16: "The cast is not good enough and the sets and costumes are false to the scene. Whether I can get others done as I want them or not is a problem." [7] Meanwhile he and the Vitagraph Company continued to exert salesmanship upon each other. Garland acknowledged the folly of expecting perfection: "My first duty is to let you make a success of our first play and reform the stage gradually." And repeatedly he urged that his stories be filmed on location in the West: "They are not 'cowboy' stories, they are stories of the high trails." His letters to Commodore Blackton ring with the same enthusiasm that once had echoed through the correspondence with Melville Stone and Ingalls Kimball. A new medium, a new day, is on the horizon. He and Vitagraph will share its glories together. [8] Colonel Brady surpassed Garland in enthusiasm, perhaps a more calculated, less sincere enthusiasm. Garland would soon be riding around in his own automobile. So would James Oliver Curwood, another Vitagraph find. So would all Vitagraph authors. Their novels would be "feature productions" with enormous sales.

As Garland recounts the episode of his movie ventures in *My Friendly Contemporaries* he permits himself to look at the record with an Olympian juggling of perspective. According to his pub-

[5] *Back-Trailers from the Middle Border* (1928), pp. 19–22.
[6] Garland to William Griffith, February 16, 1916, Garland Papers.
[7] *My Friendly Contemporaries* (1932), pp. 107–108, 110–111.
[8] Garland to J. Stuart Blackton, March 26, April 10 [1916], Garland Papers.

lished version it was on June 28 that he condemned the first run of *Hesper* as a "depressing experience." He was "deeply disheartened by the cheap and uninspired way in which the story had been filmed. Instead of the great peaks of the Rampart Range for background they had used a row of Jersey Hills. In place of my bold Rocky Mountain gold seekers and free miners, the producer had used Pennsylvania coal miners whose lamps and blackened faces were ludicrously out of place. My feeling is indicated in these lines," wrote Garland as he quoted from his contemporary diary:

The outlook for my picture plays is dark; I fear I have been led into a "pipe dream" by Brady whose sanguine nature and friendly interest have led to over-statement. His talk of "feature productions" and large sales no longer convinces me. I am bitterly disappointed. Smith is coldly indifferent, and Blackton himself has lost interest even in the "Captain," which he greatly liked when he read it in May.[9]

Certainly this disillusionment came to Garland, but obviously not in such early insights, for it was precisely on June 28 that he signed a contract with the Vitagraph Company for all rights to all past and future productions for five years, in which the Company contracted to produce no fewer than four five-reel films per year. There was a five-hundred-dollar advance each on *Hesper*, *Money Magic*, *Cavanaugh*, and *The Captain of the Gray-Horse Troop*, which were scheduled for production in that order. Garland protected himself to the extent of this clause: "Any change from the story of the book will be submitted to you and all scenarios will be submitted for your approval before being placed in rehearsal."[10]

With the prospect of wealth from the silver screen came another encouraging sign. Garland wrote jubilantly to his wife that Sullivan had "practically agreed to take four more sections of 'the Middle Border,'" and continued mysteriously: "And they took my breath away by asking me if I would accept a certain position at one hundred dollars per week. I can't tell you what it is but if it comes to a head you won't have to worry about any-

[9] *My Friendly Contemporaries,* pp. 119–20.
[10] Contract between Garland and Vitagraph Company, June 28, 1916, Garland Papers.

thing. It is not exactly an editorial position. It is bigger than that. I'll let you know just as soon as it comes to a contract." [11]

This contract did not materialize. And it was some time later that *Collier's* began again its serialization of *A Son of the Middle Border*. But Garland, in a flush of encouragement, had already determined that the time was ripe for him to remove permanently to New York.

Having sold his Chicago house, he established his family in New York in an "ugly, out-of-date, seven-room apartment," at the corner of Park Avenue and 92nd Street. The choice was made because of the location "in a good neighborhood," only two blocks from Central Park, and close to the Finch School where the Garland daughters were enrolled. For Zulime and the girls the move was "a terrible wrench," involving as it did separation from their kinfolks. It meant that the Garland girls had to give up the Taft studio as a place to work and play and the companionship of their cousins, Lorado Taft's three daughters. But Zulime went along gamely "counting the pennies, wearing her rich friends' cast-off clothes," which she was always able to remodel with a flair, and making the New York apartment the center of hospitality for a vivacious group, even when "the creamed chicken had to stretch itself, with the aid of hot biscuits and the inevitable green salad," to feed the fellow writers whom Garland brought home from the Players. [12]

They of the High Trails had just been published by Harper & Brothers. This collection of short stories had distinguished sponsors. The preface of William Dean Howells repeated the assertion of his recent critical article that Garland's shift of locale had merely broadened his canvas without weakening his techniques. In one edition a letter of Theodore Roosevelt vouched for the authenticity of the materials. And Garland's retitling of the stories attempted to throw the emphasis upon the element of characterization, labeling the various delineations of Western types: "The Grubstaker," "The Cowboss," "The Remittance Man," "The Lonesome Man," "The Trail Tramp," "The Prospector,"

---

[11] To Zulime Garland, November 10 [?], letter in possession of Isabel Garland Lord.

[12] *My Friendly Contemporaries*, p. 120; letter of Isabel Garland Lord to the author, August 25, 1956.

"The Outlaw," "The Leaser," "The Forest Ranger." Five of the stories had seen prior publication. The opening story, now "The Grubstaker," was "The Steadfast Widow Delaney" of one of Garland's earliest Colorado summers. "The Trail Tramp" was a grouping of three of the "Tall Ed Kelly" series which had appeared within the last few years in *Sunset* and in *Collier's*. Simultaneously with book publication "The Tourist" was appearing as "Emily's Horse Wrangler." [13] The stories were uneven in merit, the mark of commercial magazine slanting obvious in many. Garland's reportorial eye had caught the idiosyncrasies of his mountain characters as faithfully as it had the characteristics of his early farmers. What was lacking was the emotional identification with his subject matter which had given *Main-Travelled Roads* its vital impact. Garland, and his beloved parents, had been an integral part of the prairie world, his writing the cry of an inarticulate people. In the mountain West he remained an observer, an appreciative and sympathetic visitor, but an outsider, nonetheless. *They of the High Trails* remains a pleasant collection of competent but undistinguished stories in which a romantic objectivity wars with Garland's professed realistic intent. In general the reviewers approved of the book. The *Nation* declared: "No lover of the west could read the volume without feeling his heart lift again in the presence of her grandeurs and warm in recognition of her inimitable human kind." But the *Independent* preferred Garland's treatment of scene to his rendition of character. "Garland writes of the outdoors understandingly. But when he sets people to influencing people his insight is less true. He falls back on the accepted formulas of magazine fiction, and the men and women in his stories fail to live up to the possibilities of their setting." [14]

The proofreading on this latest collection alternated with Garland's continuing attempt to revise *A Son of the Middle Border* for further serialization or for book publication. But the firm of Harper's remained adamant in its refusal to consider the autobiographical material. Frederick Duneka was ill. George Harvey

---

[13] *They of the High Trails* (1916).
[14] *Nation,* CIII (August 10, 1916), 132; *Independent,* LXXXVI (June 19, 1916), 486. See also *New York Times,* XXI (May 14, 1916), 202; *Review of Reviews,* LIII (June, 1916), 760; *Dial,* LXI (June 22, 1916), 27.

had left the firm. And even the editorial offices were moving their location. Garland felt the old intimacy of relations crumbling. The accounting on his sales was not encouraging. For the year ending June 30, 1916, his total royalties from all the Harper titles, prior to *They of the High Trails,* were only $1,070.27, and he was forced to agree with the wisdom of the proposal that the sheets and bound copies of four volumes be remaindered. Sales, he was told, on *Cavanaugh, The Light of the Star, Money Magic,* and, despite the good reviews, on *Other Main-Travelled Roads,* had "almost ceased." [15]

With the moving-picture mirage fading and his literary career floundering, Garland looked upon the state of the nation and of the world with a jaundiced eye. The war in Europe seemed a remote and senseless striving to this Middle-Westerner. His one published comment upon it was the isolationist poem entitled "The Lure of the Bugle," in *Current Opinion* for September, 1916. Meanwhile he brooded over the futility of his existence:

A powerful wind from the south has been complaining all day in my ears, filling me with memories of the past—memories vaguely sweet and sad. Voices of the plain—of my boyhood. What does life mean? Where do we land? What is the value of the cargo we carry? Fiction seems futile in a time like this. What will come after this slaughter ends? For forty years, from 1868 to 1914, our nation enjoyed a steady, quiet advance. It cannot expect another period of the same tranquillity and prosperity. We have "The Habit of War!" News of battles is our recreation.

None of us care much about the thousands slain or captured. It has come to be merely a dramatic daily slaughter. The truth is we are getting accustomed to slaughter. We shall miss it when it stops. It will leave a sad vacancy in our morning program.

As I look round my poor little sooty flat and regard our slender stock of battered furniture, I admit my failure, and confess that I am too old to do better. I ought not to feel so, but I do. I am the least successful of my fellows. Seton, Bacheller, Tarkington—all possess handsome homes, and live as authors should, surrounded by books and pictures. I would not care if I were alone, but my daughters are growing up. I don't like to think of them living in this little cell,

[15] Royalty statement of Harper & Brothers for period ending June 30, 1916; Harper & Brothers to Garland [1916] with his notation of agreement, Garland Papers.

seven stories in the air; and yet a home in the country might mean poorer school facilities. It is a sad problem, one which I see no way of solving unless our film plays succeed. It is a curious reflection upon my standing as a writer, but the mere *possibility* of succeeding on the screen causes my friends to respect me!

This is one of my sorrowful days. Lame and lonesome, I went up to Bronx Park. The delicious woods smell and the splendid colors of oaks and elms did me good. I need contact with dirt and grass and trees. The old trailer in me is dying hard. Can I stand city life? What will this riding about in cars, this work of committees, do to me? To bring my wife and children into this noisy, dirty, dangerous town seems a crime. Manhattan will be still more dangerous next year. [16]

But the mood passed, and Manhattan was again the city of opportunities and intellectual stimulation which had induced Garland to become a permanent resident. Despite the crippling effects of his arthritis, he scheduled a marathon of committee meetings, literary luncheons, and dinners.

A life membership in the National Arts Club as incentive to build up its literary section; service on the Board of Directors of a simplified-spelling movement, endorsed by "T. R."; work with the Writers' Syndicate; campaigning for Charles Evans Hughes; speeches for the League for Political Education; all these obligations were added to those of the National Institute. There were speeches to be made to the Whitman Fellowship, to the graduating class of Maine University, and in honor of Booth Tarkington. There were excursions to Mark Sullivan's home in Westport, to York Harbor to visit Howells, to Sagamore Hill for luncheon with Theodore Roosevelt, to Columbia for dinners given by Nicholas Murray Butler, to Sing Sing to discuss prison reforms with Thomas Mott Osborne. And always the literary luncheons and the casual contacts of the Players and the Lotus Club.

Garland joined the Vigilantes, a patriotic organization, and wrote syndicated articles at its behest. In recognition of wartime dislocations he organized a Joint Committee of the Arts, composed of the presidents of seven metropolitan organizations to welcome "distinguished citizens of other shores" to New York. [17]

[16] *My Friendly Contemporaries,* pp. 124–25.
[17] *Ibid.,* pp. 107–147; *passim.*

And in the spring of 1917 he was prime mover of a dinner offered in tribute to William Dean Howells by the National Arts Club on the occasion of his eightieth birthday. Although Howells was ill in Florida, unable to attend, the crowd was record-breaking. As the letters of appreciation were read, and personal tributes rendered, hundreds of guests stood throughout the program. Garland felt great satisfaction in having given public recognition to one who had so often aided his career, and the careers of other young writers. The various tributes were bound in a handsome book for presentation to Howells, who wrote Garland in humorous appreciation of "the noble obsequies of my departed youth, which you arranged." Referring to himself as a "departed spirit" and an "ungracious ghost," he thanked his colleague for "the loving-kindness which so efficiently moved you." [18]

Howells was soon able to assume his old role of critic and mentor to Garland, this time with respect to the long-debated *A Son of the Middle Border.* For Macmillan & Company had agreed to publish Garland's revised manuscript on most favorable terms, featuring the book as one of the important publications of the fall season. Meanwhile Mark Sullivan had renewed his interest. Three more installments, frankly autobiographical, appeared in *Collier's,* bringing Garland's serial narrative through his homesteading days in Dakota. [19]

By July 20 Howells was writing excitedly from New York Harbor where he had received Garland's galley proofs:

> Unless the first 24 pages deceive me you have written one of the truest and greatest books in the world. Now indeed our life is getting into literature. But now and then your literosity gets the better of your life, and then I want to kill you. More anon. [20]

That Howells, who had previously been cool toward the prospect of Garland's autobiography, now received it with such spontaneous enthusiasm is indicative of the minor miracle accomplished by Garland's latest revisions. Somehow in the past two

[18] *Ibid.,* pp. 148–49; W. D. Howells to Garland, April 7, 1917, Garland Papers, and in *Life in Letters of William Dean Howells,* II, 370.
[19] Contract between Macmillan & Company and Garland, February 25, 1917, Garland Papers; *Collier's,* LIX (March 31, 1917), 9, 10; (April 21, 1917), 8–9; (May 26, 1917), 13–14.
[20] W. D. Howells to Garland, July 20, 1917, Garland Papers.

years the manuscript of *A Son of the Middle Border* had undergone a profound sea-change. The diffuseness, the awkwardness, of the earlier *Collier's* version had been transmuted into leisureliness and sincere fluency, an alchemy inexplicable solely in mechanical terms. Changes of pace, tightening and cutting, improved transitions, the shifting of persons, all contributed to the excellence of the new version. But more important, the manuscript at last had become true *autobiography,* imbued in every phrase with the personality of the writer, unified by a "story line" which recorded real-life experience.

It seems strange that Garland, never the most reticent of creatures, had been blocked so long by the difficulties of first-person narration. A public speaker since his boyhood, a controversialist in print, an avid cultivator of literary friendships, this recoil from the limelight seems most uncharacteristic. In truth, he had shown no diffidence in exposing on paper his most intimate concerns. The trouble began when he approached a discussion of his family relations.

Garland's close relation to his family and its emotional effect upon his writing has been variously interpreted by literary critics. It is indeed true, as R. E. Spiller avers, that "the conflict between his soldier-father's consecration to frontier hopes and the wasting poverty and toil of his mother gave him his one great theme." But that theme was never narrowly realized. It found its most direct expression in the realism of his early short stories, in his wrath against the land speculators and "the foolhardy pioneers," a wrath capable, however, of being transmuted into such forms as indignation against the cattle combines for their encroachment upon Indian lands.

Nor was Garland's psychology so limited as Mr. Spiller suggests in his remark: "The Oedipus complex was here no deep source of buried tragedy; it shaped the life of a family and created a chronicler." [21] Garland's excessive language might at times raise the suspicion of abnormality, as when, reporting his reaction to his mother's stroke, he exclaims: "At the moment I cursed the laws of man. I cursed myself. I accused my father." The important point, however, is that Garland recognized his

[21] R. E. Spiller, *et al,* eds., *Literary History of the United States,* II, 1018.

own emotion as the immediate result of shock, as being of "the moment," and that he includes in his blind accusations not only his father, but "the laws of man," and even himself. Read in their broader context such quotations cannot be considered indicative of an Oedipus complex, of anything other than a deep and abiding affection for the parent who had sympathized with the writer throughout his long struggle toward a broader life.

Moreover, the fact remains that after the death of his mother Garland's loyalties were equally intense toward his aging father, his attentions equally filial. The emotional conflict was perhaps lessened in these later years by the very processes of maturity and by the fact that in this period Garland was *able* to provide for his father the comforts which in earlier years he could only *wish* to provide for his mother. It is noteworthy also that Garland's devotion extended to other relatives of his parents' generation, to his Uncle David, for example, whom he helped to purchase a fruit farm in California. [22]

Indeed the Garland-McClintock clan was to him a veritable holy circle. To write of it directly, without the shield of fictional devices, seemed an exposure of intimacy of which he had been psychologically incapable in the early versions of his Middle Border narrative. The death of his father apparently had broken that mental taboo.

Now, with the editorial help of Mark Sullivan and of Edward Marsh of Macmillan's, Garland, shifting to the "I" of immediate experience, rewrote his narrative into the universal pioneer epic which he had so long envisioned. He opened his chronicle simply from a child's perspective:

All of this universe known to me in the year 1864 was bounded by the wooded hills of a little Wisconsin coulee, and its center was the cottage in which my mother was living alone—my father was in the war. As I project myself back into that mystical age, half lights cover most of the valley. The road before our doorstone begins and ends in vague obscurity—and Granma Green's house at the fork of the trail stands on the very edge of the world in a sinister region peopled with bears and other menacing creatures. Beyond this point all is terror and darkness. [23]

---

[22] *A Son of the Middle Border*, pp. 400, 454.
[23] *A Son of the Middle Border* (1938), p. 1.

Holding to his four-year-old viewpoint Garland recites the yet-poignant story of his father's return from the war, and fondly characterizes that intrepid woodsman and pioneer. His mother, his grandparents, his uncles and aunts, are all depicted in relation to their frontier environment, as Garland lingers nostalgically over the details of life in "the home in the coulee." Before many years have passed the pioneer impulse stirs again in the elder Garland and the family learns they are to migrate to Minnesota. Thus "the last threshing in the coulee" takes on a ceremonial aspect not known to other harvests. As the McClintocks assemble that last Thanksgiving on the Neshonoc, David's violin brings forth melodies made mystically sweet by thoughts of parting. And when he plays that old favorite

> Then o'er the hills in legions, boys,
> Fair Freedom's star
> Points to the sunset regions, boys,

Dick Garland's face shines "with the light of the explorer, the pioneer," but over the mother's countenance passes a wistful expression and a reflective shadow. Garland, writing of the occasion half a century later, lets slip his youthful viewpoint for the contemplative apostrophy of an aging man to whom illness has brought intimations of mortality:

Oh, you by the western sea, and you of the south beyond the reach of Christmas snow, do not your hearts hunger like mine tonight for that Thanksgiving Day among the trees? For the glance of eyes undimmed by tears, for the hair untouched with gray?

It all lies in the unchanging realm of the past—this land of my childhood. Its charm, its strange dominion cannot return save in the poet's reminiscent dream. No money, no railway train can take us back to it. It did not in truth exist—it was a magical world, born of the vibrant union of youth and firelight, of music and the voice of moaning winds—a union which can never come again to you or me, father, uncle, brother, till the coulee meadows bloom again unscarred of spade or plow. [24]

Near the Quaker town of Hesper, Minnesota, the Garlands settled for a season, then sold out again and rented land in Winneshiek County, while the husbandman surveyed the prospects

[24] *Ibid.*, pp. 66–67.

farther westward. Again the family moved, this time to Mitchell County, Iowa, where young Garland began his intimate acquaintance with true prairie lands and with the characters which were to people his fiction, the square-dance fiddler and the evangelist, the hired men on their Saturday nights, the toil-weary farm wives, the village lawyer and the schoolmaster. The incidents of the narrative are the simple episodes of frontier existence, the plowing and the seeding, the festivities of the County Fair, the night ride for the doctor, the death of a beloved sister. And always the battle against weather and insects:

Those years on the plain, from '71 to '75, held much that was alluring, much that was splendid. I did not live an exceptional life in any way. My duties and my pleasures were those of the boys around me. In all essentials my life was typical of the time and place. My father was counted a good and successful farmer. Our neighbors all lived in the same restricted fashion as ourselves, in barren little houses of wood or stone, owning few books, reading only weekly papers. It was a pure democracy wherein my father was a leader and my mother beloved by all who knew her. If anybody looked down upon us we didn't know it, and in all the social affairs of the township we fully shared. Nature was our compensation. As I look back upon it, I perceive transcendent sunsets, and a mighty sweep of golden grain beneath a sea of crimson clouds. The light and song and motion of the prairie return to me. I hear again the shrill myriad-voiced choir of leaping insects whose wings flash fire amid the glorified stubble. The wind wanders by, lifting my torn hat-rim. The locusts rise in clouds before my weary feet. The prairie hen soars out of the unreaped barley and drops into the sheltering deeps of the tangled oats, green as emerald. The lone quail pipes in the hazel thicket, and far up the road the cowbell's steady clang tells of the home-coming herd.

Even in our hours of toil, and through the sultry skies, the sacred light of beauty broke; worn and grimed as we were, we still could fall a-dream before the marvel of a golden earth beneath a crimson sky. [25]

Thus alternating on-the-spot reporting with contemplative backward glances Garland continues his chronicle, recording the removal of the family to the town of Osage and his own "golden days at the Seminary." His family soon returns to the farm, and at this point the narrative loses something of its universal char-

[25] *Ibid.,* pp. 171–72.

acter. For the forces of individuality have been aroused in the prairie lad, differentiating him from his neighbors and classmates by a blind urge toward further learning. Studying on his bleak Dakota homestead, reading in the Boston Public Library, Garland pursues his own charted course, a son of the Middle Border indeed, but becoming a person in his own right, an aspiring author. When he returns to the West in 1887, and again in 1888, there is no nostalgia, no remembrance of things past, only resentment for the harshness which entraps his parents in an unproductive round of toil. As autobiographer Garland faithfully records this emotional shift which underlay his early fiction:

I perceived little that was poetic, little that was idyllic, and nothing that was humorous in the man, who, with hands like claws, was scratching a scanty living from the soil of a rented farm, while his wife walked her ceaseless round from tub to churn and from churn to tub. On the contrary, the life of such a family appealed to me as an almost unrelievedly tragic futility. [26]

Into a cursory fifty pages Garland compresses the story of his budding literary career, his association with the Boston School of Oratory, with *Harper's Weekly* and with the *Arena*, throwing the emphasis of his narrative upon his growing determination to re-establish his family in the place of their origins. *A Son of the Middle Border* closes with a Thanksgiving reunion in the new Garland Homestead at West Salem. As Hamlin takes his place at the head of the table he feels himself for the first time the head of his family, and ponders: "The pen had proved itself to be mightier than the plow. Going east had proved more profitable than going west!"

My father was not entirely convinced, but I, surrounded by these farmer folk, hearing from their lips these quaint melodies, responded like some tensely-strung instrument, whose chords are being played upon by searching winds. I acknowledged myself at home and for all time. Beneath my feet lay the rugged country rock of my nativity. It pleased me to discover my mental characteristics striking so deep into this typically American soil.
Here I make an end of this story, here at the close of an epoch of western settlement, here with my father and mother sitting beside me

[26] *Ibid.,* p. 375.

in the light of a tender Thanksgiving, in our new old home and facing a peaceful future. I was thirty-three years of age, and in a certain very real sense this plot of ground, this protecting roof may be taken as the symbols of my hardearned first success as well as the defiant gages of other necessary battles which I must fight and win. [27]

Howells laid aside the last of the proof sheets which had absorbed his attention for the past two days. He reached for his pen:

York Harbor, July 22, 1917

My dear Garland:

So far as I know your book is without its like in literature. It is perfectly true to life, and beautiful with right feeling, from first to last. I wish every American, every human being might read it. Never before has any man told our mortal story so manfully, so kindly. I would like it to go on forever. But I miss galley slips, 160–161, and where are they? It often needs proof-reading.

Are you coming to see me? Say when.

Yours affectionately,

W. D. Howells. [28]

[27] *Ibid.*, pp. 466–67.
[28] W. D. Howells to Garland, July 22, 1917, Garland Papers; and in *Life in Letters of William Dean Howells,* II, 373–74.

§14§

A Literary Comeback

HOWELLS' WORDS of praise exalted Garland. He immediately passed them on to his editors, who saw their promotional possibilities. But a request for permission to quote shocked Howells into categorical refusal: "I hope to be your friendliest critic," he wrote Garland, "but not their advance agent. To let a publisher advertise from such a letter as I like to write to a brother-author would take all heart and zest out of friendship, and I *never* do it."[1]

That Howells' indignation stemmed strictly from principle rather than from a change of heart was obvious for, shortly after this exchange, he reviewed Garland's book for the *New York Times* in terms even more laudatory than those of his personal letter. Indeed, his article, which opened the Book Review Supplement and ran to 3,200 words, pulled open the full critical diapason. Ranging through the literature of autobiography—Goldoni, Alfieri, Goethe, Rousseau, Marmontel, Franklin—Howells declared all these of "thinner and narrower interest"

[1] W. D. Howells to Garland, August 4, 1917, Garland Papers.

than the "psychological synthesis" achieved by Garland, whose realism was equalled only by certain chapters of *La Terre.* "In all the region of autobiography, so far as I know it, I do not know quite the like of Mr. Garland's story of his life, and I should rank it with the very greatest of that kind in literature." [2]

The *Times* review reached Garland in a summer camp in the Catskills. All through the year his physical condition had deteriorated. A three-weeks stay in a sanitarium that spring had effected no improvement, and with the coming of the summer heat the Garlands had fled New York to take refuge near an artist colony at Onteora, New York, not far from John Burroughs' home at Roxbury. There they had found a rustic shack with a large living room and stone fireplace. Wild cherry trees and berry bushes clustered round, and in the distance across the fog-shrouded valley loomed the twin peaks of Rip Van Winkle's mountains. The delight of his daughters in the cool green silence of the woods, the therapeutic value of the mountain solitude, moved Garland to negotiate for the purchase of the lodge, which, once acquired, was promptly renamed "Camp Neshonoc" in memory of their Wisconsin valley home. [3]

The reviews of *A Son of the Middle Border* continued to roll out a paean of praise which encouraged the extravagance of acquiring new property. Wrote F. F. Kelly in the *Bookman:*

So understanding and skilled a portrayal of characteristic spiritual values gives the book added importance, makes it a contribution to our spiritual history that is well worth while.

As autobiography, it is an original and distinctive piece of work and illustrates the possibilities of varied and unique treatment to be found in the writing of American biography.

"A contribution to American autobiographical literature," reiterated the *Boston Transcript;* "a contribution to the annals of the settlement of our country," echoed the *Independent.* The *North American Review* praised its "mingling of practicality and idealism": "Nothing could be more wholesome in these times than the lesson of intellectual honesty and large sympathy

[2] *New York Times,* XXII (August 26, 1917), 309.
[3] *Back-Trailers from the Middle Border* (1928), pp. 62–67.

which is implicit in it." The *New Republic* sagaciously recognized that Garland had stumbled upon a vehicle favorable to his particular talents:

> The inventive writer, after long struggling with stiff fictional forms, suddenly discovers himself as his own best artistic form and material and bursts out into the freshness of self-revelations, without self-consciousness and yet with an insight that makes silly the legend that the American has no talent for introspection and resents its expressions. [4]

When Garland returned to New York in October he discovered that his book had created a minor literary sensation. He was overwhelmed by congratulations of friends and acquaintances, "somewhat as the friends of a prize fighter congratulate him on having recovered his 'punch'." Lorimer revived interest. Acknowledging receipt of the *Son,* which he had so often rejected, he now wrote wistfully, "I wish you had another Eagle's Heart for the *Post,* or if not that a novel which would be suitable for *The Country Gentleman,* on the stocks." This reception encouraged him in plans to produce further reminiscent works, and he set to work to edit his diaries and notes, to shape them into usable source materials. "It may be," he jotted a suggestion, "that I shall publish the diaries as they stand. They go back to 1898, and, while very condensed every page offers something to think about." [5]

Already this mining of old manuscripts had produced one long-buried nugget. While at work upon his final revisions of the autobiography Garland had unearthed a forgotten story of his early years. As the newly-founded *Art World* had asked him for a contribution, he sent along a two-page tribute to Howells as "Master Craftsman," timed for publication just after the birthday dinner, and in addition, this tattered manuscript. As consequence, in 1917 there appeared in print the story "Graven Image," [6] which Garland had first offered to Gilder of the *Century*

[4] *Bookman,* XLVI (November, 1917), 327; *Boston Transcript,* August 29, 1917; *Independent,* XCII (November 3, 1917), 256; *North American Review,* XXVI (November, 1917), 796; *New Republic,* XII (October 20, 1917), 333.
[5] *My Friendly Contemporaries* (1932), pp. 168–69; George H. Lorimer to Garland, October 2, 1917, Garland Papers.
[6] *Art World,* I (April, 1917), 411–12; II (May, 1917), 127–30.

in 1900 as "the story of a little Quaker town where I lived as a boy." As a matter of fact, Gilder had even earlier than this passed up Garland's first tentative offer of his autobiography, ignoring Garland's May 1, 1899, suggestion from London of "a sort of epic of that splendid life now passing away." Garland at the time had confided to Gilder his determination to create that "epic." "I can do it and shall do it if I never do another thing." [7]

Now, eighteen years later, that determination had been carried out, and *A Son of the Middle Border,* produced out of so much travail and discouragement, bid fair to recompense its author for all the agonies of its composition. Selling slowly at first, the volume began to make its way with steadily increasing sales. Already it was a critical success.

The temper of the times was a contributing factor to the favorable reception of a work which undeniably had intrinsic merits. The wave of patriotism engendered by our belated entrance into the European conflict had turned attention to the national heritage. Historical volumes and reminiscent sidelights upon distinctive American characteristics found favor with the public. In that year of 1917 came the establishment of the Pulitzer awards, with Richards and Elliott's *Julia Ward Howe* winning the initial prize for "the best American biography teaching patriotism and unselfish service to the people." Garland's book could hardly have appeared at a more propitious season.

In January of 1918 came the announcement of his election to the American Academy in recognition of the achievement of his autobiography. No honor could have delighted Garland more, for the National Institute and the American Academy had remained one of his dearest interests. The appointment ranged him with such old friends as Howells and Brander Matthews as a member of the "Senate," but it aligned him against those of his colleagues who still protested the principles involved in an autocratic organization. Irving Bacheller debated the issue with Garland in a long and vehement letter, denouncing the entire idea of the Academy as undemocratic. [8] But Garland held to his oft-repeated convictions:

[7] Garland to R. W. Gilder, January 23 [1900], June 12 [1900], May 1, 1899, New York Public Library.
[8] Irving Bacheller to Garland, January 30, 1918, Garland Papers.

My position is that of an intellectual aristocrat; I have no confidence in a "democratic art," if by that phrase is meant an art based on popular approval. With due regard for the welfare of the average man, I do not value his judgment upon wallpaper or rugs or paintings. Why should his verdict on a book or a play be considered something mystically sure and high and final? The Tolstoyan belief in "the intuitive rightness" of the peasant has always affected me as sentimental nonsense. I am gratified when my work appeals to a large number of my fellow republicans, but if one of my books were to have a very wide sale, I should at once lose confidence in its quality. The judgment of the millions, when it comes to a question of art, is usually wrong.

Furthermore, as one who believes in selection, I have helped to form various other clubs and societies where merit counts above success or good citizenship or social position. Wild as I may have been on political economy, I have never believed in artistic anarchy. Ethics and esthetics are separate fields of thought in my world. [9]

With his new prominence Garland found himself in increasing demand as a lecturer. Despite the difficulties of locomotion brought on by *arthritis deformans* he continued to occupy the platform, speaking to groups of servicemen and to literary assemblies on "The Middle Border," a phrase that had become almost a personal trademark. Augustus Thomas defined the area jokingly: "The Middle Border—why the Middle Border is wherever Hamlin Garland is." But Garland's own definition, formulated for the geographical edification of Bernard Shaw, ran thus:

In a sense it does not exist and never did. It was but a vaguely defined region even in my boyhood. It was the line drawn by the plow, and broadly speaking, ran parallel to the upper Mississippi when I was a lad. It lay between the land of the hunter and the harvester. [10]

Many of Garland's audiences needed no such specific blueprinting. His frontier was a part of their own collective memories. After many of his lectures the listeners crowded about him eager to tell how closely his remarks had paralleled their own experiences. His correspondents echoed the same refrain, as

[9] *Back-Trailers from the Middle Border,* pp. 78–79.
[10] *My Friendly Contemporaries,* p. 519.

members of the older generation wrote to thank him for having written "their" life stories. "There is something almost sacred in the deep-laid memories which my words call up," mused Garland. "There is a source of power here if I can lay hold upon it."[11]

Already he was at work upon a sequel to *A Son of the Middle Border*. That volume had closed with a provocative snatch of dialogue, sure indication that Garland even before its publication was planning a continuation of his chronicle.

The Garland family, reunited in West Salem, closed their Thanksgiving celebration and the celebration of their homecoming. Hamlin, leaving the next day for Chicago, asked:

"Mother, what shall I bring you from the city?"
With a shy smile she answered, "There is only one thing more you can bring me,—one thing more that I want."
"What is that?"
"A daughter. I need a daughter—and some grandchildren." [12]

With this "To be continued in our next," Garland had left his readers. Small wonder that some of them were asking for a sequel. And through 1918 Garland struggled to compose an answer to their demands, taking up his story where he had left off and carrying it along through the rich Chicago years. That summer of 1918 the family were again installed in "Camp Neshonoc," a seasonal migration which had taken the place of the old West Salem summers. Garland worked with increasing difficulties:

My shoulder is now so lame that I cannot lift my pen to the ink bottle; but by dipping the pen with my left hand and passing it to my right I am able to keep going. It is as though my right hand were a separate, feebler entity. In this desperate spirit, I toil. I *must* get this record in readable shape this summer. [13]

At this juncture help came in the offer of a physician acquaintance, Dr. Fenton B. Turck, to treat Garland by a new method which he had developed for arthritis, an injection of "a biological product, a direct stimulant of metabolism." As the treatments continued over a period of months Garland's condition de-

[11] *Ibid.*, p. 178.
[12] *A Son of the Middle Border* (1938), p. 467.
[13] *My Friendly Contemporaries*, pp. 190–191.

cidedly improved so that he could welcome the celebration of the Armistice both as an end to the world-wide slaughter and as an omen of his own returning health. Meanwhile the second volume of his autobiography had taken shape to the extent that he felt confident in proposing it for serial publication successively to Honoré Willsie, editor of *Delineator,* and to Mark Sullivan. Both rejected it.

George Lorimer wrote kindly:

"My dear Garland, I sat up until one o'clock last night to finish your book and I enjoyed every word of it, but I can't see it as a Post serial anymore than I could see The New Machiavelli, by Wells, one of my pet novels of recent years, in the weekly.

The manuscript is being expressed to Mark Sullivan as you suggest.

I wonder if we can't plan something this fall aimed directly at the Saturday Evening Post."

Garland, undismayed by this rejection, endorsed the letter to Edward Marsh of Macmillan's: "Here is the second verdict on the volume—nearly 600 pages—and all interesting even to a busy man like Lorimer." [14]

On January 15, 1919, Garland wrote Fuller reporting on his health and literary affairs: "I am almost normal once more, due apparently to the treatment of Dr. Turck. I can run down-stairs and walk quite as well as any one of my age and previous condition of servitude." As to his new book he was reconciled to spending three years on getting it into proper shape. "The other book made an impression that scares me now," he confided. [15]

The death of Theodore Roosevelt that month saddened Garland. "He was the biggest, most interesting and versatile man I ever knew. . . . He had been a dominating figure in my world for over a quarter of a century and his going leaves a vacant place in my horizon something like the sudden sinking of a mountain peak." [16] The temperamental kinship of Garland with his fellow author, the ex-President, had indeed been marked. The favorite

[14] *Ibid.,* pp. 192, 197, 213; George H. Lorimer to Garland, August 16, 1918, Garland Papers.

[15] Garland to H. B. Fuller, January 15, 1919, Garland Papers.

[16] *My Friendly Contemporaries,* pp. 214–15.

commendation of both writers had been the description "manliness," and it seemed highly appropriate that Dan Beard, speaking over the grave at Oyster Bay, quoted Garland's lines: "Do you fear the force of the wind/The slash of the rain?" [17]

But the characteristics which Roosevelt had embodied, the vigorous morality, the unreflective gusto, the explorer's kinship with the out-of-doors, were characteristics of an age fast passing from the American scene. The strenuous life was far from the ideal of the postwar generation, and Garland more and more felt himself out of tune with the times. Bobbed-haired flappers did the Charleston in speakeasies—the "new woman" indeed become a Frankensteinian monster. The theaters and the bookstalls purveyed what to Garland was frank pornography. "The stock ingredients are embezzlement, seduction, rape, adultery, incest, and a cheapening of womanly virtues. Normal human life seems not to interest publishers or play producers." And the streets of New York teemed with dark-skinned foreigners whose manner and bearing irritated Garland daily. "Manhattan is no longer American as in the days when the Knickerbocker families were its social rulers. It is American only in the other and less grateful sense of being a hodge-podge of individuals of no dignity or consequence; peasants in newly acquired finery—ancestors of the future." [18]

The intolerances of age were coming to dominate many of Garland's reactions. Speaking at Public School 42, he was shocked to find that all of its teachers were Jewish:

So long as our teachers are carrying on the tradition of the republic, there is a possibility that the pupils can be made over into Americans, but when instructors as well as pupils become alien, there is danger that the principles and policies which hold our great nation together may be weakened. In our fury of hospitality, we have opened our doors to the criminal as well as to the indigent and the illiterate, and our schools cannot take care of the aspiring children of these European peasants. It is fine that they are all so eager to become educated, but to what end will their education tend?

[17] Dan Beard, "Hamlin Garland, the Poet," *Mark Twain Quarterly*, IV (Summer, 1940), 10.
[18] *My Friendly Contemporaries*, p. 347.

In his more confident youth Garland had answered that query by assuring an audience of Boston listeners in one of his earliest lectures of "a certain dominant quality" to be found in these immigrants, "a spirit filled with the desire to amalgamate": "It is not to be expected," he wrote then, "that a Swedish, German or Irish peasant, whose ancestry for centuries have trod in their dreary round of toil, whose recreations were for the most part animal or childish, a wake or a fair, to whom books were a dry task to be forgotten as soon as possible—it is not to be expected such people will immediately subscribe for the 'Century,' organize Wordsworth Clubs, or read Hawthorne. Evolution, though marvelously swift in these cases, is not so swift as that." [19]

With the passage of the years Garland had lost faith in the processes of evolution and in the immigrants' "desire to amalgamate." But whatever his doubts about the efficacy of the educational system he found himself increasingly in demand as a school speaker. An excerpt from his autobiography, "Going to School in Iowa in 1871," appeared in the *Education Review*. [20] He travelled to Pennsylvania State College to speak to the students of Fred Lewis Pattee, to Sweet Briar College, and to the University of North Carolina, en route for a visit with Irving Bacheller in Florida, and wondered at the thoughts of the grim-faced returning Negro soldiers he saw on the trains:

In imagination I went with them to the low bare cabins of their parents. I sat among them while they told their stories of battles, boasting perhaps of the white women who had overlooked their color, while their worshipful mammies stared with eyes of wonder. Would such men return to the position which the white South insisted upon? [21]

Garland could find no trace of the Old South of the literature of its novelists, but felt at home in the small villages as he had not done since leaving Wisconsin:

[19] *Ibid.*, p. 207; "The Present and the Future," unpublished MS in Garland Papers.
[20] *Education Review*, LIV (December, 1919), 435–39.
[21] *My Friendly Contemporaries*, p. 180; *ibid.*, pp. 23–33; *Back-Trailers from the Middle Border*, p. 116.

The South through which I passed is young, vital, buoyant, and American. . . . It was like revisiting my home town. After the heterogeneous mixture of New York, it was a pleasure to meet once more the men and women who know what pioneering means and what our history has been. I am a philanthropist—in theory—and should have no race prejudices; but I like my own kind—at least I enjoy meeting a blond, gray-eyed citizen now and again. I grant the black-eyed people the same prejudice regarding me. [22]

At an earlier lecture at the Horace Mann School, Garland in a facetious mood had enlivened his talk by a rendition of "O'er the Hills in Legions, Boys."—"It was all on a dangerously intimate plane, but my auditors liked it, and with no reporters in evidence I permitted myself to be almost as funny as I could." [23] Thereafter, on many occasions, Garland diversified his program in true chautauqua fashion. To one of his sponsors in Cleveland, for a tour which would include Albany, Cincinnati, and Columbus, Garland wrote describing his proposed offering as "a more or less humorous informal discourse without manuscript concerning almanacs, cow milking, ballads—and any other subject which comes into my head. I may even break into song. I may also read a little from the Middle Border book. Thus far people have not gone to sleep on it." [24] Such ebullience spoke of returning health and self-confidence.

But some of Garland's discourses were of more serious nature. With his old enthusiasm for causes he had thrown himself into the work of the Roosevelt Memorial Association, speaking frequently in behalf of an organization pledged to raise ten million dollars to construct a Roosevelt monument in Washington and to make of Oyster Bay a national shrine after the example of Mount Vernon. For *Everybody's Magazine* he wrote out his recollections of his hero, from the days of their first meeting in New York, when Roosevelt was the Commissioner of Police pardoning "Lemuel Barker," the negligent police officer, to the time of a hospital visit shortly before Roosevelt's death. The essay was in Garland's best anecdotal vein, justifying its informal approach by the conceit that Roosevelt in the eighties had been his fron-

[22] *My Friendly Contemporaries*, p. 233.
[23] *Ibid.*, p. 186.
[24] Garland to "Professor Benton," February 3 [1919], Garland Papers.

tier "neighbor." At the time of Garland's homesteading venture Roosevelt had been ranching in Dakota. In the conceptions of the border, Garland insisted, the proximity of a hundred miles constituted "neighboring." On the anniversary of the President's death a more sober tribute from Garland appeared in the *Mentor.* [25]

With his passion for organization Garland now determined to make of his benefactor Dr. Turck a public institution. With Augustus Thomas and H. G. Murray he formed the "Publication Committee of the Turck Foundation for Biological Research" and set out to preach the gospel of Turck's *"cytosts"* and *"anticytosts."* The physician, however, was apparently as strong-willed an individualist as his patient, "A genius with all the peculiarities of genius," Garland described him. Their correspondence indicates that they were often at cross purposes and Garland once reversed the roles by prescribing testily for his physician to get away from his manuscript, get back to research, and act like "a dignified scientist in speech and in writing." [26]

Needless to say, the Turck Foundation joined the limbo of Garland's many aborted educational projects. One part of the difficulty may have been Turck's lack of confidence in an advisor who was simultaneously dabbling with the occult. Although Turck "detested the word 'psychic' " and considered Garland's experiments foolish, [27] Garland had again turned to active participation in the American Psychical Society. For *McClure's* he wrote an article on "The Spirit World on Trial," and joined in the acclaim which greeted Sir Oliver Lodge on his American lecture tour. [28]

But if the Turck Foundation, and even the Roosevelt Memorial Association, gained little ground, the affairs of the National Institute of Letters progressed in a fashion most gratifying to Garland, who was now its acting secretary. Archer M. Huntington had become its benefactor and there were plans afoot for the

[25] *Everybody's Magazine,* XLI (October, 1919), 9–16; *Mentor,* VII (February 2, 1920), 1–12.

[26] "Bulletin of the Turck Foundation for Biological Research," Vol. 1, No. 1, and Garland-Turck correspondence, Garland Papers.

[27] *Forty Years of Psychic Research* (1936), p. 349.

[28] *McClure's,* LII (March, 1920), 33–34; *Touchstone,* "The Coming of Sir Oliver Lodge," VI (January, 1920), 217.

erection of a permanent building on West 155th Street. Also Garland had a new field of organizational activity, having been recently elected to membership in the austere Century Club. [29]

Meanwhile he struggled with the recalcitrant manuscript of the second volume of his autobiography. It was refractory material which he had set himself to handle, the story of his courtship and the early years of his marriage, a difficult subject to handle with taste and objectivity. His was, in a sense, the problem that plagues all autobiographers, and even biographers, the inevitable progression which threatens a falling off of interest once the subject has attained his majority. For the experiences of boyhood, whatever the locale, are universals; the experiences of manhood, always particulars. The joys of childhood and the dreams of youth are of the common fund of knowledge, the struggles of maturity belong too largely to a particular class or occupation, and, to the majority of readers, can appeal only through a vicarious participation. While Garland's Chicago years would automatically interest other writers, it was difficult to imbue them with a more general appeal. Moreover, he was attempting to carry out his original scheme of making his reminiscences not so much the story of one man as the chronicle of a family, a family representative of a strand of American culture. It was a difficult problem he posed: "In relating my own joys and cares, I shall be delineating the lives of other families in the West and elsewhere. As the first volume dealt with the centrifugal forces of American life—the era of exploration—so in this volume the centripetal forces, the passion for cities and crowds, must find expression." [30]

As Garland thus relived his past the days at West Salem came to seem to him a halcyon period. The narrowness and frustrations of Western life faded into the distance and in the foreground grew "The Fairy World of Childhood" of his daughters. From the perspective of twenty years it seemed at times to Garland as though the city lights which had lured him East had been a will-o'-the-wisp. As he wrote, the sunlight fell upon the Homestead making it now the fabled house of the golden windows.

[29] *My Friendly Contemporaries,* pp. 327, 267. See Irving Bacheller to W. D. Howells on proposing Garland to the Century Club, May 26, 1918, Garland Papers.
[30] *My Friendly Contemporaries,* p. 174.

As the story progressed into the more immediate present, through the intimate sorrow of his mother's death to the "mustering out" of his father, Garland found it increasingly difficult to strike the proper balance between sentiment and objectivity. Thus it was consoling to have his friend Albert Bigelow Paine's approval, "You have handled the chapter on the 'Choosing of the Daughter' with taste and candor," and to know that Harold Latham of Macmillan's was eager for the book's completion.

On May 3, 1920, Garland came from an interview with his publishers "half resolved to forego serialization," trusting to the added sales which Latham assured him would result from immediate book publication before the impact of the first volume had been dissipated. [31] Nonetheless, he continued to try for magazine serialization. That month Ellery Sedgwick of the *Atlantic,* although he had encouraged submission of the manuscript, was forced to turn it down as unsuited to his space requirements. Later Garland submitted it to the *Century.* [32] And continually he revised in the hope of achieving the success of his earlier volume.

In periods of disillusionment with his sequel Garland turned to what appeared to him a simpler task, the writing of the history of his family in the years prior to the Civil War. In that remote era there was more play for his imagination, and the story of western migrations awakened an emotional response which communicated itself to his writing. When weary of one manuscript he turned to the other, alternating from the boyhood of his father to the childhood of his daughters. "It now appeared that this new manuscript which I called *The Trail-Makers* might serve as a fictive introduction to the other two books." [33]

During the New York winters there was much play-going for the Garlands, for now Garland's elder daughter had come to share her father's enthusiasm for the theater. She was beginning to appear in school plays and showed every indication of being stage-struck. As the two constituted themselves a pair of dramatic critics attending the current productions, Garland recorded his impressions. O'Neill's dramas he viewed with mixed opinions,

[31] *Ibid.,* pp. 187, 292.
[32] Ellery Sedgwick to Garland, May 5, 1920, Garland Papers; *My Friendly Contemporaries,* p. 343.
[33] *Back-Trailers from the Middle Border,* p. 125.

preferring Tarkington's *Seventeen,* the pieces of his old friend Augustus Thomas, and the sentimentalities of Barrie. [34]

The ranks of Garland's colleagues were thinning. At all of the editorial offices there were new faces. Henry M. Alden died on October 7, 1919. "For over sixty years," wrote Garland, "he was connected with *Harper's Magazine,* and for over forty years he sat in his dusty office, a plain little room, hardly more than a stall, with the ceaseless grind and jar of the elevated road filling his ears. He seemed not to mind this tumult, but his visitors found it deafening. Now he is in silence." Six months later Garland suffered a more personal loss. "William Dean Howells is dead. To write that sentence is to write an end to the longest and most important friendship of my life." After the funeral Garland continued: "So ends the material part of my great friend. No death since that of my father had so deeply affected me. Howells was more than an elder brother; he was a spiritual guide, an arbiter in many cases of dispute." [35]

The next day Edgar Chamberlin wrote offering one hundred fifty dollars for an article on "Howells' Boston" for the next week's *Transcript,* and Garland promptly entrained for Boston. As he wandered down Commonwealth Avenue and Beacon Street, out to Cambridge, reliving the days of his "Meetings with Howells," he found it "disheartening to realize that Boston had almost forgotten Howells, that few remain who knew him in Cambridge." [36] It was a melancholy pilgrimage and Garland could reflect that of the giants of his youth there remained only rugged old John Burroughs.

Burroughs, always a favorite of the Garland children, who regarded him, like Santa Claus, as "a kind of household saint," was yet a frequent visitor to Camp Neshonoc. "Oom John" had kept up with the times. One day Garland looked out to see Burroughs, his shock of white hair and beard flying in the wind, "engaged in maneuvering a snorting, sputtering, protesting 'flivver' into a position of repose on the steep slope of my front yard. He

[34] *My Friendly Contemporaries,* pp. 185, 242, 269, 284, 332–33.

[35] *Ibid.,* pp. 258, 294–95. The last two sentences are indicated by parentheses as a 1932 addendum.

[36] E. Chamberlin to Garland, May 12, 1920, Garland Papers; *My Friendly Contemporaries,* pp. 298–304; "Howells' Boston," *Boston Transcript,* May 22, 1920.

looked like an up-to-date Santa Claus as with a smile of pride he shut off his engine." He explained that the car was the gift of Henry Ford, who each year presented him with a new model and took away the old.

The Garlands also had acquired an automobile, which only Mary Isabel understood sufficiently to enjoy driving. Since it had been purchased with the proceeds of one of Garland's psychic articles it had been christened "The Spook," and for want of a garage was sheltered in the Cheyenne tepee in which Garland had once done his writing in the camp at Eagle's Nest. With this transportation the family was able to explore the Catskills at their leisure and to call upon their friends of the artist colony. At Roxbury, Burroughs received them, the porch piled high with woodchuck skins which he was patiently tanning for an overcoat. His home was but a dilapidated cottage and the great naturalist looked like any farmer. "His baggy trousers, his mouse-hide shoes, his faded sweater and rustic speech fitted in with the bare walls and stark simplicity of his home." But the talk was of subjects the two men held in common, books and the world of nature. To Garland's mind, Burroughs was "the writer first, the naturalist only second."

Then in March of 1921 came the word that Burroughs too was dead, en route home from the West. Garland attended the funeral services, and in his habitual response to death, began to spearhead arrangements for a more permanent memorial to his old friend. In the same reaction pattern he wrote for the *Century* the sort of article which was coming to be expected of him on such occasions, the intimate, anecdotal recollections of his association with "My Friend, John Burroughs." [37]

Now there was no one left with whom he could talk over the old days, no one who had known Whitman and Lowell and the Boston which was "the hub of the intellectual universe." True, there were the younger critics with whom he could indulge in literary conversations. Fred L. Pattee had warmed his heart by admitting that he made great use of *Crumbling Idols* in his classroom teaching. Professor Benjamin Shambaugh at Iowa Uni-

[37] *My Friendly Contemporaries*, pp. 347–50; *Back-Trailers from the Middle Border*, pp. 145–50. The quotations are from "My Friend, John Burroughs," *Century*, CII (September, 1921), 731–42.

versity welcomed the son of the Middle Border as a distinguished historian. Young Carl Van Doren (whom Garland took, on first meeting, to be a newspaper reporter, from his request for a story on the new Academy building) seemed "an especially admirable type, vigorous in mind and body, sanely sympathetic in his judgments and wholly American in his point of view." But the two men differed radically in some of their opinions. *Main Street* was a case in point. Garland thought it a "disturbing and depressing book." [38] Appointed in 1921, however, with Stuart Sherman and Robert Morss Lovett to recommend to the Pulitzer Prize Committee the best novel of 1920, he concurred in the choice of *Main Street*, a recommendation ignored by that Committee which selected instead Edith Wharton's *The Age of Innocence*. [39] Despite the furor which followed this selection and the publication of the correspondence, Garland unofficially held to his low opinion of the Lewis novel:

It is true, amazingly true, up to a certain point, but it fails to convince simply because the writer is not quite large enough, not quite generous enough, to fuse the minute, distressing details into something noble. The characters are too much like puppets, types rather than persons. In the more individualized figures the author fails to convince, for the reason that he does not hold to the lines of his characters. As for the town, the same methods applied to any country would yield a similar result. There is also something bitter in this writing, something vengeful. [40]

As Mr. Van Doren would point out, this was strange criticism to come from the lips of the author of *Main-Travelled Roads*.

Garland's work as a member of the Pulitzer prize committee necessarily kept him in touch with current literature. For the play award he was happy to join in a unanimous decision for Zona Gale's work, *Miss Lulu Bett*, the dramatization of a commonplace Wisconsin family, calculated to appeal to Garland. [41] That year the prize for biography went to the work of another old friend for *The Americanization of Edward Bok*, a book for

[38] *My Friendly Contemporaries,* pp. 181, 387, 315–16, 368–69, 382, 337.
[39] Harrison Smith, ed., *From Main Street to Stockholm,* p. 203n.
[40] *My Friendly Contemporaries,* p. 330.
[41] *Ibid.,* p. 375.

which Garland's *A Son of the Middle Border* had done a bit towards paving the way.

It is possible to read into this award, in a knowledge of the backstage maneuverings of prize committees, the reason for the long deferring of publication of Garland's second autobiographical volume. In the interlocking of Academy and Pulitzer prize committee memberships there well may have been a tacit agreement that after the award to Bok the way would be clear for a recognition of Hamlin Garland. Garland's own published reminiscences reflect, however, only a desire to improve his manuscript as reason for its long gestation. But the three years of which he had spoken to Fuller as the optimum period for its composition had come and gone before the book came into print.

He had wanted to call it *A Son of the Middle Border, II*. But when the book was brought out in September of 1921, the title was changed, on advice of his publishers, to *A Daughter of the Middle Border*. Garland had never been so agitated over the publication of a book since the days of his first beginnings. His correspondence with Harold Latham assumed a querulous note as he questioned the publicity arrangements and the advertising appropriations. At one juncture he was interfering boldly with promotional matters, suggesting advertisements at his own expense and frankly soliciting his friends for testimonials.

Latham's replies were in the bedside manner which editors reserve for just such periods of accouchement. With infinite patience he explained the details of the publicity campaign, advising Garland of the folly of newspaper advertising at his own expense. [42] Macmillan's were certainly doing their best to capitalize on their, at this moment, difficult author. The previous year, in recognition of the Grant centenary, they had brought out from Garland's plates a new edition of his Grant biography, which to date had sold only some two hundred copies. But *A Son of the Middle Border* was selling in the thousands four years after publication date, and they were sanguine of an equal response to the *Daughter*. Indeed, at this time, Latham suggested a republication of certain earlier titles, *Rose of Dutcher's Coolly, Main-Travelled Roads, Prairie Songs, A Spoil of Office, The Eagle's Heart,*

[42] Harold Latham to Garland, correspondence of 1920–1921, Garland Papers, in particular, letters of December 30, 1921, January 20, 1922.

Crumbling Idols, The Captain of the Gray-Horse Troop, and *Boy Life on the Prairie.* Since Harper & Brothers owned rights in several of these, Garland approached them on the matter of a release, but was unable to conclude an agreement at a price which Macmillan's would approve, particularly since Harper's was reluctant to relinquish *Boy Life on the Prairie.* [43]

As *A Daughter of the Middle Border* appeared Garland alternated between hopes and fears. Six months before publication date, which was set for his sixty-first birthday, he was sanguine. "It begins to look like a 'go.' " But by the time the book had been out three months he was forced to admit that it was both a critical and financial failure. "Only a half dozen reviews of it have come in, and these were written by my personal friends. The whole outlook is humiliatingly dark." [44]

Garland's appraisal of the book's reception was only too accurate, although his friends attempted to fill out the review lists. J. E. Chamberlin dutifully discussed the volume in the *Transcript,* querying the intent of the title. Was "the daughter" intended to be Garland's mother, or his wife, both of whom played such important roles in the story? "It is a strange book . . . pure literary autobiography, sometimes egotistic, frequently direct and simple to the point of naïveté, but interesting and for the most part really significant in its record of American intellectual development." Further than this the honest old newspaper man could not go in praise of his protégé's narrative.

"Henry B." in the *Freeman* loyally praised the *Daughter* as "a successful sequel." Mr. Van Doren perceptively discussed the man behind the book, concluding that it was from Garland's "filial instincts that he derives his peculiar power," the ability to make of his paternal and maternal relatives "the most vivid families in American literature." [45] A few scattering reviews and elsewhere a bored silence.

In desperation Garland wrote to Albert Shaw, pleading for a notice: "I wish you would write of the two books as a unit for

---

[43] Harold Latham to Garland, October 17, 1921, Garland Papers.
[44] *My Friendly Contemporaries,* pp. 358, 381.
[45] *Boston Transcript,* December 10, 1921, p. 7; *Freeman,* IV (November 9, 1921), 210; *Nation,* CXIII (November 13, 1921), 601–602.

that is what they are. Someday I hope to have them printed in India paper and in one binding." [46] The idea of linking the inferior volume to the more successful became an obsession with Garland. But Macmillan's, with a slow seller on their lists, were in no mood to add to the cost of their investment. A few months later they agreed to a scheme of combining the two books in a boxed volume. [47] But by this time the news was out that the Pulitzer award had gone to Hamlin Garland, nominally at least for *A Daughter of the Middle Border.*

As belated recognition of Garland's 1917 achievement the prize was appropriate, and the honor did much to revive his spirits after the fiasco of the recent volume. He had further cause of self-congratulation, for Harper & Brothers, their interest awakened by their competitor's achievements with Garland, now offered to bring out a book of his Indian stories and to get out a new "Border Edition" of Garland's works in twelve volumes.

Edward Marsh, who had gone to Harper's, was editor for this new project. From the older "Sunset Edition" four titles were carried forward: *Main-Travelled Roads, Rose of Dutcher's Coolly, Boy Life on the Prairie,* and *The Eagle's Heart.* For *The Trail of the Goldseekers* was substituted the juvenile version *The Long Trail. Other Main-Travelled Roads* replaced the volumes from which its stories had been drawn, *Prairie Folks* and *Wayside Courtships. They of the High Trails* was included, and the other five volumes were made up from novels of the 1903–1914 period, with *Money Magic* retitled *Mark Haney's Mate.*

With the publication date of this revival set for May 4, Garland rebounded into ebullience, attempting to set up a promotional scheme whereby the *Review of Reviews* should give the entire twelve-volume set as a subscription premium. [48] He also began to plan a summer for his family in Europe, to be financed by the Pulitzer prize of one thousand dollars and the receipts from sale of his Oklahoma lands. Real estate prices were in their

[46] Garland to Albert Shaw, January 23, 25 [1922], New York Public Library. Shaw complied in the March issue of the magazine, Vol. XLV, pp. 419–24.

[47] Harold Latham to Garland, January 20, April 14, 1922, Garland Papers.

[48] Edward C. Marsh to Albert Shaw, March 15, 17, 1922, New York Public Library.

post-war boom and Garland had cashed in to become "one of the creatures my father both feared and hated 'a bond-holder fattening on the labor of others'."

Garland's motivations for the European tour were complex. It was to be a bribe for Mary Isabel, who was that spring graduating from Finch and who had announced her intention of going on the stage. Her father found his theatrical enthusiasm waning when it was a case of his daughter's entering the field. With the promise of six months in England he bargained for a year's postponement of her stage debut, offering in its stead an assistant's part in his lecture appearances. [49] But Garland had another end in view in his excursion. Despite the warning of the public's lack of interest in his family chronicle, he was stubbornly determined to produce yet another volume of the series. If the material was not suitable for literary purposes, he would make it suitable. He attributes the suggestion to Yale's historian Allen Johnson in a reminiscent sequence which has something of the flavor of ventriloquism.

In the spring of 1922 he was in correspondence with William Lyon Phelps of Yale over the matter of the Pulitzer play award (it was with reluctance that he went along with the committee's selection of the depressing "Anna Christie"). [50] In February he was in New Haven to speak to the Yale Y.M.C.A., under the sponsorship of Dr. Turck's young son. At lunch with Phelps and Allen Johnson the latter expressed interest in Garland's conception of the centripetal forces in American history, and suggested an extension of the idea of "back-trailing."

"How long has it been since you visited London?"
"Sixteen years."
"That is too long to be away from your ancestral home. . . . I value your chronicle and hope you will bring it down to date. Why not take it to England as an extension of your back-trailing?" [51]

Whether or not this conversation was as Garland remembered it, the idea of *making* his own life story of sufficient interest to

[49] *Back-Trailers from the Middle Border*, pp. 171–81.
[50] W. L. Phelps to Garland, April 25, 1922, Garland Papers.
[51] *My Friendly Contemporaries*, p. 392.

justify its literary recording was involved in his scheme of voyaging abroad. As a writer of fiction he had roamed in far places in search of material. Now that he had become his own material, the logic of travel was even more imperative!

On May 31, 1922, Garland sailed from Quebec, armed with the inevitable sheaf of letters of introduction, with the suggestion of McClure that he do a "Conversation with H. G. Wells" in the pattern of the old Field and Riley interviews, [52] and with the acclaim of being a member of the American Academy of Letters and the most recent recipient of the Pulitzer Prize for Biography.

[52] S. S. McClure to Garland, November 30, 1921, Garland Papers.

§15§

The Hall of Mirrors

As GARLAND was scheduling his sailing date he was interrupted by a caller, a young girl doing research for a master's degree at Wisconsin University. It was something of a surprise to Garland to realize that he alone was to be the subject of her thesis. He was both flattered and repelled at the notion that his work was to be "the subject of a careful historical monograph, precisely as though I were a personage in English literature." "I have suddenly become a veteran," he admitted, "almost a venerable person! It is hard for me to accept that view of myself and my work. I have so long been a 'promising writer'!" [1]

In more august critical circles Garland's work was likewise beginning to attract comment. American literature had at last become respectable in academic circles. Doctorates were now given in a field which not a generation before had been considered unworthy of undergraduate credit. And a body of critical literature was growing up on Americana in which the place of Garland was

[1] *My Friendly Contemporaries* (1932), p. 407.

beginning to be debated fervently. Articles appeared in scholarly journals, the *Sewanee Review*, the *Yale Review*—even in college textbooks—evaluating the literary revolt of the eighteen nineties, and the precise impact of "veritism." The occasion of the Pulitzer Prize award and the publication of the "Border Edition" underlined the scope of Garland's work and provoked additional critical articles in the book review supplements of the papers.

In the *Yale Review* Zona Gale reciprocated handsomely Garland's recent patronage. With uncritical enthusiasm she fulsomely praised all of his reprinted volumes. "Their unashamed provincialism is their glory." The autobiographical volumes she ranked with *The Education of Henry Adams* as source books of American history. "He is at his best in his picture of the daughter of the Middle Border, Isabelle McClintock, and his relationship to her—his mother, the eternal mother, wise, weak, loving, tribal." [2]

Another feminine admirer wrote in the *New York Times* of "A Middle West Chronicler": "More than any other writer the student of the up-building of our great Middle States will have to turn to Hamlin Garland for a picture, faithful and sincere of that stupendous adventure." "The Middle Border" appeared to her "a more felicitous descriptive title" than "The Border Edition" as, ignoring the competitions of publishers, she expressed the hope that one day Garland's autobiographical books would appear as part of the same edition. [3]

There were less enthusiastic strains in the chorus of criticism that the early twenties brought forth. Garland had the dubious honor, along with five fellow members of the National Institute, of winning a place of prominence in H. L. Mencken's *Prejudices*.

"The case of Hamlin Garland belongs to pathos in the grand manner," pontificated Mencken. "What ails him is a vision of music, a sedative strain of bawdy music over the hills. . . . The vision in his youth tore him from his prairie plow and set him to

[2] Zona Gale, "Among the New Books," *Yale Review*, n.s. XI (July, 1922) 852–56.

[3] Hildegarde Hawthorne [a granddaughter of Nathaniel Hawthorne, whose husband was part Cherokee Indian], "A Middle West Chronicler," *New York Times* Book Review Supplement, July 30, 1922, p. 10.

clawing the anthills at the foot of Parnassus. He became an elo-
cutionist—what in modern times would have been a chautau-
quan. . . . The natural goal of the man was the evangelical
stump." To include him in the ranks of the artists is ridiculous.
"No more grotesque miscasting of a diligent and worthy man is
recorded in profane history," announced Mencken gleefully.
"One follows the progress of the man with the constant sense
that he is steering by faulty compasses, that fate is leading him
into paths too steep and rocky—nay, too dark and lovely—for
him." *A Son of the Middle Border* is "in substance, a document
of considerable value—a naïve and often highly illuminating contribution to the history of the American peasantry. It is, in form,
a thoroughly third-rate piece of writing—amateurish, flat, banal,
repellent." [4]

Fred Lewis Pattee also had some qualms about the evangelical
character of Garland's work. Fortunately in his volume on *The
Development of the American Short Story* Pattee was obliged to
comment only upon his friend's short fiction, which he treated
with courtesy and with caution:

> The spirit of the reformer was often stronger in Garland than his
> sense of art. . . . His permanency, however, rests almost wholly upon
> these thirty short stories of his first inspiration. How much of their
> value depends upon the materials used, upon the fact that they
> record with truth the spirit of a vanished episode, that was enormous-
> ly picturesque, it is perhaps too early to determine. [5]

With a keen insight for the biographical factors involved Mr.
Van Doren discussed Garland in the *Nation* under the general
heading of "Contemporary American Novelists," pointing out
that while Garland's instincts clashed with those of his migratory father, the migratory impulse in his own blood combined
with a revulsion from the stifling conditions of frontier life to
send Garland upon a different Odyssey, which was in effect but
another version of the search which had sent Henry James to
England. As a writer Garland "had been kindled by Howells in

[4] H. L. Mencken, *Prejudices, First Series,* pp. 134–38.
[5] Fred L. Pattee, *The Development of the American Short Story* (New
York, 1923), pp. 315–16.

Boston to a passion for realism which carried him beyond the suave accuracy of his master to the sombre veracity" of his early books, a veracity "more than sombre. It was deliberate and polemic." *"Main-Travelled Roads* did what *Main Street* was to do thirty years later," maintained Mr. Van Doren. Both challenged the myth of rural beauties and rural virtues. Though the comparison was apposite, Garland could never be brought to admit any similarity between his work and that of Sinclair Lewis.

To Mr. Van Doren Garland's novels of his middle period were a mistaken enterprise. He had followed "the false light of local color to the Rocky Mountains," become "a visiting enthusiast for the 'high trails' and let himself be roused by a fervor sufficiently like that from which he had earlier dissented." "He came to lay so much emphasis upon outward manners that he let his plots and characters fall into routine and formula." But with *A Son of the Middle Border* Garland came into his own again:

> His enthusiasms might be romantic but his imagination was not; it was indissolubly married to his memory of actual events. The formulas of his mountain romances, having been the inventions of a mind not essentially inventive, had been at best no more than sectional; the realities of his autobiography, taking him back again to "Main-Travelled Roads" and its cycle, were personal, lyrical, and consequently universal. All along, it now appeared, he had been at his best when he was most nearly autobiographical: those vivid early stories had come from the lives of his own family or of their neighbors; "Rose of Dutcher's Coolly" had set forth what was practically his own experience. . . .
>
> In a sense "A Son of the Middle Border" supersedes the fictive versions of the same material. They are the original documents and "Son," the final redaction and commentary.
>
> This autobiographical method, applied with success in "A Daughter of the Middle Border" to his later life, brings into play all his higher gifts and excludes his lower. Under slight obligation to imagine, he runs slight risks of succumbing to those conventionalisms which often stiffen his work when he trusts to his imagination. . . . Dealing chiefly with action, not with thought, he does not tend so much as elsewhere to solve speculative problems with sentiment instead of with reflection. . . . If it is difficult to overprize the documentary value of his saga of the Garlands and the McClintocks and of

their son who turned back on the trail, so is it difficult to overpraise the sincerity and tenderness and beauty with which the chronicle was set down. [6]

All this critical furore reached Garland but faintly for the Atlantic rolled between him and New York's literary excitements. Later he would assess it and be influenced by it. In his further reminiscences his comments on his mountain novels would have a defensive ring, and when he considered his prairie narratives he would imbue them with a more conscious intent of "social history" than had been present in their composition. The hindsight of a septuagenarian who had read the critics would differ from the viewpoint of the unrecognized young writer. But in that halcyon summer of 1922 Garland moved untroubled in a society to which America was a place of subsidiary rights and lecture tours and where his personal acquaintance was of more importance than any critical acclaim.

Before his boat docked at Southampton Garland had written letters announcing his arrival, to Barrie, to Kipling, to Shaw, and to Zangwill, and almost immediately he was caught up in a round of calls and dinners, interspersed with attempts to locate a flat in which to install his wife and daughters who were to follow him in a few weeks. He was guest of honor at a Piccadilly woman's club, elected an honorary member of the P.E.N. Club. But it was at the Authors' Club that he was in the habit of lunching. One thing that amazed Garland was the lack of intercourse between well-known figures in the literary world. That James Barrie should not be acquainted with Joseph Conrad passed his belief. Barrie, however, suggested Galsworthy as a possible go-between to Conrad, and urged Garland to present his letter of introduction from Henry Cabot Lodge to Lord Balfour.

Thus it was that no sooner were Zulime and the girls installed in a Kensington flat, complete with English housekeeper, than the Garlands were off for a luncheon at the historic Palmerston mansion of Arthur Balfour. Thereafter the Garland girls had an Arabian Nights summer of entertainments and visits with the famous. Their first call was upon Peter Pan in neighboring Ken-

[6] Carl Van Doren, "Contemporary American Novelists," *Nation*, CXIII (November 23, 1921), 596–97.

sington gardens. There was the pageantry of the trooping of the colors. A. A. Milne came to luncheon at their flat. Kipling gave them a conducted tour of Bodiam Castle. During a weekend in Sussex with Conan Doyle they visited Battle Abbey. And Doyle showed them a silver plate set in his floor where his dead son had spoken to him. [7]

Zulime had developed a lead of her own which provided the Garlands a glimpse of another world. At the Fourth of July dinner of the P.E.N. Club Zulime was seated next to the Maharajah of Jahlawar. "At the close of the dinner," Garland reported, 'I found my wife talking with an East Indian, a superb figure in a robe of embroidered satin and wearing a snowy turban, in the center of which blazed a glorious diamond." It turned out that His Royal Highness was in England with his family taking a doctor's degree from Oxford. An invitation for the Americans to visit him followed, and in the Maharajah's car with a coronet on the radiator Hamlin and Zulime rolled through Oxford's twisted streets. [8] On a second visit the Garlands took their daughters and found on the table of the Indian's rented villa a complete morocco-bound edition of Garland's works awaiting his autograph. The juxtaposition of contrasts was all a writer could wish for in the way of material. Garland wrote:

Whether any of my ancestors ever studied at Magdalen or not, I cannot say, but if they did, I hope their ghosts, lingering about its beautiful doorways, had the grace to smile as they saw my daughters walking by, conducted by an Oriental prince in turban and Tuxedo, whilst I bare-headed and rapt with the beauty of it all, followed with a mounting sense of the amazing character of our parade. [9]

With Zulime and the girls Garland took many a sight-seeing excursion, but he could not forsake his habit of club life. The Authors' Club, the Savile Club, the Savage Club, the Reform Club, were all habitual lunching places. Naïvely he observed:

As I come and go in the clubs which used to seem inaccessible, I wonder if something has not gone out of them. Has the war broken down their walls—or made their gates less forbidding? Surely none of

[7] *My Friendly Contemporaries,* pp. 418–26, 437, 442–46, 474, 479–80.
[8] *Ibid.*, pp. 460–61, 536–38.
[9] *Back-Trailers from the Middle Border* (1928), p. 239.

these I have entered can be called formal or formidable. They are reserved, but they are not exclusive or aristocratic—as they are made to appear in novels. They are all filled with hard-working professionals of one kind or another. [10]

Garland met Conrad, as he had hoped. He recorded that to his amazement the Pole said "I have written for years with the thought in my mind 'What will Hamlin Garland think of my books?' but I had given up all hope of seeing you." Conrad talked of the last days of Stephen Crane, who, he assured Garland, "often spoke of you with respect and gratitude." Wickham Stead, editor of the *London Times,* and a friend of Mark Sullivan, proved an interesting companion, and with Edmund Gosse, upon whom Garland called on business of the Academy, there began an acquaintance which progressed as years passed. A meeting with H. G. Wells, however, proved a fiasco. At the same dinner at which Zulime annexed the Maharajah Garland was seated directly opposite "a plump, bullet-headed man with a thin, high, falsetto voice. This was H. G. Wells, who civilly offered to share his bottle of wine with me. I thanked him and explained that I seldom drank wine. He then attempted to talk with me, but his weak, husky pipe failed to reach me." [11] So ended the project of writing up a "real conversation" with H. G. Wells.

For his daughters Garland was able to bring about miracles of introductions. Constance aspired to be an artist, an illustrator, and her ideal was Arthur Rackham, who had done the drawings for her favorite books of fairy tales. Garland arranged a call upon Rackham in his Primrose Hill studio where the artist, mindful of his own daughter, talked to Constance "as a teacher might, advising her in matters relating to pen-and-ink illustration." [12] To please Mary Isabel the Garlands entrained for Salisbury to look up Maurice Hewlett, the author of the girls' favorite "Richard Yea-and-Nay." Some of the constraint which marked this encounter is obvious in Garland's remembrance of it. "To relate this small, sad man with the richly woven tapestries of his medieval romances was not easy. His manner was that of a literary editor who refuses to talk shop. That he was interested and

[10] *My Friendly Contemporaries,* pp. 458–59.
[11] *Ibid.,* pp. 491, 499, 439, 505, 460.
[12] *Ibid.,* p. 503.

somewhat embarrassed was evident. Few Americans seek him out and he was curious to know the reasons for our coming." But, according to Garland, Hewlett's British reserve softened under the flattery of girlish eagerness and he gave the tourists a card to the current owners of the rectory where his books had once been written, so that they could see his old study. [13]

There was a certain lack of spontaneity in many of the Garlands' experiences in England, for Garland *père* was only incidentally concerned with showing his family the sights. He was primarily conscious of the need for building up "literary materials." On September 4, he noted in his journal:

> I am working each morning on the third volume of my Middle Border chronicle which for the moment we are calling "The Back Trailers." There is a certain advantage in being three thousand miles from the scene of my narrative. This is not an easy book to write, for part of it deals with New York City and the London part will run along the beaten track of English travel. All that will save it from being trite will be my contact with distinctive and interesting personalities. English landscapes, English cities, do not greatly change from year to year, but authors and artists do. I shall rough out the early chapters and revise them in the light of my diaries after my return. Six weeks of our stay remain and they are likely to be richer in experiences than any that have gone before. [14]

The six weeks passed quickly in another round of visits from Shaw, Conrad, Masefield, Barrie, and Arnold Bennett, as Garland continued his avid note-taking to play Boswell to all these Johnsons. The highlight of the trip for the girls was the event of having Sir James Barrie as a dinner guest and receiving a return invitation to lunch. When the date arrived Barrie was suffering from a severe cold, but exerted himself to make the occasion pleasant for the girls, showing them pictures of his adopted sons, and a photograph which the Queen had autographed for him. Garland appreciated the effort of his host:

> He could very justly have called the luncheon off, but he knew how deeply disappointed my daughters would have been and so went through a meal which he could not share and did his heroic best to interest us all. I never think of it without a feeling of admiration for

[13] *Ibid.,* pp. 464–67.
[14] *Ibid.,* p. 506.

his courage and a sense of gratitude for his consideration. My girls would have been broken-hearted by a postponement of this visit for the end of our vacation was near. [15]

Four days before sailing date Sir Arthur and Lady Conan Doyle came to lunch. "Hearty, wholesome, joyous, and sane, Doyle was in sharp contrast to Hewlett whose vogue has passed, and to Masefield, who dealt in a commodity for which there was little demand." As the two families sat plotting the course for the Doyles to take on a proposed tour of the western United States, Garland reflected that no one would ever have taken them for spiritualists. "No one listening would have considered either of us in the slightest degree a man of the séance room. He was an athlete, an outdoor man, and so was I in my degree—and a horseman besides." [16]

When the family sailed October 14 each of the Garland girls carried a five-pound box of candy, the gift of the author of *Peter Pan*.

Garland's account of his 1922 summer excursion in *Back-Trailers of the Middle Border* was objected to by Fuller as too much of a "set piece." Indeed the author's emphasis upon the celebrities encountered places the narrative at the other extreme from the recounting of homely episodes which had marked the beginnings of his Middle Border chronicle. Fuller had advised at the time of composition:

Above all, I don't want the account of the first London visit to seem naif. Drum it in beyond doubt that you took the Albert Gate flat very largely for the sake of the children, and make it clear that most of the reactions are theirs, with father (who had "been there before") as somwhat the indulgent and amused spectator. He can resume his own proper character when it comes to his dealings with the great ones of the London literary world. [17]

Fuller's plea for sophistication added to Garland's normal penchant for name-dropping produced a document which as biography must be taken with large grains of salt. The corrective touches lie in Garland's less guarded admissions as to things

[15] *Ibid.*, p. 527.
[16] *Ibid.*, p. 542.
[17] H. B. Fuller to Garland, June 8 [?], Garland Papers.

British, and in what may be read between the lines of his account of his reception in the mother country.

In the autumn of 1922 Garland again took up his chautauqua round across the United States. Now his lectures were embellished by the appearance of Mary Isabel as assistant reader. In hoop skirt, with hair in a net, she would appear in Civil War garb as an evocation of her grandmother. Later in the program she shifted into an old gown of her mother's, the period dress of the nineties, with puffed sleeves and long train. "In this costume she spoke with utter simplicity a chapter from *A Daughter of the Middle Border* . . . 'The Fairy World of Childhood,' and her auditors enjoyed the complex experience of hearing a daughter read, in the character of her mother, a prose analysis of her childhood composed by her own father." [18] Thus the Garlands of the Middle Border presented themselves to their audience as figures repeating themselves in a series of reflecting mirrors.

In November the Garland team toured Wisconsin and Iowa returning to New York for the holidays and for a January engagement at Town Hall. There Mary Isabel left the troupe to join Walter Hampden's company where for a time she played bit parts in a Broadway production of *Cyrano*. Her father continued his Middle Border lecture alone, ranging through Illinois, Missouri, Tennessee, Oklahoma, Texas, and as far as California. With Mary Isabel absent the performance must have sunk to a stereotyped routine which Garland persisted in repeating solely for the purpose of accumulating funds for another family summer in Europe. [19]

One Oklahoman has given a candid report of his recollections of a Garland lecture:

I recall how Hamlin Garland, a professional pioneer (as it seemed to us), once addressed our college assembly and read a paper (doubtless some speech he had given before ladies' clubs in the East) boasting of his pioneer ancestry—and left his audience of pioneers stone cold. Then our neighbor, John Homer Seger, the old Indian agent, who had driven Hamlin Garland, was invited to speak. Seger got up

---

[18] *Back-Trailers from the Middle Border*, p. 274.
[19] *Ibid.*, p. 278; *Afternoon Neighbors* (1934), pp. 20–28.

and entranced us by the hour with true stories of Indian life and of his own pioneer endeavor set in our own Plains country. [20]

But the lecture tour had served its purpose and the Garlands were enabled to spend another summer in England. It held not the excitement of the previous visit but rather the familiar charm of repetition. Garland was in more contemplative mood. In Westminster he brooded: "Those of us who come from the pine-board shanties of the Mid-West plains are awed by the shadows of these arches. Some of us are oppressed by them. We escape into the shadeless present with a sense of relief."

The clue to English literary society yet eluded him. Mark Sullivan, he admitted "is about the only man in London with whom I can actually neighbor. It is not easy for an old fellow like me to make new friends. I am not in touch with English newspaper men or with the younger generation, and like so many authors I tend to grow solitary as my years increase. Gosse and Galsworthy are exceptions. They both go out of their way to be of personal use—so does Doyle but most English writers and artists keep to their studios and see their admirers and co-workers but seldom." [21]

To the list of Garland's loyal friends in England must be added Barrie, who again entertained the family, this time for a weekend at his summer home in the Cotswolds. But not even the author of *Peter Pan* was sufficient inducement to the Garland girls to prolong their stay in England. The interests of their young lives lay, after all, in America, and they were eager to return home, although their father might have lingered. He protested: "I thought I was bringing with me three steam-engines to drive me along; and all I have is three sand bags!"[22] In August Garland took a reluctant leavetaking of a land to which he had become greatly attached:

While this summer has not reached the ecstatic level of last year, it has been rich in experience, and as I look for the last time from my study window out over the city at the rounded Surrey hills, so familiar to me now, I experience a pang of fear that I may never revisit them.

[20] W. S. Campbell, *The Booklover's Southwest,* p. 243.
[21] *Afternoon Neighbors,* pp. 36, 37.
[22] *Ibid.,* pp. 67–69; Conversation with Constance Garland Doyle, January 21, 1957.

There is so much yet to be seen, so many interesting and kindly folk to be met, and such delightful friendships offering, that the thought of leaving them all behind saddens me. The only anodyne for this ache of regret is the vague and unexpressed hope of returning next year. At the age of sixty-three, however, "next year" is not under bond to fulfill any promise. [23]

Back in New York where Henry Fuller had been occupying the Garland apartment the two old friends discussed the charm of Europe. The man who had once posed for the portrait of Abner Joyce admitted:

"I now realize that the man who stays too long amid fortunate circumstances in the Old World, is certain to find himself discontented with his vexatious life in the New. Having gained the comparative outlook of a cosmopolite, he loses interest in the social doings of his home town."

To this Fuller tartly said, "That's what I've been saying to you for twenty years."

"I know you have, and you put it into all your books. At that time your comment was treasonable. Now, as a result of two summers in England, I find myself in danger of gaining your point of view."

He laughed. "You returned just in time. Better not go again." [24]

Notwithstanding this advice Garland did go abroad the following two summers, but, without the companionship of his family, the pleasure of travel soon palled, and he at last abandoned what had been more than a half-hope of following in the footsteps of other distinguished American authors by becoming an expatriate.

While Garland was experimenting with British residence his *Book of the American Indian* had gone to press. He had wanted Harper's to bring it out as part of the "Border Edition," but Edward Marsh, who had selected Frederick Remington as illustrator, thought that the book would do better in a de luxe art edition designed to feature Remington's pictures. Garland, who as a youth had yearned to have the western painter illustrate his books, now was out of sympathy with Remington's approach:

My design was directly opposite to that of Remington, who carried to the study of these hunters all the contempt, all the conventional

[23] *Afternoon Neighbors*, p. 100.   [24] *Ibid.*, pp. 110–11.

notions of a hard and rather prosaic illustrator. He never got the wilderness point of view. His white hunters were all ragged, bearded, narrow between the eyes, and his red men stringy, gross of feature and cruel. I recognized no harmony between his drawings and my text, but as I was poor and my publishers agreed that they could not publish the book as I wished to have it done, I laid my manuscript on their editorial desk and went away. (It may interest the reader to know that the editors were right and that they sold more than ten times the number of copies I had anticipated.) [25]

It is interesting that the London *Times* rather agreed with Garland at this point, suggesting that the material might well have appeared in two volumes, one an album of Remington drawings and one of Garland's text. [26] Yet, as produced, the book was an attractive addition to the Garland canon.

The majority of its stories had been published in various magazines twenty and twenty-five years earlier, when Indian characterizations based on real observation had scarcely made an appearance in American fiction. At that time Garland had sounded a new note by his insistence on treating the Indian as an individual. His "Spartan Mother" [27] reluctantly relinquishing her son to the white man's school, his agency nurse "sheathed in the boiler-iron of her own superstitions," his Indian chiefs meta-

---

[25] *My Friendly Contemporaries*, pp. 409–410. For another comment on Remington, see *Roadside Meetings*, p. 394.

[26] London *Times* Literary Supplement, December 27, 1923, p. 908.

[27] It has been suggested that Garland improperly used materials of the Indian agent John Homer Seger in these stories. Walter S. Campbell (under his penname of Stanley Vestal) in editing Seger's *Early Days Among the Cheyenne and Arapahoe Indians* ("Bulletin of Oklahoma University" [Norman, 1924], reprinted Norman, 1934) made this caustic statement in his foreword: "Mr. Hamlin Garland, who is certainly qualified to appraise valuable literary material, has drawn freely upon Mr. Seger's stories in the past (e. g. *The Spartan Mother*), and has recently confessed to me that he intends to rehandle others in a forthcoming volume." The parallelisms between Garland's stories and materials in the Seger autobiography are indisputable. Professor Campbell makes the further statement that on many occasions as a boy he had "sat up half the night listening to his [Seger's] stories." Garland had had the same experience and in *Companions on the Trail* (pp. 143–44) recounts how he once had a stenographer take down Seger's stories, and attempted to find a publisher for this "confused tangle of valuable material." Later, with Seger's consent he "used a few of the incidents as suggestions for short stories," although he continued to urge his friend to work up his own autobiography. The extensive correspondence between Seger and Garland, ranging from 1902 until the former's death, confirms this ac-

morphosed into awkward plowmen as they learned "to walk the white man's road," were fresh contributions to American literature. Garland, without religious orientation, could not interpret so ably as would later writers, the inner life of the Indian, but in social problems his apprehension of their dilemma was instinctive and sympathetic. His own experiences in shifting from the freedom of the frontier to the restrictions of cities had left him in high degree cognizant of the difficulties of the clash of cultures.

Three of his stories and one longer "epic" were original publications. "The Blood Lust," dealing with a Cheyenne's revenge for the loss of his daughter by the wholesale sacking of a border town, must have been too realistic for *Harper's Weekly, Frank Leslie's Magazine,* or the *Ladies' Home Journal,* where the earlier stories had appeared. "The Remorse of Waumdisapa" was a sketch footnoted "A substantially true account of an incident well-known to bordermen," and dealt with fratricide among the Indian chiefs. "A Decree of Council" had a comic touch. Big Nose, having gambled away all of his property including both of his wives, appeals to the tribal council for restitution. That body gives him back one wife, the termagant, with the decree that he shall never remarry. Doubtless the editorial taboo against polygamy kept this amusing story earlier unpublished.

In "The Silent Eaters" Garland revived the "epic" of Sitting Bull which had absorbed his thoughts at the turn of the century, when his recent visit to Standing Rock reservation had given him access to the accounts of the agency schoolteacher and one of the tribal annalists. Garland's version of the statesmanship of Sitting Bull is given in the words of the son of one of the "silent eaters," that religious group which sparked the ill-fated uprising. His hero has been criticized by one authority as "too flawless," his rendition of native life before the coming of the white man "too idyllic." But, adds the critic, "it must of course not be forgotten that the whole is dominated by the contrast between a native's retrospect of his unhindered roaming of the prairies and the

---

count. Professor Campbell maintains that the Seger manuscript which was furnished him required practically no editing. On the other hand, the Seger materials remaining in the Garland Papers are chaotic and at best semiliterate.

present life of enforced labor within the bounds of the reservation." [28]

In 1923 when *The Book of the American Indian* appeared these stories written so many years before were forced to stand comparison with the work of Mary Austin, Oliver La Farge, Charles Lummis, Stanley Vestal, Frank Waters, and others. But the book, with Remington's pictures (which likewise were largely reprints from that earlier era), was well received. The *New York Times* remarked that the state of the Indians was yet a disgrace, and of Garland's stories: "If they do no more than prick our conscience as to a national responsibility toward an ancient race which, as the Indian bureau reminds us, is slowly increasing, then they will bring the greatest honor to a distinguished American writer." [29] Albert Keiser dedicated his 1933 volume *The Indian in American Literature* to "Hamlin Garland, Friend of the American Indian," calling Garland's work "one of the most systematic as well as sympathetic treatments of the American native and his problem." [30] In considering the general critical disparagement of Garland's middle period, it is well to consider that these Indian stories were written, though only ephemerally published, in the years when he was producing the series of Western novels, then critically acclaimed, now completely scorned.

That winter of 1923 Garland was again upon the lecture circuit. At Minnesota College he encountered a ghost from his past. After his speech a "handsome dark-eyed woman of seventy, or thereabouts," came up the aisle to meet him, and shaking hands introduced herself as "Agnes Davis of Burr Oak." He searched for a familiar feature and found it at last in eyes still velvety black. Was this the "Agnes" of his impassioned poem "Homeward Bound" of 1889? But now it develops that she had been a mature sixteen to Garland's hero-worshipping thirteen when he last saw her:

I could not recall that she had ever spoken to me directly, but I had admired her as one of the loveliest of all the neighborhood girls. She was in truth, the calm-voiced maid who stopped the fight in my story

---

[28] Albert Keiser, *The Indian in American Literature,* p. 284.
[29] *New York Times,* October 14, 1923.
[30] Keiser, *op. cit.,* Dedication and p. 279.

"The Sociable at Dudley's." How could she relate Hamlin Garland, the novelist of sixty-three, with the uncouth boy of thirteen who "spoke a piece" at the Burr Oak schoolhouse? Nevertheless, she did, and something fine and sweet was in her voice, something which prose is quite unable to express.

And so across a gulf of fifty years the two old people reminisced. Agnes could exhibit with pride her two grandchildren, but in the end there was little they had to say to each other. [31]

With the excuse of arranging for French translations of his works Garland went abroad again in the summer of 1924, to meet Dr. Friman Roz, who wished Dunod to publish *The Captain of the Gray-Horse Troop* and other works of Garland's. Despite scheduled addresses and the brief companionship of Henry Fuller, Garland found himself homesick for his family. "I have many acquaintances here," he wrote in London, "but few friends, and I suspect that I am a kind of obligation even to the oldest of my friends." Even Fuller, he had declared earlier, irritated him in many ways, "but he is, notwithstanding, the most satisfactory companion of my old age." In 1925 Garland again made the experiment of a solitary summer abroad. He was bored. Only a temporary membership in the Athenaeum Club, where he had never so much as lunched before, convinced him that the summer "had not been without its climax." But he returned to America with the reflection: "I was in danger of coming to like England too well. I am cured." [32]

By now Garland's financial position was secure. With a school edition of the *Son* and a reprint edition of the *Daughter* he was practically independent of the magazine market and could publicly thumb his nose at the slick commercial magazines. He did so with enthusiasm in an article in the May, 1924, *Bookman* entitled "Limitations of Authorship in America." "After all," he admitted, speaking as "one whose work has suffered from commercial considerations," "authors write for publication, and the conditions which govern the distribution and sale of books and magazines have more to do with determining the form and spirit

[31] *Afternoon Neighbors,* pp. 126–27.
[32] *Ibid.,* pp. 175, 179, 130, 265, 270. Apparently the translation arrangements fell through. Later, however, (see Bibliography) some of Garland's Indian stories appeared in French journals.

of a nation's literature than most historians are willing to admit."

Garland's complaint was that of *O tempora, O mores*. He insists that in the eighties he wrote his stories with no thought of the editor. "Besides," he continues, "Aldrich, Gilder, Alden were men of letters. . . . the monthly magazine was not yet a topical monthly journal." Times have changed, and not for the better, he complains. "I permit myself to think that American literature should somehow be considered quite apart from its effect on the sale of underwear or safety razors. . . . [not as] a narrow rill of text meandering down a wide plain of advertising." [33]

Garland could now afford such a declaration of independence. For in addition to his steady royalties there were ample lecture fees, and the mirage of movie rights which had danced so tantalizingly on the horizon a decade earlier now rematerialized in unexpected fashion. As damages for a pirated picture version of *Cavanaugh* Garland recovered a round ten thousand dollars. [34]

Not only were European summers becoming a reality but the family could acquire a more permanent home in the Catskills. In the Onteora Park co-operative community, which hitherto had welcomed the Garlands as neighbors but not as full-fledged members, the family located a twelve-room house for sale, a two-story red brick building upon a rocky ledge, which they occupied with much gusto, naming it "Grey Ledges." [35] Here the girls could entertain their young men while their father watched the process of their emergence into womanhood with all the pride and qualms which parents universally experience.

Mary Isabel was again appearing with her father in lecture appearances, and employing herself in typing his manuscript of *The Trail-Makers of the Middle Border*. It was a book in which Garland produced further illusions with his reflecting mirrors, recounting the story of his father's migration from Maine to Boston, thence to Wisconsin where he joined forces with the McClintocks. In this introduction to the Middle Border autobiographies the author was dealing with events which had come down to him in fireside reminiscence. To indicate that fictional license

[33] *Bookman*, LIX (May, 1924), 257–61.
[34] *Afternoon Neighbors*, p. 275.
[35] *Back-Trailers from the Middle Border*, pp. 245–49; *Afternoon Neighbors*, pp. 272–75.

had supplied the details, he converted the Garlands into the "Grahams" and the McClintocks into the "McLanes." But the story was essentially the factual one which he had sketched into *A Son of the Middle Border,* and which had furnished the basis for some of his short stories. The second half of the narrative deals with "Dick Graham's" experiences as a scout of Grant's army and ends with the homecoming, the point at which *A Son of the Middle Border* had begun.

Published in 1926 the volume drew good reviews. [36] A considerable part of the charm of the new volume was attributable to the drawings which accompanied the text, full-page renditions of the progenitors of the clan, imaginative sketches for the chapter heads and tailpieces, all from the pen of young Constance Garland, who thus after her own fashion joined in the family act. *Trail-Makers of the Middle Border* recaptured for its author some of the acclaim which had greeted *A Son of the Middle Border.* One enthusiastic reader went so far as to propose the creation of an organization of "Sons of the Middle Border," to be composed of all those whose fathers had been trailmakers—a sort of regional F.F.V. or D.A.R. fraternity. [37]

At the June, 1926, commencement exercises of the University of Wisconsin Garland received the doctorate which had been offered him earlier, but which a trip to England had prevented his accepting. [38] Travelling alone to Madison to receive the honor Garland rapidly became disillusioned over the perfunctory character of the proceedings. The room assigned him at the University Club was dark and odorous, "not at all such a lodging as a more or less distinguished author and prospective Literary Doctor might reasonably expect to enjoy." At a small dinner given him by the English Department he was chagrined to see that only one other man had donned a Tuxedo for the affair. He thought

[36] *Bookman,* LXIV (November, 1926) 349; New York *Herald Tribune,* Book Section, October 26, 1929, p. 25; *Boston Transcript,* November 13, 1926, p. 3; *Independent,* CXVII (December 11, 1926), 681; *Saturday Review,* III (November 6, 1926), 270.

[37] Henry C. Taylor to Garland, carbon copy to Albert Shaw, November 22, 1926, New York Public Library.

[38] *Afternoon Neighbors,* pp. 30, 328. In the first case Garland dates the proffer of the degree as on May 17, 1923. Later he speaks of the same offer as being "in the spring of 1924."

the auditorium where the exercises were held "smelled like a livery stable," and that the address of President Frank Glenn "was unconventional as the building." In fact, he considered it "a bit Bolshevik." Only the attentions of his friend Zona Gale, now a regent of the University, saved the occasion from utter fiasco in Garland's mind. For when he stepped forward to receive his hood the applause was "only a polite greeting," himself "just another claimant of a diploma." Summing up his reactions he wrote wryly: "With the modesty which has always—or nearly always—characterized me, I hope the press of the State will at least print my name on the list of those who have contributed to the literature of Wisconsin." Later he added: "I don't think it did— no one knew of it except as I told them." [39]

Macmillan & Company, however, made sure that their author's honorary degree was called to the attention of the public. George Brett had become convinced that the *Trail-Makers* merited a special promotional campaign, [40] and a handsome brochure on "Hamlin Garland. A Son of the Middle Border" was soon in preparation. Its lead paragraph recited the fact of Garland's latest honor: "On June 21, the University of Wisconsin conferred upon Hamlin Garland the degree of Doctor of Letters," and quoted from the citation of Professor Frederic Logan Paxson:

Hamlin Garland is the novelist of our northwest farmer country. For thirty-five years his easy pen has worked at the life of our people. . . . Fiction is often the truest history and formal biography as such, but what we value today, and what our children will value in years to come is his verisimilitude to life. His writings are works of art, but they are also documents which may become the source of history.

The publisher's blurb continued with a summary of Garland's career down to the publication of the *Trail-Makers*. Roosevelt's endorsement was quoted, as were reviews of the earlier Middle Border books by Howells, by Carl Van Doren, and the London *Times*. Fuller's article from the *Freeman* was reprinted. The jaunty style of Henry B.'s epistles is missing from this somewhat awkward formal tribute. (Perhaps he intended the solemnity of this article to serve as belated amends for the irony of "Abner Joyce.")

[39] *Ibid.*, pp. 328–32.   [40] *Ibid.*, pp. 349–50.

No surviving friend will need to make an appeal through the literary weeklies for material to use in "The Life and Letters of Hamlin Garland"; the manner [*sic*] has been attended to most completely by Mr. Garland himself.

In a new field, in almost a new form, he moves with freshness, originality, confidence. ... He has regained all the better among his earlier qualities, and has added others to them.

J. E. Chamberlin contributed to the pamphlet a friendly reminiscent sketch of "The Hardy of the West," recalling Garland's early days when "he had broken into life in Boston in the cheekiest way that a boy possibly could":

It was characteristic of him that he could walk up to the house of Edwin Booth on the hill, linger until some chance opening had revealed to him a hat-rack, a mirror and possibly a dark figure passing through the hall before the door closed again, and then go back to his little attic room and write a glowing and perfectly plausible essay on "The Art of Edwin Booth," which people would want to listen to.

Expanding into criticism Chamberlin described Garland as "by instinct too much the artist to be a reformer. Too much, if you analyze his work, a romanticist to narrow his soul with ethical or social problems." The comparison with Hardy is made on the basis of regionalism. "But it does not seem to me that Garland has created great characters as Hardy has done. He has described great scenes. ... Garland's people are as real as flesh and blood, but they are commonplace people, just as he found them. All except some great Indians." After devoting two pages to a discussion of Garland's Indian writings, Chamberlin concludes of "The Silent Eaters": "It is the extraordinary merit of Garland that he has sung this Indian Iliad with the voice of the Indian himself." [41]

This collection of tributes was handsomely adorned by Macmillan's with profuse illustrations: a frontispiece of Garland; one of Constance's book illustrations, "The Reunited Family"; a photograph of Mary Isabel in lecture costume; a picture of "The Homestead"; Garland "in his Cheyenne Teepee Smoking the Peace Pipe, 1899"; "Garland on the Klondike"; pictures of

[41] *Hamlin Garland. A Son of the Middle Border.* Macmillan pamphlet. [n. d.]. Copy in Garland Papers.

Zulime, of Isabel Garland, of the new home "Gray Ledges." For once Garland could not complain of the extent of his advertising appropriation.

The first edition of the *Trail-Makers*, a printing of fifteen thousand, was sold out before publication, and in the author's estimation, "the book sold well, but not as well as the firm's campaign deserved." [42] Ten years later, with the title still moving a hundred or so copies per year, it was reproduced in a cheap edition which found its way to the jobbers in bulk lots of 1,500 and 2,500. When it is considered that this pamphlet advertised also the *Son* and the *Daughter*, as well as the *Grant* reprint, it probably proved a profitable investment for the publishers. At all events, in 1937 on the occasion of a second doctorate for Garland from the University of Southern California, the brochure was reprinted with an expanded text, bringing Garland's achievements up to date and with a substitution of more recent photographs of the Garland family. [43]

After seeing the *Trail-Makers* through the press Garland continued to work in desultory fashion upon his fourth autobiographical volume *Back-Trailers from the Middle Border* and to edit his diaries with a view to future publication. The New York apartment on Fifteenth Street, which he had so long complained against as crowded and uncomfortable, was being torn down to make way for a more modern structure. Perversely, Garland considered this an outrage, and only with much grumbling moved his city residence to a new apartment building on Cathedral Parkway. The erection of St. John's Cathedral across the roadway provided a compensating factor. But the sense of disgust with New York living persisted, moving him to nostalgia for "the quiet, order and cleanliness of London." "From the standpoint of a Londoner or a Parisian this Cathedral group is a pitiful showing, but we must make the most of what we have. The older I grow, the more deeply I long for the historic, the settled,

---

[42] *Afternoon Neighbors*, pp. 347, 350.

[43] Macmillan royalty statements to Garland, July 28, 1936 (for fiscal year ending April 30, 1936); July 29, 1937 (for fiscal year ending April 30, 1937); and July 29, 1938 (for fiscal year ending April 30, 1938), Garland Papers. The second edition of the Macmillan brochure is also in the Garland Papers.

the permanent. I am filled with hunger as I think of the lovely old towns of England."

With Fuller, who was a frequent visitor, he became a sidewalk superintendent of the erection of the Cathedral, making a matutinal inspection trip "to mark from day to day the layers of stone which the swarming workmen, like so many heroic ants, deposit." The two aging writers sat in the sun of the unfinished quadrangle, dreaming of the completed project which they could not hope to live to see. [44]

Even the affairs of the American Academy filled Garland with despondency as the inexorable years moved on. He was called upon to present the Howells medal for fiction to Mary E. Wilkins Freeman. Contrasting the deaf and broken old lady now at his side with the radiant young woman he had known thirty-five years before, Garland complained it was "a little like the ceremony of pinning a gold cross on the bosom of a disabled soldier in a forgotten war." [45]

The Academy might honor women, but to admit them to membership in the National Institute was an innovation which alarmed Garland. "Writers and artists of the rank of Anna Hyatt, Cecilia Beaux and Edith Wharton are beyond dispute eligible but the question is—will the election of women bring a schism in the Institute?" [46] Garland's one-time militant feminism had sharply faded as his daughters matured. "Having no son," he wrote on the occasion of Constance's graduation from Finch, "I was ambitious for both my daughters. I granted them freedom of action. I expected them to marry, but I hoped to see them famous. That this was illogical and contradictory I granted." [47]

The issue of marriage versus a career settled itself quickly enough for both girls. Mary Isabel quoted her mother: "I'd rather be a first-class wife than a fourth-class artist. That's the way I feel about it." And in May of 1926 she married a young tenor Hardesty Johnson, whom she had met three years before in England. The young couple worked up a program for voice and

[44] *Afternoon Neighbors,* pp. 310–11.
[45] *Ibid.,* pp. 318–19.
[46] *Ibid.,* p. 353.
[47] *Back-Trailers from the Middle Border,* p. 349.

violin using some of Garland's ballads. As Garland took his seat
in their audience to observe the traditions of his family thus
carried forward by yet another generation he sighed sentimental-
ly: "I wish Uncle David might have listened. Perhaps he did!" [48]

Constance now succeeded to Mary Isabel's place as costumed
reader for the Middle Border lecture. That winter their tour led
them to Detroit. Garland had begun writing occasional articles
for the *Dearborn Independent* and it logically followed that he
and Constance should be entertained by the Ford organization.
On the night of their lecture there was scheduled at the Dearborn
plant a musical revival, and the Garlands were whisked from the
platform at the conclusion of their performance to attend the
festivities at Dearborn. Constance, still in her hoop skirt, was
soon dancing one of the old-fashioned squares to the tune of dulcimer and fiddle, with Henry Ford as her partner. The next day
as the Garlands were shown through the Ford Museum with its
collection of frontier relics, Ford joined the party and soon he
and Garland were capping quotations from the old McGuffey
readers.

Completely captivated by the magnate's efforts to preserve the
frontier life they both had known, Garland returned home to
write an article praising Ford's historical interests. He found
that none of his editorial friends would print it.

If I had written a slurring article, calling Ford a tyrant, a despot,
a monopolist and a merciless money-grabber I've no doubt it would
have been acceptable. As I had only seen the human, kindly side of
this man I was unable to attack him. On the contrary I found in him
the man John Burroughs liked and journeyed with. [49]

Constance was not long to be her father's assistant. In September of 1927 she too married. [50] Her choice was a grandson of the
founder of Harper & Brothers. Thus Garland had the satisfaction
of knowing that his sons-in-law belonged, the one by vocation
and the other at least by heritage, to the circle of the arts. But
with this marriage of his second daughter the family circle definitely dissolved. Garland grew increasingly restive, dissatisfied

[48] *Ibid.*, pp. 355–56.
[49] *Afternoon Neighbors*, pp. 359–68.
[50] *Ibid.*, p. 442.

with his surroundings and impatient with his writing. On November 12, 1927, he wrote despondently:

> Nothing remains but to go on doggedly making books, although I am perfectly well aware that none of them will appeal to the casual reader with greater power than those I have already published—probably they will have less and less appeal. . . . I am told that my books go into libraries and will be studied after my death as social records, but these younger opportunists build castles and buy yachts with the royalties on their tales of lust and war. To be read after one's death is cold comfort—but what if even that is denied me? [51]

The loyal Fuller labored to break this mood, continually urging Garland to complete his *Back-Trailers*, writing long letters of criticism and advice:

> Send on anything. Send on everything. Will reread the whole Ms. if you wish, and will comment and annotate as far as you desire and as broadly as the occasion may require. As for PROPORTION, I am satisfied—judging from the four-fifths I have read and the one-fifth I have heard sketched out. The English part will not be too big, if followed by four American chapters; and it's a good thing to separate the two visits by an "at home" chapter—England thus seeming less of a set piece.
>
> BALANCE seems assured, but will depend on the fulness of the concluding chapters, and on their tone. You are not merely winding up a single book, but a whole series of books. Gravity, poise, a touch of the diapason—that's about the order I place with you. Quietude, reverie, retrospection—oh, how I'm crowding it on you!
>
> "INJUDICIOUS ADMISSION." Well, now you know you have already set the tone in your previous books. As I seem to recall having written somewhere, you employ a manly frankness that has no need for concealment.

To this epistle Fuller added a note some days later advising "touch-and-go references in present book to both English and American friends, leaving the essential and best for future use." His final word of advice was this: "Don't get locoed. There's no need. And DO learn to make allowances for these varying moods of yours."

Under Fuller's goading the manuscript took final shape. By

[51] *Ibid.*, p. 454.

Thanksgiving Fuller was sure that it was "the best of the four, and the best you have ever done." The novels of the middle period "take quite secondary rank—though they did save your soul from the Lorimers, et al." But this book need not be the end. If Latham has expressed an interest in the diaries, "seize a favorable moment and strike out the general plan." [52] Surely a competent literary agent, if not a great editor, was lost to American letters when Henry Fuller devoted his time to writing travel sketches!

But his enthusiasm for *Back-Trailers from the Middle Border* was unduly weighted by Garland's need of encouragement at the moment. The fourth volume of the series suffers in comparison with the earlier volumes. True, it is the most carefully wrought of the series. There is more art. But the matter is slight, too slight. In this volume Garland carried the history of his family from the time of his father's death in 1914 almost to his immediate present. But the travels of a successful novelist, the concerns of his growing daughters, have none of the representative character of the struggle of the pioneer family who had formed the original cast of actors. One follows the activities of the younger generation with a sense of personal acquaintance, but the continuity is too much of the variety provided by present-day radio serials.

Garland strove valiantly to inject into his sequel the qualities of "quietude, reverie, retrospection" which Fuller had recommended. But Garland was essentially of an unreflective nature. His mature reading had been limited to current novels and to memoirs of fellow writers. From an unstocked mind he could produce, aside from descriptive reporting, only platitudes.

"Contentment with an inland American town may be due either to lack of comparative knowledge, or to a deep philosophy, or to resignation born of need." Garland making his uneasy *apologia pro vita sua* is unconvincing in urging his thesis of an inevitable "centralizing force" which "cannot be checked even though it strips the West of its creative sons." [53] For as the book progresses nostalgia becomes the dominant note, with Garland summing up in this fashion:

[52] H. B. Fuller to Garland, June 8 [1928], June 18 [1928], Thanksgiving, 1928, Garland Papers.
[53] *Back-Trailers from the Middle Border,* pp. 303, 321.

Notwithstanding all that I have written here, I am too much the veritist to deny that our concepts of the past are partial. That our forefathers and foremothers lived in a world as real as our own and with far greater hardships is true. It is probable that their hours of rejoicing were fewer than ours, and yet I shall go on believing that they enjoyed a more poetic world than that in which I live, that they had more courage and less enfeebling doubt. [54]

The reviewers on the whole were kind to what they must have considered an old performer's last bow to the public. The whole series, declared J. E. Chamberlin, had "decided merit and significance." The closing volume was "wholly delightful" reported the *New York Times.* Allan Nevins of the *Saturday Review,* who had complained that the preceding volume lacked "the pulse and color" of *A Son of the Middle Border,* was sympathetic to Garland's swan song, calling it "essentially an intellectual and spiritual biography. If not as exciting as the record of the crusading years it has a mellow fulness. . . . The intimacy of this record, occasionally breaking into naïveté, is always appealing and sometimes touching." [55]

As with any sequel, *Back-Trailers* provokes comparison with its predecessors. Of *Trail-Makers* the *Literary Review* had said: "There are times when the reader forgets it is fiction. . . . As in real life certain persons appear for a brief moment to play their little parts in the scheme, then to disappear forever, like ships in the night." [56] The reverse is true of Garland's final volume. Intended as fact, it reads like fiction. For there is a contrived effect, a straining toward the dramatic, in the latter half of the book. In England Garland dutifully enacted the episodes which he would later convert into "personal history." Thus they became fact. Likewise he enacted his closing scene for *Back-Trailers from the Middle Border,* but his stage was set, his players arranged, with all the care of a producer planning a final curtain. The verisimilitude is that of the stage, not that of the street.

To Henry Ford, Garland had confided his need: "I feel something in your Sudbury Inn restoration which may help me in the

---

[54] *Ibid.,* p. 370.

[55] *Boston Transcript,* November 24, 1928, p. 4; *New York Times,* January 13, 1929, pt. 2; *Saturday Review,* V (December 8, 1928), 453.

[56] *Literary Review,* November 6, 1926, p. 3.

final chapter of my book. It may also aid my daughter in her illustration of this volume."

With Constance, then, Garland spent a weekend at the Wayside Inn, among the replicas of frontier buildings which Ford had created. Constance sketched the scene, placing her father and mother in high-backed chairs before the Longfellow fireplace. Later Garland and Zulime returned to act out the parts assigned. Looking about the room at the pine chairs and tables, the family Bible reposing on its stand, Garland gave Zulime her cue: "We have rounded the circle," he said. "We are at the source of our family history."

At nine o'clock, after the doors were closed, my wife and I had the silent tavern all to ourselves. For two hours we sat before the fireplace described by Longfellow, watching its flames die down and the embers of the logs grow gray. There was something mystically beautiful in this hour of communion with our sires, and I recovered in it the mood with which the fourth volume of my chronicle should close. [57]

With the house lights thus artfully lowered that old trouper Garland stepped forward to deliver his curtain speech:

Some say it is all an illusion, this world of memory, or imagination, but to me the remembered past is more and more a reality, a joyous, secure reality. . . . Rejoicing in the mental law which softens outlines and heightens colors, I have written faithfully, in the hope of adding my small part to the ever-increasing wealth of our home-spun national history. [58]

[57] *Afternoon Neighbors*, pp. 405–407, 498–500.
[58] *Back-Trailers from the Middle Border*, p. 378.

❧ 16 ❧

A Literary Nomad

LIKE MANY ANOTHER seasoned actor Garland continued to repeat his "farewell tour." Sixty-eight, when *Back-Trailers* appeared, he was yet to publish six more volumes, not to mention articles and reprints. While this fourth volume of "personal history" was still in production he was being encouraged by George Brett and Harold Latham to write a series of literary reminiscences based on the diaries which he had faithfully kept throughout the years. [1] It was a project which Garland had often considered in one form or another. In an early notebook of 1902 under the heading "Joyous Hours" occurs this jotting: "A book might be written giving in chapters long or short the best of my experience, the joys that came. It could be biographical and yet free from all tiresome and egotistical details—could have a wide range." [2]

Again in 1926 he noted: "In going over these diaries of mine, I find in them a story which might be called 'Paternity,' for from the coming of my first child, I have set down from time to time

---

[1] *Afternoon Neighbors* (1934), pp. 491–96.
[2] Notebook, 1902, Garland Papers.

... brief paragraphs which chronicle the development of my little daughter." By the next year the project had crystallized to the extent that Garland was tentatively revising the journals for publication, making excerpts from "over eight hundred pages of my diaries (those from 1900 to 1906)."

Whether these excerpts *are* of general interest can be determined only by trying them on some reader who is mildly interested in me and my books. At their lowest valuation these entries form a fairly comprehensive literary chronicle. [3]

The Macmillan readers to whom the excerpted journals were submitted agreed. But the editors turned Garland aside from his intention of publishing the diaries as such. They insisted that he write a literary narrative based on his records. With this goal before him, Garland arose each morning early and by five o'clock was at work at his desk.

My fiction is finished. I shall write no more verse or history, but in these thirty volumes of diaries I see at least two volumes of literary report and comment. These books will contain a summing-up of what I have seen and heard, along with a statement of what I have accomplished. If I can do this task well it will close my career honorably. [4]

Much of the work of selection and compilation had already been accomplished in years gone by. Earlier articles on "Meetings with Howells," "Whitman at Seventy," "Stephen Crane as I Knew Him," "My Neighbor, Theodore Roosevelt," were almost ready-made chapters for the book. To augment the diaries was the wealth of Garland's hoarded correspondence, the early letters of Sarah Orne Jewett, Bret Harte, E. W. Howe, Joseph Kirkland, Mary Wilkins Freeman, and Howells, the rare scrawl of Stephen Crane, the notes from Shaw, from Barrie, from Henry James. To tap this fund of literary source material Macmillan's was willing to pay augmented royalties, and the *Bookman* eagerly scheduled publication for October, 1929, of the first installment of "Roadside Meetings, the Adventures of a Literary Nomad." [5]

[3] *Afternoon Neighbors,* pp. 303, 420.
[4] *Ibid.,* p. 524.
[5] Royalty statements of Macmillan Company to Garland, Garland Papers; *Bookman,* LXX and LXXI (October, 1929–July, 1930).

With his usual ebullience Fuller welcomed the news of Garland's new venture: "Yes, I'll fall in somewhere
$$\left\{\begin{array}{l}\text{behind}\\\text{beyond}\\\text{below}\end{array}\right\}$$ Howells, and be glad to." [6] Fuller had cause of his own for rejoicing. After years of virtual inactivity in a sudden throe of creative energy he had produced two books in the early months of 1929. The first, consisting of sixteen chapters—35,000 words—he had written (and typed himself) in eighteen days! Two months later he delivered to his publisher Alfred Knopf a second manuscript of 60,000 words. Knopf accepted both and planned on reprinting earlier Fuller titles. [7] So Fuller wrote jauntily of both his own and Garland's prospects:

My new Italian thing [*Gardens of This World*] was written just to please myself and a dozen more people who've been asking me to do something in my Earlier Manner. . . . I expect to read and re-read it to my dying day. As I say, it's written for myself.

The other book [*Not on the Screen*] . . . it's a *righthanded* version of a lefthanded "film" society story.

Now for your reprints—with all the slapjacks turned over right in the front window. Well, I guess that's the last best way to realize on earlier work. "Fifteen thousand edition"! A juvenile of "the Trail Makers"! New Roads, Main travelled by H. G. and C. H. G.! Wow! [8]

Harper's had on the agenda for Garland a sixth edition of *Main-Travelled Roads,* and for advice on the matter of its table of contents he turned to his old and trusted companion, asking: Should he add to the time-tested early stories "The Fireplace"? Fuller replied on June 11, 1929: "Is it not over-long for the final story? Is it not 'slightly story bookish'? It is a beautiful thing, even if over-ingenuous and *voulu* (consult Z. T. G. here!); in fact, ask *her* what *she* thinks, about it all." [9]

Disregarding Fuller's questions Garland decided on inclusion of "The Fireplace" in the new edition of *Main-Travelled Roads,* which he urged be illustrated by Constance. Her drawings "have a quaint old-fashioned wood-cut effect," he wrote to Harry

[6] H. B. Fuller to Garland, June 10, 1929, Garland Papers.
[7] Constance M. Griffin, *Henry Blake Fuller* (1939), p. 69.
[8] H. B. Fuller to Garland, June 10, 1929, Garland Papers.
[9] H. B. Fuller to Garland, June 11 [1929], Garland Papers.

Haynes of Harper's, "which is not only highly appropriate but economical to print." "This book has been published thirty-eight years and will sell for thirty-eight years longer [10] and I want to have a suitable edition made this year while I am able to supervise it and while my daughter is able to illustrate it." [11]

Six weeks later Fuller was dead, alone in his Chicago rooming house, as he had been alone for most of his days. *Gardens of This World,* which he had written for the purpose of reading and re-reading, was not yet off the press. But Garland, grieving, found consolation in the fact that Fuller had known the satisfaction of his two last acceptances: "I like to think of him going away in the glory of that victory." [12]

With Fuller gone, Garland was at a loss for a trusted friend and literary advisor. The place of Henry B. in his life could never be filled. But as time went on Garland came to turn most often, for the critical advice and literary discussion once provided by Fuller, to a younger colleague, the "author of two or three essays of rare quality," Mr. Van Wyck Brooks. Meeting Brooks for the first time on New Year's Day of 1926 Garland reported:

I found him quite in character with his writing, although he mani-fested a measure of shyness curiously at variance with the elegance and subtlety which I felt in his writing. His delicacy of workmanship is in direct opposition to the slang-whanging of his contemporaries. In this regard he reminded me of Henry Fuller. [13]

The ranks of Garland's associates were indeed thinning. [14] Of the old guard Irving Bacheller remained the closest in friendship. For several years the Garlands spent the months of February and March with him in Winter Park, Florida, and even toyed with the idea of making a home in that more equable climate. But Garland's younger daughter had gone with her husband to live

[10] Garland's boast was probably accurate. A new edition of *Main-Trav-elled Roads* was published by Harper & Brothers in 1956.

[11] Garland to Harry Haynes, June 2 [1929], Garland Papers.

[12] *Afternoon Neighbors,* p. 550.

[13] *Ibid.,* p. 302.

[14] The continuity and the quotations of the next few pages have been taken from an unpublished manuscript "Fortunate Exiles" in the Garland collection. Interrupted by Garland's death it is in a chaotic state and page references would be an impossibility.

in Hollywood, and in 1928 and again in 1929, the Garlands travelled out to visit her. When Mary Isabel and Hardesty also announced their intention of living on the West Coast, Garland succumbed to the lure of California and purchased a lot adjoining his daughter's with the intent of building a home in Laughlin Park, Los Angeles.

By November of 1929 Garland, in New York, was in a frenzy packing, going through old correspondence, throwing away bushel baskets of letters and culled manuscripts. His wife was leaving on a trip to Egypt along with her brother Lorado Taft, so that Hamlin Garland made the trip cross-continent alone save for the Maltese poodle Blinkie ensconced in the baggage car. As icy storms delayed the train Garland foraged food for his dog. He might have been reminded of the journey thirty years before when he had travelled in reverse direction with the care of his horse Ladrone on his mind. After the rigors of this winter passage the sunshine of the City of the Angels was a welcome sight, and Garland settled down contentedly with Mary Isabel to supervise the construction of his new home.

On the site graced by "twelve noble olive trees" he planned a rambling structure of California colonial style. As building progressed on the twenty-thousand dollar structure he was in a reckless mood of extravagance, enlarging the plan of his study, adding brick to the terraces. The sale of his copy of *Maggie* and the Riley autograph helped finance these additions. Garland explained his willingness to part with such personal mementoes: "My girls are not keenly interested even in the signatures of Barrie and Kipling. They just don't have the autograph sense."

On April 16 he and Zulime were able to move into their new home, which included on its lower floor an entrance hall, a beamed music room, living room, and dining room. An iron-railed staircase led to the L-shaped upper story which provided bedrooms and a spacious study. Garland rejoiced in the view from his windows:

Mt. Hollywood stood directly to the north, a wooded peak some fifteen hundred feet high, and two of my windows opened toward it. To the east, Mt. Lone and Mt. Wilson, and in favorable lights the snowy dome of San Antonio, ten miles high, loomed above the green walls of my neighboring eucalyptus trees.

Still unwilling to cut all ties with the East, Garland envisioned this only as a winter home. Yet on his next trip to New York he noted again the city's alien quality in contrast with Los Angeles, which was filled with "transplanted Mid-Westerners." "My closest friends," he observed, "Irving Bacheller, John Van Dyke, Augustus Thomas, Albert Paine, are all white with years." Garland himself was snowy-haired, his mustache a bar of white against his weathered skin. But the old plainsman carried himself erect and moved with a leonine dignity.

In Onteora Zulime fell seriously ill and the couple hastily retraced their steps to New York. As he watched by her bedside Garland read Edgar Wallace novels "by the dozen." Friends proposed a seventieth birthday dinner but Garland replied that he was eating "the bitter bread of loneliness and old age." "I am in no mood for a birthday dinner when Zulime may not be able to go to it." Nonetheless, thirty or forty friends gathered at Yama Farms with Garland to celebrate the occasion.

The alarm of Zulime's attack, which was diagnosed as Parkinson's disease, convinced Garland that his program of commuting annually across the continent was too strenuous for their years. He gave up the New York apartment, and in view of his proposed exile, resigned from active membership in the American Academy:

I may be shirking the battle of life but I feel no guilt in doing so. I've done my share of the fighting. I have earned a furlough. This does not mean a cessation of effort. I shall continue to work as long as I can drive a pen. At times, I realize that my value in the life of New York is an illusion. I am not missed.

Meanwhile *Roadside Meetings* had appeared in book form. Said Garland: "One's first publication is a tremendous event, the third less important, the tenth negligible." This was by conservative count Garland's thirty-sixth full-length volume. To include separate editions would double or treble the account. *Companions on the Trail,* the second volume of diaries, covering the period from 1900 to 1913, was returned for revision to Garland in California in December, 1930, at a time when banks all over the country were closing their doors. Despite the financial situation Macmillan planned an edition of 10,000 copies.

The publication of Garland's reminiscences set off in some quarters a fiery blast of protest. The reviewers of the *Nation* led the attack, with C. Hartley Grattan condemning *Roadside Meetings:*

Once upon a time Mr. Hamlin Garland was aflame with passion for social justice. . . . Once upon a time he was a literary radical. Now he can covertly sneer at the active writers: our present day school of pornographic fiction. Once he was a veritist and a proponent of local color and looked toward the future. Now he is a member of the American Academy and rests on his laurels. [15]

The next year Granville Hicks carried on the charge for the *Nation* damning *Companions on the Trail* as "the dullest of the six" autobiographical books, filled with incidents which are "trivial and narrated with merciless prolixity." Reviewing Garland's career, he recalled when his fiction was among the finest, "direct, comprehensive, moving, and savagely honest. Scarcely a word of it was propaganda." "And now," he lamented, "Hamlin Garland, member of the American Academy, as the title page proudly states, is self-satisfied, fastidious, undemocratic, out of sympathy with every vital movement in contemporary life." [16]

The *Nation's* reviews were not entirely typical of contemporary reaction, [17] but they sounded a note which would be repeated again and again in connection with Garland's work. "Just for a handful of silver he left us," would become the complaint of many a liberal reformer or academic critic, struggling to explain Garland's "decline from realism." Among the least charitable interpretations given has been that of Mr. Bernard I. Duffey, who accuses Garland of pursuing literary success always "by playing the main chance." Basing his arguments chiefly on the Gilder correspondence Mr. Duffey maintains that Garland's writing was "shaped by the vagaries of editorial taste," with Garland seeming "from the beginning never to hesitate over any necessary compromise." According to this interpretation most of

[15] "Ex-Literary Radical," *Nation,* CXXXI (October 1, 1930), 351.
[16] "Garland of the Academy," *Nation,* CXXXIII (October 21, 1931), 435.
[17] See W. A. White in *Books,* September 21, 1930, p. 1, September 27, 1931, p. 1; New York *Evening Post,* September 27, 1930, p. 2; *Boston Transcript,* December 19, 1931, p. 2; *Saturday Review,* VIII (October 10, 1930), 187.

Garland's realism and his reform work was due entirely to suggestions from Flower. [18]

That the reverse was true has been pertinently suggested by a colleague of Mr. Duffey's. Mr. James D. Koerner promptly pointed out that Flower was attracted *to* Garland by the realism of work already produced. [19] And the fact remains that Garland offered to the *Arena* stories which in the majority of cases had previously been rejected by Gilder. The sanest comment on the entire problem of Garland's shift in method and subject matter is probably that of Mr. Edward Wagenknecht in his recent *Cavalcade of the American Novel:*

That there was an element of worldly wisdom in the change he made is no doubt true, but it is not necessary to become hysterical about it. Writers do not usually turn away from their native material until they have exhausted the use they can make of it, and the truth of the matter is that, outside of *Main-Travelled Roads,* Garland's strongest social and economic convictions had never directly inspired his best work. Moreover, his radicalism was an agrarian radicalism; he belonged to the old Jeffersonian school. It was never possible for him to follow the labor movement along any of its later lines of development; both his temperament and his convictions forbade this. [20]

"As a matter of fact," wrote Garland himself in 1895, in an insight particularly applicable to his own future case, "literary power is not personal, it is at bottom sociological. The power of the writer is derived from the society in which he lives, like the power of a general which springs from the obedience of his army. When society changes, when his audience dies, the writer's power passes away." [21] Certainly, after 1895, when began Garland's alleged defection from the ranks of the true reformers, American society changed with great rapidity. Garland's philosophy changed, if at all, in somewhat the opposite direction from the popular trend of ideologies. Vernon Parrington well analyzed Garland's inevitable rejection of naturalism and industrializa-

[18] "Hamlin Garland's 'Decline' from Realism," *American Literature,* **XXV** (March, 1953), 69–74. See also Claude Simpson, "Hamlin Garland's Decline," *Southwest Review,* XXVI (January, 1941), 223–234.
[19] *American Literature,* **XXVI** (November, 1954), 427–32. For rebuttal, see *ibid.,* pp. 433–35.
[20] *Cavalcade of the American Novel,* p. 211.
[21] *Crumbling Idols* (1895), pp. 184–85.

tion and his consequent unpopularity: "While America was driving towards regimentation and industrialization he travelled backward in time to recover a vanishing world of individualism, and the distance rapidly widened between them." [22]

No one was more aware than Garland of the gulf which loomed between him and the audiences of the 1930's. It was the burden of his constant complaint. But he stubbornly maintained with the Scotsman, "Everybody's out of step but me." Of the critics of *Roadside Meetings* who wanted him to display "the iconoclastic mood of the 1890's," he commented mildly, "They forget that forty years is a long time for any mood to endure." [23]

Companions on the Trail recorded Garland's early married years, their scenes, Chicago, West Salem, the mountain West, with brief interludes in New York City. Inherently the material was much less interesting than that of the previous volume. Moreover, this sequel picked up at that point where Garland had settled to his daily habit of journalizing, [24] and in revision he was loath to depart from the chronological form. The resultant volume was, it must be admitted, prolix. Latham kept throwing his editorial weight toward compression, but the best compromise that could be effected was a holding of the book to five hundred pages.

By now Garland's project of printing *two* volumes of diaries had expanded indefinitely. Faithfully, Latham labored with him over a third volume, tentatively titled "The Silver Road." Garland's untidy manuscripts had never been an editor's delight. Now as his script grew more indecipherable, his attitude toward details more Olympian, this project must have appeared to Latham interminable as the labors of Sisyphus. Tactfully he suggested the excising of such phrases as "the kikes of Tannersville," the softening of comments on Vachel Lindsay and Edgar Lee Masters, the regularization of spellings. "Please *do* make up your mind. Shall it be Mary Isobel, or Isabel?" [25] In 1932 this book appeared as *My Friendly Contemporaries*, bringing the

[22] Vernon Parrington, *Main Currents of American Thought*, III, 299–300.
[23] "Fortunate Exiles," Garland Papers.
[24] The originals of these diaries are not available.
[25] Harold Latham to Garland, June 23, 1931, September 28, 1931, Garland Papers.

Garland record down to 1923. But Garland was working merrily along on another volume, *Afternoon Neighbors.*

In these published journals there is much of incidental interest to the student of literature, but the garrulity of old age mars many of the passages. Garland's pet prejudices are aired and re-aired, his aversion to "alien citizens," his disparagement of "the school of pornography" in novel and drama. One curious evolution has occurred in Garland's style. As a young writer he was among those who considered dialect, the differentiation of regional speeches, as of utmost importance. He would argue at length with Gilder over the substitution of "Yes" for "Yup" in a story. But as he transcribed and amplified his journals, throwing into direct quotations the substance of many a past intercourse, his feeling for the cadences of speech seems entirely to have deserted him. In these books farmer and statesman, Mid-Westerner and Scotsman, youth and graybeard, all speak in the same rounded periods: the platform voice of Hamlin Garland. Dialogue, as a device of characterization, is lost, as every spoken word takes on the didactic accents of the author. This ventriloquism produces puppet figures, and the monotony of monologue accounts in large part for the tedious effect of these literary reminiscences.

Garland was still appearing frequently on the platform, although his commercial lecture tours had been abandoned. There were speeches, however, to be made to all manner of civic groups and educational institutions. On April 20, 1931, he records a marathon of appearances in Iowa City. At nine-thirty he made a radio address. As luncheon guest of the president of the University he spoke briefly. At three-thirty there was another radio address to the women of the state. At four he spoke to a round-table meeting of students and citizens. At seven there was his scheduled address to the Hamlin Garland Club in the Student Union Building. And all these various engagements involved transportation in violent rain showers. Garland, although past seventy—"The Cape of Storms"—was perdurable under the torments inflicted on the speakers of the lecture circuit. For a week later he appeared at Wesleyan University for two more speeches, and the following day addressed the Ohio State Historical Society on "The Western March of Settlement."

Although forced to cancel a series of lectures at Columbia University because of Zulime's ill health Garland was able to fulfill an engagement at the University of Hawaii which provided the relaxation of a sea voyage with the acclaim of being hailed on territorial soil as "The Dean of American Letters." [26] For the once jesting title of the Herne's Boston parlor had now become Garland's accepted designation. In writing to Katherine Herne of the honors of his old age Garland still used the ancient sobriquet, signing himself, "Faithfully yours, 'The Dean.' " "I am now in motion pictures," he told this friend of his youth, "that is to say, a young man out here has made a kind of biographical film of my home and my family. It is a record which will outlast one generation, and that is about all the history a man can claim these days." [27]

For the main, Garland forewent long lecture excursions to stay with Zulime, who to the distress of her family felt unable to go in society. Intermittently he worked upon *Afternoon Neighbors,* although Latham wrote that "the bottom had fallen out of the book market," and Bacheller complained that the literary market was "dead as my grandmother." [28] There were days in Los Angeles when the smog rolled in, when Garland felt that he had been mistaken in uprooting himself from the Eastern literary scene. Days when he was restless and disoriented, when the local writers' club seemed "evanescent and wholly commercial," Los Angeles in about the same state of literary stagnation as the Chicago of 1894. Then Garland complained: "News of my dying generation comes to me now like tales of shipwreck on remote seas."

But on other days the sun shone. He could watch the Sunday afternoon polo game, or play a bit of tennis, bask on the terrace in silent companionship with Constance's two children, or drive with Zulime to the country to enjoy the spectacle of the desert's flowering. Franklin Garland was now in Hollywood, playing character bits in the movies and his companionship was valuable to Hamlin. [29]

[26] "Fortunate Exiles," Garland Papers.
[27] Garland to Katherine Herne, May 10 [?], Garland Papers.
[28] "Fortunate Exiles," Garland Papers; Irving Bacheller to Garland, September 21, 1932, Garland Papers.
[29] "Fortunate Exiles," Garland Papers.

On September 14, 1933, on the occasion of his seventy-third birthday, Garland was tendered one of those memorial dinners which he had so often arranged in his time. Dr. Robert Millikan, a friend of Chicago days, now head of California Institute of Technology, presided. Will Rogers, as principal speaker, relieved Garland by being "humorous without being farcical." Garland in his response teased Rogers about his ignorance of Cherokee affairs and over a recent accident of the film star vis-à-vis a wooden horse. One of the journalists present reported the exchange: "Garland is the only man we know who has been able to give Will Rogers as good as he sent." Another local reporter awed by the Jovian majesty of the honored guest estimated that "every noted writer in world literature contributed congratulations to be read at the banquet." There were indeed friendly letters from Kipling, Shaw, Tarkington, Brand Whitlock, Christopher Morley, Nicholas Butler, John Erskine, and many others, to be cherished in Garland's collection of autographs. [30]

In 1934 appeared the fourth volume of reminiscences, *Afternoon Neighbors,* dealing with the decade of the twenties. As Garland's journals passed that point of time at which the Middle Border autobiographical series had ended the author saw fit to drop the chronological scheme of his reminiscences and deal in narrative fashion with the events from his 1924 summer in England to his removal to California .These later chapters recapture some of the flavor of intimate revelation which had given charm to the early autobiographies and to *Roadside Meetings.* At seventy-five the magician's hand had not entirely lost its cunning, and the illusions of his mirrors are sometimes as dazzling as of old.

But the sales of the volume were negligible. Year by year a few copies found their way into libraries, where they often repose with pages uncut. In Garland's lifetime *My Friendly Contemporaries* and *Companions on the Trail* never repaid the advances which Macmillan's had made upon them. Yet to another writer the four volumes of literary memoirs afford a fascinating study in their variations upon a theme. Carl Van Doren had pointed out that *A Son of the Middle Border* was "the final re-

---

[30] *Afternoon Neighbors,* pp. 556–57; Los Angeles *Herald,* September 15, 1933, II, 1. Many of the congratulatory letters (Garland Papers) were addressed to Gaylord Beaman, who arranged the dinner.

daction and commentary" upon Garland's earlier fictive versions of the same material, for which his short stories should be considered "the original documents." But the pattern is even more complex, and the hand was quicker than the eye. These four reminiscent volumes in actuality are the source material of *A Daughter of the Middle Border* and *Back-Trailers,* and to some extent of *A Son of the Middle Border.* In the sense that art is fiction, the Middle Border books are, to confute Mr. Van Doren, the fictionalized version of Garland's life, now revealed in the true "original documents."

Nor with their publication had Garland exhausted the possibilities of variations upon his main themes. In 1935 there appeared *Joys of the Trail,* a handsome volume put out by the Chicago Bookfellows (of which Garland was one of the founders). It was a "final redaction" of the old *McClure's* article "Hitting the Trail," which had appeared in intermediate form as "Vanishing Trails" in 1905. The Clio Press of Iowa City, Iowa, with Frank L. Mott acting as editor, brought out, also in 1935, a volume *Iowa, O, Iowa,* containing reprints of early Garland poems, with three new poems added. Harper & Brothers produced in the same year a new edition of the juvenile volume *The Long Trail,* which included as lagniappe a reprint of that 1880 favorite "The Return of a Private."

And Garland was fulfilling his pledge that he would work "as long as he could drive a pen." In the "Afterword" to *Afternoon Neighbors* he had written:

> At this point I rest—not for lack of material (for several volumes of unused dated records still remain) but for the reason that this break in my lifelines, this establishment of a new routine under serener skies seems a logical point at which to set the words *To Be Continued,* and to say as Howells once said to me with a smile of deep meaning, "If I live long enough I shall write my later life." [31]

In 1936 Garland was still busily engaged in writing his "later life" under the title of "Fortunate Exiles." But as the lines of his narration grew closer and closer to the vanishing point when past and present would be one, the difficulties of composition multiplied. Latham wrote in gentle criticism of the early chapters sub-

---

[31] *Afternoon Neighbors,* p. 589.

mitted to him: "It is all very pleasantly written, all very agreeable reading, but it has not the social significance or the power
of everything else of yours." [32] Indeed, the angles between Garland's mirrors of illusion had narrowed so acutely that the reflections were becoming distortions, no longer images of reality.

Many of his day-to-day experiences were his adventures in
psychic research, materials impossible to interweave with personal reminiscence. He determined to abandon his journals and
in their stead to publish a report upon his lifetime of experimentation with the occult. Macmillan's had already signed a contract for the publication of this volume and had given him a five-
hundred-dollar advance. [33] In 1936 there appeared *Forty Years
of Psychic Research,* a labor of love on Garland's part, and an
effort of faith on the part of his publishers. It sold better than
might have been expected, with a considerable foreign sale adding to the totals.

It was the summary record of Garland's encounters with mediums and clairvoyants throughout the years, as he put it in his
preface, his "psychic log-book" to complement the "literary log-
books." In thus arranging his material Garland was following
the advice of Henry Fuller—advice from beyond the grave. For
Garland reports on a 1933 séance in which "Fuller" discussed
the project of the book: " 'A good idea,' " came the voice from the
luminous cone held to Garland's ear, " 'but let the incidents in
the book spell out something. The trouble with your "Shadow
World" was the lack of sequence. It was chronologically jum-
bled.' " [34]

What Garland spelled out as the conclusion of his forty years
of psychic research was not what might have been expected from
the tone of many of his reports. Summing up, and foreswearing
further discussion, he wrote:

While it would not be quite true to say that as an investigator I am
at the point from which I started forty-five years ago, I shall no doubt
disappoint some of my readers when I confess to a state of doubt.

[32] Harold Latham to Garland, May 25, 1936, Garland Papers.
[33] Harold Latham to Garland, May 17, 1935, June 12, 1935, Garland
Papers.
[34] *Forty Years of Psychic Research,* p. 344.

The shadow of death, once so remote, has become a cloud across my pathway, so close that I can almost touch it with my hand. Questions which are wholly "academic" at thirty-one, become concretely personal at seventy-five. The problem of survival has for me, to-day, a significance which it did not have when I began my researches forty-five years ago.

As I bring this record of many personal experiences to a close I am urged by my friends to state my conclusions. To them I must reply: "I have no conclusions. I am still the seeker, the questioner."

In writing of my doubts, I have no wish to weaken any other man's faith; I am merely stating the reasons which prevent me from accepting the spiritist interpretation of psychic phenomena, phenomena which I have abundantly proven to exist—I am still questioning the identity of the manifesting intelligences. My dissent is not upon the phenomena but upon their interpretation.

Now finally, if you ask me bluntly, "What is the present status of your belief?" I must repeat that I am still the experimentalist, the seeker, and that I find myself most in harmony with those who say: "All these movements, voices, forms, are biodynamic in character. They are born of certain unknown powers of the human organism. They are thought-forms—resultants of mind controlling matter. They all originate in the séance room, and have not been proven to go beyond it. [35]

The publication of this volume brought Garland again into correspondence with others working in similar areas. Professor J. B. Rhine expressed interest in Garland's "hypothesis alternative to that of the survival hypothesis." Having investigated some of the mediums whom Garland discusses, he commented that though "unable to feel the confidence in Captain Fife of the Margery case that you felt compelled to hold, we are unable to find any such loop-hole in your astounding Mrs. Smiley case." A young man whom Garland has recently recommended to him as worthy of attention he dismisses as "probably fraudulent." [36]

For Garland, despite his avowed intention of publishing no more on the subject, was deeply engrossed in further experimentation. Indeed, his resolution was no sooner written than regretted, for while the manuscript of Forty Years was yet in

[35] Ibid., extracted from pp. 394–95.
[36] J. B. Rhine to Garland, June 26, 1936, Garland Papers.

Latham's editorial hands, Garland began a series of adventures in the occult which he immediately wanted to include as addenda to that volume. Latham, uneasy as to the turn his author's enthusiasms were taking, discouraged this suggestion. [37]

Garland, it seemed, had become fascinated with the history of a woman (then dead) who had had the ability to make "spirit photographs" and to find hidden caches of money. Directed by her "voices," she had turned up certain artifacts, apparently long-buried, crude crosses, which no museum could identify. Garland engaged another medium, a Mrs. Sophie Williams, in the hopes of reproducing such experiences, finding other such crosses. He did.

His ghostly advisor in the enterprise was an early Spanish priest, Father Junípero Serra, and his guide, the deceased medium Mrs. Violent Parent. As Garland devised and put into play "test" after "test" to validate his experiences, the roster of materializations climbed to include Fuller, Lorado Taft, Conan Doyle, William Stead, and dozens of others, even to the skeptic Dr. Turck. The "spirits" led Garland into expeditions across country, up onto cactus-covered hills, down into rugged canyons, to recover with pick and shovel at least sixteen of the controverted artifacts. Play by play, with stenographic records of some séances, with diagrams to indicate the wiring of microphone attachments designed to prevent collusion by Mrs. Williams, Garland wrote up his incredible researches and presented them to Macmillan's.

Latham replied cautiously to the first offerings. "I know you won't like to have me say this, but I can't help being a bit suspicious of the medium. . . . So, for the moment, I am not taking up the book officially. Don't you think I am right in postponing it until we can meet all possible objections?" [38]

Garland labored frantically to buttress his proofs. He assembled affidavits from the living medium, from physicians and friends who had known her work, statements from neighbors of the deceased Mrs. Parent, witnesses of *her* explorations, a chemical analysis of the crosses, a letter from the *Museo Nacional de*

[37] Harold Latham to Garland, December 22, 1936, Garland Papers.
[38] Harold Latham to Garland, December 22, 1936, Garland Papers.

Arqueologia, Historia y Ethnografía of Mexico City, suggesting a mid-seventeenth century origin of the artifacts. [39]

Meanwhile Stewart White, who had participated in some of the séances, was egging Garland on toward publication, criticizing and approving the manuscript, which bore working titles indicative of Garland's lapse from scientific objectivity: "Mechanical Proofs of Survival," "Objective Evidence of Human Survival." [40] At this point Garland sought to sell some articles about his discoveries, suggesting to a literary agent that while Macmillan's was likely to take the final book there was "sensational news value in what I am doing." [41]

Latham was the epitome of tactfulness in dealing with Garland's more and more insistent letters, but at last, on August 6, 1937, he gently but firmly closed the Macmillan door. The manuscript, he wrote "is absorbing as a mystery novel, but despite the best of efforts and the friendliest and most affectionate feeling for you, we simply don't believe it." [42] Stewart White was indignant that Macmillan's was thus "afraid of the book." "Don't they know the trends of modern thought? Why, even the run-of-the-mill newspaper reviewers have, *without exception,* treated the Betty Book seriously and with respect." [43]

Unofficially Latham continued to try to place Garland's manuscript. But after various rebuffs from publishing houses he wrote on April 4, 1938, "I am afraid you are right in thinking that publishers suspect that you are the victim of a clever woman."

At last Dutton's agreed to publish, provided Garland would forego royalties on the first 1,500 copies. Upon the signing of a contract there followed an astounding and pitiable correspond-

---

[39] *The Mystery of the Buried Crosses* (1939), Appendices, pp. 317–351.

[40] White to Garland, correspondence of 1937–38, Garland Papers. The working titles were mentioned in a letter from Harold Latham to Garland, June 1, 1937.

[41] Garland to W. K. Wing, author's representative, June [?], 1937, carbon copy in Garland Papers.

[42] Harold Latham to Garland, August 6 and August 14, 1937, Garland Papers.

[43] S. E. White to Garland, August 14, 1937, Garland Papers. Reference is to "*The Betty Book:* excursions into the world of other-consciousness made by Betty between 1919 and 1936, now recorded by Stewart Edward White—N.Y.: E. P. Dutton, 1937," which went through three printings.

ence between Garland and "Dear John"—John Macrae, president of Dutton's. [44] On one day Garland would write as the hard-
headed and experienced author, discussing arrangements for the
medium Mrs. Williams to share in royalties after deduction of
his costs ($700.00 with $300.00 advance to his collaborator). On
the next day he would be reporting more fantastic séances and
absurd proposals to bolster the "evidential value" of his account.
Once he excitedly reported contact with Amelia Earhart, whose
disappearance had made recent headlines, and asked Macrae to
stand by to organize a search based on his information. Another
day he wrote in confident vein of having "been last night with
Henry Fuller," relaying Fuller's suggestion that the final chapter of the book take the form of a round-table discussion of "Life
in the Fourth Dimension" with Fuller presiding and all the cast
of characters, including Father Serra, contributing their impressions. This last idea Macrae firmly vetoed. In the spring of 1939,
with the publication of the book *The Mystery of the Buried
Crosses* imminent, Macrae was still playing out his role of confidant, reiterating, with one can understand what motives, the
need for secrecy, urging Garland not to rush into premature
revelation to journalists of his great discoveries.

In these episodes Garland was experiencing an emotional up-
heaval similar to that which he had once described in his interpretation of the last days of Sitting Bull. That old chieftain, who
had rejected Christianity, was at last drawn toward supernatural
belief. According to Garland, the chief's "clear mind could not
accept the new religion, yet his heart desired it deeply." The Bull
refused to be "pushed into" the fanaticism of the tribal Ghost
Dancers, but as other resources failed he at times assumed the
posture of a believer. "Now he was equally cautious," wrote Garland as biographer, "only he was older, with a deeper longing to
be comforted." [45] One can only look upon Garland's own deflec-
tions from the scientific attitude in a similar spirit of charity.

Before the book was actually through the press its author had
reacted somewhat from his excesses, for it carried a "Personal

[44] Garland to John Macrae, correspondence of May 13, 1938–June 19,
1939, Garland Papers.
[45] *Book of the American Indian* (1924), pp. 25–51.

Afterword" more characteristic of Garland's normal expression:

As I close the presentation of my evidence at the end of two years of study and exploration, I find myself not very far advanced beyond the point from which I set out. Nevertheless, I make claim to definite progress. I think my readers will agree that by the aid of Sophia Williams and her voices, I have assembled a valuable mass of evidence, testimony which points to a solution of the problem involved, although beneath every mystery a still more insoluble mystery remains.

I have keenly enjoyed the experience of these years of sunlit experiment and open-air exploration, and I trust my readers will find a like pleasure in the reading of my chronicle.

The good old Earth, notwithstanding all its storms, floods, and wars, seems as solid as when I began my study of the Invisible World forty-seven years ago. I still find it difficult to believe in an intangible universe, a fourth-dimensional plane from which these inexplicable voices appear to come, and yet when Henry Fuller and Father Serra speak to me, I am convinced—momentarily—of their reality. When they tell me that I am surrounded by scores of mission padres, eager to prove their possession of continuing life and memory, I reply in good faith, but as I break the connecting current and go out upon the street, swarming with business men and pleasure-seekers, I lose that faith. I find myself still the doubter, still the investigator, demanding proof and still more proof. I return to my desk each morning, resolved upon further experiment and exploration.

I close with a word of warning IF this spirit world exists, consideration of it should be left to elderly people and experimentalists like myself. After all, the normal man is properly concerned with commerce, sport, and mechanical progress. To foster in the young an overwhelming interest in a fourth-dimensional universe will not do. The only life we definitely know is here. As one of my invisible friends said of his life on earth, "I had a hope but no expectancy of life on another plane," and perhaps that is the best that we who are scientifically-minded can achieve.

As I ride among the cactus-covered hills, it is easy for me to visualize the time when primitive men climbed to the mountain tops to worship the sun. The earth is no longer commonplace to me. It suggests the faith of the millions who have dissolved into its dust. "We are not dead, we are not far, we are here," one of the padres said to me.

I do not pretend to have solved the problems involved in the discovery of these barbaric buried amulets; I merely present them. I am nearing my final *entrada,* but I do not expect death to explain life.

If it does, I shall certainly attempt to share my wisdom with those I leave on this side of the dark river, just as those heroic priests have tried to do with me.

Psychic mysteries still allure me, as distant mountain ranges allured me in my youth. As a mental pioneer, I am still moved to cultivate unknown valleys and tunnel unnamed ranges.

Unlike the true frontiersman, few of us who seek the borderlands of human life are able to overtake the forms which flee, or touch the hands which beckon. Perhaps it is better so—the never-ending joy of the seeking remains. [46]

Edwin Markham, writing to Garland at about this time and after a severe illness, meditated the same questions:

Life is a mystery to me, and my last experiences increase my feeling of its mystery. Who devised this drama of our mortal days? Well, it will soon be over for all of us and then we will pass on to another climb into the infinite. Whatever happens, always think of me as yours in an abiding friendship. [47]

There were other enduring friendships to brighten Garland's days, correspondents with whom he could exchange long, leisurely letters in the assurance of complete understanding. There was Albert Shaw, who had moved with the *Review of Reviews* to the *Literary Digest*. There was Irving Bacheller in Florida, and Harold Latham in New York, who continued to look after the business interests of his one-time author. There was particularly Mr. Van Wyck Brooks, who took the time to write long discussions of literary questions, arguing at one time that Howells' flair of prudishness had its part in the present "brutalness," at another time gracefully relaying to Garland a story of William McFee's of the old days when *Rose of Dutcher's Coolly* had been forbidden him by the headmaster of his boarding school. [48]

The fact that *Buried Crosses* had not the flair to make a commercial success such as that achieved by the *Betty Book*—or in more recent times by *The Search for Bridie Murphy*—did not

[46] *The Mystery of the Buried Crosses,* pp. 313–14.
[47] Edwin Markham to Garland, February 8, 1938, Garland Papers.
[48] Van Wyck Brooks to Garland, January 17, 1937, August 1, 1938, Garland Papers.

trouble Garland's equanimity. As the author of more than forty volumes he was no longer surprised by the vagaries of public taste. Macrae confessed that it was not being taken at all by the booksellers, but Garland clipped the review of the *Psychical Journal* and contented himself with defending vehemently to the Department of Internal Revenue his expense deductions on research for a book "which involved a good deal of motoring, and a very unusual amount of correspondence." [49]

"I have seen fashions in painting, sculpture, music and architecture wax and wane," he wrote in an article in 1939 on "Literary Fashions Old and New," "and I have had something to do with celebrating some of these fashions when they came and I have rejoiced when some of them passed. In my small way a reformer in politics, a veritist in art, and an evolutionist in science, I have wrought unceasingly to record some part of these changes.

"As a writer I have always been among the minority. I believe in dignity, decorum and grace, and I decline to honor those who pander to the appetite of millions. . . . In such judgments [of salacious fiction] the voice of the people is not the voice of God. I do not accept popular judgment on wall paper. Why should I do so when a book is in question." [50]

With such a Jovian dismissal of his readers Garland turned to the problem of disposing of his accumulated papers. The Library of Congress suggested itself as a possible repository, but Garland shied away from the idea that there his collection would probably be dispersed among different departments. [51] At one time he was in the notion of burning all his papers. He wrote to Van Wyck Brooks, disturbed because a "young enthusiast" had been "nosing through my records on the theory that he can write a publishable thesis about me." Garland had warned this professor that he was "wasting his time," and to Brooks confided his perplexities. [52] Brooks had the obvious reaction of a literary historian, and replied in haste:

[49] Garland to Bureau of Internal Revenue, December 8, 1939, carbon copy in Garland Papers.
[50] *Think*, IV (March, 1939), 24–27.
[51] Garland to Herbert Putnam, December 6, 1938, Garland Papers.
[52] Garland to Van Wyck Brooks, August 31, 1939.

But it horrifies me to think that you have considered burning those papers. I certainly agree with the relatives who say "preserve every scrap." They are all bound to have some use and value, and it seems to me that future students ought to have the right to see them. Nor do I see how you can escape a biography. In another thirty years your life will stand for a whole phase of American history.

It must be a problem, of course, to know what to do with a nice young man who has "no power as a writer." But his enthusiasm and knowledge must count for much, and, if he is competent to arrange the papers, could there not be some understanding by which your daughter perhaps might collaborate with him? And, in any case, it would be extremely useful to have the facts and the documents well compiled. Even if the work were dull, it would stand as a basis for the really good biographer who will certainly appear.

Continuing with reassurances as to Garland's place in literary history, Mr. Brooks insisted that if a future biographer had "trouble in finding a publisher, the author will be to blame, not the subject. So I can only beg you to withhold your hand when there is any question of destroying papers." [53]

If Garland had seriously considered such a move, the intervention of a distinguished literary historian prevented the holocaust, and his collection—including the Santa Clara artifacts which Macrae urged be kept together for their "evidential value" [54]—were assigned to the University of Southern California, which had recently honored Garland with another doctorate of letters.

From time to time Garland made desultory notations on his manuscript of "The Fortunate Exiles," which had been abandoned midway in his enthusiasm for psychic records. Apparently he had no serious intention of trying to publish it. He continued his interest in matters occult, but in calmer fashion. Once as he scrambled over the California hillsides hunting psychic artifacts he turned to his daughter with a wry grimace, "Most men of my age," he chuckled, "play golf." [55]

Hamlin Garland, yet erect of figure, with his mane of white hair and luxuriant mustaches, was a familiar sight pacing along

[53] Van Wyck Brooks to Garland, September 10, 1939, Garland Papers.
[54] John Macrae to Garland, November 10, 1939, Garland Papers.
[55] Conversation with Constance Garland Doyle, January 21, 1957.

De Mille Drive—a phenomenon in that land of motor transport. Observers noted his resemblance to Hawthorne. Others said he looked like Mark Twain. Cyril Clements claimed he was the image of Longfellow. At all events Garland bore the hallmark of a famous writer. He was considered a distinguished host and was a welcome guest at any dinner table. In 1940 in the first week of March he was scheduled for appearances as guest of honor and speaker at two literary dinners, but on the Friday he was stricken with a cerebral hemorrhage, and died the following Tuesday, March 5, 1940. [56]

Professional author to the end, he had just received a check for an article on Walt Whitman, in which he passed on to another generation of writers that creed which he had learned from the failing sage of Camden:

Don't depict evil for its own sake. Make it a foil as Shakespeare did. His evil is always a foil for purity. Somewhere in your play or novel, let the sunshine in. [57]

[56] Carroll Sibley, "Hamlin Garland, Delightful Host," *Mark Twain Quarterly*, IV (Summer, 1940), 6; Los Angeles *Times*, March 5, 1940, p. 1.
[57] "Let the Sunshine In," *Rotarian*, LV (October, 1939), 11.

Bibliography

TABLE OF SYMBOLS FOR GARLAND'S WORKS

AN   *Afternoon Neighbors.* New York: Macmillan & Company, 1934.

BAI   *Book of the American Indian.* New York: Harper & Brothers, 1923.

BL   *Boy Life on the Prairie.* New York: Macmillan & Company, 1899.

CI   *Crumbling Idols.* Chicago: Stone & Kimball, 1894.

DMB   *A Daughter of the Middle Border.* New York: Macmillan & Company, 1921.

IOI   *Iowa, O, Iowa.* Iowa City: Clio Press, 1935.

JT   *Joys of the Trail.* Chicago: The Bookfellows, 1935.

MTR-1   *Main-Travelled Roads.* Boston: Arena Publishing Company, 1891.

MTR-2   *Main-Travelled Roads.* Chicago: Stone & Kimball, 1893.

MTR-3   *Main-Travelled Roads.* New York: Macmillan & Company, 1899.

MTR-4   *Main-Travelled Roads.* New York: Harper & Brothers (Sunset Edition), 1909.

MTR-5   *Main-Travelled Roads.* New York: Harper & Brothers (Border Edition), 1922.

MTR-6   *Main-Travelled Roads.* New York: Harper & Brothers, 1930.

MTR-7   *Main-Travelled Roads.* New York: Harper & Brothers, 1956.

OMTR   *Other Main-Travelled Roads.* New York: Harper & Brothers, 1910.

PF-1   *Prairie Folks.* Chicago: F. J. Schulte & Company, 1893.

PF-2   *Prairie Folks.* New York: Macmillan & Company, 1899.

PS   *Prairie Songs.* Chicago: Stone & Kimball, 1893.

RM   *Roadside Meetings.* New York: Macmillan & Company, 1930.

SMB   *A Son of the Middle Border.* New York. Macmillan & Company, 1917.

TGS   *The Trail of the Goldseekers.* New York: Macmillan & Company, 1899.

THT   *They of the High Trails.* New York: Harper & Brothers, 1916.

WC   *Wayside Courtships.* New York: Appleton & Company, 1897.

CHRONOLOGY OF MAJOR GARLAND PUBLICATIONS

There are many variant titles in the Garland canon. In this chronology of his publications a title is listed under the first known year of publication and its earliest form, followed by a list of periodicals or volumes in which it later appeared, the Garland publications being designated by the symbols in the Table. Where a later title differs materially from the original title, it is given in parentheses immediately following the symbol of the collection. Stories and poems have not been traced through outside anthologies.

Many fugitive pieces of writing have been omitted, such as Garland's book reviews, which appeared in the *Arena,* the *Boston Evening Transcript,* the *Standard,* and elsewhere; his political reporting in the *Standard;* and his letters to such journals as the *Boston Evening Transcript* and the *New York Times.* The more important of these have been noted in documentation in the preceding chapters.

Mr. Donald Pizer, to whom I am indebted for the specific Philadelphia *Press* references below, has recently published an excellent detailed bibliography of Garland's newspaper and periodical publications for the years 1885–1895. (*Bulletin of Bibliography,* XXII, No. 2 [January–April, 1957], 41–44).

PROSE
1885
"Ten Years Dead," *Every Other Saturday* (Boston), II (March 28, 1885), 97–99.
1887
"Carlyle as a Poet," *Boston Evening Transcript,* August 2, 1887, p. 5.
1888
"Holding Down a Claim in a Blizzard," *Harper's Weekly,* XXXII (January 1, 1888), 66–67.
"Boy Life on the Prairie: I. The Huskin'," *American Magazine* (Brooklyn), VII (January, 1888), 299–303; "II. The Thrashin'," (March, 1888), 570–77; "III. The Voice of Spring," (April, 1888), 683–90; "IV. Between Hay an' Grass," VIII (June, 1888), 143–55; "V. Meadow Memories," (July, 1888), 296–302.
"A Common Case," *Belford's Magazine,* I (July, 1888), 188–99; *Standard,* July 28, 1888, p. 6; *WC* and *OMTR* ("Before the Low Green Door").
"American Novels." *Literary News,* IX (August, 1888), 236–37.
"Boy Life on the Prairie: VI. Melons and Early Frost," *American Magazine* (Brooklyn), VIII (October, 1888), 712–17.
"Mrs. Ripley's Trip," *Harper's Weekly,* XXXII (November 24, 1888), 894–95; *MTR*-1 to *MTR*-7; *Golden Book,* XIII (April, 1931), 45–49.

1889
"The Greek Play," *Boston Evening Transcript,* May 1, 1889.
"Whitman at Seventy," New York *Herald,* June 30, 1889, p. 7
"Under the Lion's Paw," *Harper's Weekly,* XXXIII (September 7, 1889), 726–27; *Standard,* September 28, 1889, pp. 12–13; *MTR*-1 to *MTR*-7.
"Truth in the Drama," *Literary World,* XX (September 14, 1889), 307–308.
"Old Sid's Christmas," *Harper's Weekly,* XXXII (December 28, 1889), 1038–40.
"The Teacher," in *Camden's Compliments to Walt Whitman,* ed., Horace Traubel, Philadelphia, 1889, pp. 40–42.

1890
"Mr. Howells' Latest Novels," *New England Magazine,* II, n. s. (May, 1890), 243–50.
"Drifting Crane," *Harper's Weekly,* XXXIV (May 31, 1890), 421–22; *PF*-1 and *PF*-2.
"Among the Corn Rows," *Harper's Weekly,* XXXIV (June 28, 1890); *MTR*-1 to *MTR*-7; *Golden Book,* II (July, 1925), 88–98.
"Ibsen as a Dramatist," *Arena,* II (June, 1890), 72–82; *CI*.
"Mr. Herne's New Play," *Boston Evening Transcript,* July 8, 1890, p. 6; reprinted by Donald Pizer in *American Literature,* XXVII (May, 1955), 264–67.
"Under the Wheel" (drama), *Arena,* II (July, 1890), 182–229; excerpts in *Standard,* July 30, 1890, pp. 6–7; in pamphlet form, 1890; novelized as *Jason Edwards.*
"The Return of a Private," *Arena,* II (December, 1890), 97–113; *MTR*-1 to *MTR*-7; *The Long Trail* (1935).

1891
"A New Declaration of Rights," *Arena,* III (January, 1891), 157–84; in pamphlet form, 1891.
"The Test of Elder Pill," *Arena,* III (March, 1891), 480–501; *PF*-1, *PF*-2 and *OMTR* ("Elder Pill, Preacher").
"Going for the Doctor," *Youth's Companion,* LXIV (March 12, 1891), 151.
"The Question of an Independent Theatre," *Boston Evening Transcript,* April 29, 1891, p. 6.
"The Morality of Margaret Fleming," *Boston Evening Transcript,* May 7, 1891, p. 6.
"The New Drama," *Boston Evening Transcript,* May 9, 1891, p. 12.
"A Spring Romance," *Century,* XLII (June, 1891), 296–302; *PF*-1 ("William Bacon's Hired Man"); *PF*-2 and *OMTR* ("William Bacon's Man"); *Golden Book,* IX (April, 1929), 72–78.
"A Prairie Heroine," *Arena,* IV (July, 1891), 223–46; *PF*-1 ("Sim Burns' Wife"); *PF*-2 and *OMTR* ("Lucretia Burns").

"An Evening at the Corner Grocery," *Arena,* IV (September, 1891), 504–512; *PF*-1 and *PF*-2 ("Village Cronies").
"Mr. and Mrs. Herne," *Arena,* IV (October, 1891), 543–60.
"Uncle Ripley's Speculation," *Arena,* V (December, 1891), 125–35; *PF*-1 ("Uncle Ethan's Speculation"); *MTR*-3 to *MTR*-7 ("Uncle Ethan Ripley").
"The Branch Road," first appeared in *MTR*-1; *MTR*-1 to *MTR*-7.
"Up the Coolée," first appeared in *MTR*-1; *MTR*-1 to *MTR*-7.
Main-Travelled Roads. Boston: Arena Publishing Company, 1891.

1892

"A Spoil of Office," *Arena,* VI (January–May, 1892), 253–68, 376–400, 495–522, 619–44, 749–74, VI (June, 1892), 104–32.
"A Queer Case," *Youth's Companion,* LXV (March 3, 1892), 105–106; (March 10, 1892), 121–22; (March 17, 1892), 133–34.
"The Alliance Wedge in Congress," *Arena,* VI (March, 1892), 447–57.
"Ol' Pap's Flaxen," *Century,* XLIII, 743–51, 912–33; XLIV, 39–47 (March–May, 1892); as *A Little Norsk* (1892).
"Daddy Deering," *Belford's,* VIII (April, 1892), 152–61; *PF*-1 and *PF*-2.
"At the Brewery," *Cosmopolitan,* XIII (May, 1892), 34–42; *PF*-1 ("Saturday Night on the Farm").
"Psychography," *Psychical Review,* I (August, 1892), 43–44.
"Salt Water Day," *Cosmopolitan,* XIII (August, 1892), 387–94.
"Under the Dome of the Capitol: a Prose Etching," *Arena,* VI (September, 1892), 468–70; *WC* ("The Prisoned One").
"The West in Literature," *Arena,* VI (November, 1892), 669–76; *CI.*
"An Experiment in Psychography," *Psychical Review,* I (November, 1892), 136–37.
"Forgetting," *Ladies' Home Journal,* X (December, 1892), 17; *WC* ("The End of Love is Love").
Jason Edwards. Boston: Arena Publishing Company, 1892.
A Member of the Third House. Chicago: A. J. Shulte & Company, 1892.
A Little Norsk: Ol' Pap's Flaxen. New York: D. Appleton & Company, 1892.
A Spoil of Office. Boston: Arena Publishing Company, 1892.

1893

"Sounds, Voices, and Physical Disturbances in the Presence of a Psychic," *Psychical Review,* I (February, 1893), 226–29.
"The Future of Fiction," *Arena,* VII (April, 1893), 513–24; *CI.*
"Before the Overture," *Ladies' Home Journal,* X (May, 1893), 13; *WC* ("At the Beginning").
"A Short-Term Exile," *Literary Northwest,* III (July, 1893), 303–15; *WC* ("A Fair Exile").
"A Dialogue between Eugene Field and Hamlin Garland," *Mc-*

Clure's, I (August, 1893), 195–204; digested in *Review of Reviews,* VIII (September, 1893), 334.

"Literary Emancipation of the West," *Forum,* XVI (October, 1893), 156–66; *CI.*

"Western Landscapes," *Atlantic Monthly,* LXXII (December, 1893), 805–809.

"Report of Dark Séances," *Psychical Review,* II (November, 1893), 152–171 [with others].

"A Graceless Husband," *Northwestern Miller,* December, 1893, 51–63; *WC* ("The Owner of the Mill Farm").

"A Pioneer Christmas," *Ladies' Home Journal,* XI (December, 1893), 11.

"The Sociable at Dudley's," first appeared in *PF*-1; *PF*-1 and *PF*-2.

Prairie Songs. Cambridge: Stone & Kimball, 1893.

Prairie Folks. Cambridge: Stone & Kimball, 1893.

1894

"The Land Question and Its Relation to Art and Literature," *Arena,* IX (January, 1894), 165–75.

"Boy Life in the West," *Midland Monthly,* I (February, 1894), 113–22.

"A Dialogue between James Whitcomb Riley and Hamlin Garland," *McClure's,* II (February, 1894), 219–34; digested in *Review of Reviews,* IX (March, 1894), 356.

"God's Ravens," *Harper's Monthly,* LXXXIX (June, 1894), 142–48; *MTR*-5 to *MTR*-7.

"The Single Tax in Actual Application," *Arena,* X (June, 1894), 52–58.

"An American Tolstoi. Hamlin Garland describes a visit to Joaquin Miller's Farm," *Philadelphia Press,* June 17, 1894.

"Homestead and Its Perilous Trades," *McClure's,* III (June, 1894), 1–20.

"Productive Conditions of American Literature," *Forum,* XVII (August, 1894), 690–98.

"Old Mosinee Tom," New York *Press,* November, 1894, Pt. VI, p. 4.

"A Lynching in Mosinee," New York *Press,* November 11, 1894; *Pocket Magazine,* II (July, 1896), 5–6.

"Mount Shasta," *Midland Monthly,* December, 1894, pp. 481–83.

"Only a Lumberjack," *Harper's Weekly,* XXXVIII (December 8, 1894), 1158–59; *WC* and *OMTR* ("An Alien in the Pines").

"Woman in the Camp: A Christmas Sketch," *Arena,* XI (December, 1894), 90–97.

"The Land of the Straddle Bug," *The Chap-Book,* II (November 15, 1894–February 15, 1895); novelized as *Moccasin Ranch,* 1901; "La Ferme du Moggason," *Revue Politique et Littéraire,* LV (July 28–October 27, 1917).

Impressions on Impressionism. Chicago: Central Art Association, Autumn, 1894.

Five Hoosier Painters. Chicago: Central Art Association, Winter, 1894.

Crumbling Idols: Twelve Essays on Art. Chicago: Stone & Kimball, 1894.

1895

"Art Conditions in Chicago," *Catalogue, United Annual Exhibition,* Chicago, January 24, 1895, pp. 5–8.

"The Wapsypinnicon Tiger," *Philadelphia Press,* February 28, 1895, p. 11; *PF-2.*

"Night Landing," *Midland Monthly,* III (February, 1895), 142–43.

"My Grandmother of Pioneer Days," *Ladies' Home Journal,* XII (April, 1895), 10.

"Work of an Art-Association in Western Towns," *Forum,* XIX (July, 1895), 606–609.

"A Grim Experience," *Philadelphia Press,* August 24, 1895, p. 11.

"Evangel in Cyene," *Harper's Monthly,* XCI (August, 1895), 375–90; *WC* and *OMTR* ("A Preacher's Love Story").

"Edward Kemeys," *McClure's,* V (July, 1895), 120–31; McClure Syndicate.

"Grace," *Philadelphia Press,* October 17, 1895, p. 9; *PF-2* ("A Day of Grace").

"Opposites," *Bookman,* II (November, 1895), 196–97; *WC* ("A Sheltered One").

Rose of Dutcher's Coolly. Chicago: Stone & Kimball, 1895.

1896

"A Girl from Washington," Bacheller Syndicate, copyrighted, January 16, 1896.

"Into the Happy Hunting Ground of the Utes," *Harper's Weekly,* XL (April 11, 1896), 350–51; Albert Bigelow Paine Syndicate as "Among the Utes."

"Among the Moki Indians," *Harper's Weekly,* XL (August 15, 1896), 801–807; Albert Bigelow Paine Syndicate.

"The Most Mysterious People in America," *Ladies' Home Journal,* October, 1896, pp. 5–6; Albert Bigelow Paine Syndicate.

"The Dance at Acoma," Albert Bigelow Paine Syndicate; probably "The Prairie in the Sky" which Garland erroneously said was published in *Harper's Weekly* (*A Daughter of the Middle Border,* p. 20).

"Captain Hance," Bacheller Syndicate, October 27, 1896.

"The Whole Troop Was Water Drunk," Bacheller Syndicate, November 7, 1896.

"A Division in the Coulé," Bacheller Syndicate, New York *Press,* November 1, 1896, p. 3; *PF-2* ("Aidgewise Feelin's"); *OMTR.*

"A Stern Fight with Cold and Hunger," Bacheller Syndicate, copyrighted, November 16, 1896.
"The Early Life of Ulysses S. Grant," *McClure's*, VIII (December, 1896), 125; McClure and Company Syndicate.

1897

"Grant at West Point," *McClure's*, VIII (January, 1897), 195; McClure and Company Syndicate; digested as "Grant as a Cadet," *Living Age* (January 9, 1897), 143–44.
"Upon Impulse," *Bookman*, IV (January, 1897), 428–32; *WC*.
"Grant in the Mexican War," *McClure's*, VIII (February, 1897), 366.
"Grant's Quiet Years at Northern Posts," *McClure's*, VIII (March, 1897), 402.
"Grant's Life in Missouri," *McClure's*, VIII (April, 1897), 514.
"Grant at the Outbreak of the War," *McClure's*, IX (May, 1897), 601.
"Grant's First Great Work in the War," *McClure's*, IX (June, 1897), 721.
"A Girl of Modern Tyre," *Century*, XXI, n.s. (July, 1897), 401–43; *WC* and *OMTR* ("A Stop-over at Tyre").
"Grant in a Great Campaign," *McClure's*, IX (July, 1897), 805.
"Grant: His First Meeting with Lincoln," *McClure's*, IX (August, 1897), 892.
"The Spirit of Sweetwater," *Ladies' Home Journal*, XIV (August–October, 1897); in book form, 1898; expanded to *Witch's Gold*, 1906.
"Joe, the Navajo Teamster," *Youth's Companion*, LXXI (November 18, 1897), 579–80.
"The Story of Buff," *Youth's Companion*, LXXI (December 2, 1897). 606–607.
"The Creamery Man of Molasses Gap," *Outlook*, LVII (December 4, 1897), 838–45; *MTR*-3 to *MTR*-6.
"The Stony Knoll," *Youth's Companion*, LXXI (December 18, 1897), 635.
"A Meeting in the Foothills," first appeared in *Wayside Courtships*, 1897.
"The Passing Stranger," first appeared in *Wayside Courtships*, 1897.
Wayside Courtships. New York: D. Appleton & Company, 1897.
A Member of the Third House. New York: D. Appleton & Company, 1897.
A la troisième chambre. Mme. Alice Foulon de Vaultx (trans.). Paris: C. Lévy, 1897.
Jason Edwards. New York: D. Appleton & Company, 1897.
A Spoil of Office. New York: D. Appleton & Company, 1897.

1898

"The Doctor," *Ladies' Home Journal*, XI (December, 1897–March, 1898).

"Ho, for the Klondike," *McClure's*, X (March, 1898), 443–54; digested in *National Geographic*, IX (April, 1898), 113–16.

"The Grant and Ward Failures," *McClure's*, X (April, 1898), 498–505.

" 'A Good Fellow's' Wife," *Century*, LV (April, 1898), 937–52; *MTR*-5 to *MTR*-7.

"Ulysses S. Grant, His Last Year," *McClure's*, XI (May, 1898), 86–96.

"Sam Markham's Wife," *Ladies' Home Journal*, XV (July, 1898), 8; *MTR*-3 to *MTR*-7 ("A Day's Pleasure").

"General Custer's Last Fight as Seen by Two Moon," *McClure's*, XI (September, 1898), 443–48.

The Spirit of Sweetwater. New York: Doubleday & McClure Company, 1898.

Ulysses S. Grant: His Life and Character. New York: Doubleday & McClure Company, 1898.

1899

"Rising Wolf, Ghost Dancer," *McClure's* XII (January, 1899), 241–48; *BAI.*

"Hitting the Trail," *McClure's*, XII (February, 1899), 298–304; revised as "Vanishing Trails," *University Record* (University of Chicago), X (1905), 53–61.

"The Man at the Gate of the Mountains," *Ladies' Home Journal*, XVI (August, 1899), 9–10; "Le Vengeur," *Revue Politique et Littéraire*, LXXIII (May 4, 1935), 312–16.

"I. Zangwill," *Conservative Review*, II (November, 1899), 402–12.

"Impressions of Paris in Times of Turmoil," *Outlook*, LXIII (December 16, 1899), 968–73.

"Black Ephram," first appeared in *PF*-2.

Boy Life on the Prairie. New York: Macmillan & Company, 1899.

Prairie Folks. New York: Macmillan & Company, 1899.

Main-Travelled Roads. New York: Macmillan & Company, 1899.

The Trail of the Goldseekers. New York: Macmillan & Company, 1899.

1900

"Electric Lady," *Cosmopolitan*, XX (May, 1900), 73–83.

"The Eagle's Heart," *The Saturday Evening Post*, CLXXII–CLXXIII (June 16–September 8, 1900).

"Stephen Crane: A Soldier of Fortune," *The Saturday Evening Post*, CLXXIII (July 28, 1900), 16–17.

"Big Moggasen," *Independent*, LII (November 1, 1900), 2622–24; *BAI.*

"People of the Buffalo," *McClure's*, XVI (December, 1900), 153–59; recast as "The Storm-Child," *BAI.*

"Jim Matteson of Wagon Wheel Gap," *Century*, LXI (November, 1900–April, 1901); as *Her Mountain Lover*, 1901.

"Bad Medicine Man," *Independent,* LII (December 6, 1900), 2899–2904.
The Eagle's Heart. New York: D. Appleton & Company, 1900.

1901
"The Drummer-Boy's Alarum," *The Saturday Evening Post,* CLXXIII (March 9, 1901), 7.
"Homeward Bound," *Living Age,* CXXIX (June, 1901), 594–96; from *Her Mountain Lover.*
"A Tale of a Tenderfoot," *The Saturday Evening Post,* CLXXIV (August 24, 1901), 8–9.
"Herne's Sincerity as a Playwright," *Arena,* XXVI (September, 1901), 282–84.
"The Captain of the Gray-Horse Troop," *The Saturday Evening Post,* CLXXIV (December 14, 1901–March 29, 1902).
Her Mountain Lover. New York: The Century Company, 1901.

1902
"The River's Warning," *Frank Leslie's,* LIII (January, 1902), 297–304; *BAI.*
"Delmar of Pima," *McClure's,* XVIII (February, 1902), 340–48.
"The Red Man's Present Needs," *North American Review,* CLXXIV (April, 1902), 476–88.
"The Steadfast Widow Delaney," *The Saturday Evening Post,* CLXXIV, (June 14, 28, 1902); *THT* ("The Grub-staker").
"Hippy, the Dare-Devil," *McClure's,* XIX (September, 1902), 474–80.
"Automobiling in the West," *Harper's Weekly,* XLVI (September 6, 1902), 1254.
"Sitting Bull's Defiance," *McClure's,* XX (November, 1902), 35–40.
"New Medicine House," *Harper's Weekly,* XLVI (December 6, 1902), 36–37; *BAI.*
"Culture or Creative Genius," *Outlook,* LXXII (December 6, 1902), 780–81.
The Captain of the Gray-Horse Troop. New York: Harper & Brothers, 1902.

1903
"The Work of Frank Norris," *Critic,* XLII (March, 1903), 216–18.
"Sanity in Fiction," *North American Review,* CLXXVI (March, 1903), 336–48.
"Nistina," *Harper's Weekly,* XLVII (April 4, 1903), 544–45; *BAI.*
"Lone Wolf's Old Guard," *Harper's Weekly,* XLVII (May 2, 1903), 716–18; *BAI.*
"The Faith of His Fathers'," *Harper's Weekly,* XLVII (May 30, 1903), 892–93.
"Outlaw," *Harper's Weekly,* XLVII (June 13, 1903), 972–73.

"The Story of Howling Wolf," *BAI; Revue Politique et Littéraire*, LXXI (February 18–March 4, 1933), 103–107, 138–43 ("Histoire de l'Indian Loup Hulant," trans. Mme. P. Chène).

"The Red Man as Material," *Booklovers' Magazine*, II (August, 1903), 196–98.

"Iron Khiva," *Harper's Weekly*, XLVII (August 29, 1903), 1416–19; *BAI; Revue Politique et Littéraire*, LXXVII (February, 1939), 56–60 ("La Maison d'Ecole des Hommes Blancs," trans. Mme. P. Chène).

"The Wife of a Pioneer," *Ladies' Home Journal*, XX (September, 1903), 8, 42; as *A Pioneer Mother*, 1922.

Hesper. New York: Harper & Brothers, 1903.

1904

"The Light of the Star," *Ladies' Home Journal*, XXI (January–May, 1904).

"Little Squatters," *Youth's Companion*, LXXVIII (June 9, 23, 1904).

"Two Stories of Oklahoma," *Century*, LXVIII (June, 1904), 328–29.

"Marshall's Capture," *Harper's Weekly*, XLVIII (December 19, 1904), 34–40.

The Light of the Star. New York: Harper & Brothers, 1904.

1905

"Tyranny of the Dark," *Harper's Weekly*, XLIX (January 28–May 13, 1905).

"Spartan Mother," *Ladies' Home Journal*, XXII (February, 1905), 10, 50; *BAI*.

"Doctor's Visit," *Pall Mall Magazine*, XXXV (May, 1905), 558–90.

"Building a Fireplace in Time for Christmas," *Country Life in America*, VIII (October, 1905), 645–47.

"Mark Haney's Mate," [Chaps. I–VI], *Saturday Evening Post*, CLXXVIII (November 18, 1905), 1–3, 27–32.

"Fireplace," *Delineator*, LXVI (December, 1905), 1051–56; *MTR*-4 to *MTR*-6, ("Martha's Fireplace").

"Vanishing Trails," *University Record* (University of Chicago), X (1905), 53–61.

The Tyranny of the Dark. New York: Harper & Brothers, 1905.

1906

"The Long Trail; a Story of the Klondike," *Youth's Companion*, LXXX–LXXXI (December 6, 1906–February 7, 1907).

"The Noose; a Story of Love and the Alien," *The Saturday Evening Post*, CLXXVIII (June 6, 1906), 3–5, 18.

Witch's Gold (expanded from *The Spirit of Sweetwater*). New York: Doubleday & Page, 1906.

Trail of the Goldseeker. New York: Macmillan & Company, 1906.

1907

"In That Far Land," *Circle,* II (October–November, 1907), 204–205; 298–300.

"Red Plowman," *Craftsman,* XIII (November, 1907), 180–82.

"Money Magic," *Harper's Weekly,* LI (August 7–October 12, 1907).

Money Magic. New York: Harper & Brothers, 1907.

The Long Trail; a Story of the Northwest Wilderness. New York: Harper & Brothers, 1907.

1908

"The Healer of Mogalyon," *Circle,* III (March, 1908), 140–45.

"The Shadow World," *Everybody's Magazine,* VIII–IX (April–October, 1908).

"The Outlaw and the Girl," *Ladies' Home Journal,* XXV (May–July, 1908); *THT* ("The Outlaw").

"A Night Raid at Eagle River," *Century,* LXXVI (September, 1908), 725–34; *THT* ("The Cow-Boy").

"Shadow World Prize Winners," *Everybody's Magazine,* IX (November, 1908), 665–79.

The Shadow World. New York: Harper & Brothers, 1908.

1909

Moccasin Ranch: A Story of Dakota (from "The Land of the Straddle-Bug"). New York: Harper & Brothers, 1909; *Revue Politique et Littéraire,* LV (July 28–October 27, 1917), ("La Ferme du Moggason").

Sunset Edition. Harper & Brothers, 10 vols. (*Boy Life on the Prairie, The Eagle's Heart, Jason Edwards, A Little Norsk, Main-Travelled Roads, Prairie Folks, Rose of Dutcher's Cooley, A Spoil of Office, Trail of the Gold-Seekers, Wayside Courtships.*)

1910

"My Aim in Cavanaugh," *World's Work,* XX (October, 1910), 1356–59.

Cavanaugh, Forest Ranger. New York: Harper & Brothers, 1910.

Other Main-Travelled Roads. New York: Harper & Brothers, 1910.

1911

" 'Starring the Play,' " *Nation,* XCIII (July 20, 1911), 54.

"My First Christmas Tree," *Ladies' Home Journal,* XXVIII (December, 1911), 13.

Victor Olnee's Discipline. New York: Harper & Brothers, 1911.

1912

"Middle West—Heart of the Country," *Country Life,* XXII (September 15, 1912), 19–24, 44.

1913

"Nugget," *Sunset,* XXX (April, 1913), 335–42.

"Poet of the Sierras," *Sunset,* XXX (June, 1913), 765–70.
"The New Chicago," *Craftsman,* XXIV (September, 1913), 555–65.
"Kelly Afoot," *Sunset,* XXXI (November, 1913), 919–26; *THT,* "The Trail Tramp"; *L'Illustration,* 1939 ("Le Vagabond," trans., Ferron-Chène).

1914

"Partners for a Day," *Colliers,* LII (March 14, 1914), 5–6; *THT* ("The Trail Tramp").
"A Son of the Middle Border: A Personal History: I, Half-Lights," *Colliers,* LIII (March 28, 1914).
"Stephen Crane as I Knew Him," *Yale Review,* III (April 1, 1914), 494–506.
"A Son of the Middle Border: A Personal History: II, Following the Sunset," *Colliers,* LIII (April 18, 1914).
"A Son of the Middle Border: A Personal History: III, Woods and Prairie Lands," *Colliers,* LIII (May 9, 1914).
"A Son of the Middle Border: A Personal History: IV, The Passing of the Prairie," *Colliers,* LIII (June 27, 1914).
"A Son of the Middle Border: A Personal History: V, Lincoln Enters Hostile Territory," *Colliers,* LIII (August 8, 1914).
"On the Road with James A. Herne," *Century,* LXXXVIII (August, 1914), 574–81.
The Forester's Daughter. New York: Harper & Brothers, 1914.

1915

"Kelley of Brimstone Basin," *National Sunday Magazine,* March 28, 1915, pp. 387–88; 392–94; *THT* ("The Trail Tramp").
"The Ranger and the Woman," *Colliers,* LV (July 24–August 28, 1915).

1916

"Emily's Horse Wrangler," *Colliers,* LVII (August 5, 19, 1916); *THT* ("The Tourist").
"The Remittance Man," "The Lonesome Man," "The Prospector," "The Leaser," first published, *THT.*
They of the High Trails. New York: Harper & Brothers, 1916.

1917

"A Son of the Middle Border," *Collier's,* LIX (March 31, 1917), 9–10; (April 21, 1917), 8–9; (May 26, 1917), 13–14.
"Meetings with Howells," *Bookman,* XLV (March, 1917), 1–7.
"William Dean Howells: Master Craftsman," *Art World,* I (April, 1917), 411–12.
"Graven Image," *Art World,* II (May, 1917), 127–30.
A Son of the Middle Border. New York: Macmillan & Company, 1917.

1918

"A Word about Bacheller," *American,* LXXXV (April, 1918), 19.

1919

"Reading Aloud to the Child," *Kindergarten Primary Magazine,* XXXI (January, 1919), 134.

"My Neighbor, Theodore Roosevelt," *Everybody's Magazine,* XLI (October, 1919), 9–16, 94.

1920

"Theodore Roosevelt," *Mentor,* VII (February 2, 1920), 1–12.

"The Spirit World on Trial," *McClure's,* LII (March, 1920), 33–34.

"Howells' Boston," *Boston Transcript,* May 22, 1920.

"Ulysses S. Grant," *Mentor,* VIII (July, 1920), 1–11.

"The Coming of Sir Oliver Lodge," *Touchstone,* VI (January, 1920), 217.

Ulysses S. Grant: His Life and Character. New York: Macmillan & Company, 1920.

1921

"A Great American" [Howells], New York *Evening Post,* Literary Review (March 5, 1921), 1–2.

"My Friend, John Burroughs," *Century,* CII (September, 1921), 731–42.

A Daughter of the Middle Border. New York: Macmillan & Company, 1921.

1922

Commemorative Tribute to James Whitcomb Riley. New York: American Academy of Arts and Letters, 1922.

A Pioneer Mother. Chicago: The Bookfellows, 1922.

Border Edition. New York: Harper & Brothers, 12 vols. (*Main-Travelled Roads, Other Main-Travelled Roads, Boy Life on the Prairie, Rose of Dutcher's Coolly, The Eagle's Heart, Captain of the Gray-Horse Troop, Hesper, Cavanaugh, Forest Ranger, The Long Trail, Mark Haney's Mate [Money Magic], The Forester's Daughter, They of the High Trails.*)

1923

"Mid-Western Sculptor: The Art of Lorado Taft," *Mentor,* XI (October, 1923), 19–24.

"The American Academy of Arts and Letters," *Bookman,* LVIII (November, 1923), 89–92.

"Pioneers and City Dwellers," *Bookman,* LVIII (December, 1923), 369.

"The Blood Lust," "The Remorse of ѵѵaumdisapu," " A Decree of Council," and "The Silent Eaters," first published in *BAI.*

"Introduction," *The Autobiography of David Crockett.* New York: C. Scribner's Sons (Modern Students' Library), 1923.

A Son of the Middle Border. New York: Macmillan & Company (School Edition), 1923.

Book of the American Indian. New York: Harper & Brothers, 1923.

1924

"Limitations of Authorship in America," *Bookman*, LIX (May, 1924), 257–61.

1925

"Memories of Henry George," *Libertarian*, V (November, 1925), 280.

1926

"The White Weasel," *Dearborn Independent*, XXVII (December 18, 1926), 4, 5, 27.

A Daughter of the Middle Border. New York: Grosset & Dunlop, 1926.

Trail Makers of the Middle Border. New York: Macmillan & Company, 1926.

Boy Life on the Prairie. New York: Allyn & Bacon, 1926.

1927

"John Burroughs," *World Review*, IV (June 6, 1927), 265.

"Doris Ullman's Photographs," *Mentor*, XV (July, 1927), 42–44.

"The Dark Side of the Moon," *Dearborn Independent*, July 2, 1927, pp. 3, 18, 19.

"Recollections of Roosevelt," *Roosevelt As We Knew Him*, F. S. Wood, ed. Philadelphia: John C. Winston Co., 1927.

Westward March of American Settlement. Chicago: American Library Association, 1927.

"Stuart Pratt Sherman," *Commemorative Tribute to William LeRoy Metcalf*, Royal Cortissoz, ed. New York: American Academy of Arts and Letters, 1927.

1928

"I Don't Know What Happened at Those Séances," *American*, CV (March, 1928), 42–43, 142–48.

Back-Trailers from the Middle Border. New York: Macmillan & Company, 1928.

Prairie Song and Western Story: Selections, Stella S. Center, ed. ("Academy Classics for Junior High Schools"). Boston: Allyn & Bacon, 1928.

1929

"Songs and Shrines of Old New England," *Current Literature*, VI (March 25–29, 1929), 38–40.

"Roadside Meetings of a Literary Nomad," *Bookman*, LXX and LXXI (October, 1929–July, 1930).

"The Value of Melodious Speech," *Emerson Quarterly*, IX (November, 1929), 5, 6, 22.

1930

"Fortunate Coast," *Saturday Evening Post*, CCII (April 5, 1930), 31.

"Books of My Childhood," *Saturday Review*, VII (November 15, 1930), 347.
Main-Travelled Roads. New York: Harper & Brothers, 1930.
Roadside Meetings. New York: Macmillan & Company, 1930.

1931
"Some of My Youthful Enthusiasms," *English Journal*, XX (May, 1931), 355–62.
"William Dean Howells," *American Writers on American Literature*, John Macy, ed., New York: H. Liveright, 1931.
Companions on the Trail. New York: Macmillan & Company, 1931.

1932
My Friendly Contemporaries. New York: Macmillan & Company, 1932.

1934
Afternoon Neighbors. New York: Macmillan & Company, 1934.

1935
"La Vengeur," Mme. P. Chène, trans., *Revue Politique et Littéraire*, LXXIII (May 4, 1935), 312–16.
"The Westward March of Settlement," *Frontier Times*, XII (August, 1935), 499–505.
Iowa, O, Iowa. Iowa City: Clio Press, 1935.
Joys of the Trail. Chicago: The Bookfellows, 1935.
The Long Trail (with "The Return of a Private"). New York: Harper & Brothers, 1935.

1936
Forty Years of Psychic Research. New York: Macmillan & Company, 1936.

1937
"A Man Most Favored," *Mark Twain Quarterly*, I (Summer, 1937), 3.
"Homage to the Pioneers," *Stepladder*, XXIII (September, 1937), 162–63.
"Houtan, le Courrier Rouge," Mme. P. Chène, trans., *Revue Politique et Littéraire*, LXXV (December 18, 1937), 777–78.
"We Go Up The Hill," *Stepladder*, XXIII (December, 1937), 218–19.

1938
"Two Excellent Bookmen," *Stepladder*, XXIV (January, 1938), 3.

1939
"Let the Sunshine In," *Rotarian*, LV (October, 1939), 8–11.
"Literary Fashions, Old and New," *Think*, IV (March, 1939), 14, 24–27.
The Mystery of the Buried Crosses. New York: E. P. Dutton & Company, 1939.

1940

"Quiet Acceptance," *Mark Twain Quarterly*, III (Spring, 1940), 11.
"Dan Beard and the Scouts," *Mark Twain Quarterly*, IV (Summer, 1940), 12.
"Twain's Social Conscience," *Mark Twain Quarterly*, IV (Summer, 1940), 13.

Posthumous

"James Whitcomb Riley," "Stuart Pratt Sherman," "John Charles Van Dyke," "Augustus Thomas," *Commemorative Tributes of the American Academy of Arts and Letters* (1905–14). New York: American Academy, 1942.
Main-Travelled Roads. New York: Harper & Brothers, 1956.

POETRY

"Edwin Booth," *Boston Evening Transcript,* January 2, 1886, p. 7.
"Prairie Memories," *American* (Brooklyn), V (October 6, 1886), 653; *PS; BL* (untitled).
"Logan at Peach Tree Creek," *Boston Evening Transcript,* January 1, 1887, p. 6; *PS; PF-2.*
"Beneath the Pines," *American* (Brooklyn), VII (November, 1887), 87; *PS.*
"Lost in the Norther," *Harper's Weekly,* XXXI (December 3, 1887), 883; *PS; BL.*
"My Cabin," *American* (Brooklyn), VII (December, 1887), 232; *PS; IOI.*
"The Coming Storm," *Boston Evening Transcript,* March 28, 1888, p. 6.
"Paid His Way," *America,* I, No. 7 (May 19, 1888), 6; *PS; PF-2.*
["A Tribute of Grasses: to W. W."], *Boston Evening Transcript,* November 15, 1888, p. 6; *PS; Rotarian,* LV (October, 1939), 9; excerpt *RM.*
"A Wind from the East Sea," *Standard,* March 7, 1889, p. 7.
"Apology," *Literary World,* XX (June 8, 1889), 192; *PS; BL* ("A Prologue").
"Points of View," *Standard,* June 22, 1889, p. 15.
"A Dakota Wheat Field," *Youth's Companion,* LXII (July 18, 1889), 366; *PS* ("A Dakota Harvest Field"); *BL* ("A Western Harvest Field").
"The Average Man," *America,* II (July 25, 1889), 526; *Outlook,* DXIII (September 2, 1889), 75.
"By the River," *Youth's Companion,* LXII (August 15, 1889); *Standard,* August 31, 1889, p. 13; *PS; IOI.*
"Scepterless Kings," *Standard,* August 17, 1889, p. 9.
"The Single Tax Cat," *Standard,* September 7, 1889, p. 15.

"She Passed Me on the Street," *Arena,* II (July, 1890), 187; *Jason Edwards.*

"Music Land; at a Symphony," *New England Magazine,* III n. s. (January, 1891), 628–30.

"In Winter Night," *Literary Northwest,* II (December, 1892), 96; *PF-2* ("An afterword: Of Winds, Snows and the Stars").

"Ridge of Corn," *Harper's Weekly,* XXXVII (August 12, 1893), 763; *PS; BL; IOI* ("Corn Shadows").

"The Cool, Gray Jug," *Harper's Weekly,* XXXVII (August 19, 1893), 786; *PS; BL; IOI; SMB.*

*"A Summer Mood," *New England Magazine,* IX n.s. (September, 1893), 64; *PS; BL.*

"Prairie Fires," *Youth's Companion,* LXVI (September 14, 1893), 444; *PS; BL.*

"Sport," *New England Magazine,* IX n. s. (October, 1893), 240; *PS.*

"Prairie Chickens," *Independent,* LXV (October 5, 1893), 1329, and LXV (December 10, 1908), 1410; *PS; BL; IOI.*

"A Human Habitation," *Arena,* IV (December, 1893), 130; *PS.*

"The West Wind," *PS.*

"Coming Rain on the Prairie," *PS; BL.*

*"Massauga—the Meadow Rattlesnake," *PS; BL; IOI.*

"Spring on the Prairie," *PS.*

"A Song of Winds," *PS.*

"Indian Summer," *PS; IOI.*

"Color in the Wheat," *PS; BL; Bookman,* LXX (December, 1924) 394; *RM; IOI.*

"The Meadow Lark," *PS; IOI.*

"The Hush of the Plains," *PS.*

"Settlers-Portrait," *PS; PF-1; PF-2; OMTR.*

"Pioneers," *PS; PF-1; PF-2.*

"Drought," *PS.*

"At Dusk," *PS; IOI.*

*"A Winter Brook," *PS; IOI.*

"The Voice of the Pines," *PS; IOI.*

*"The Herald Crane," *PS; BL; IOI.*

"Sundown," *PS.*

*"In the Autumn Grass," *PS; BL; Craftsman,* XIII (1907), 182; *IOI.*

*"Dreams of the Grass," *PS; TGS* ("In the Grass").

"Meadow Memories," *PS; BL.*

"The Whip-poor-will's Hour," *PS; IOI.*

"Atavism," *PS.*

"In a Lull in the Splendors of Brahms," *PS.*

*This poem and others similarly indicated were printed in *Midland Monthly,* I, 22–27, as "Selections from the Advance Sheets of a Book of Poems by Hamlin Garland." Other periodicals of December, 1893, printed selections from these same advance sheets.

"The Passing of the Buffalo," *PS; IOI.*
"Home from the City," *PS; McClure's,* VIII (November, 1896), 96.
*"April Days," *PS; PF-2.*
"A Mountain-side," *PS.*
"In August," *PS; BL; IOI.*
"The Blue Jay," *PS; BL.*
"The Mountains," *PS.*
"The Striped Gopher," *PS; BL; IOI.*
"The Prairie to the City," *PS.*
"A River Gorge," *PS.*
"Altruism," *PS.*
"Return of the Gulls," *PS.*
"Early May," *PS; IOI.*
*"The Wind's Voice," *PS.*
"On the Mississippi," *PS.*
"A Brother's Death Search," *PS.*
"Spring Rains," *PS; BL.*
"The Noonday Plain," *PS.*
"Midnight Snows," *PS; PF-2; OMTR; DMB.*
"In Stacking-Time," *PS; BL; IOI.*
"A Town on the Plain," *PS.*
"In the Gold Country," *PS.*
"Home from the Wild Meadows," *PS; BL; IOI.*
"Fighting Fire," *PS; IOI.*
*"Boyish Sleep," *PS; BL.*
"The Herdsman," *PS; BL.*
"Rushing Eagle," *PS.*
"September," *PS.*
"The Stampede," *PS.*
"The Gray Wolf," *PS; TGS* ("The Gaunt Gray Wolf").
"Plowing," *PS; BL; IOI; SMB.*
"Moods of the Plains," *PS.*
"Ladrone," *PS; BL.*
"Across the Picket Line," *PS; PF-2.*
"Then It's Spring," *PS; PF-2; BL.*
*"Horses Chawin' Hay," *PS; PF-2; IOI.*
"Growing Old," *PS; PF-2.*
"A Farmer's Wife," *PS; PF-2; IOI.*
"Pom, Pom, Pull-away," *PS; BL; IOI.*
"Goin' Back T'morrer," *PS; PF-2.*
"On Wing of Steam," *PS.*
"My Prairies," *PS; Review of Reviews,* VIII (December, 1893), 130.
"Midway on the Trail," *PS.*
"Wagner," *The Chap-Book,* III (October 1, 1895), 379–80.
"Cry of the Artist," *The Chap-Book,* IV (November 15, 1895), 7–8.
"The Golden Seekers," *McClure's,* XII (April, 1899), 505; *TGS*
    ("The Gold Seekers").

"The Long Trail," *McClure's,* XII (April, 1899), 505, *TGS.*

"The Freeman of the Hills," *McClure's,* XII (April, 1899), 506; *TGS.*

"Do You Fear the Wind?" *McClure's,* XII (April, 1899), 507; *TGS; Chicago University *Record,* X (1905).

"The Loon," *McClure's,* XIII (May, 1899), 65; *TGS.*

"Camp Fires," *McClure's,* XIII (May, 1899), 65; *TGS.*

"O, the Fierce Delight," *McClure's,* XIII (May, 1899), 66; *TGS.*

"Relentless Nature," *McClure's,* XIII (May, 1899), 67; *TGS; RM.*

"A Mountain Pass," *McClure's,* XIII (May, 1899), 67; *TGS.*

"The End of the Trail," *McClure's,* XIII (May, 1899), 67; *TGS; DMB.*

"Cry of the Age," *Outlook,* LXII (May 6, 1899); LXXII (November 29, 1902), 740. *Saturday Review,* X (July 29, 1933), 22; stanza on motto page of *CI.*

"The Ute Lover," *Century,* LVIII (June, 1899), 218–20; *TGS.*

"The War of Race," *PF-2.*

"Beacons through the Gloom," *Outlook,* LXII (July 1, 1899), 527.

"The Vulture of the Plains," *BL; TGS.*

"The River," *BL.*

"In the Days When the Cattle Ran," *BL.*

"November," *BL.*

"Anticipation," *TGS.*

"Where the Desert Flames with Furnace Heat," *TGS.*

"The Cow-boy," *TGS.*

"From Plain to Peak," *TGS.*

"Momentous Hour," *TGS.*

"A Wish," *TGS;* Chicago University *Record,* X (1905).

"The Gift of Water," *TGS.*

"Mounting," *TGS.*

"The Eagle Trail," *TGS.*

"Moon on the Plain," *TGS.*

"The Whooping Crane," *TGS.*

"Yet Still We Rode," *TGS.*

"Abandoned on the Trail," *TGS.*

"Siwash Graves," *TGS.*

"Line Up, Brave Boys," *TGS.*

"A Child of the Sun," *TGS; Rotarian,* LVIII (May, 1941), 6 ("Give Me the Sun").

"The Faithful Broncos," *TGS.*

"The Whistling Marmot," *TGS.*

"The Clouds," *TGS.*

"The Great Stikeen Divide," *TGS.*

"Devil's Club," *TGS.*

"In the Cold Green Mountains," *TGS.*

"The Greeting of the Roses," *TGS.*

"The Footsteps in the Desert," *TGS.*

"So This Is the End of the Trail to Him," *TGS*.
"The Toil of the Trail," *TGS;* excerpt, *RM*.
"The Coast Range of Alaska," *TGS*.
"The Voice of the Maple Tree," *TGS*.
"A Girl on the Trail," *TGS*.
"The Lure of the Desert," *TGS*.
"This Out of All Will Remain," *TGS*.
"Death in the Desert," *Munsey,* XXV (June, 1901), 395.
"Oh, the Good Days on the Trail," Chicago University *Record,* X (1905); *DMB*.
"Manhattan," *Century,* LXXII (June, 1906), 301.
"The Stricken Mountaineer," *Century,* LXXIV (October, 1907), 928–30. "The Stricken Pioneer," *Rotarian,* LV (June, 1940), 6; excerpts, *DMB; RM*.
"The Magic Spring; Lines read in acceptance of the Punch Bowl," *The Cliff Dwellers' Yearbook for 1911,* Chicago, 1911, p. 37.
"Lure of the Bugle," *Current Opinion,* LXI (September, 1916), 199–200.
"Oh, Maids to Whom I Never Spoke," *DMB*.
"Once I Threatened the World with Fire," *DMB*.
"It Touched Me More Than I Can Say or Ought," *RM*, 1930.
"As Shadows Lengthen," *AN*.
"Plowman of Today," *IOI; Rotarian,* LV (September, 1939), 6.
"The Sword Two-edged," *IOI; Rotarian,* LXI (November, 1942), 53.
"The Prisoned Pool," *IOI; Rotarian,* LXIV (April, 1944), 26.
"Vanishing Trails," *IOI; JT*.
"Adventurous Boyhood," *Frontier Times,* XII (August, 1935), 503.

PRINCIPAL PRIMARY SOURCES
UNPUBLISHED

The major portion of the unpublished materials used in this study are from the Garland Papers in the Doheny Library, University of Southern California.

Various other manuscript materials have been consulted in the New York Public Library, chief among these the Garland-Gilder correspondence, which in part is included in that institution's "Century Collection." Since this particular correspondence has been a subject of controversial interest in evaluations of Garland an attempt has been made in annotation to indicate as precisely as possible the sources quoted. These letters, however, are largely undated and un-numbered, and are divided among several collections of the New York Public Library. Their chronological sequence, therefore, has been subject to authorial interpretation based upon content and upon correlation with Garland's manuscripts and the other half of the correspondence contained in the Garland Papers.

PRINCIPAL SECONDARY SOURCES

Ahnebrink, Lars. *The Beginnings of Naturalism in American Fiction.* [Uppsala] Cambridge (Massachusetts): Harvard University Press, 1950.

Beer, Thomas. *Stephen Crane.* New York: Knopf, 1933.

Campbell, W. S. *The Booklover's Southwest.* Norman: Oklahoma University Press, 1955.

Chew, Samuel C. *Fruit Among the Leaves.* New York: Appleton-Century-Croft, 1950.

Dennis, Charles H. *Eugene Field's Creative Years.* New York: Doubleday, 1924.

Dove, John R. "The Significance of Garland's First Visit to England," *University of Texas Studies in English,* XXXII (1953), 96–109.

Edwards, Herbert. "Herne, Garland, and Henry George," *American Literature,* XXVIII (November, 1956), 359–67.

Field, Eugene. *Sharps and Flats,* Vol. I. New York: C. Scribner's Sons, 1900.

Flanagan, John T. "Hamlin Garland Writes to His Chicago Publisher," *American Literature,* XXIII (January, 1952), 448–53.

Fuller, Henry B. *Under the Skylights.* New York: Appleton, 1901.

Garland, James Gray. *Garland Genealogy.* Biddleford, Maine, 1897.

Goldstein, J. S. "Two Literary Radicals: Garland and Markham in Chicago, 1893," *American Literature,* XVII (May, 1945), 152–60.

Griffin, Constance M. *Henry Blake Fuller.* Philadelphia: University of Pennsylvania Press, 1939.

Henson, Clyde E. "Joseph Kirkland's Influence on Hamlin Garland," *American Literature,* XXIII (January, 1952), 458–63.

Howells, Mildred, ed. *Life in Letters of William Dean Howells.* New York: Doubleday, 1928.

Howells, William Dean. *The Minister's Charge.* Boston: Houghton-Mifflin, 1886.

Keiser, A. *The Indian in American Literature.* New York: Oxford University Press, 1933.

Kramer, Sidney. *A History of Stone & Kimball and Stone & Company.* Chicago: N. W. Forgue, 1940.

McElderry, B. R. "Hamlin Garland and Henry James," *American Literature,* XXIII (January, 1952), 433–46.

Matthews, Brander. *These Many Years.* New York: Scribner's, 1917.

Mencken, Henry L. *Prejudices, First Series.* New York: Knopf, 1919.

"Mme. Blanc" [Th. Bentzon]. "Un Radical de la Prairie," *Revue des Deux Mondes,* CLVII (1900), 170–77.

Parrington, Vernon. *Main Currents of American Thought.* New York: Harcourt, Brace, 1927.

Pattee, Fred L. *The Development of the American Short Story.* New York: Harper's, 1923.

Pizer, Donald. "Herbert Spencer and the Genesis of Hamlin Garland's Critical System," *Tulane Studies in English*, VII (1957), 153–168.

——. "Hamlin Garland: Newspaper and Periodical Publications, 1885–1895: A Bibliography," *Bulletin of Bibliography*, XXII (January–April, 1957), pp. 41–44.

——. "Crane Reports Garland on Howells," *Modern Language Notes*, LXX (January, 1955), 37.

Simpson, Claude. "Hamlin Garland's 'Decline' from Realism," *American Literature*, XXV (March, 1953), 69–74.

Spiller, R. E., et al, eds. *Literary History of the United States*, New York: Macmillan, 1946.

Thompson, Slason. *Eugene Field: A Study in Heredity and Contradictions*. New York: Scribner's, 1901.

Traubel, Horace. *With Walt Whitman in Camden*. 4 Vols. Boston: Small, Maynard, 1906–53.

Van Doren, Carl. "Contemporary American Novelists," *Nation*, CXIII (November 23, 1921), 596–97.

Wagenknecht, E. C. *Cavalcade of the American Novel*. New York: Holt, 1952.

Index

INDEX

Riley, James W.: 56, 69–70, 74, 112
Rogers, Will: 298
Roosevelt, Theodore: meets Garland, 130–31; entertains him, 178; and *They of the High Trails*, 228; dies, 245–46; Garland's tributes to, 248–49; mentioned, 142, 175, 206, 215, 231, 278
Roz, Dr. Firman: 275

St. Gaudens, Augustus: 193
Saturday Evening Post: and *The Eagle's Heart*, 164, 165; and *Captain of the Gray-Horse Troop*, 175; rejects *Son of the Middle Border*, 217; mentioned, 201, 241
Saturday Review: 285
Schindler, Rabbi Solomon: 66
Schulte, F. J. & Company: as Garland's publisher, 68, 93, 95, 97
Scribner's: 31
Sedgwick, Ellery: 251
Seger, John Homer: 172, 179, 269, 272 n
Seton, Ernest Thompson: 130, 181
Sewanee Review: 261
Shambaugh, Benjamin: 253
Shaw, Albert: 178, 179, 256, 306
Shaw, Bernard: 157, 192, 196, 197, 264, 267
Sherman, Stuart: 254
Single-Tax, Single-Taxers: 36–37, 43, 45, 51, 54, 63, 65, 69, 112, 192. *See also* George, Henry
Sitting Bull. *See* Works of Hamlin Garland, "The Silent Eaters"
"Smiley, Mrs." (medium): 75, 179, 188, 212, 301
Southern Magazine: 101
Spencer, Herbert: 10, 66
Spiller, R. E.: quoted, 103
Standard. See George, Henry
Stanley, Henry M.: 157
Stead, William: 189, 190, 256, 302
Stedman, Edmund C.: 137, 193
Stevenson, Robert Louis: 114
Stockton, Frank: 128
Stone, Herbert: 95, 97, 102, 114, 132, 201
Stone, Melville E.: 95, 104
Stone & Kimball: publishes Garland, 95–100, 103–104, 123, 128;

and *The Chap-Book*, 113–14; failure of, 132, 137, 155; mentioned, 104, 106, 134, 140, 152, 164
Stouch, Major George: 172
Stuart, Ruth McEnery: 129
Sullivan, Mark: 219–20, 224, 231, 234, 245, 266, 270
Sunset Magazine: 213, 229

Taft, Don Carlos: 162
Taft, Lorado: 105, 106, 107, 112, 157, 167, 192, 201, 291, 302
Taft, Zulime. *See* Garland, Zulime Taft
Taine, Hippolyte Adolphe: 100
Tarbell, Ida M.: 128
Tarkington, Booth: 152, 252
Theatre Society of Chicago: 211
Thomas, Augustus: 156, 249, 252, 292
Tolstoi, Leo Nikolaevitch: 26, 90
Traubel, Horace: 37, 38, 39
Turck, Dr. Fenton B.: 244–45, 249, 302
Turner, Frederick J.: 83
Twain, Mark: 24, 193

University of Chicago: 83, 182, 193, 194

Van Doren, Carl: quoted, 263; mentioned, 254, 256, 262–63, 278, 298
Van Dyke, John: 292
veritism: 91, 103, 104, 163, 207, 214, 293, 294. *See also* naturalism; Garland, Hamlin, as realist
Verlaine, Paul: 114
Véron, Eugene: *Esthetics*, 101
Vestal, Stanley. *See* Campbell, Walter
Vitagraph Company: 225–28

Wagenknecht, Edward: quoted, 294
Wallace, Edgar: 292
Wallace, Lew: 87, 179
Warner, Charles Dudley: 156
Washington, Booker T.: 198
Waters, Albert: 274
Webster, Daniel: 6
Wells, H. G.: 55, 114, 259, 266
West Salem, Wis.: 82, 99–100, 117, 124, 141, 145, 149, 151, 159, 163,